PERFECT WORLD

9

Rie Aruga

Research Help /
Kazuo Abe (Abe Kensetsu Inc.)

contents

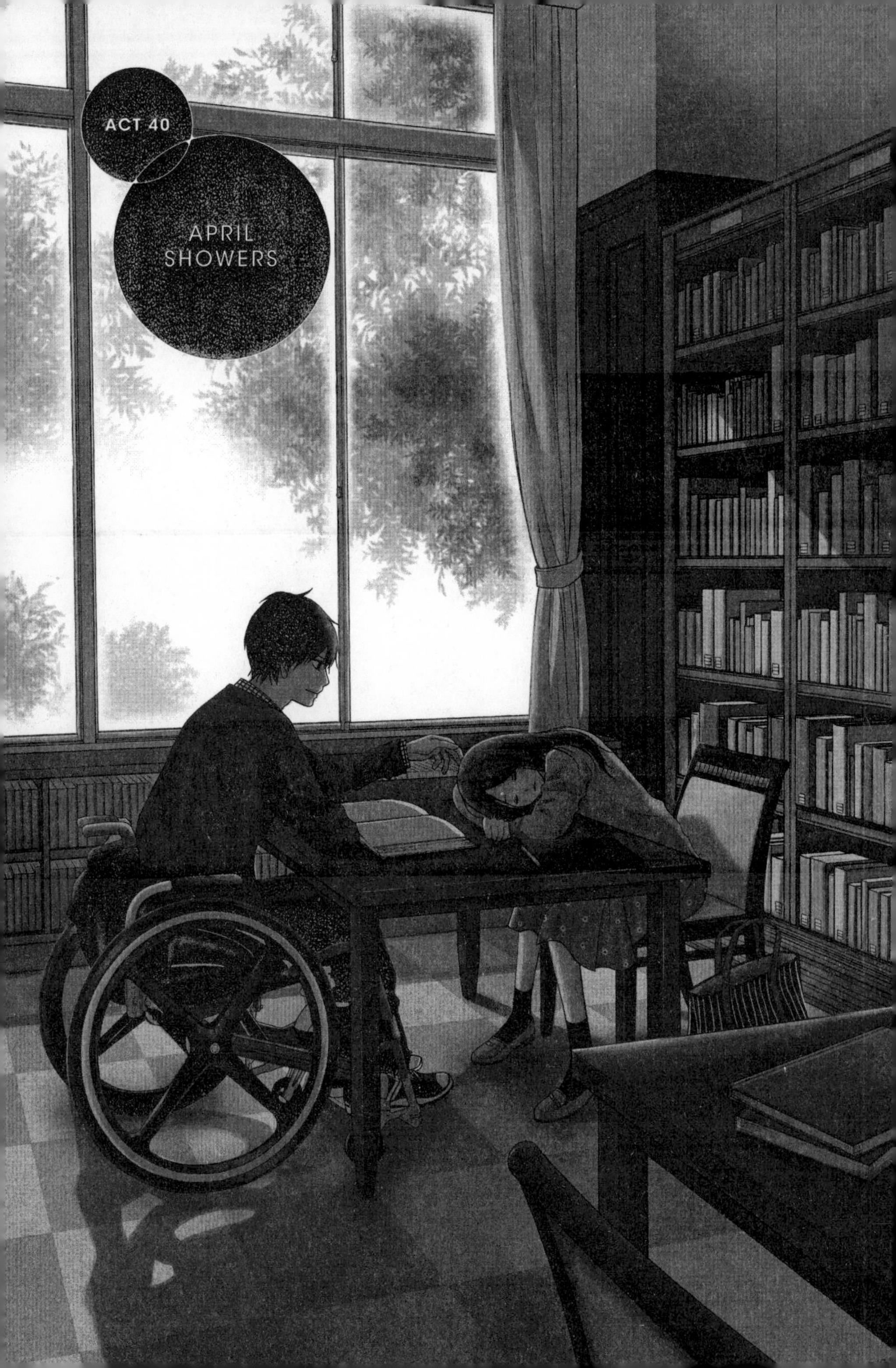
ACT 40
APRIL SHOWERS

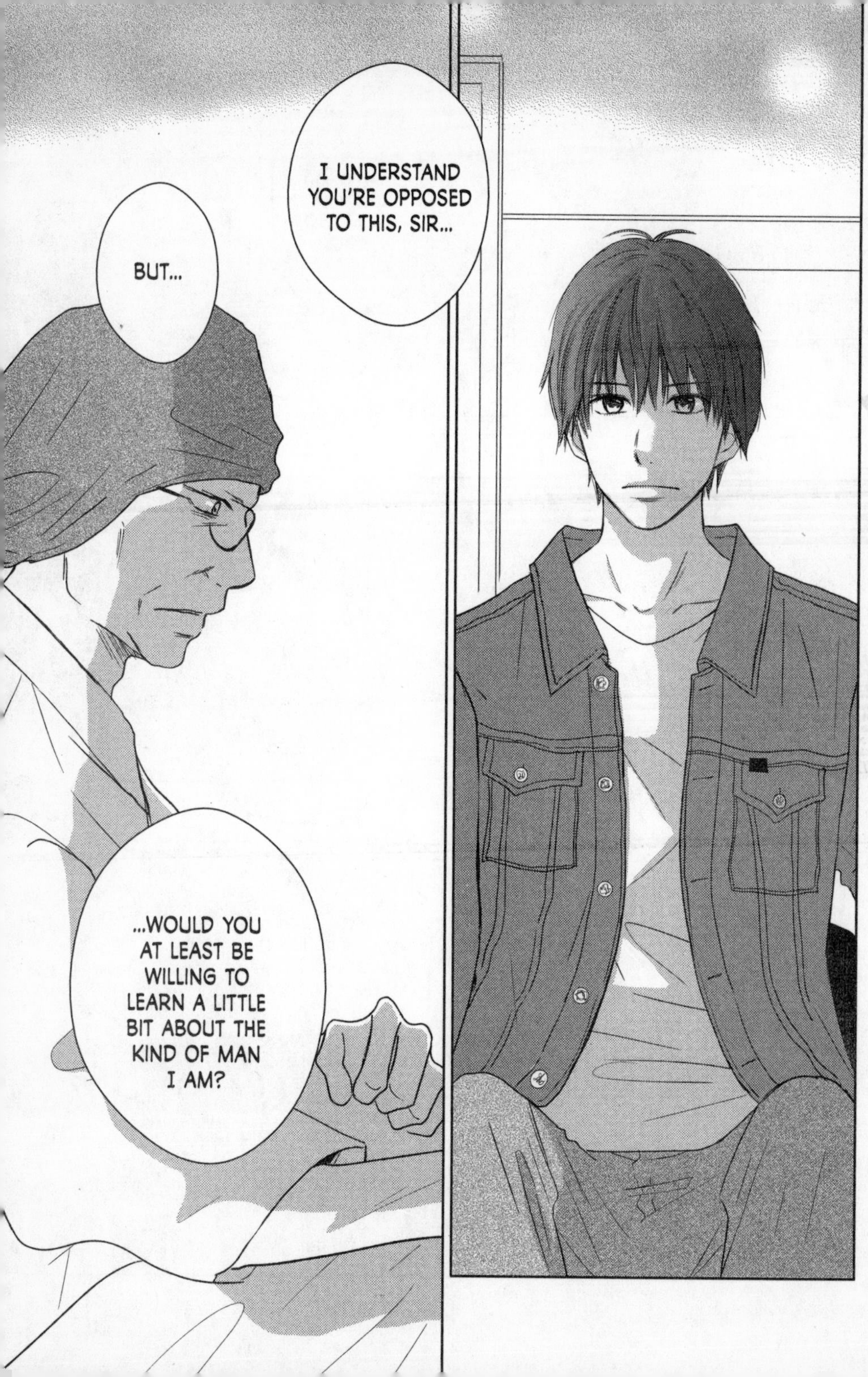
I UNDERSTAND YOU'RE OPPOSED TO THIS, SIR...
BUT...
...WOULD YOU AT LEAST BE WILLING TO LEARN A LITTLE BIT ABOUT THE KIND OF MAN I AM?

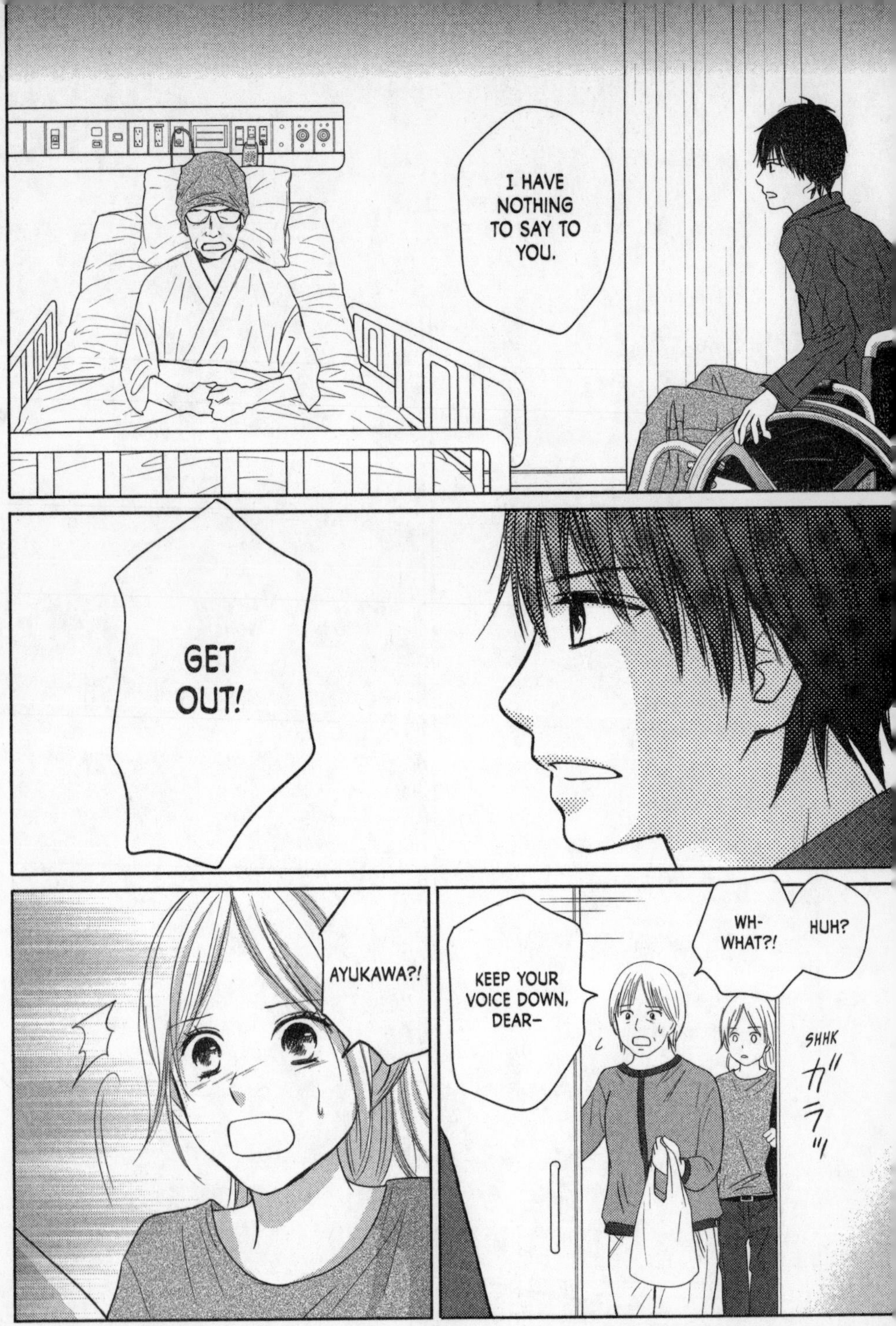
I HAVE NOTHING TO SAY TO YOU.
GET OUT!
HUH?
WH- WHAT?!
SHHK
ガラッ
KEEP YOUR VOICE DOWN, DEAR–
AYUKAWA?!

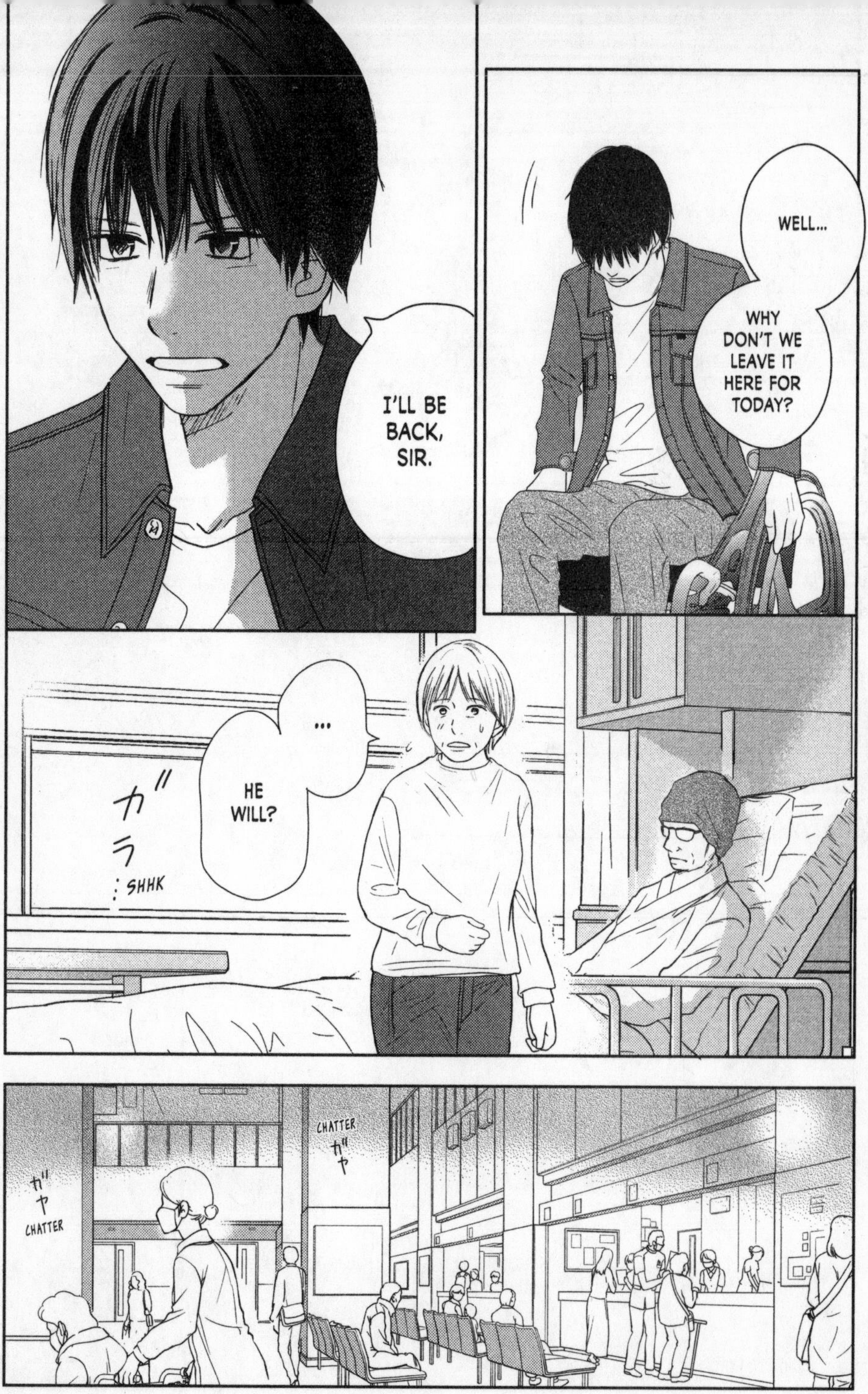
WELL...
WHY DON'T WE LEAVE IT HERE FOR TODAY?
I'LL BE BACK, SIR.
...
HE WILL?
ガラ
SHHK
CHATTER
ガヤ
ガヤ
CHATTER

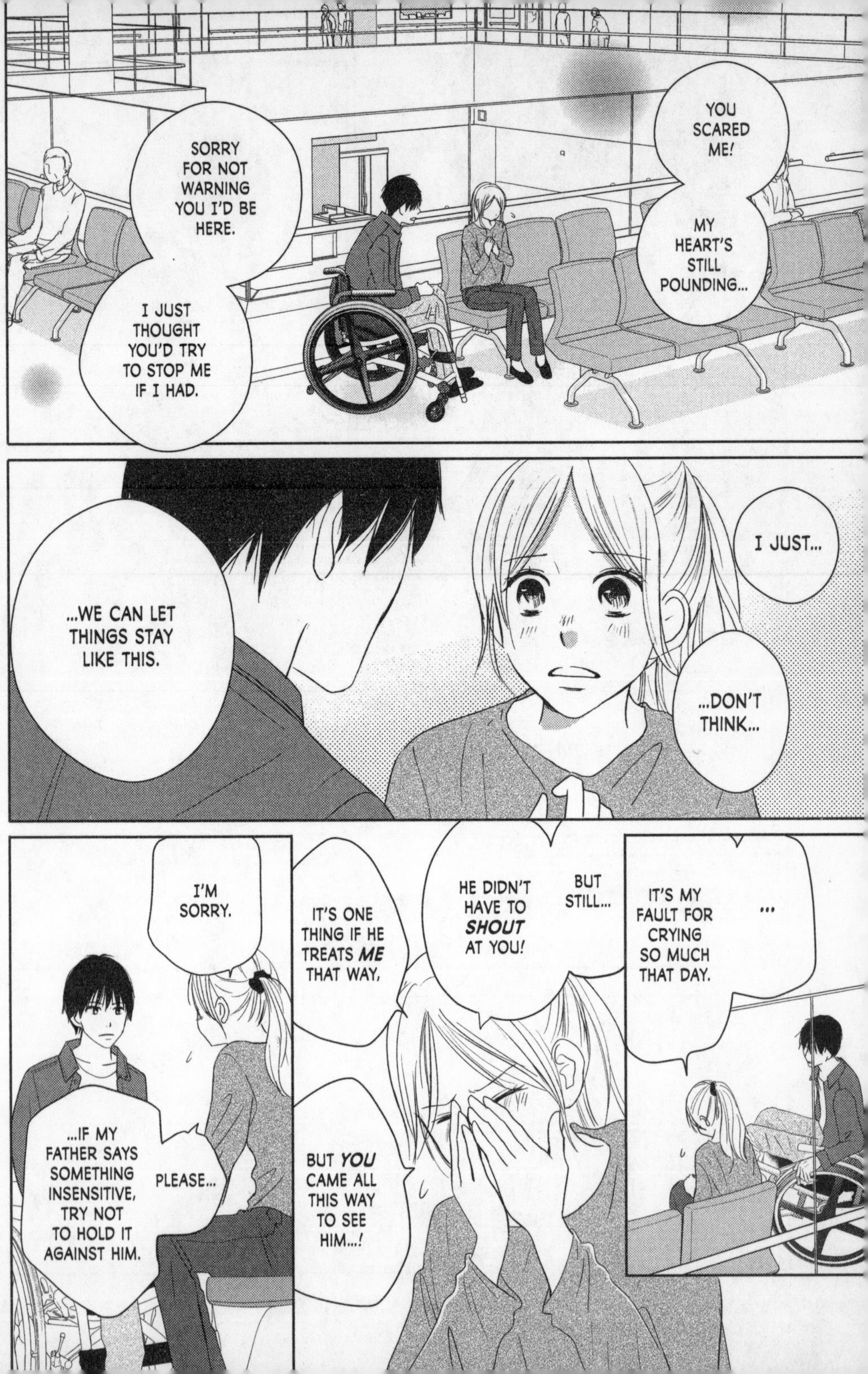
YOU SCARED ME!
MY HEART'S STILL POUNDING...
SORRY FOR NOT WARNING YOU I'D BE HERE.
I JUST THOUGHT YOU'D TRY TO STOP ME IF I HAD.
I JUST...
...DON'T THINK...
...WE CAN LET THINGS STAY LIKE THIS.
...
IT'S MY FAULT FOR CRYING SO MUCH THAT DAY.
BUT STILL...
HE DIDN'T HAVE TO *SHOUT* AT YOU!
IT'S ONE THING IF HE TREATS *ME* THAT WAY,
BUT *YOU* CAME ALL THIS WAY TO SEE HIM...!
I'M SORRY.
PLEASE...
...IF MY FATHER SAYS SOMETHING INSENSITIVE, TRY NOT TO HOLD IT AGAINST HIM.

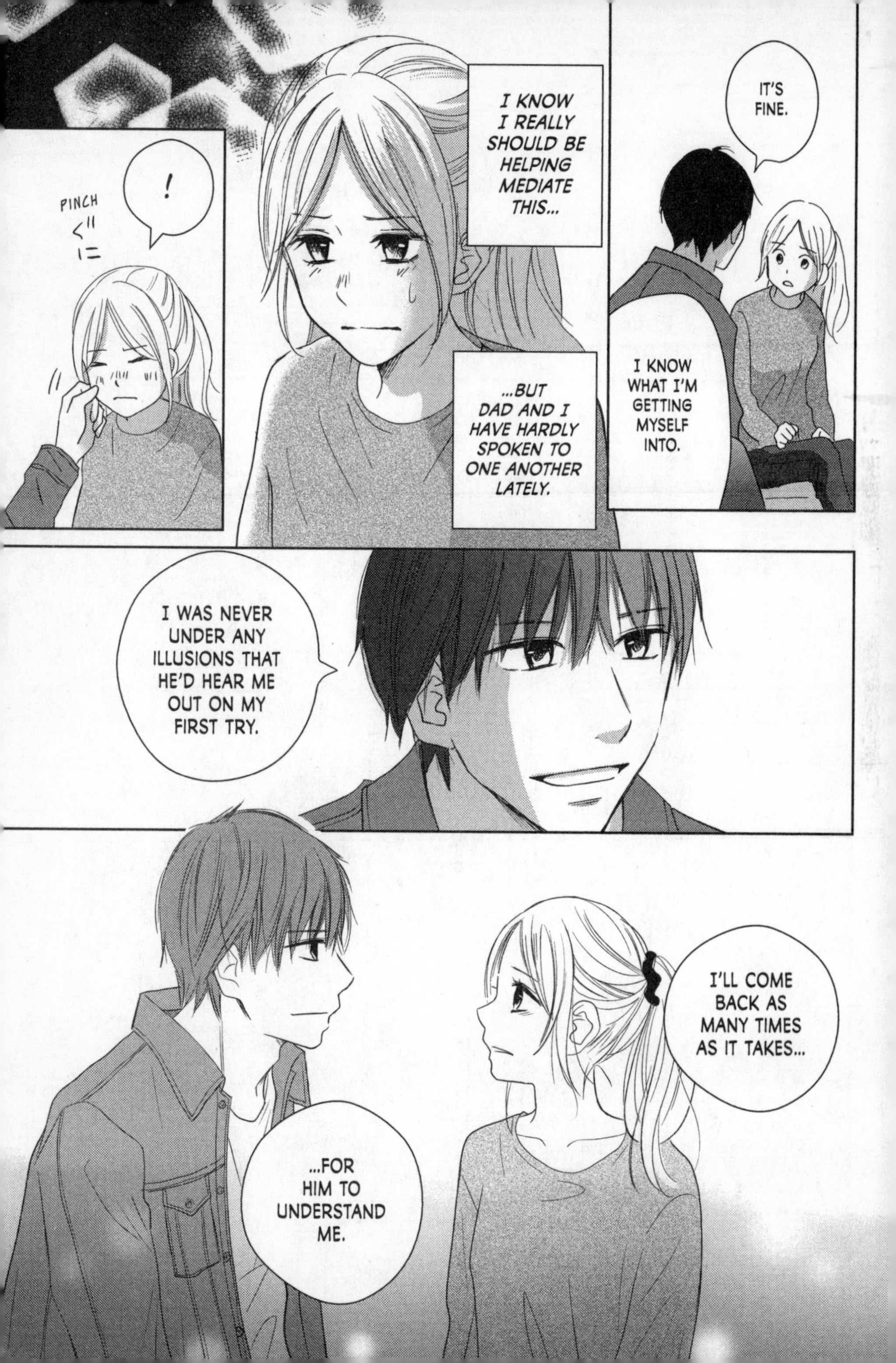
IT'S FINE.
I KNOW WHAT I'M GETTING MYSELF INTO.
I KNOW I REALLY SHOULD BE HELPING MEDIATE THIS...
...BUT DAD AND I HAVE HARDLY SPOKEN TO ONE ANOTHER LATELY.
PINCH
ぐに
!
I WAS NEVER UNDER ANY ILLUSIONS THAT HE'D HEAR ME OUT ON MY FIRST TRY.
I'LL COME BACK AS MANY TIMES AS IT TAKES...
...FOR HIM TO UNDERSTAND ME.

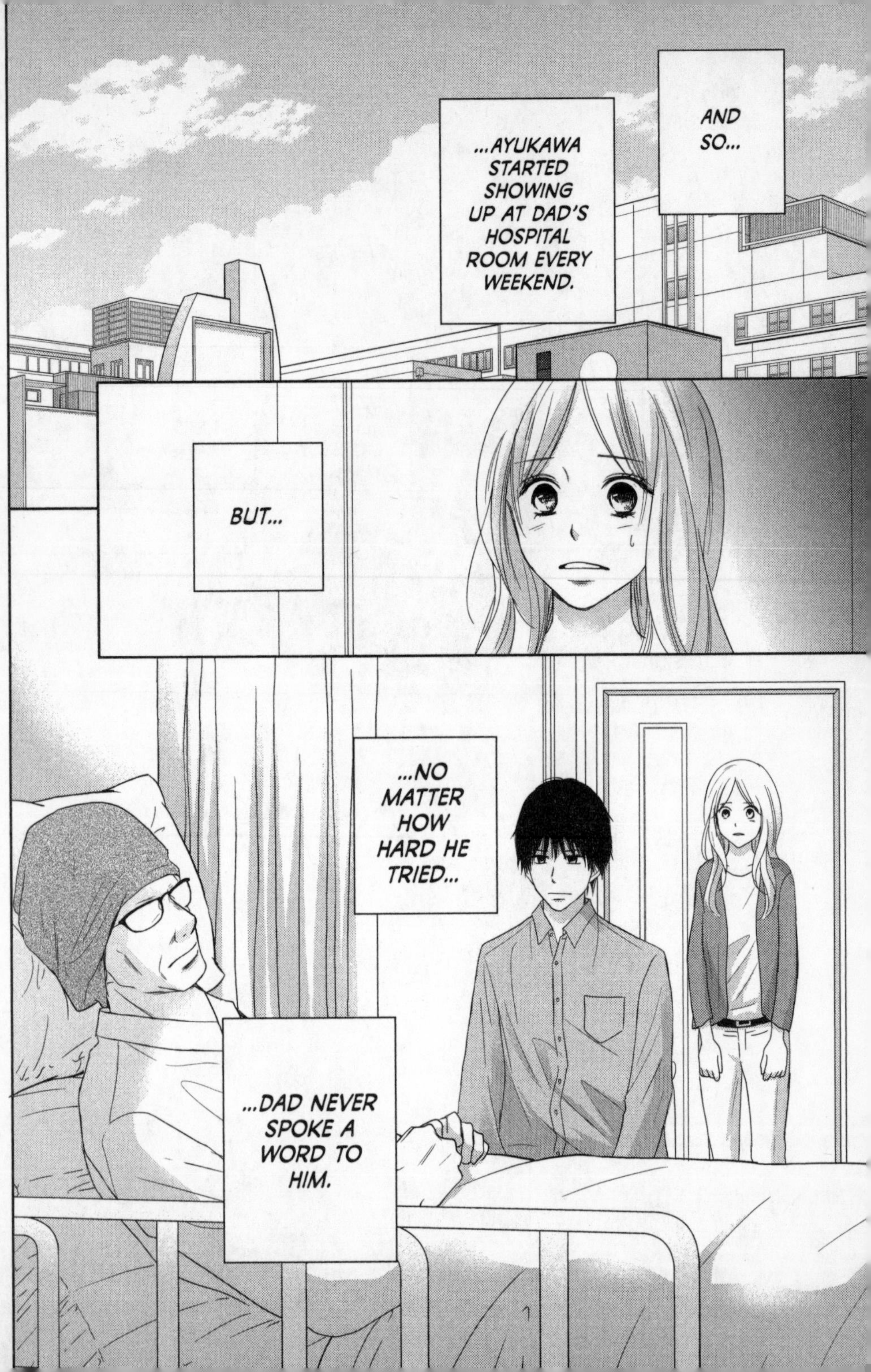
AND SO...
...AYUKAWA STARTED SHOWING UP AT DAD'S HOSPITAL ROOM EVERY WEEKEND.
BUT...
...NO MATTER HOW HARD HE TRIED...
...DAD NEVER SPOKE A WORD TO HIM.

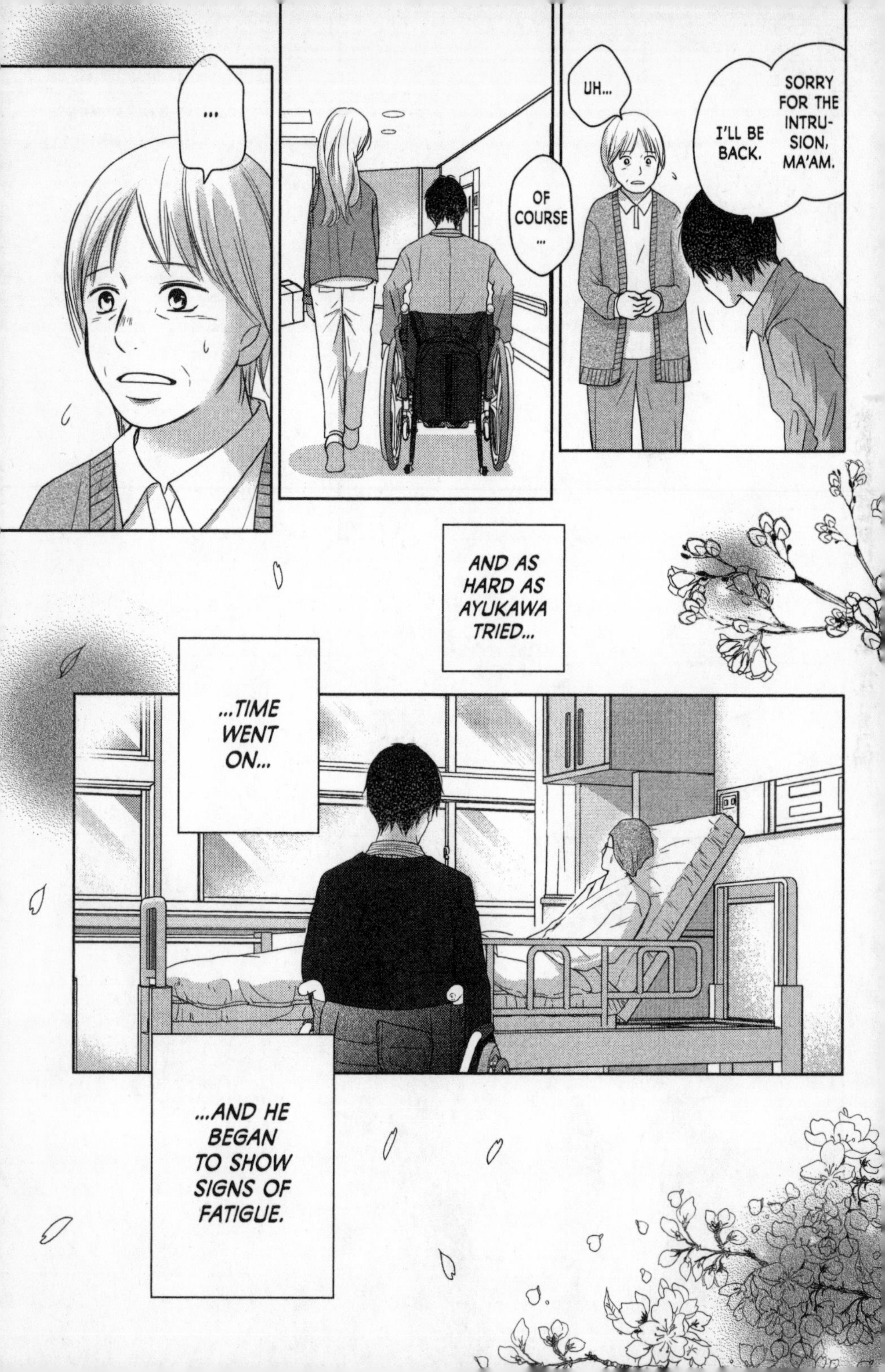
SORRY FOR THE INTRU-SION, MA'AM.
I'LL BE BACK.
UH...
OF COURSE...
...
AND AS HARD AS AYUKAWA TRIED...
...TIME WENT ON...
...AND HE BEGAN TO SHOW SIGNS OF FATIGUE.

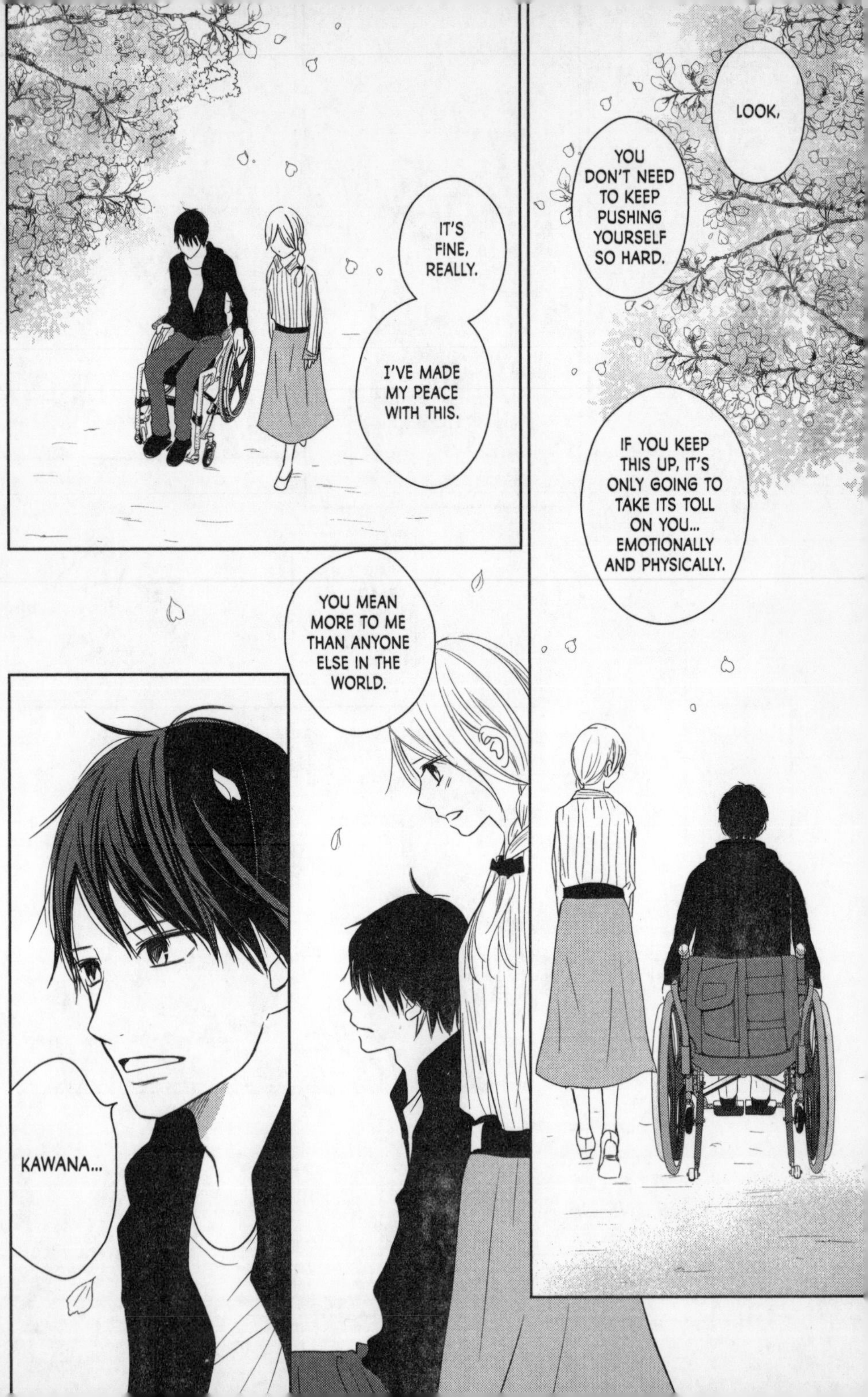
LOOK,
YOU DON'T NEED TO KEEP PUSHING YOURSELF SO HARD.
IF YOU KEEP THIS UP, IT'S ONLY GOING TO TAKE ITS TOLL ON YOU... EMOTIONALLY AND PHYSICALLY.
IT'S FINE, REALLY.
I'VE MADE MY PEACE WITH THIS.
YOU MEAN MORE TO ME THAN ANYONE ELSE IN THE WORLD.
KAWANA...

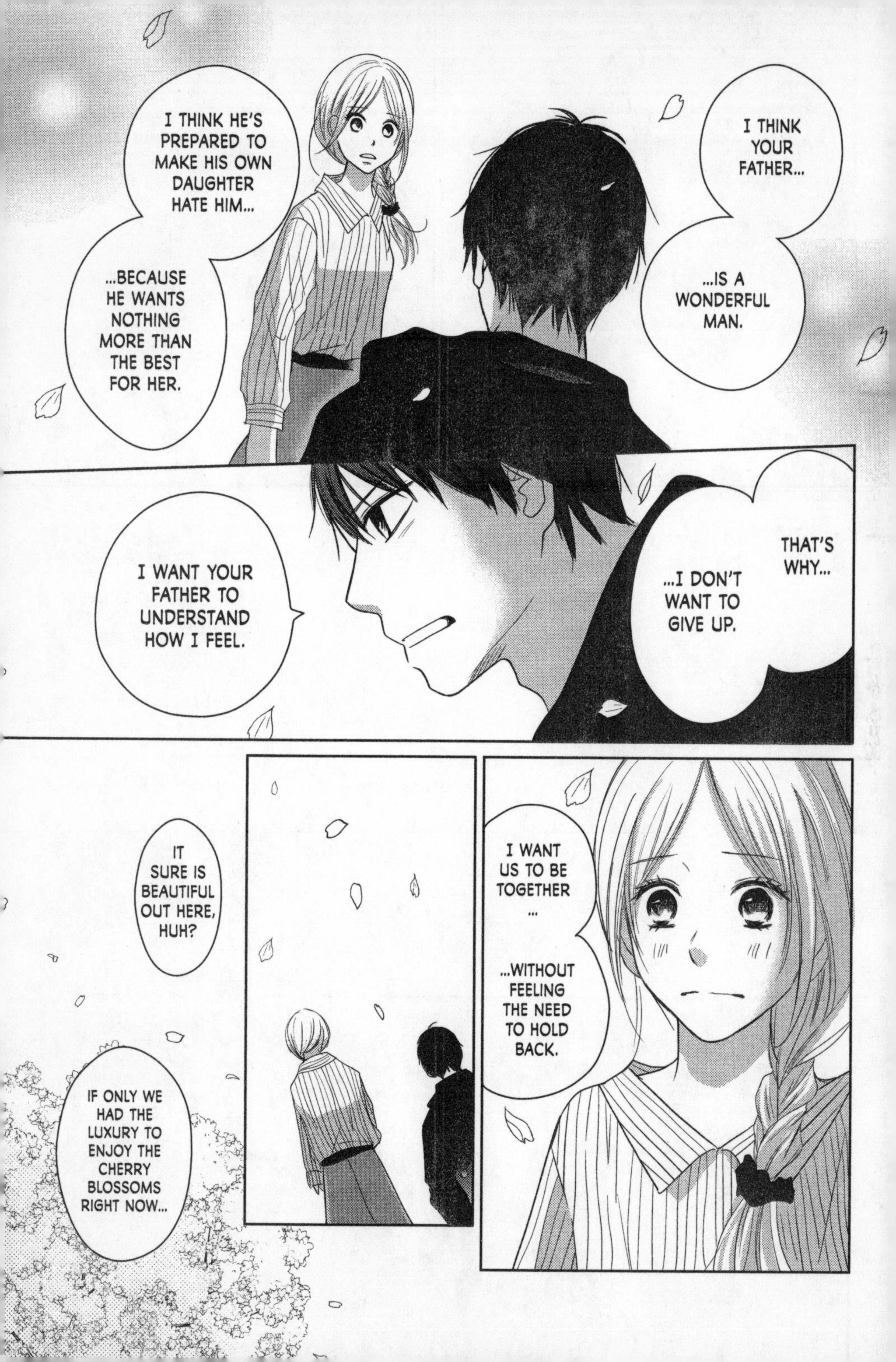
I THINK YOUR FATHER...
...IS A WONDERFUL MAN.
I THINK HE'S PREPARED TO MAKE HIS OWN DAUGHTER HATE HIM...
...BECAUSE HE WANTS NOTHING MORE THAN THE BEST FOR HER.
THAT'S WHY...
...I DON'T WANT TO GIVE UP.
I WANT YOUR FATHER TO UNDERSTAND HOW I FEEL.
I WANT US TO BE TOGETHER ...
...WITHOUT FEELING THE NEED TO HOLD BACK.
IT SURE IS BEAUTIFUL OUT HERE, HUH?
IF ONLY WE HAD THE LUXURY TO ENJOY THE CHERRY BLOSSOMS RIGHT NOW...

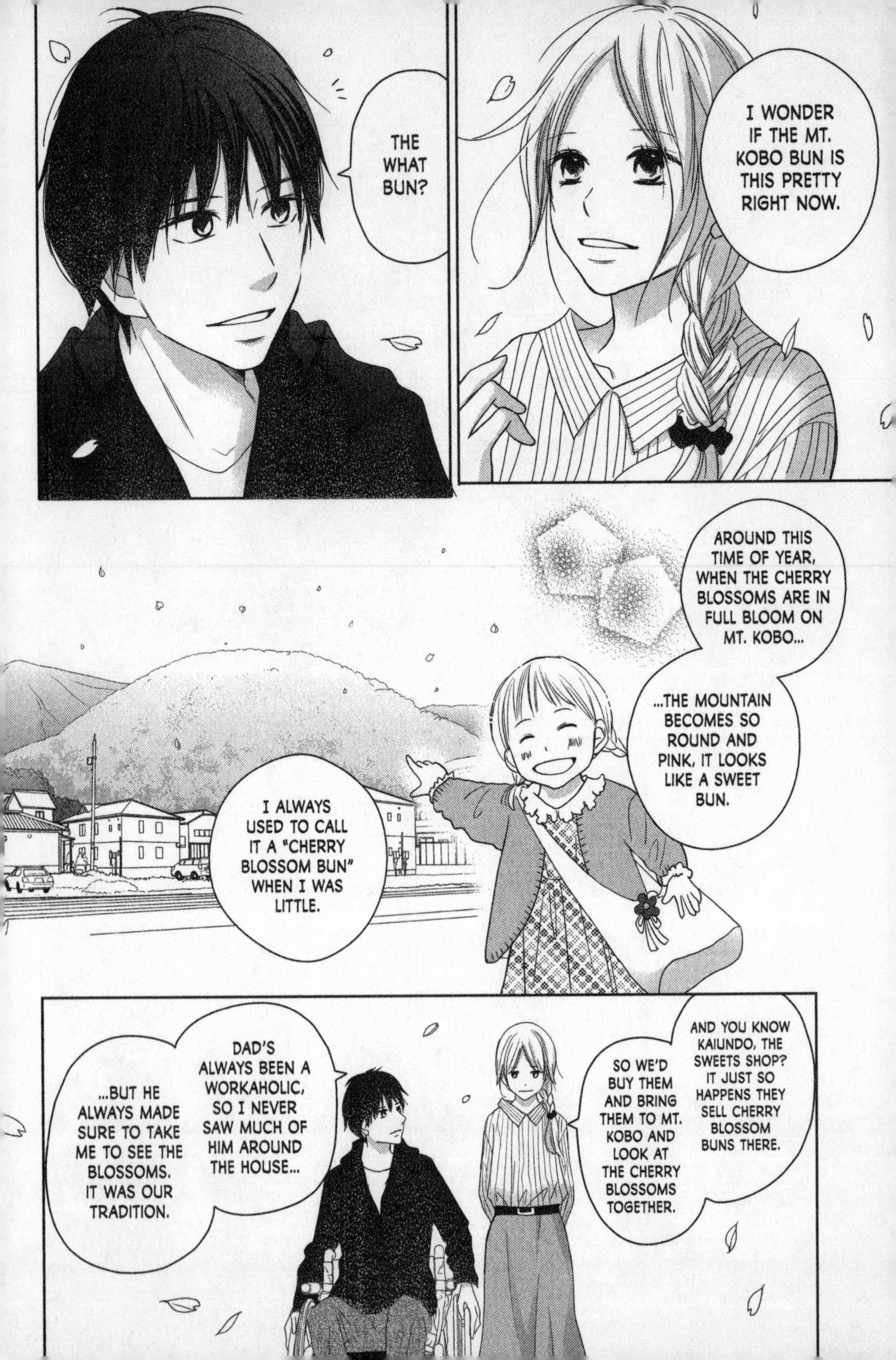
I WONDER IF THE MT. KOBO BUN IS THIS PRETTY RIGHT NOW.
THE WHAT BUN?
AROUND THIS TIME OF YEAR, WHEN THE CHERRY BLOSSOMS ARE IN FULL BLOOM ON MT. KOBO...
...THE MOUNTAIN BECOMES SO ROUND AND PINK, IT LOOKS LIKE A SWEET BUN.
I ALWAYS USED TO CALL IT A "CHERRY BLOSSOM BUN" WHEN I WAS LITTLE.
AND YOU KNOW KAIUNDO, THE SWEETS SHOP? IT JUST SO HAPPENS THEY SELL CHERRY BLOSSOM BUNS THERE.
SO WE'D BUY THEM AND BRING THEM TO MT. KOBO AND LOOK AT THE CHERRY BLOSSOMS TOGETHER.
DAD'S ALWAYS BEEN A WORKAHOLIC, SO I NEVER SAW MUCH OF HIM AROUND THE HOUSE...
...BUT HE ALWAYS MADE SURE TO TAKE ME TO SEE THE BLOSSOMS. IT WAS OUR TRADITION.

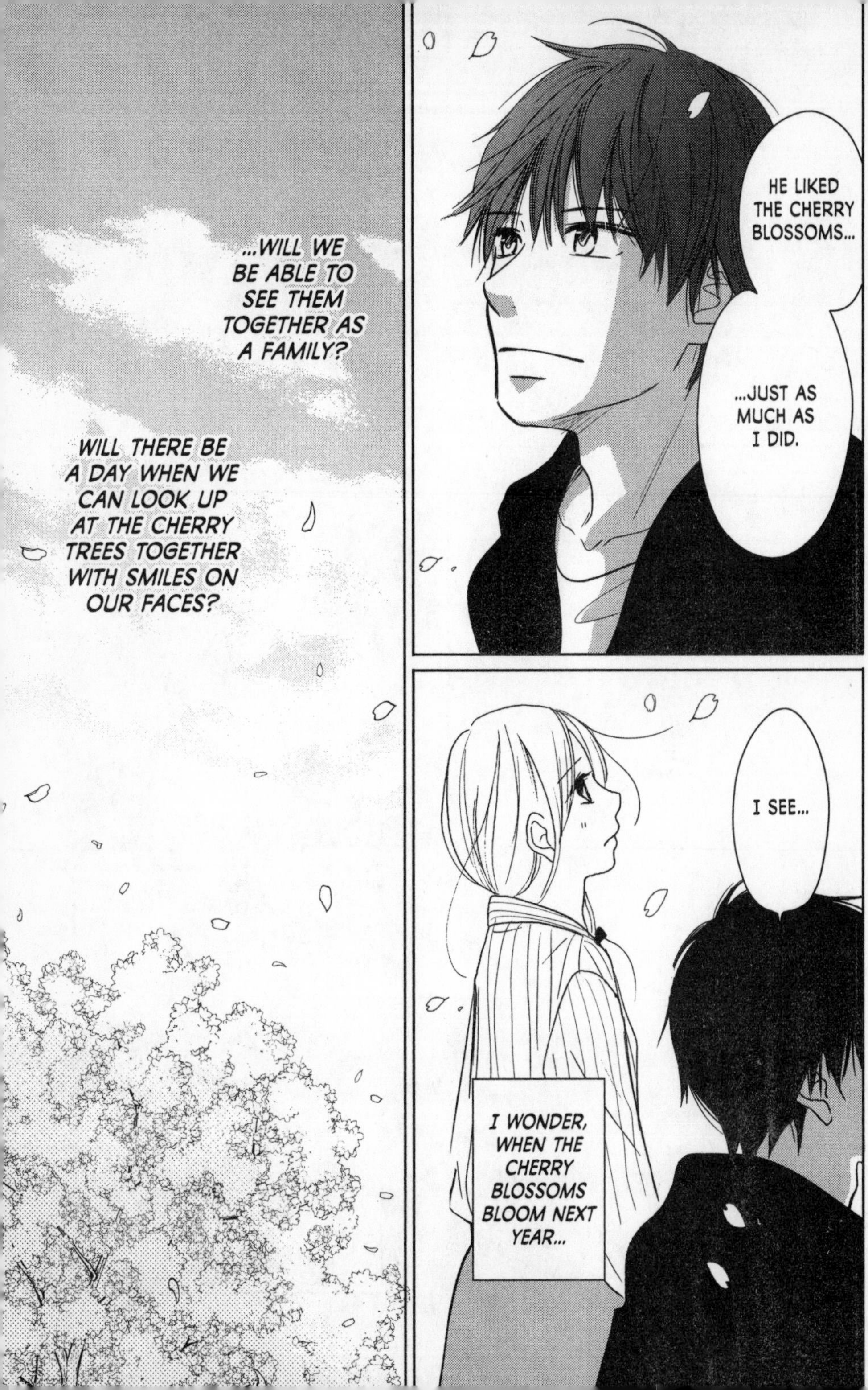
HE LIKED THE CHERRY BLOSSOMS...
...JUST AS MUCH AS I DID.
I SEE...
I WONDER, WHEN THE CHERRY BLOSSOMS BLOOM NEXT YEAR...
...WILL WE BE ABLE TO SEE THEM TOGETHER AS A FAMILY?
WILL THERE BE A DAY WHEN WE CAN LOOK UP AT THE CHERRY TREES TOGETHER WITH SMILES ON OUR FACES?

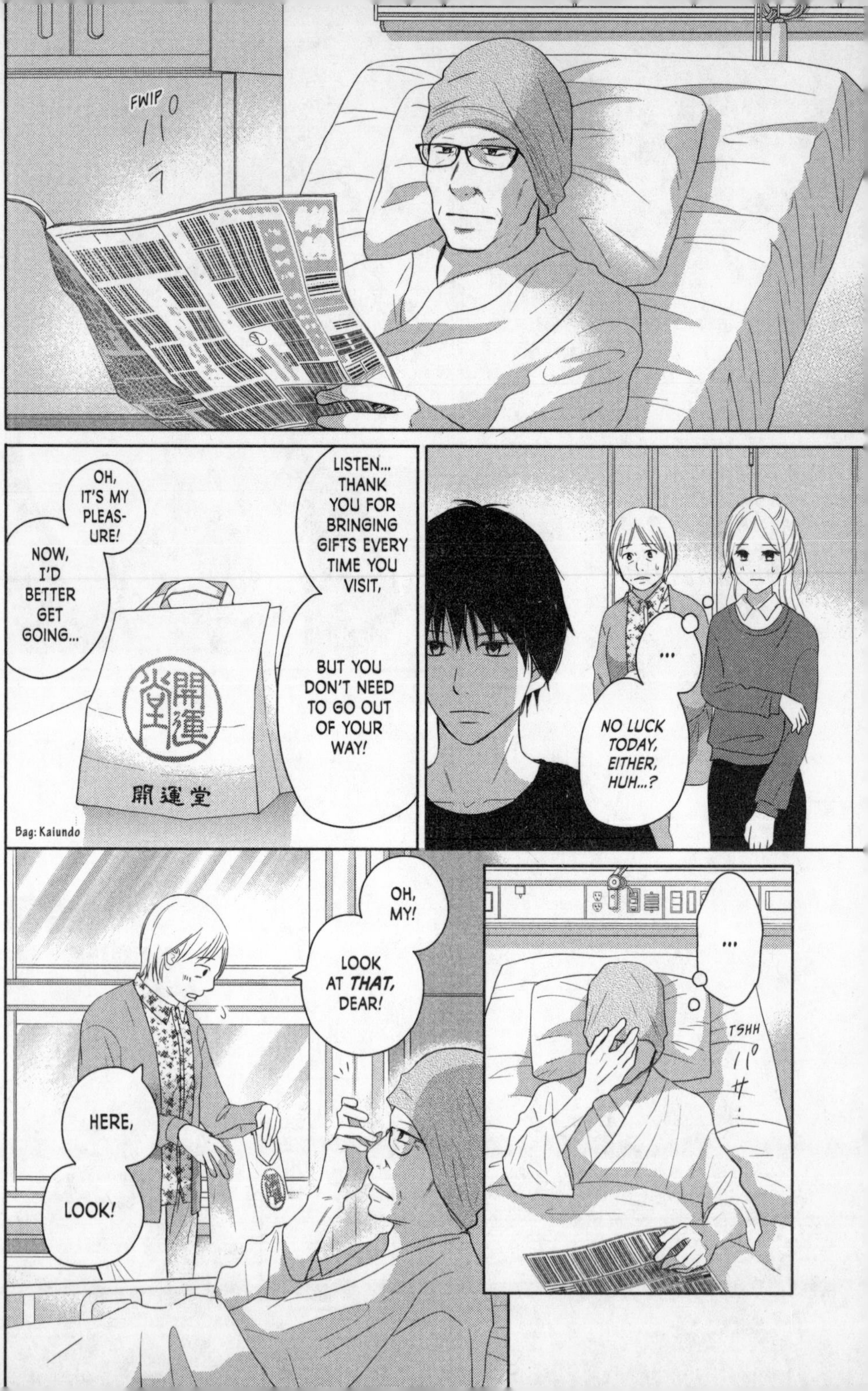
FWIP
パラ
...
NO LUCK TODAY, EITHER, HUH...?
LISTEN... THANK YOU FOR BRINGING GIFTS EVERY TIME YOU VISIT,
BUT YOU DON'T NEED TO GO OUT OF YOUR WAY!
OH, IT'S MY PLEASURE!
NOW, I'D BETTER GET GOING...
開運堂
Bag: Kaiundo
...
TSHH
パサ...
OH, MY!
LOOK AT THAT, DEAR!
HERE,
LOOK!

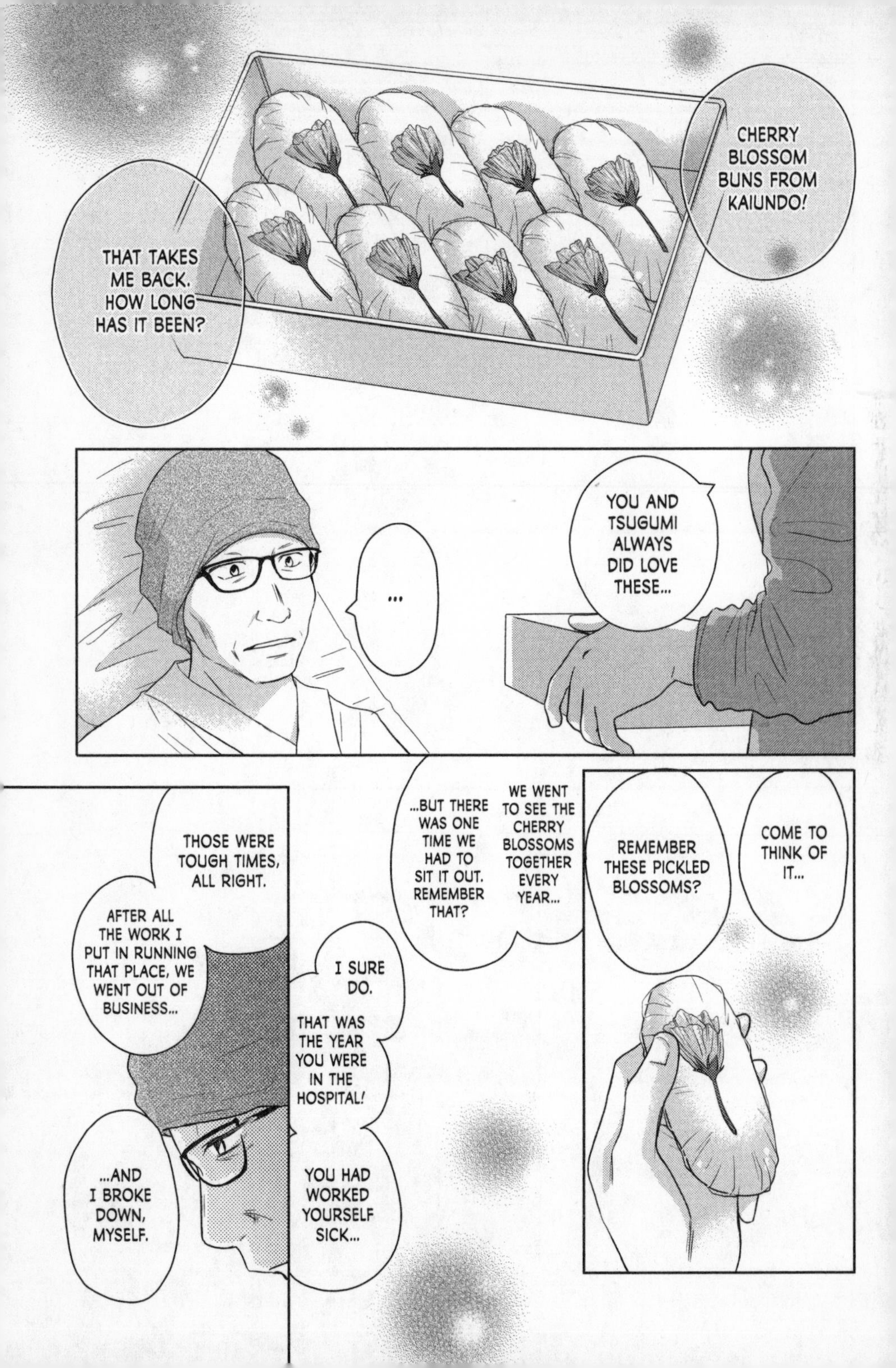
CHERRY BLOSSOM BUNS FROM KAIUNDO!
THAT TAKES ME BACK. HOW LONG HAS IT BEEN?
YOU AND TSUGUMI ALWAYS DID LOVE THESE...
...
COME TO THINK OF IT...
REMEMBER THESE PICKLED BLOSSOMS?
WE WENT TO SEE THE CHERRY BLOSSOMS TOGETHER EVERY YEAR...
...BUT THERE WAS ONE TIME WE HAD TO SIT IT OUT. REMEMBER THAT?
I SURE DO.
THAT WAS THE YEAR YOU WERE IN THE HOSPITAL!
THOSE WERE TOUGH TIMES, ALL RIGHT.
AFTER ALL THE WORK I PUT IN RUNNING THAT PLACE, WE WENT OUT OF BUSINESS...
YOU HAD WORKED YOURSELF SICK...
...AND I BROKE DOWN, MYSELF.

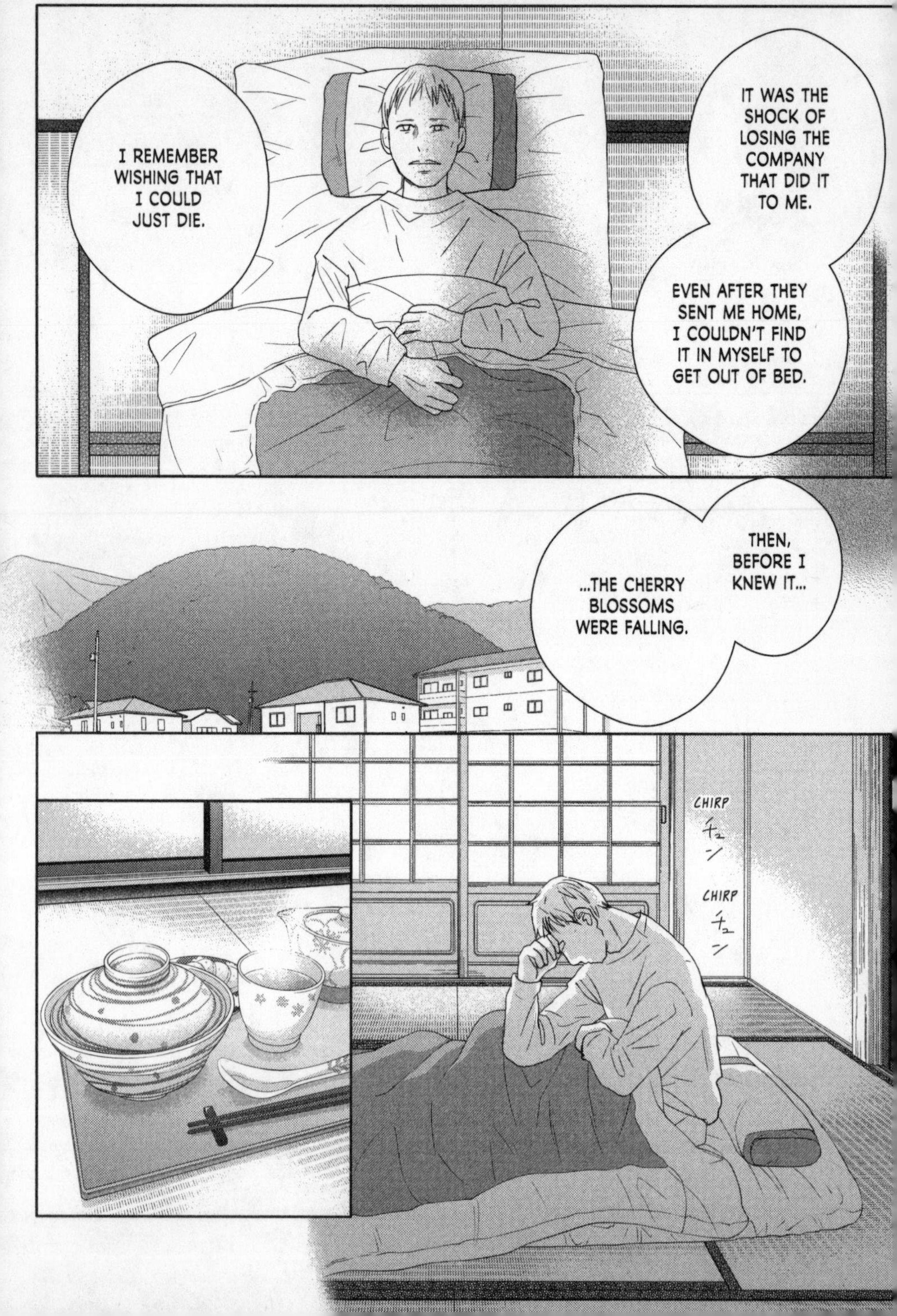
IT WAS THE SHOCK OF LOSING THE COMPANY THAT DID IT TO ME.
EVEN AFTER THEY SENT ME HOME, I COULDN'T FIND IT IN MYSELF TO GET OUT OF BED.
I REMEMBER WISHING THAT I COULD JUST DIE.
THEN, BEFORE I KNEW IT...
...THE CHERRY BLOSSOMS WERE FALLING.
CHIRP
チュン
CHIRP
チュン

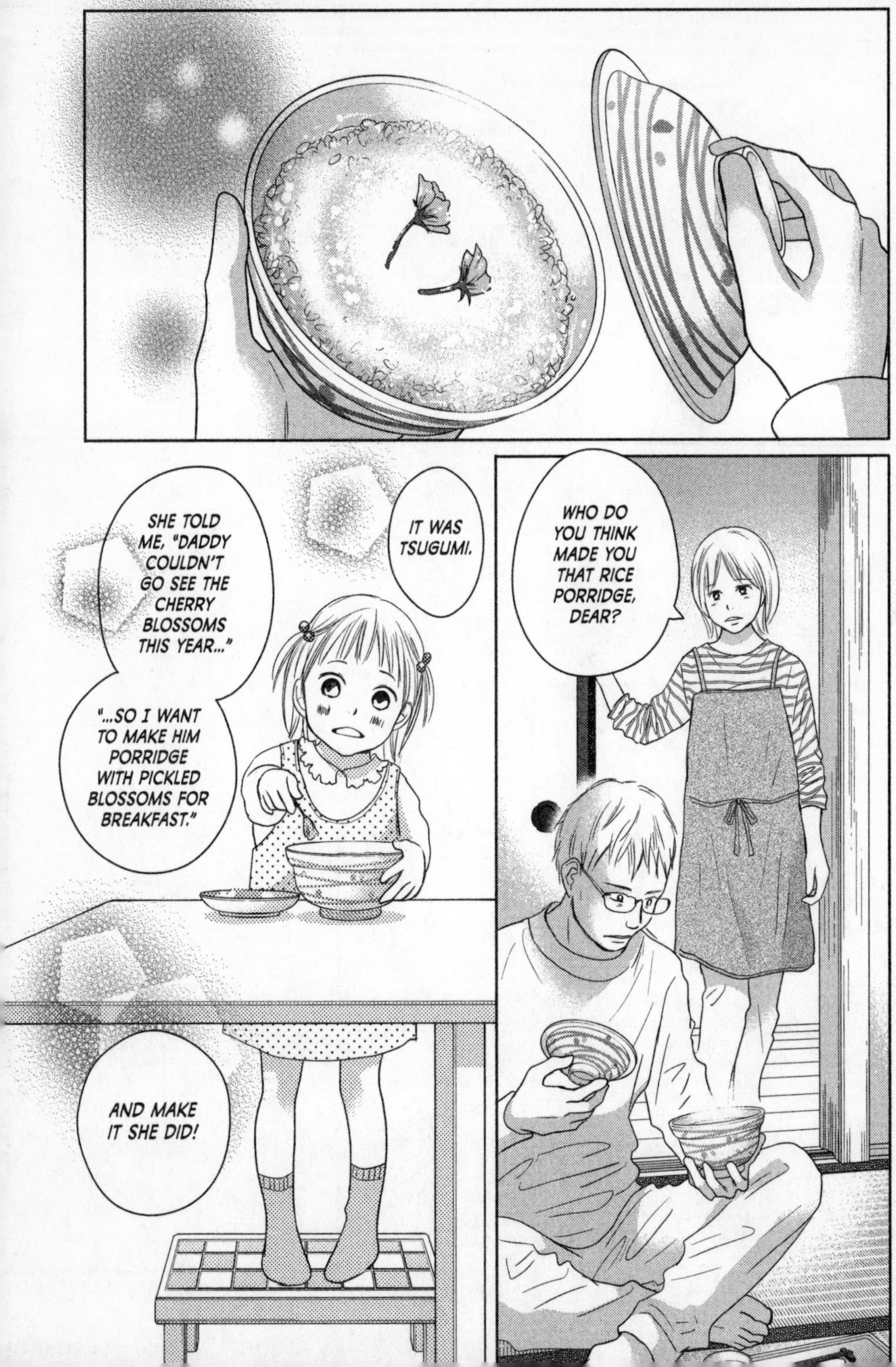
WHO DO YOU THINK MADE YOU THAT RICE PORRIDGE, DEAR?
IT WAS TSUGUMI.
SHE TOLD ME, "DADDY COULDN'T GO SEE THE CHERRY BLOSSOMS THIS YEAR..."
"...SO I WANT TO MAKE HIM PORRIDGE WITH PICKLED BLOSSOMS FOR BREAKFAST."
AND MAKE IT SHE DID!

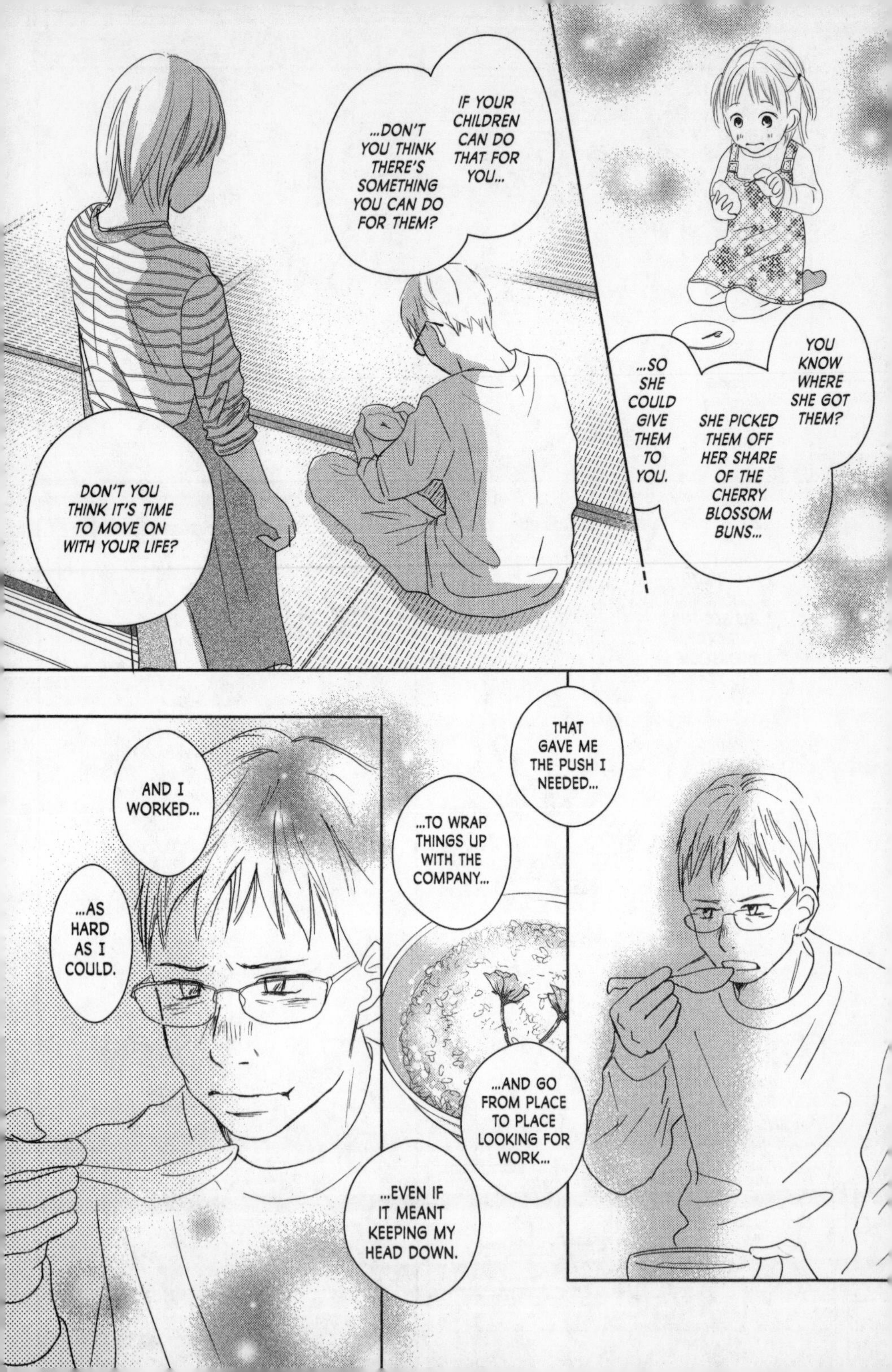
YOU KNOW WHERE SHE GOT THEM?
SHE PICKED THEM OFF HER SHARE OF THE CHERRY BLOSSOM BUNS...
...SO SHE COULD GIVE THEM TO YOU.
IF YOUR CHILDREN CAN DO THAT FOR YOU...
...DON'T YOU THINK THERE'S SOMETHING YOU CAN DO FOR THEM?
DON'T YOU THINK IT'S TIME TO MOVE ON WITH YOUR LIFE?
THAT GAVE ME THE PUSH I NEEDED...
...TO WRAP THINGS UP WITH THE COMPANY...
...AND GO FROM PLACE TO PLACE LOOKING FOR WORK...
...EVEN IF IT MEANT KEEPING MY HEAD DOWN.
AND I WORKED...
...AS HARD AS I COULD.

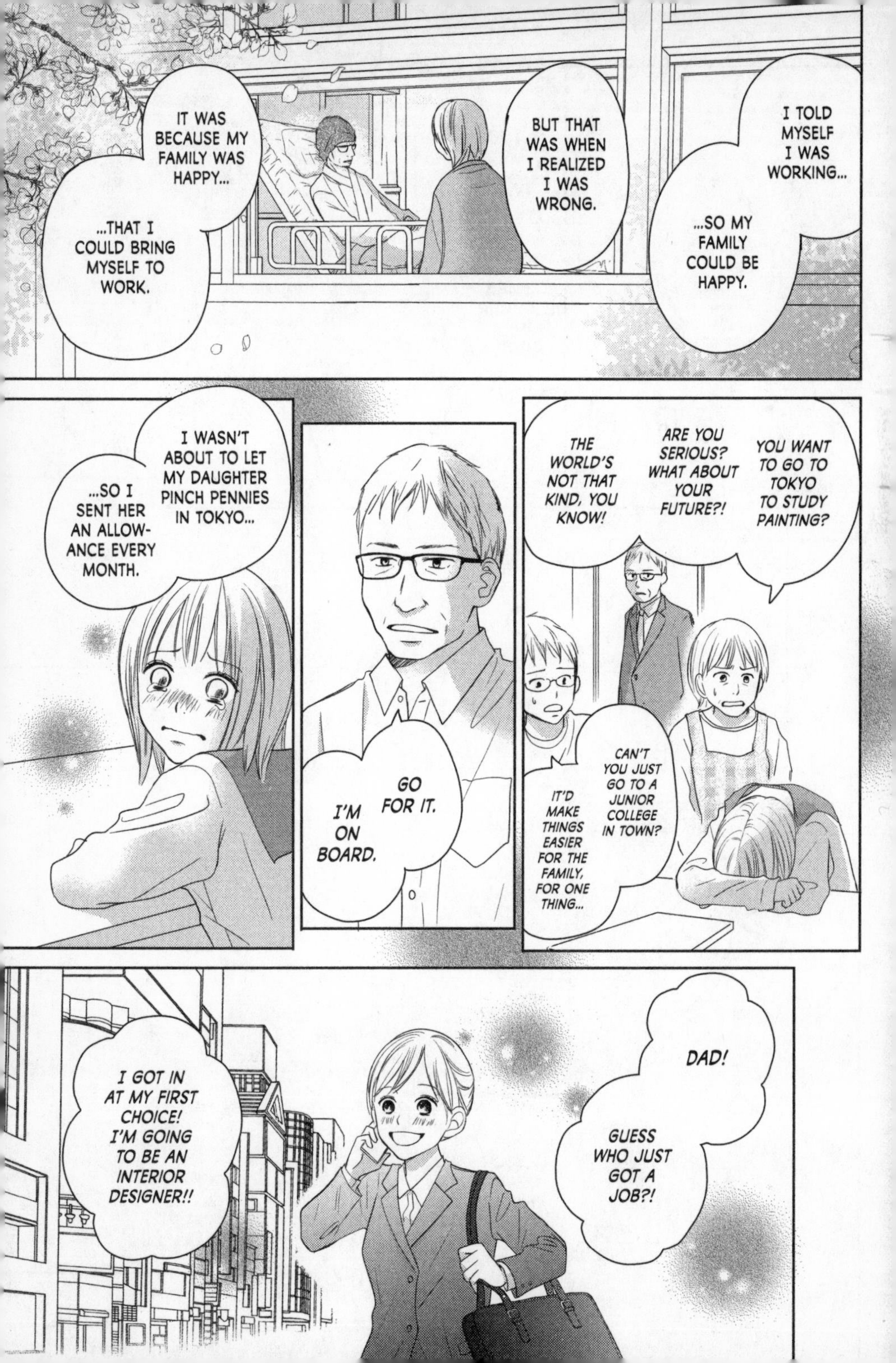
I TOLD MYSELF I WAS WORKING...
...SO MY FAMILY COULD BE HAPPY.
BUT THAT WAS WHEN I REALIZED I WAS WRONG.
IT WAS BECAUSE MY FAMILY WAS HAPPY...
...THAT I COULD BRING MYSELF TO WORK.
YOU WANT TO GO TO TOKYO TO STUDY PAINTING?
ARE YOU SERIOUS? WHAT ABOUT YOUR FUTURE?!
THE WORLD'S NOT THAT KIND, YOU KNOW!
CAN'T YOU JUST GO TO A JUNIOR COLLEGE IN TOWN?
IT'D MAKE THINGS EASIER FOR THE FAMILY, FOR ONE THING...
GO FOR IT.
I'M ON BOARD.
I WASN'T ABOUT TO LET MY DAUGHTER PINCH PENNIES IN TOKYO...
...SO I SENT HER AN ALLOWANCE EVERY MONTH.
DAD!
GUESS WHO JUST GOT A JOB?!
I GOT IN AT MY FIRST CHOICE! I'M GOING TO BE AN INTERIOR DESIGNER!!

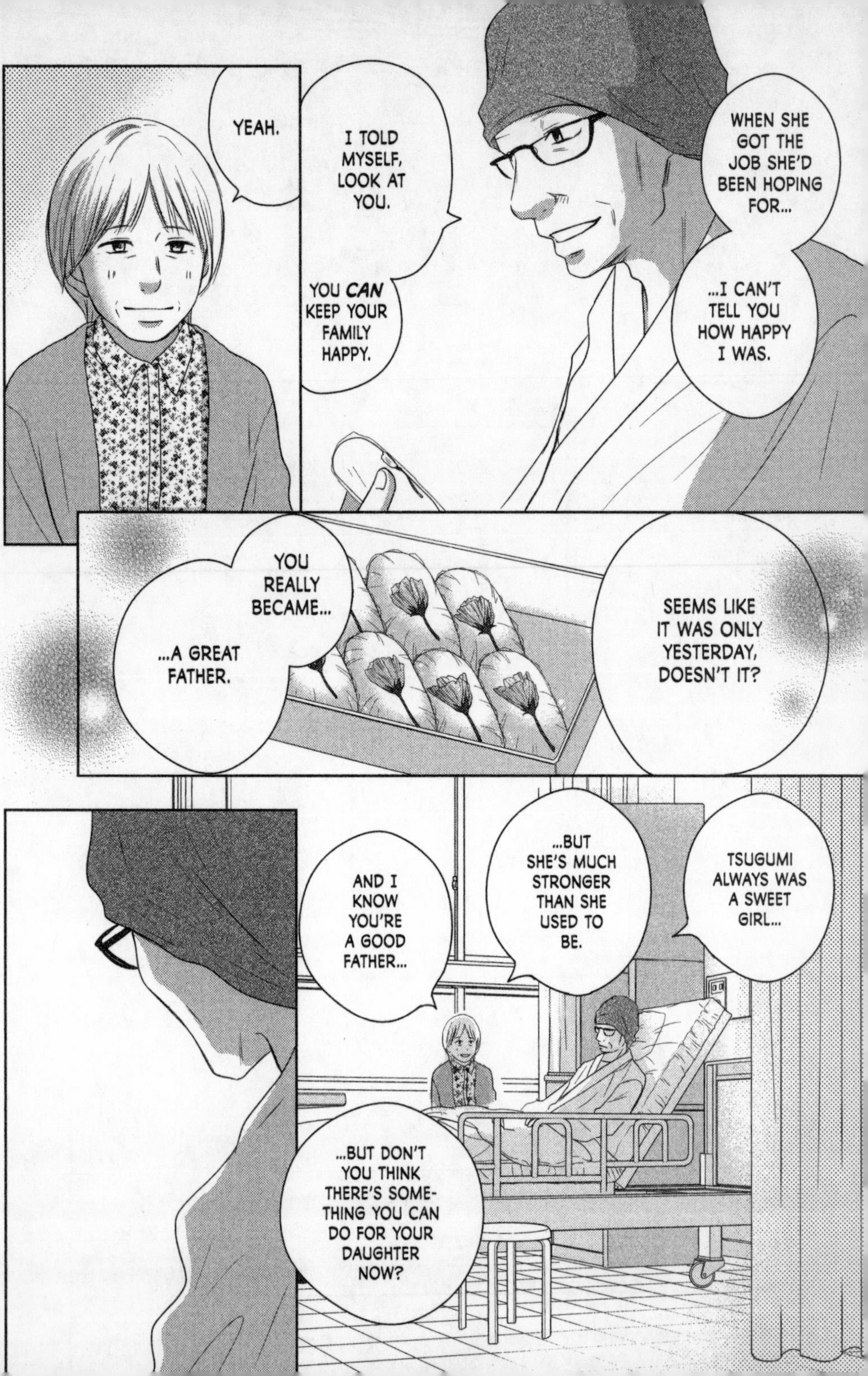
WHEN SHE GOT THE JOB SHE'D BEEN HOPING FOR...
...I CAN'T TELL YOU HOW HAPPY I WAS.
I TOLD MYSELF, LOOK AT YOU.
YOU *CAN* KEEP YOUR FAMILY HAPPY.
YEAH.
SEEMS LIKE IT WAS ONLY YESTERDAY, DOESN'T IT?
YOU REALLY BECAME...
...A GREAT FATHER.
TSUGUMI ALWAYS WAS A SWEET GIRL...
...BUT SHE'S MUCH STRONGER THAN SHE USED TO BE.
AND I KNOW YOU'RE A GOOD FATHER...
...BUT DON'T YOU THINK THERE'S SOME-THING YOU CAN DO FOR YOUR DAUGHTER NOW?

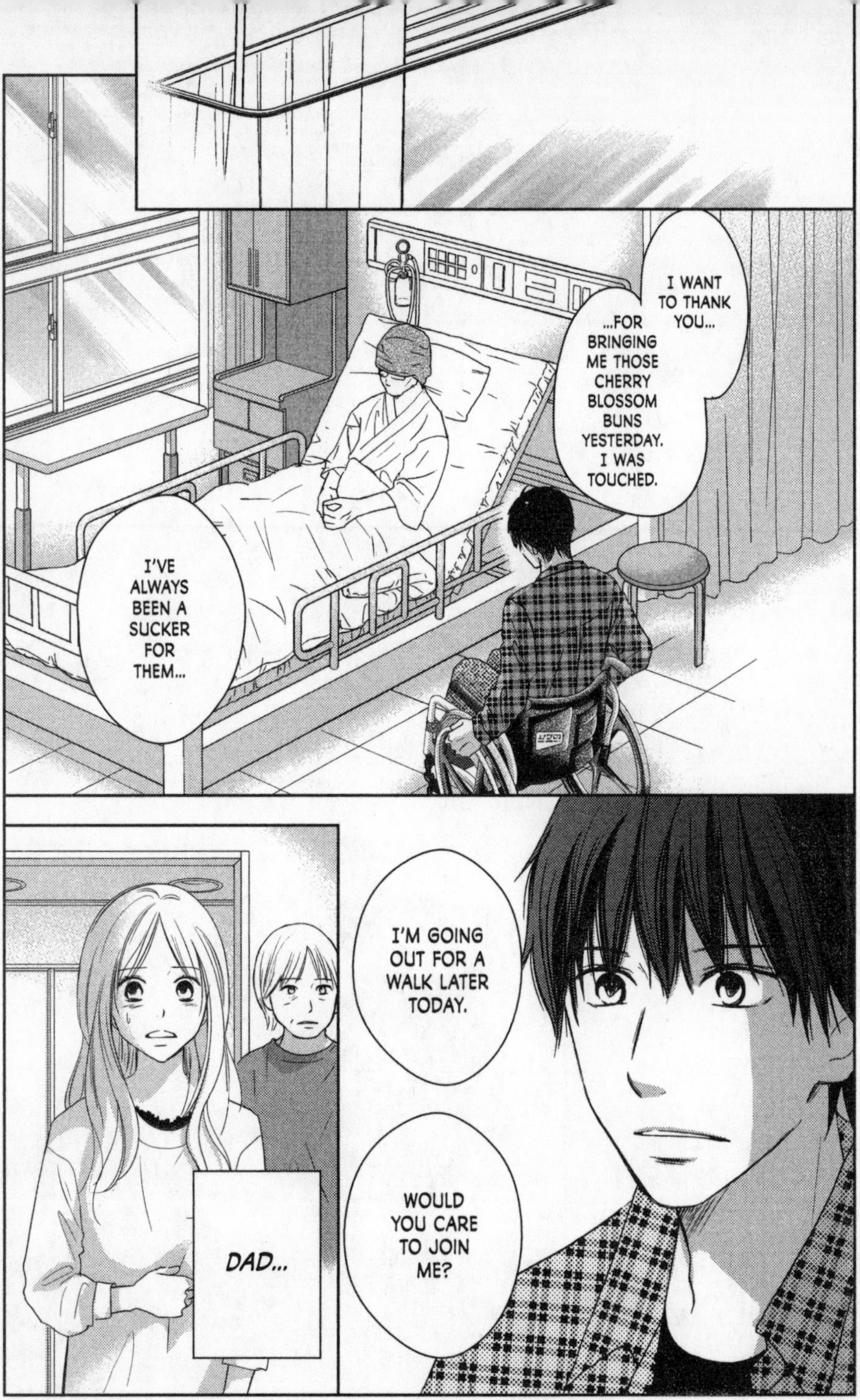
I WANT TO THANK YOU...
...FOR BRINGING ME THOSE CHERRY BLOSSOM BUNS YESTERDAY. I WAS TOUCHED.
I'VE ALWAYS BEEN A SUCKER FOR THEM...
I'M GOING OUT FOR A WALK LATER TODAY.
WOULD YOU CARE TO JOIN ME?
DAD...

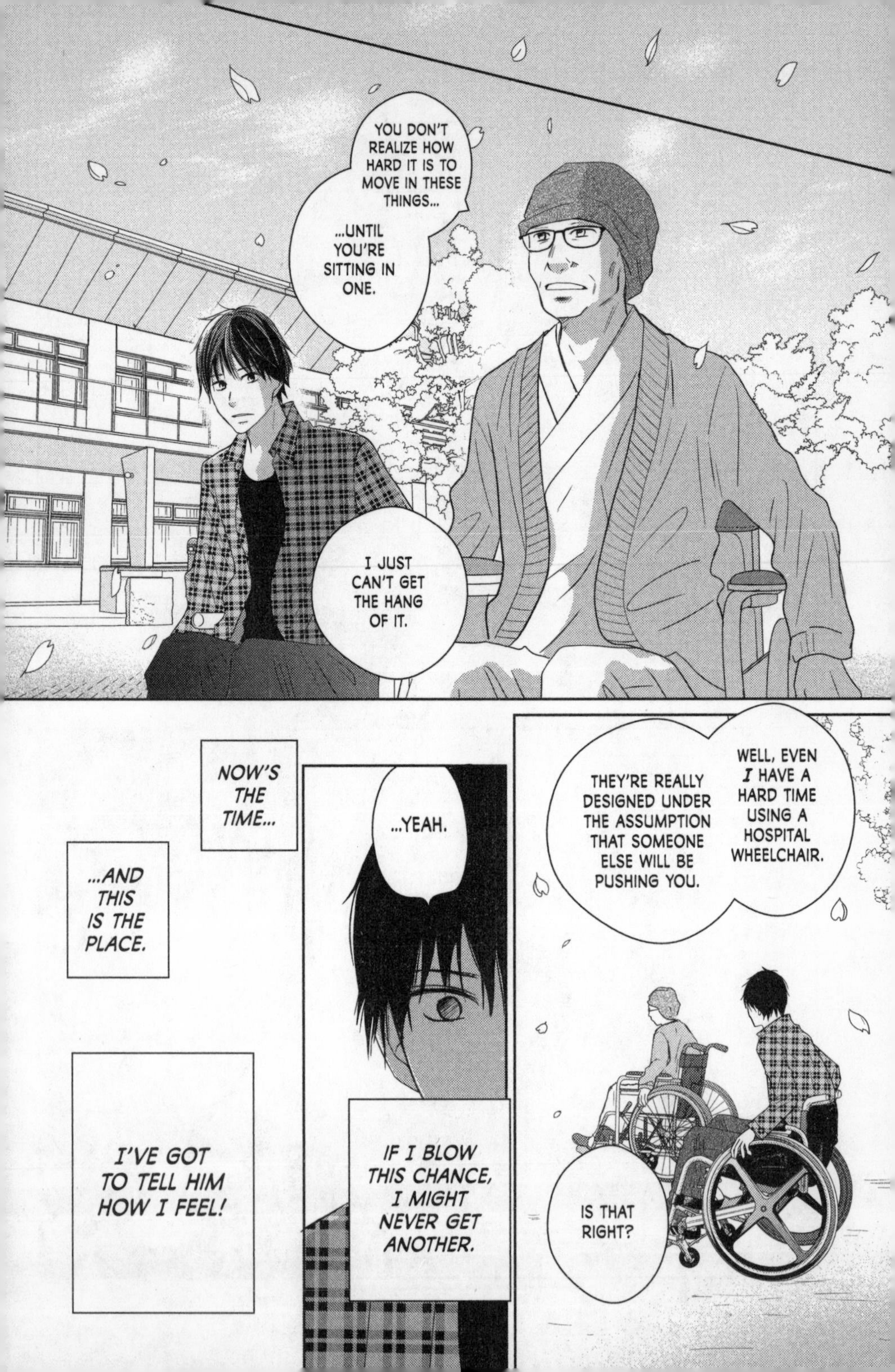
YOU DON'T REALIZE HOW HARD IT IS TO MOVE IN THESE THINGS...
...UNTIL YOU'RE SITTING IN ONE.
I JUST CAN'T GET THE HANG OF IT.
WELL, EVEN *I* HAVE A HARD TIME USING A HOSPITAL WHEELCHAIR.
THEY'RE REALLY DESIGNED UNDER THE ASSUMPTION THAT SOMEONE ELSE WILL BE PUSHING YOU.
IS THAT RIGHT?
...YEAH.
IF I BLOW THIS CHANCE, I MIGHT NEVER GET ANOTHER.
NOW'S THE TIME...
...AND THIS IS THE PLACE.
I'VE GOT TO TELL HIM HOW I FEEL!

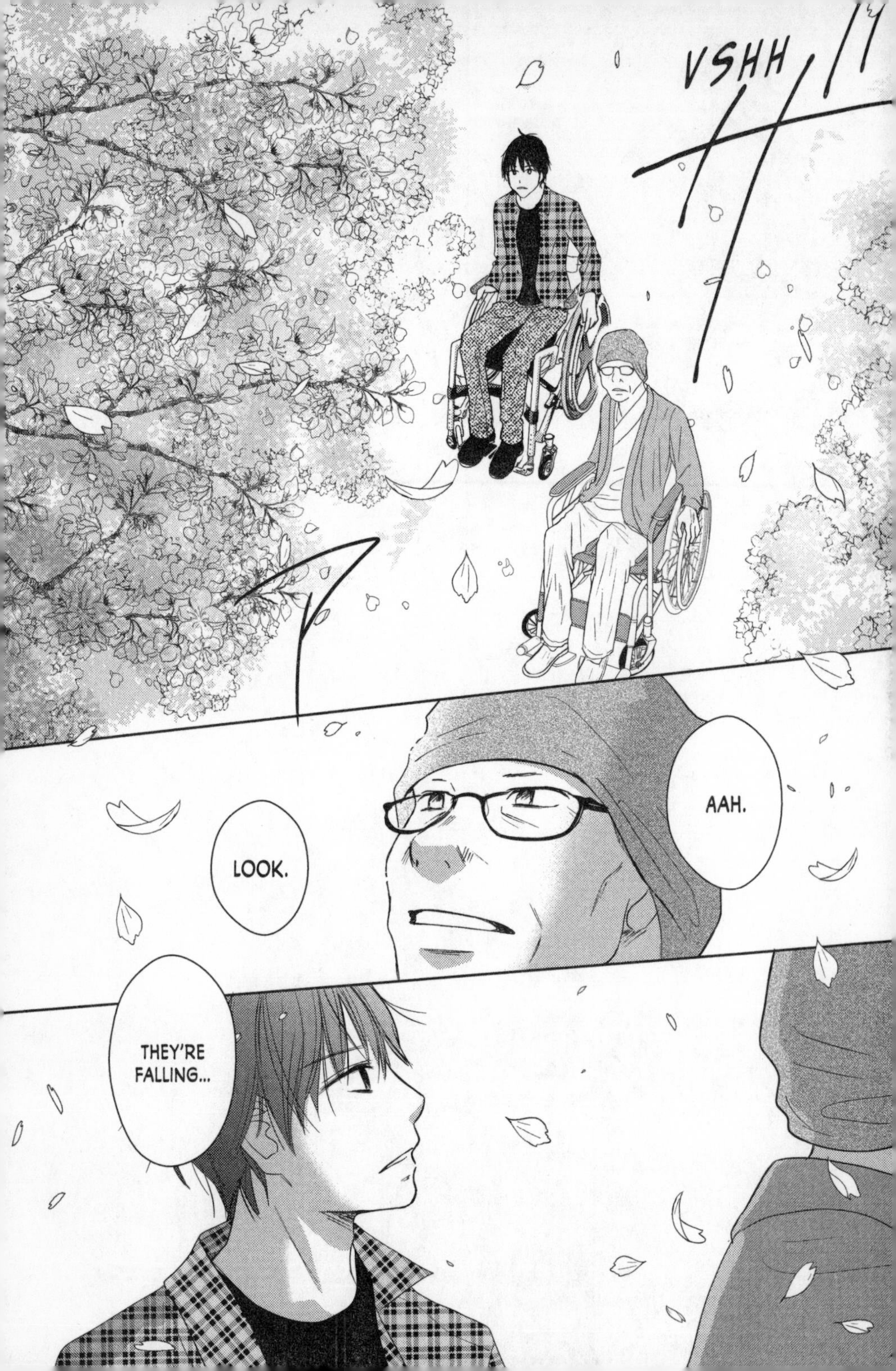
VSHH
AAH.
LOOK.
THEY'RE FALLING...

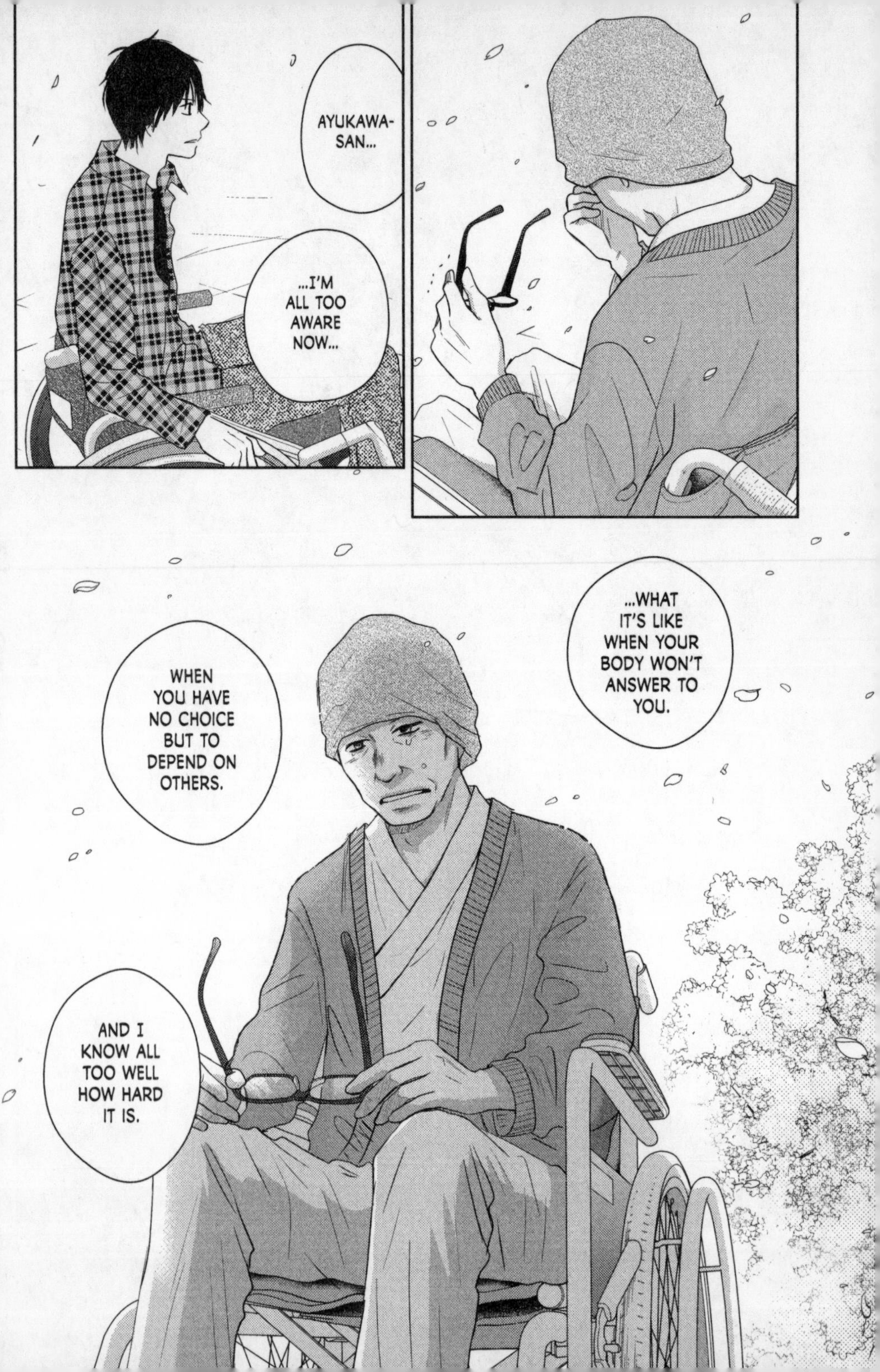
AYUKAWA-SAN...
...I'M ALL TOO AWARE NOW...
...WHAT IT'S LIKE WHEN YOUR BODY WON'T ANSWER TO YOU.
WHEN YOU HAVE NO CHOICE BUT TO DEPEND ON OTHERS.
AND I KNOW ALL TOO WELL HOW HARD IT IS.

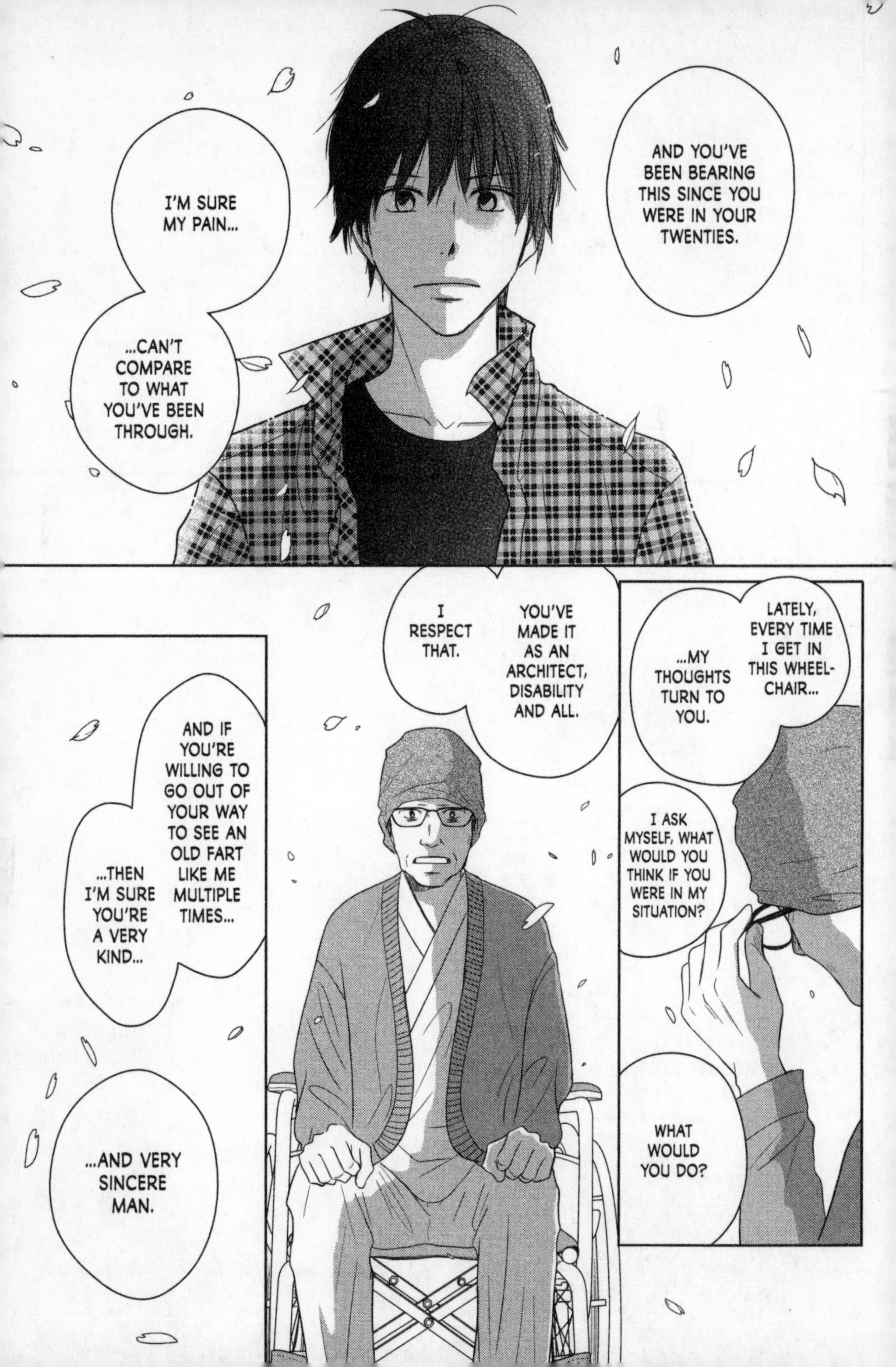
AND YOU'VE BEEN BEARING THIS SINCE YOU WERE IN YOUR TWENTIES.
I'M SURE MY PAIN...
...CAN'T COMPARE TO WHAT YOU'VE BEEN THROUGH.
LATELY, EVERY TIME I GET IN THIS WHEEL-CHAIR...
...MY THOUGHTS TURN TO YOU.
I ASK MYSELF, WHAT WOULD YOU THINK IF YOU WERE IN MY SITUATION?
WHAT WOULD YOU DO?
YOU'VE MADE IT AS AN ARCHITECT, DISABILITY AND ALL.
I RESPECT THAT.
AND IF YOU'RE WILLING TO GO OUT OF YOUR WAY TO SEE AN OLD FART LIKE ME MULTIPLE TIMES...
...THEN I'M SURE YOU'RE A VERY KIND...
...AND VERY SINCERE MAN.

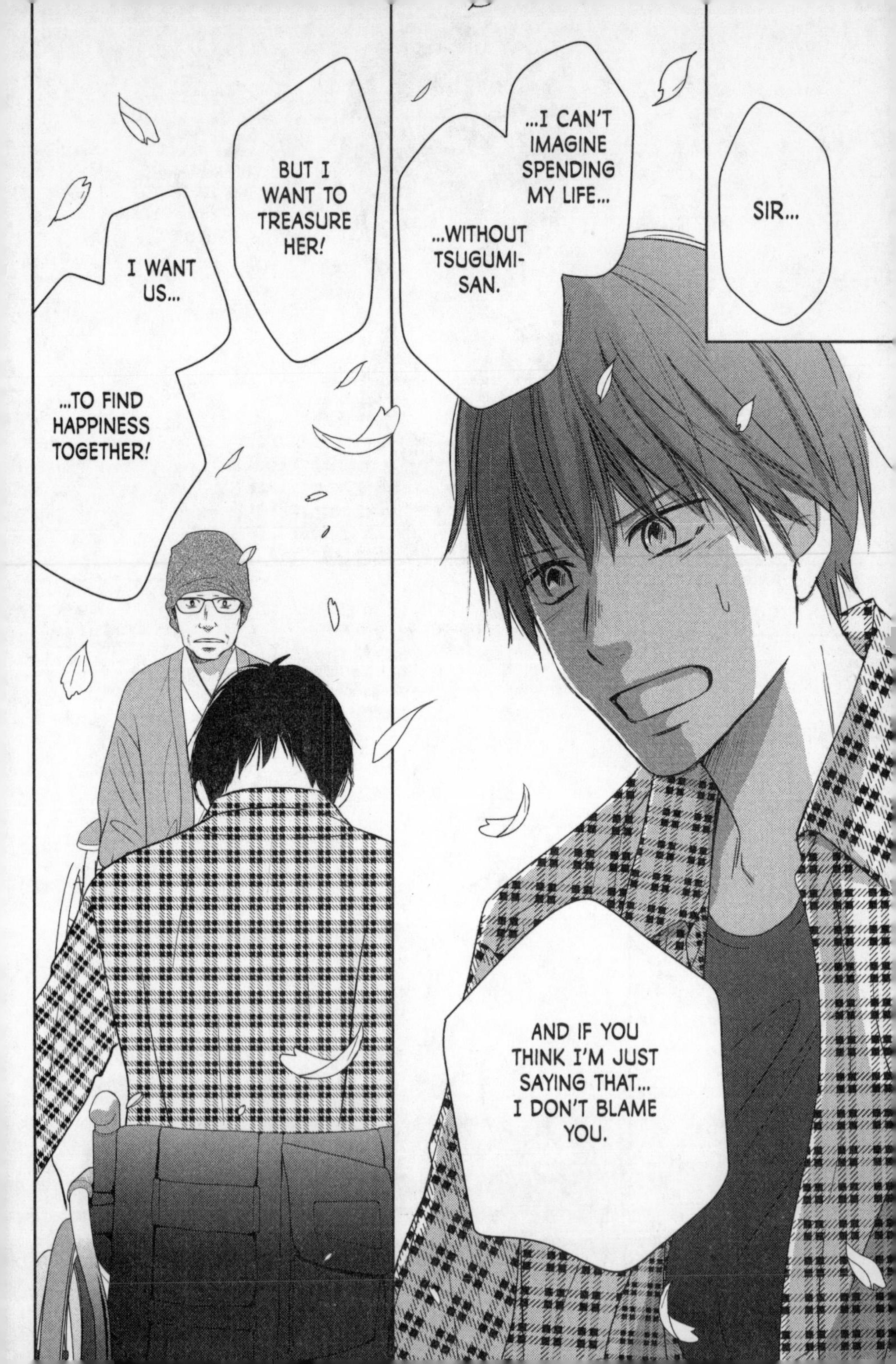
SIR...
...I CAN'T IMAGINE SPENDING MY LIFE...
...WITHOUT TSUGUMI-SAN.
AND IF YOU THINK I'M JUST SAYING THAT... I DON'T BLAME YOU.
BUT I WANT TO TREASURE HER!
I WANT US...
...TO FIND HAPPINESS TOGETHER!

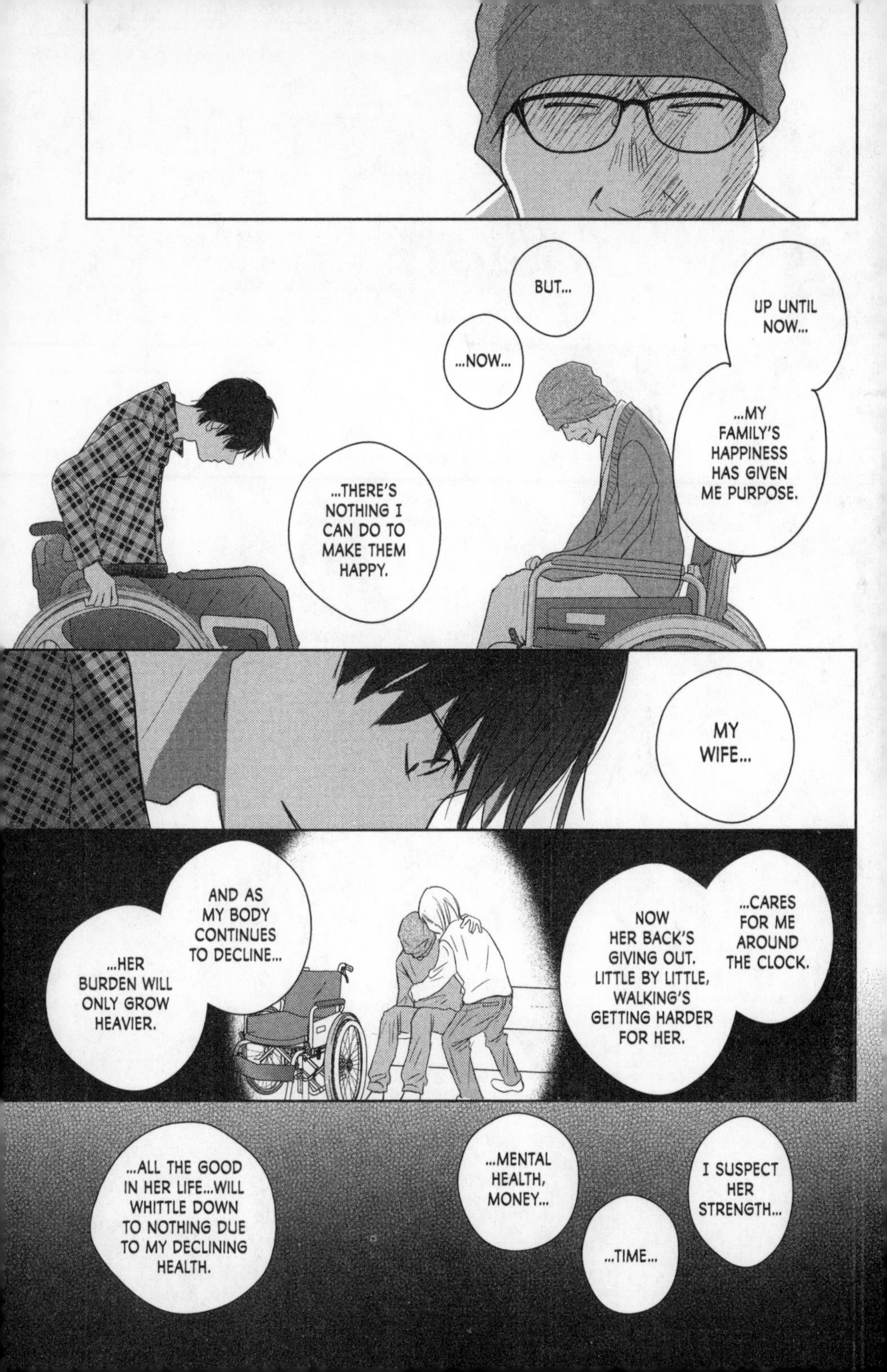
UP UNTIL NOW...
...MY FAMILY'S HAPPINESS HAS GIVEN ME PURPOSE.
BUT...
...NOW...
...THERE'S NOTHING I CAN DO TO MAKE THEM HAPPY.
MY WIFE...
...CARES FOR ME AROUND THE CLOCK.
NOW HER BACK'S GIVING OUT. LITTLE BY LITTLE, WALKING'S GETTING HARDER FOR HER.
AND AS MY BODY CONTINUES TO DECLINE...
...HER BURDEN WILL ONLY GROW HEAVIER.
I SUSPECT HER STRENGTH...
...MENTAL HEALTH, MONEY...
...TIME...
...ALL THE GOOD IN HER LIFE...WILL WHITTLE DOWN TO NOTHING DUE TO MY DECLINING HEALTH.

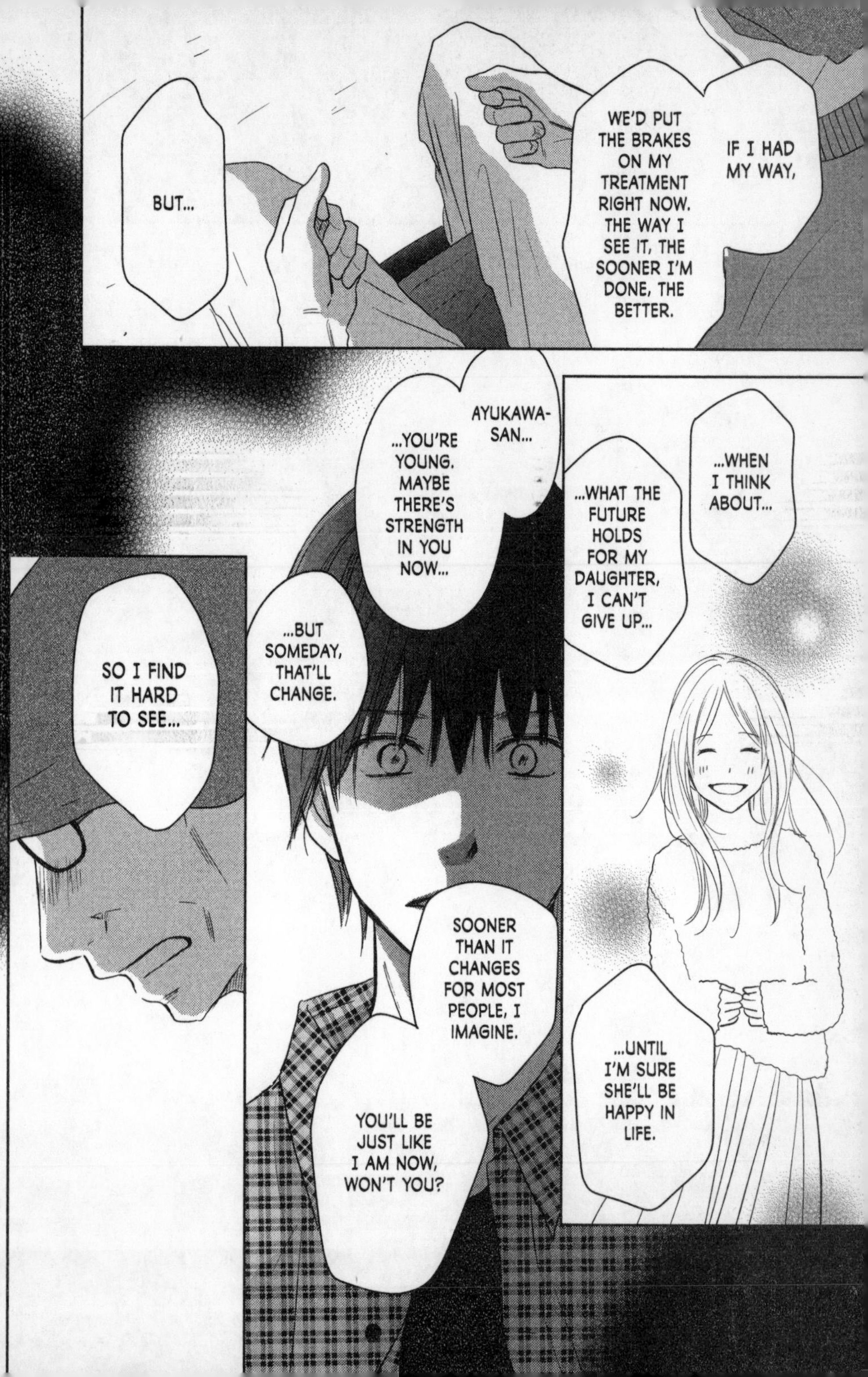
IF I HAD MY WAY,
WE'D PUT THE BRAKES ON MY TREATMENT RIGHT NOW. THE WAY I SEE IT, THE SOONER I'M DONE, THE BETTER.
BUT...
...WHEN I THINK ABOUT...
...WHAT THE FUTURE HOLDS FOR MY DAUGHTER, I CAN'T GIVE UP...
...UNTIL I'M SURE SHE'LL BE HAPPY IN LIFE.
AYUKAWA-SAN...
...YOU'RE YOUNG. MAYBE THERE'S STRENGTH IN YOU NOW...
...BUT SOMEDAY, THAT'LL CHANGE.
SOONER THAN IT CHANGES FOR MOST PEOPLE, I IMAGINE.
YOU'LL BE JUST LIKE I AM NOW, WON'T YOU?
SO I FIND IT HARD TO SEE...

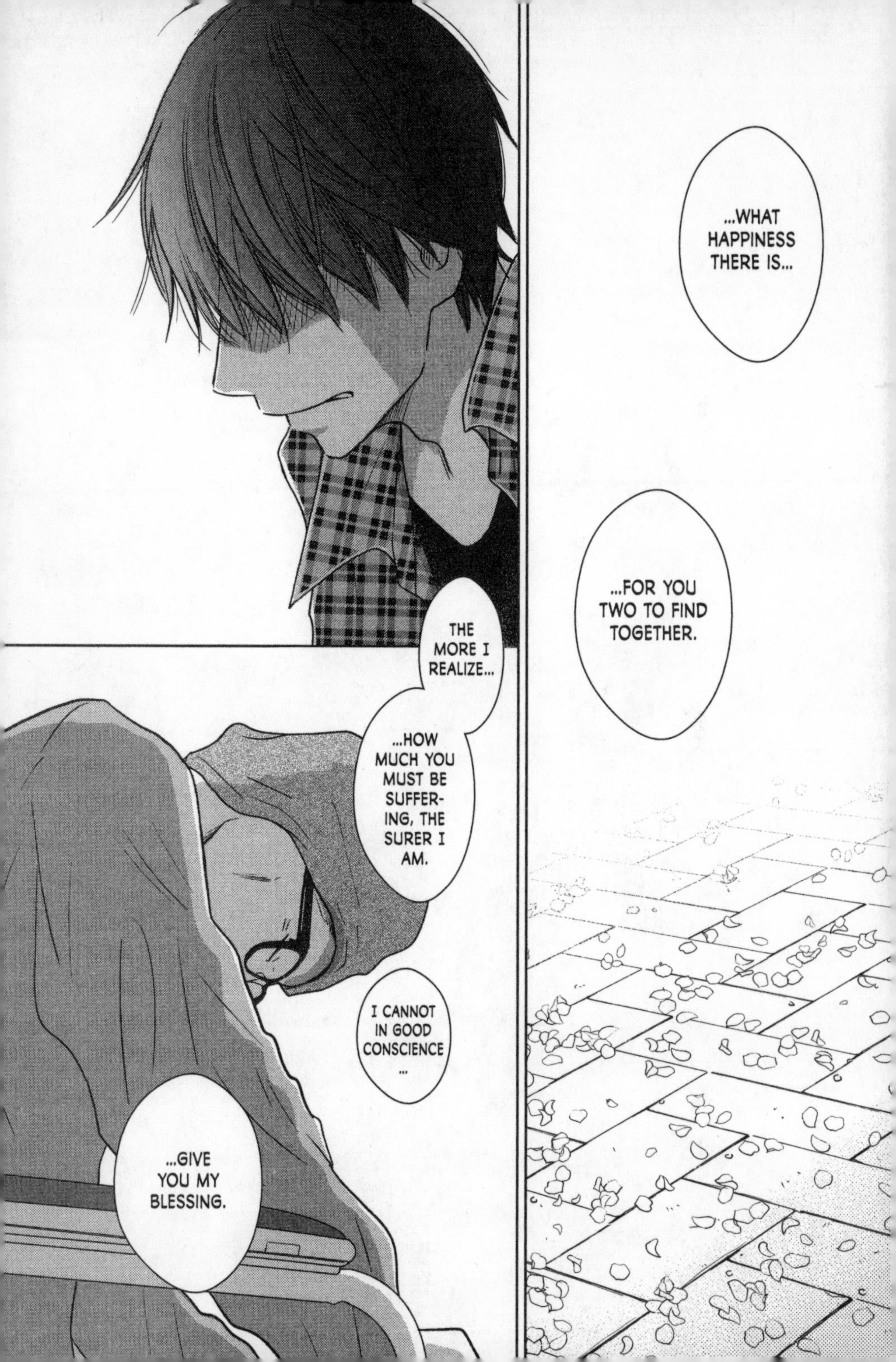
...WHAT HAPPINESS THERE IS...
...FOR YOU TWO TO FIND TOGETHER.
THE MORE I REALIZE...
...HOW MUCH YOU MUST BE SUFFER-ING, THE SURER I AM.
I CANNOT IN GOOD CONSCIENCE ...
...GIVE YOU MY BLESSING.

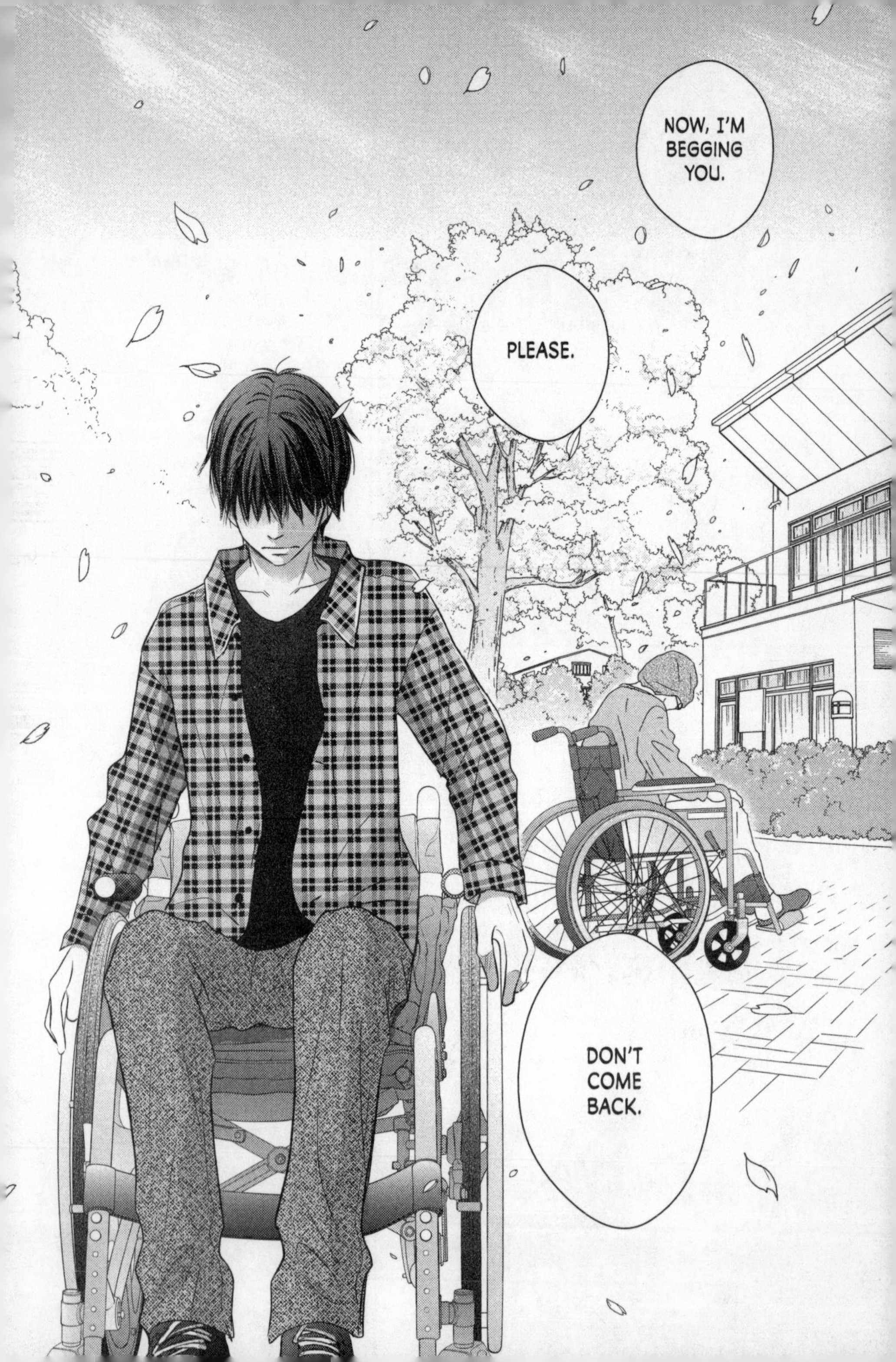
NOW, I'M BEGGING YOU.
PLEASE.
DON'T COME BACK.

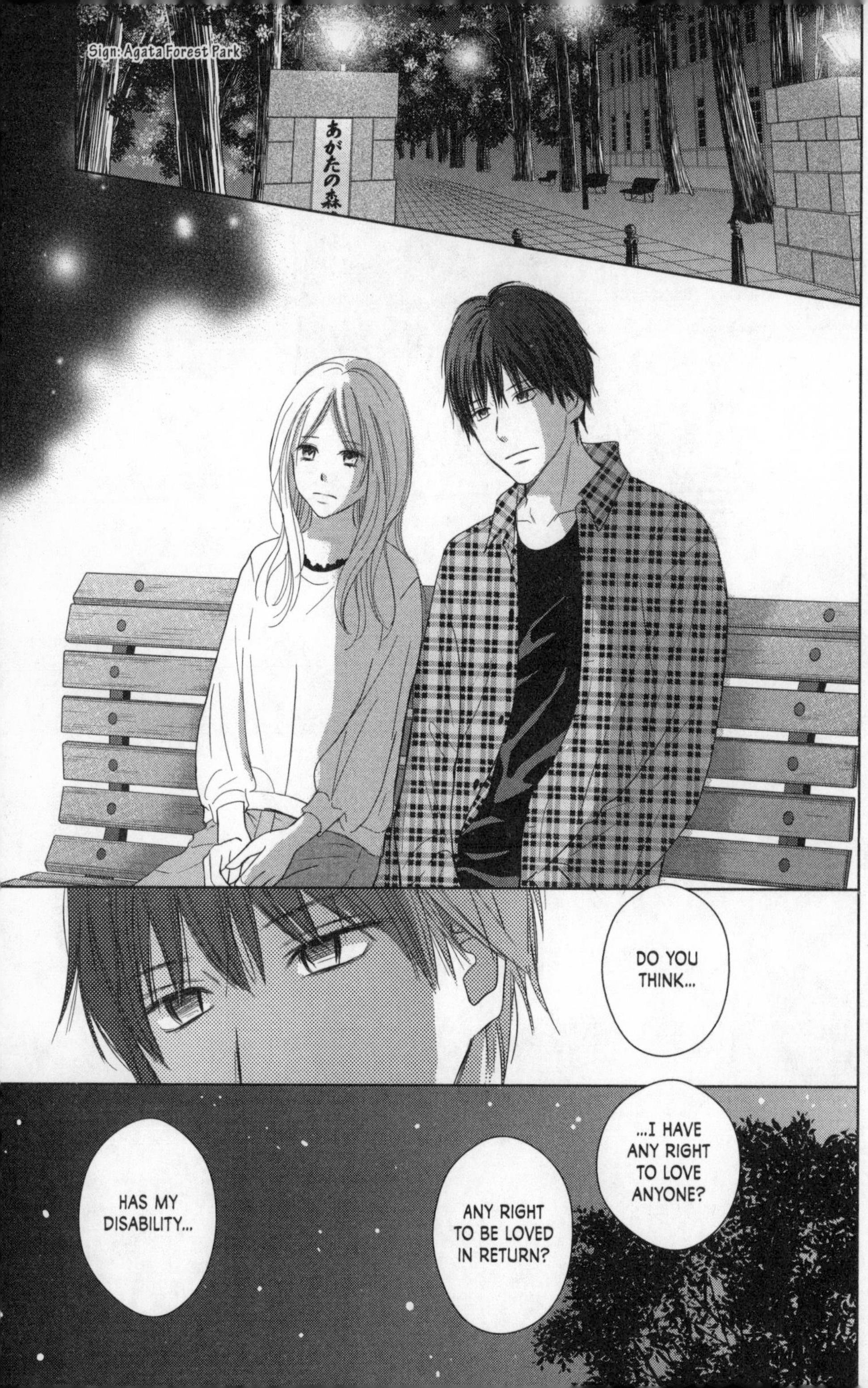
Sign: Agata Forest Park
あがたの森
DO YOU THINK...
...I HAVE ANY RIGHT TO LOVE ANYONE?
ANY RIGHT TO BE LOVED IN RETURN?
HAS MY DISABILITY...

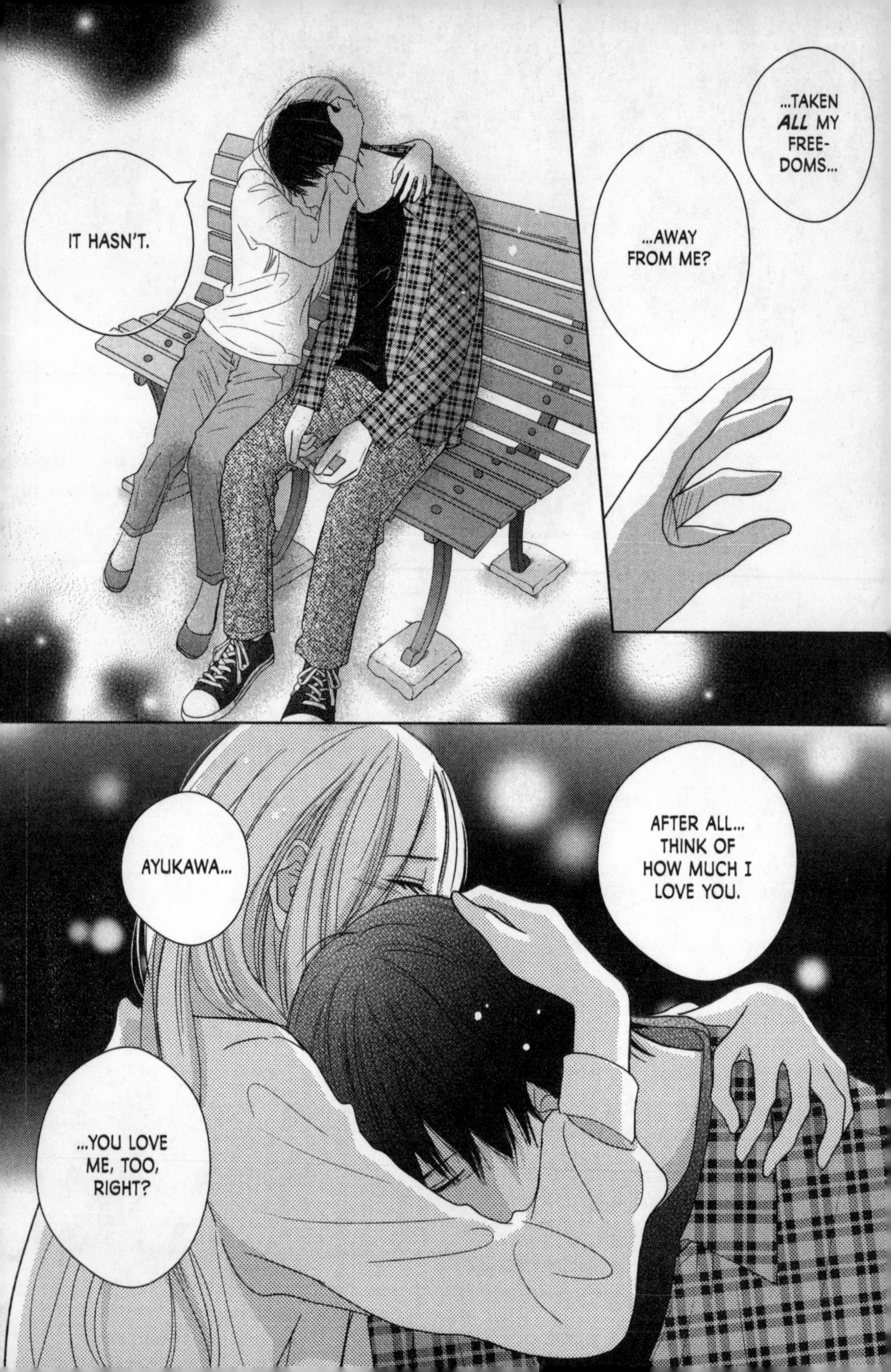
...TAKEN ALL MY FREE-DOMS...
...AWAY FROM ME?
IT HASN'T.
AFTER ALL... THINK OF HOW MUCH I LOVE YOU.
AYUKAWA...
...YOU LOVE ME, TOO, RIGHT?

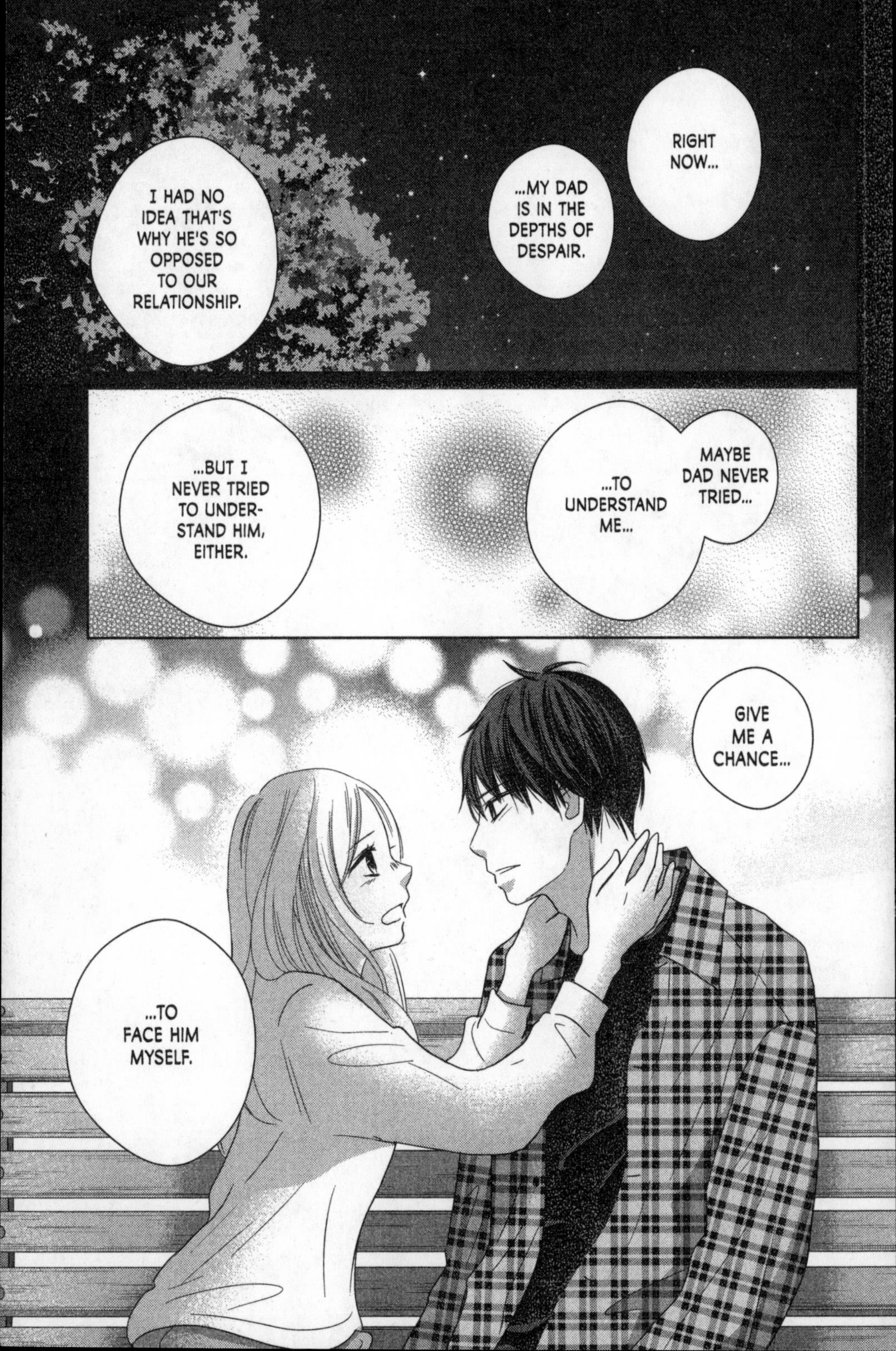
RIGHT NOW...
...MY DAD IS IN THE DEPTHS OF DESPAIR.
I HAD NO IDEA THAT'S WHY HE'S SO OPPOSED TO OUR RELATIONSHIP.
MAYBE DAD NEVER TRIED...
...TO UNDERSTAND ME...
...BUT I NEVER TRIED TO UNDER-STAND HIM, EITHER.
GIVE ME A CHANCE...
...TO FACE HIM MYSELF.

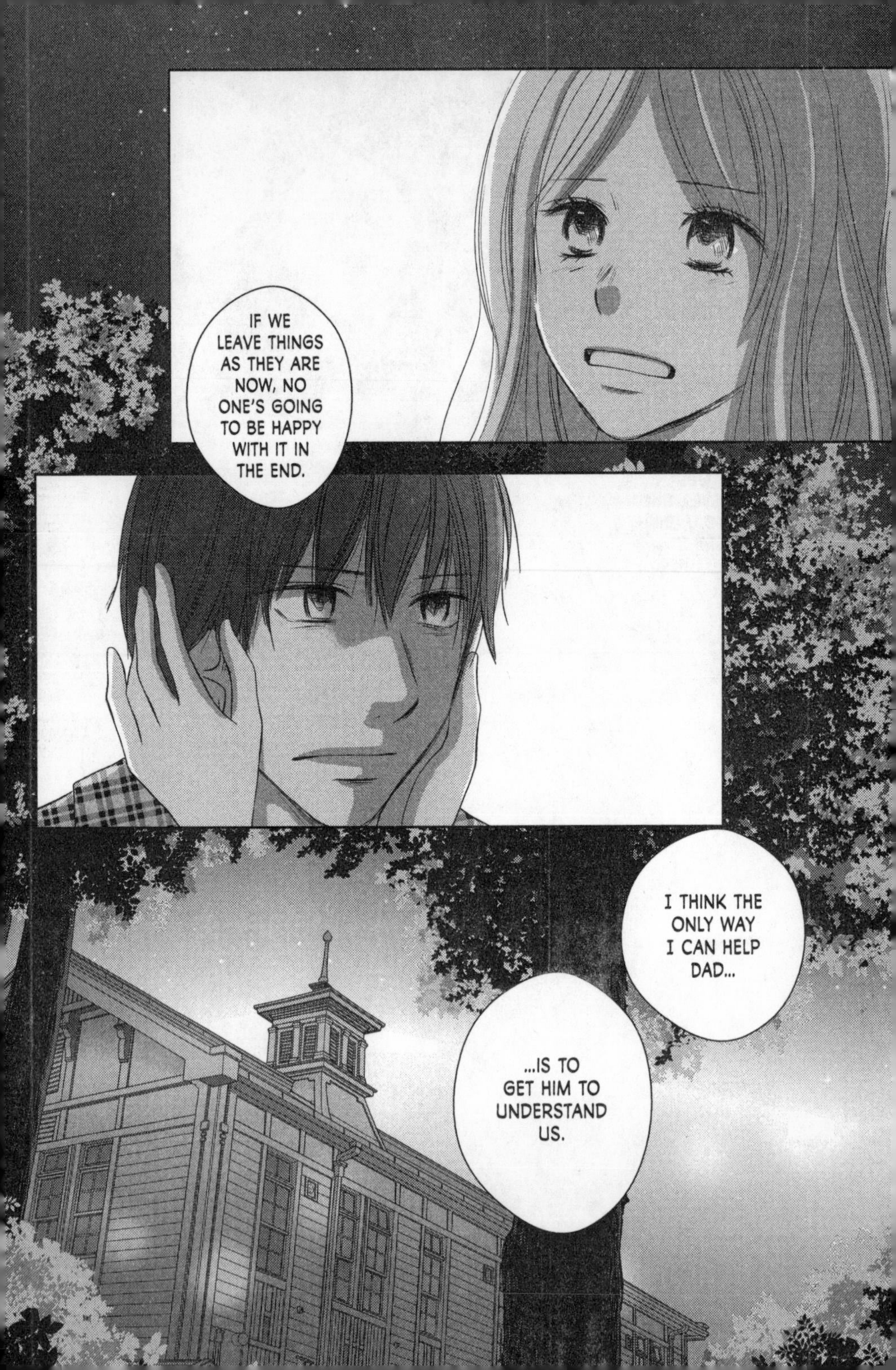
IF WE LEAVE THINGS AS THEY ARE NOW, NO ONE'S GOING TO BE HAPPY WITH IT IN THE END.
I THINK THE ONLY WAY I CAN HELP DAD...
...IS TO GET HIM TO UNDERSTAND US.

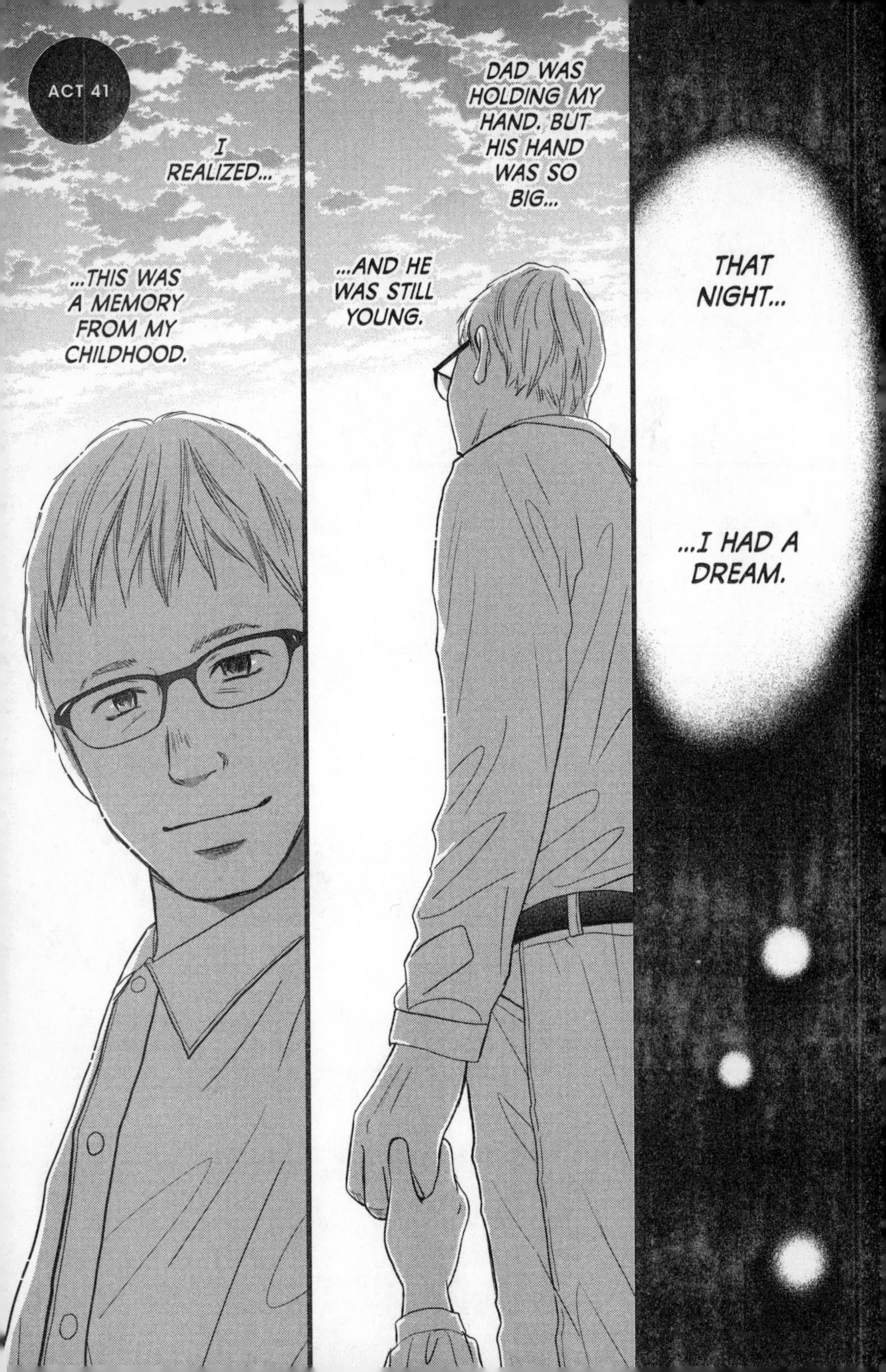
THAT NIGHT...
...I HAD A DREAM.
DAD WAS HOLDING MY HAND. BUT HIS HAND WAS SO BIG...
...AND HE WAS STILL YOUNG.
ACT 41
I REALIZED...
...THIS WAS A MEMORY FROM MY CHILDHOOD.

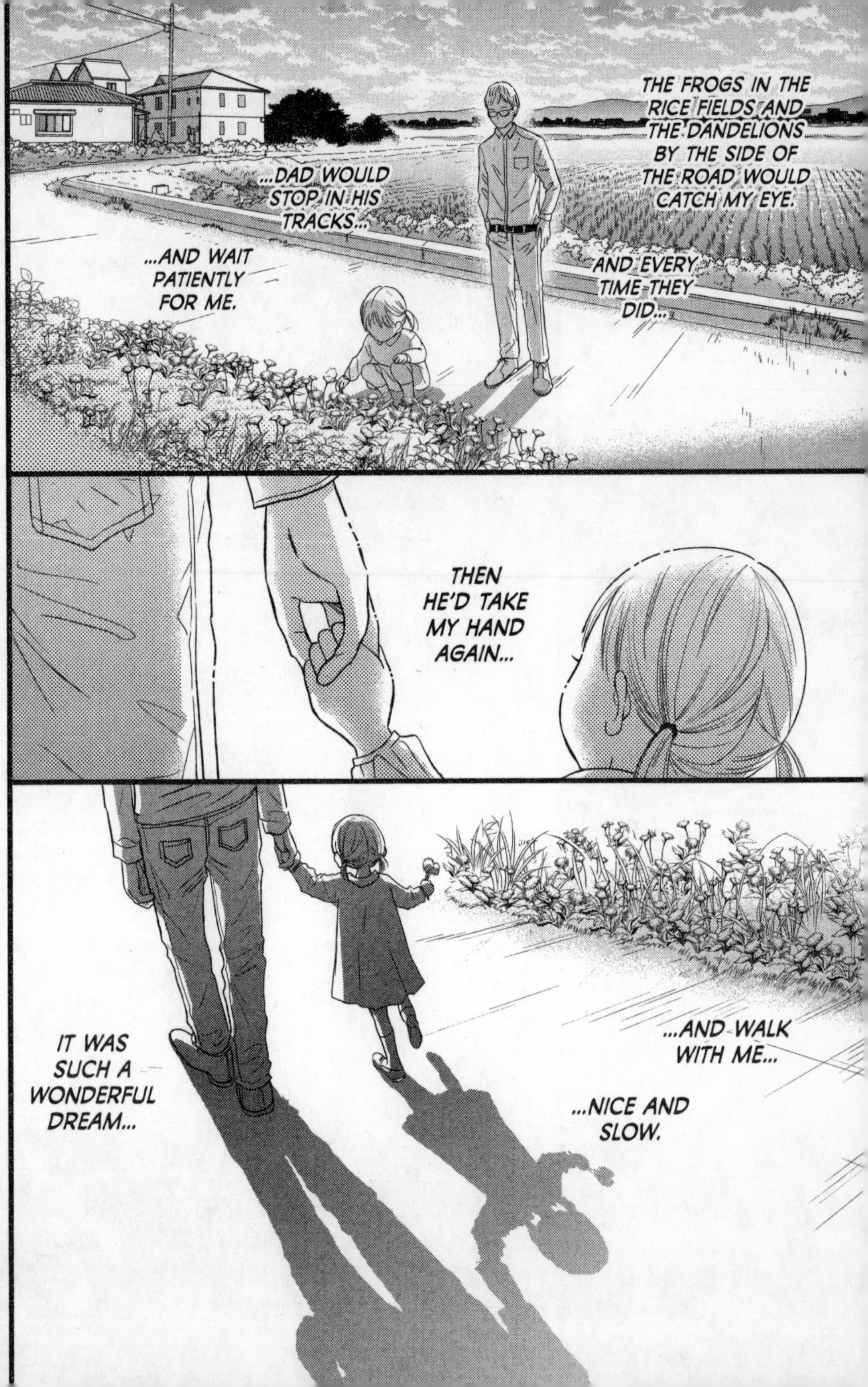
THE FROGS IN THE RICE FIELDS AND THE DANDELIONS BY THE SIDE OF THE ROAD WOULD CATCH MY EYE.
AND EVERY TIME THEY DID...
...DAD WOULD STOP IN HIS TRACKS...
...AND WAIT PATIENTLY FOR ME.
THEN HE'D TAKE MY HAND AGAIN...
...AND WALK WITH ME...
...NICE AND SLOW.
IT WAS SUCH A WONDERFUL DREAM...

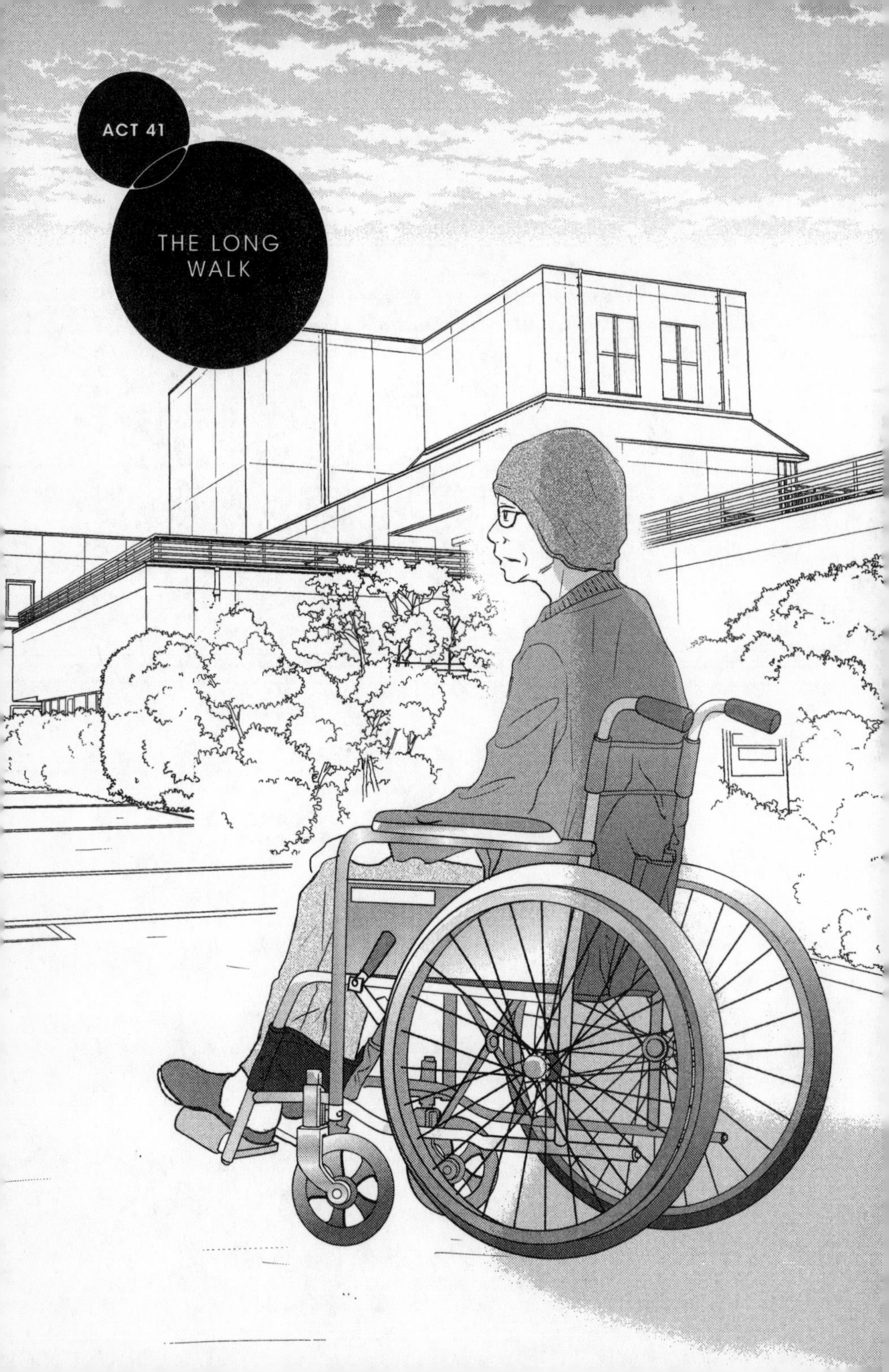
ACT 41
THE LONG WALK

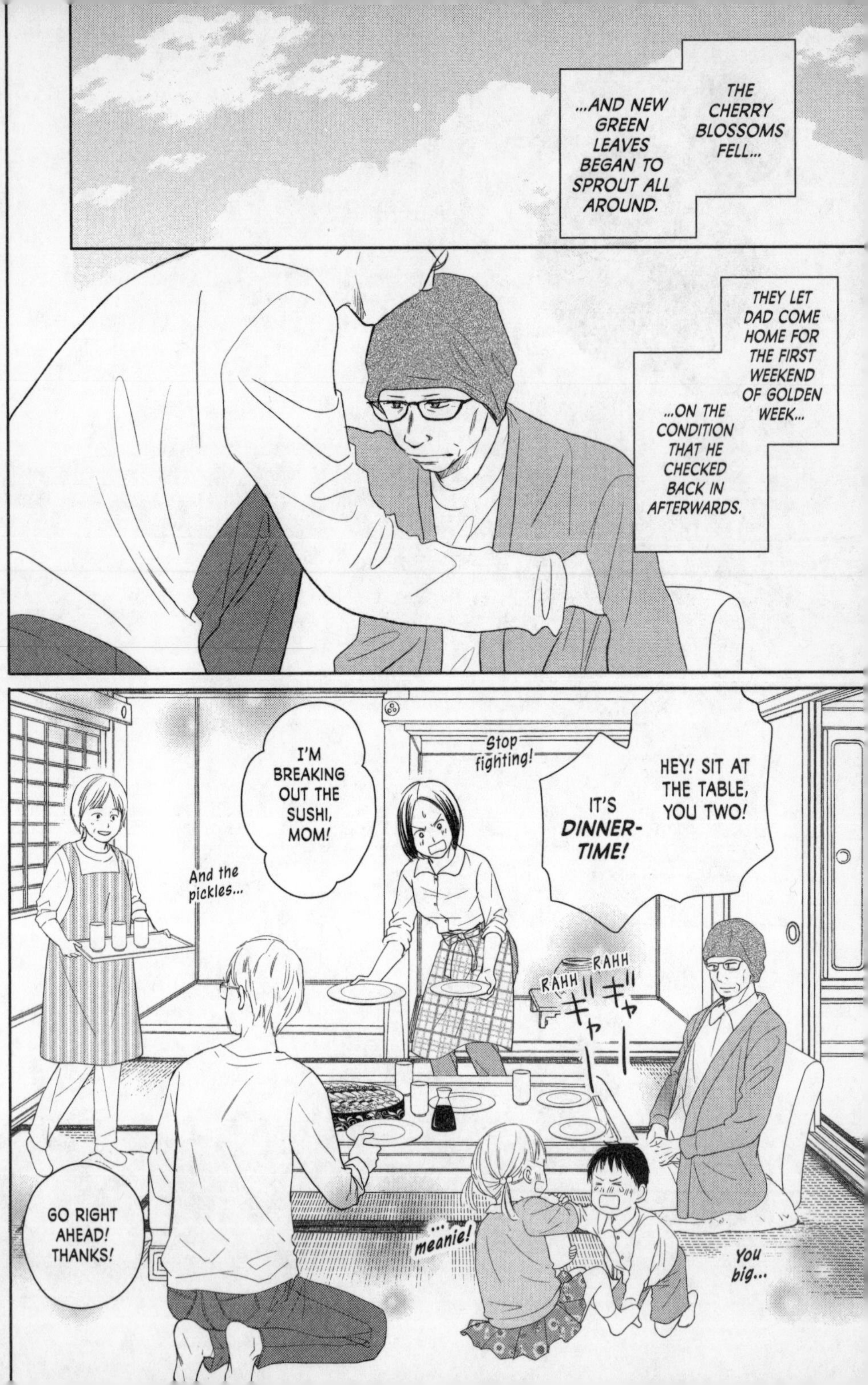
THE CHERRY BLOSSOMS FELL...
...AND NEW GREEN LEAVES BEGAN TO SPROUT ALL AROUND.
THEY LET DAD COME HOME FOR THE FIRST WEEKEND OF GOLDEN WEEK...
...ON THE CONDITION THAT HE CHECKED BACK IN AFTERWARDS.
HEY! SIT AT THE TABLE, YOU TWO!
IT'S DINNER-TIME!
Stop fighting!
RAHH
RAHH
ギャー
ギャー
I'M BREAKING OUT THE SUSHI, MOM!
And the pickles...
You big...
... meanie!
GO RIGHT AHEAD! THANKS!

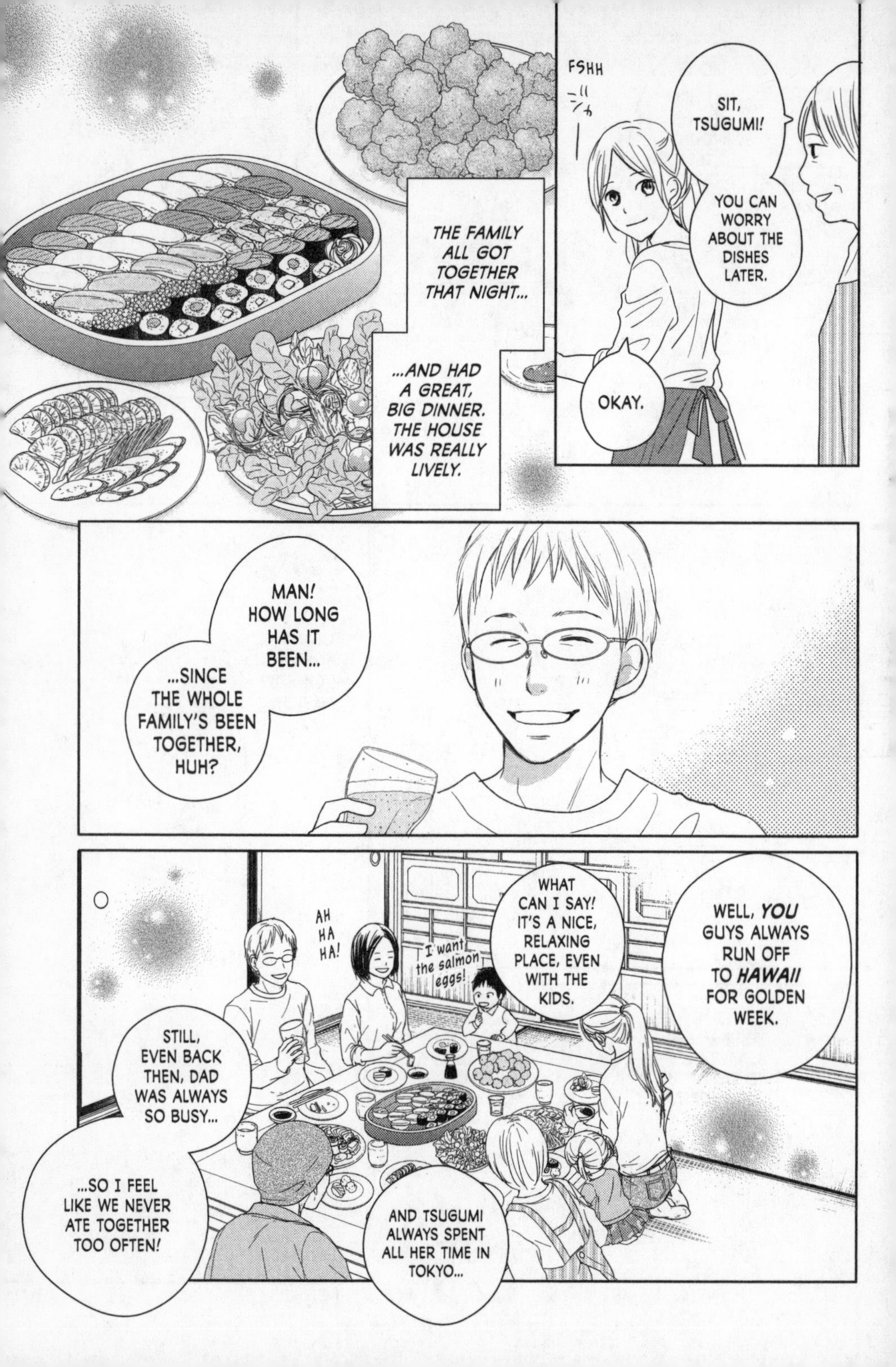
FSHH
SIT, TSUGUMI!
YOU CAN WORRY ABOUT THE DISHES LATER.
OKAY.
THE FAMILY ALL GOT TOGETHER THAT NIGHT...
...AND HAD A GREAT, BIG DINNER. THE HOUSE WAS REALLY LIVELY.
MAN! HOW LONG HAS IT BEEN...
...SINCE THE WHOLE FAMILY'S BEEN TOGETHER, HUH?
WELL, *YOU* GUYS ALWAYS RUN OFF TO *HAWAII* FOR GOLDEN WEEK.
WHAT CAN I SAY! IT'S A NICE, RELAXING PLACE, EVEN WITH THE KIDS.
I want the salmon eggs!
AH HA HA!
STILL, EVEN BACK THEN, DAD WAS ALWAYS SO BUSY...
AND TSUGUMI ALWAYS SPENT ALL HER TIME IN TOKYO...
...SO I FEEL LIKE WE NEVER ATE TOGETHER TOO OFTEN!

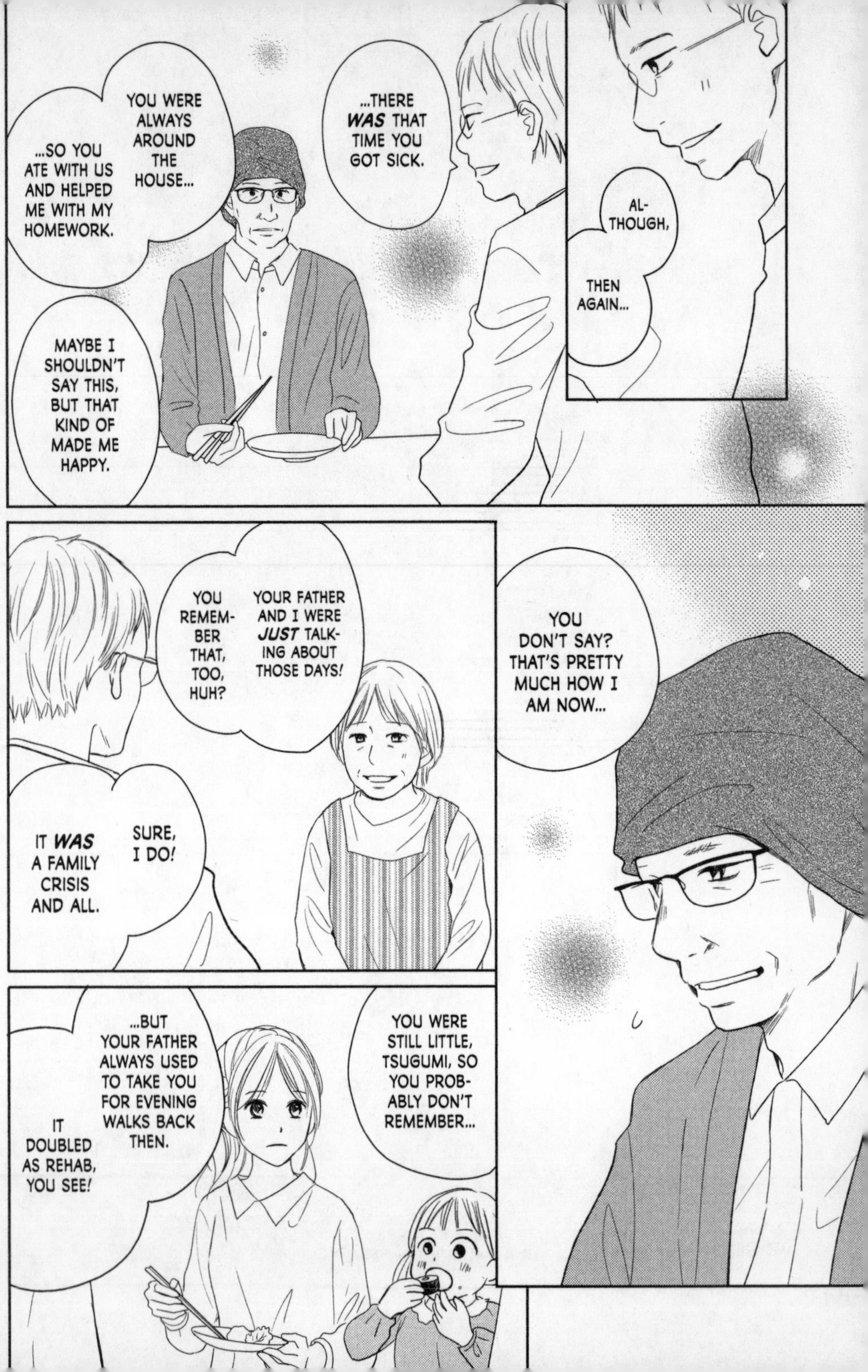
ALTHOUGH,
THEN AGAIN...
...THERE *WAS* THAT TIME YOU GOT SICK.
YOU WERE ALWAYS AROUND THE HOUSE...
...SO YOU ATE WITH US AND HELPED ME WITH MY HOMEWORK.
MAYBE I SHOULDN'T SAY THIS, BUT THAT KIND OF MADE ME HAPPY.
YOU DON'T SAY? THAT'S PRETTY MUCH HOW I AM NOW...
YOUR FATHER AND I WERE *JUST* TALKING ABOUT THOSE DAYS!
YOU REMEMBER THAT, TOO, HUH?
SURE, I DO!
IT *WAS* A FAMILY CRISIS AND ALL.
YOU WERE STILL LITTLE, TSUGUMI, SO YOU PROBABLY DON'T REMEMBER...
...BUT YOUR FATHER ALWAYS USED TO TAKE YOU FOR EVENING WALKS BACK THEN.
IT DOUBLED AS REHAB, YOU SEE!

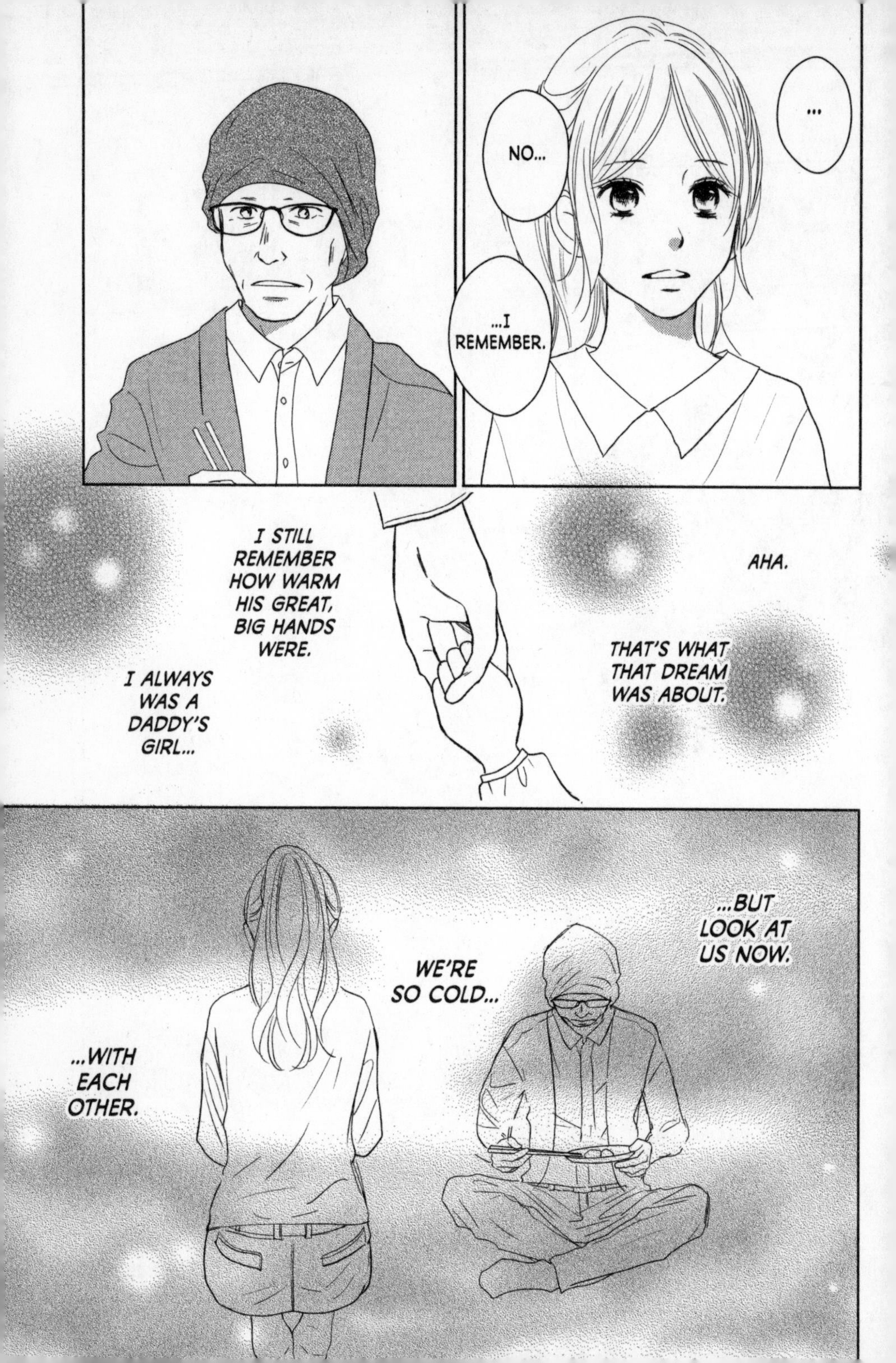
...
NO...
...I REMEMBER.
AHA.
THAT'S WHAT THAT DREAM WAS ABOUT.
I STILL REMEMBER HOW WARM HIS GREAT, BIG HANDS WERE.
I ALWAYS WAS A DADDY'S GIRL...
...BUT LOOK AT US NOW.
WE'RE SO COLD...
...WITH EACH OTHER.

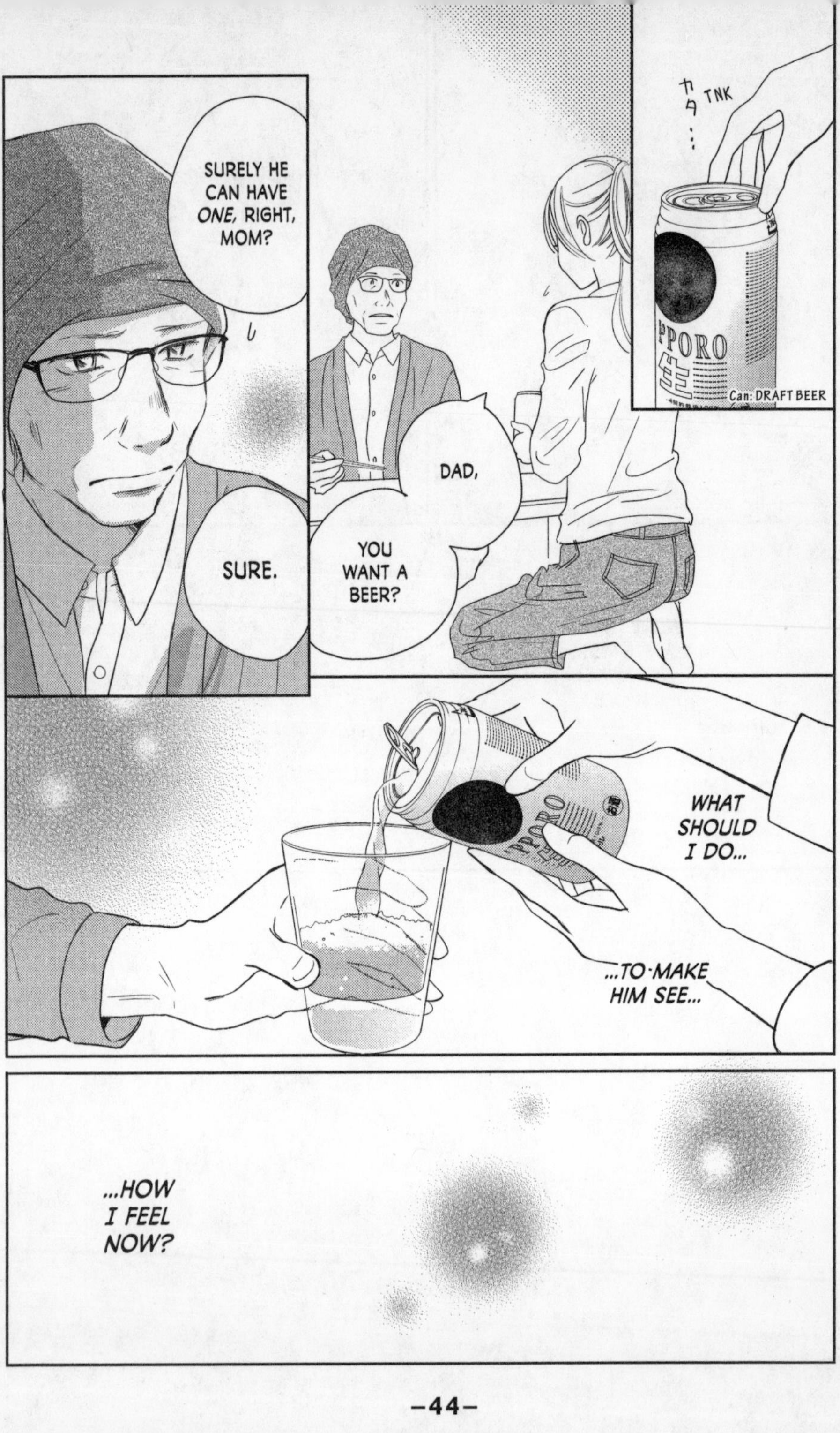

カタ…
TNK
Can: DRAFT BEER
DAD,
YOU WANT A BEER?
SURELY HE CAN HAVE *ONE*, RIGHT, MOM?
SURE.
WHAT SHOULD I DO...
...TO-MAKE HIM SEE...
...HOW I FEEL NOW?

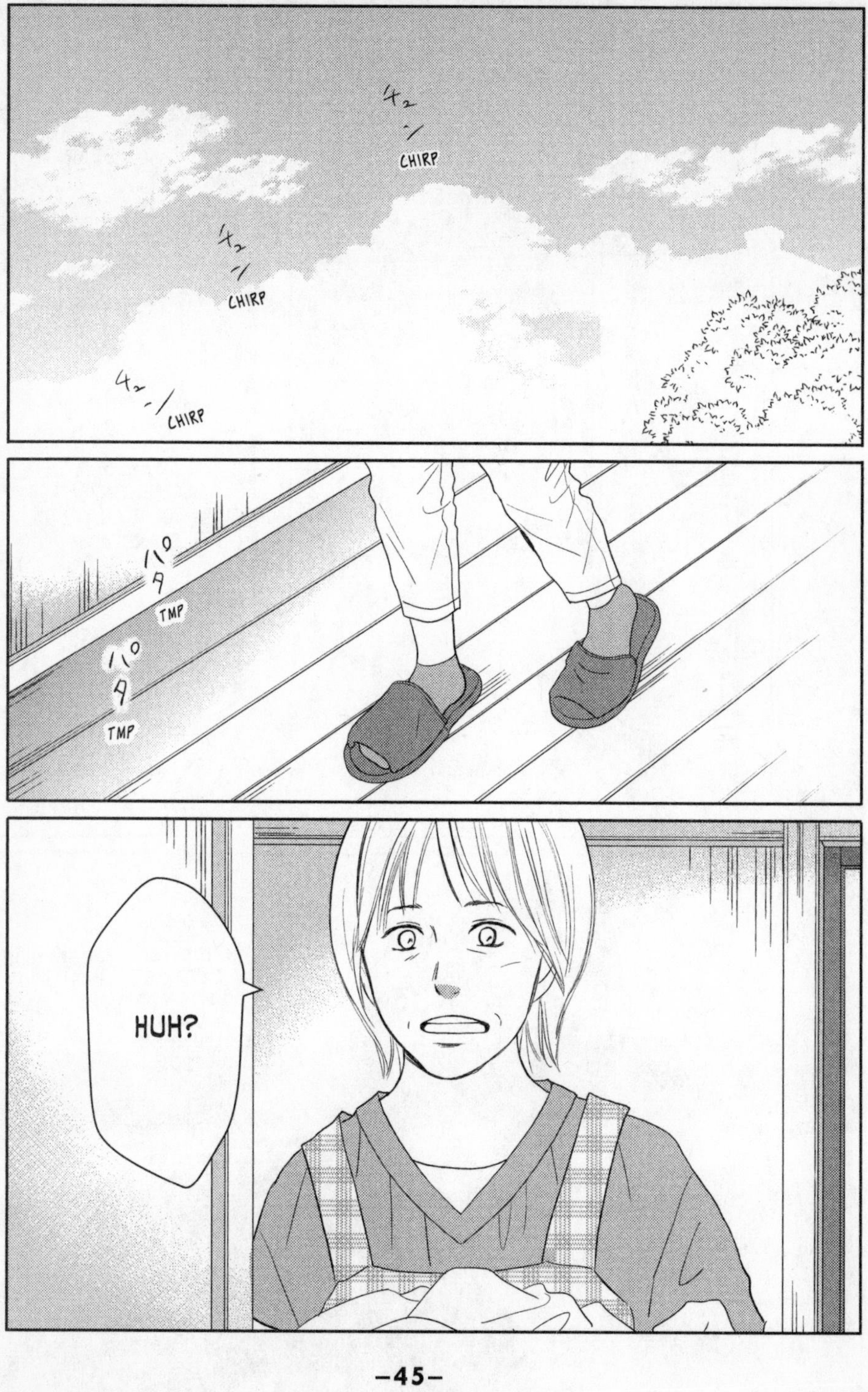

チュン
CHIRP
チュン
CHIRP
チュン
CHIRP
パタ
TMP
パタ
TMP
HUH?

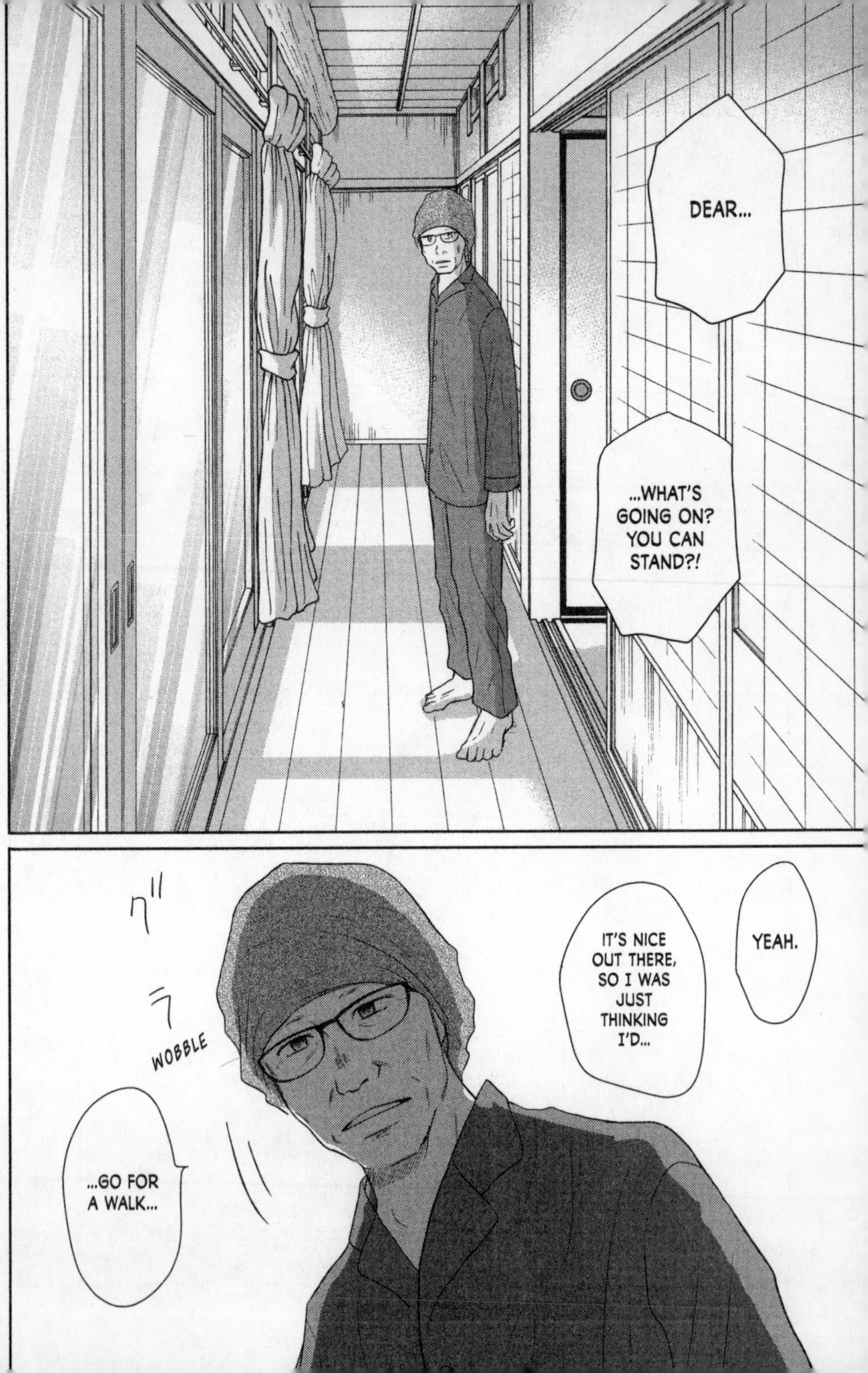
DEAR...
...WHAT'S GOING ON? YOU CAN STAND?!
YEAH.
IT'S NICE OUT THERE, SO I WAS JUST THINKING I'D...
グラ
WOBBLE
...GO FOR A WALK...

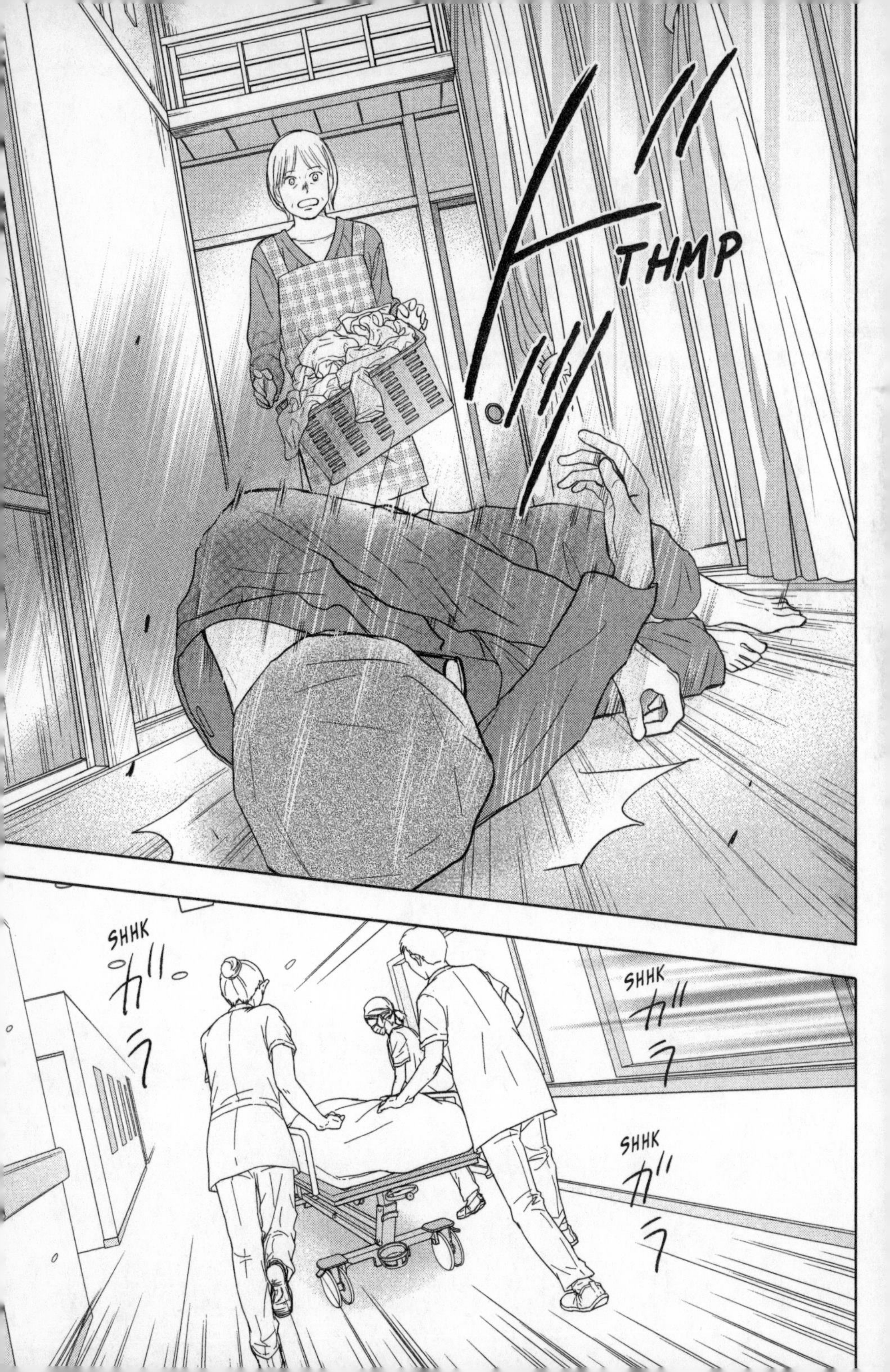
THMP
SHHK
ガラ
SHHK
ガラ
SHHK
ガラ

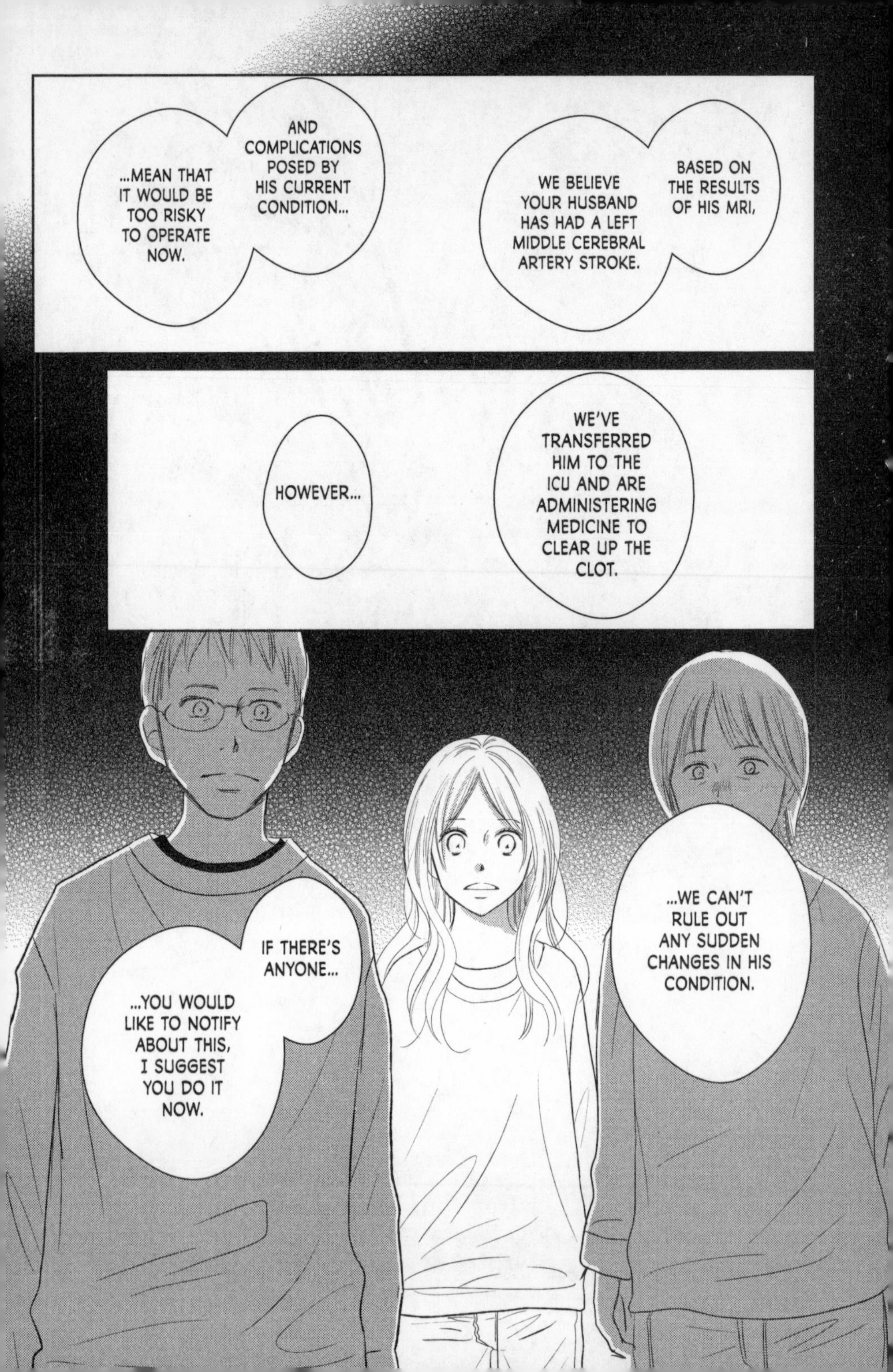
BASED ON THE RESULTS OF HIS MRI,
WE BELIEVE YOUR HUSBAND HAS HAD A LEFT MIDDLE CEREBRAL ARTERY STROKE.
AND COMPLICATIONS POSED BY HIS CURRENT CONDITION...
...MEAN THAT IT WOULD BE TOO RISKY TO OPERATE NOW.
WE'VE TRANSFERRED HIM TO THE ICU AND ARE ADMINISTERING MEDICINE TO CLEAR UP THE CLOT.
HOWEVER...
...WE CAN'T RULE OUT ANY SUDDEN CHANGES IN HIS CONDITION.
IF THERE'S ANYONE...
...YOU WOULD LIKE TO NOTIFY ABOUT THIS, I SUGGEST YOU DO IT NOW.

BUT...

...HE SEEMED LIKE HE WAS HAVING SO MUCH FUN LAST NIGHT...

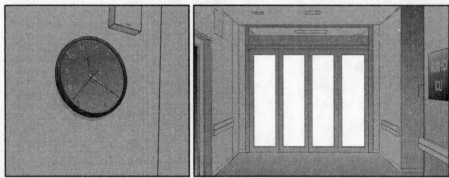

WHY...

...DID I PUT SO MUCH SPACE BETWEEN US FOR SO LONG?

I KNEW DAMN WELL...

...WE DIDN'T HAVE FOREVER.

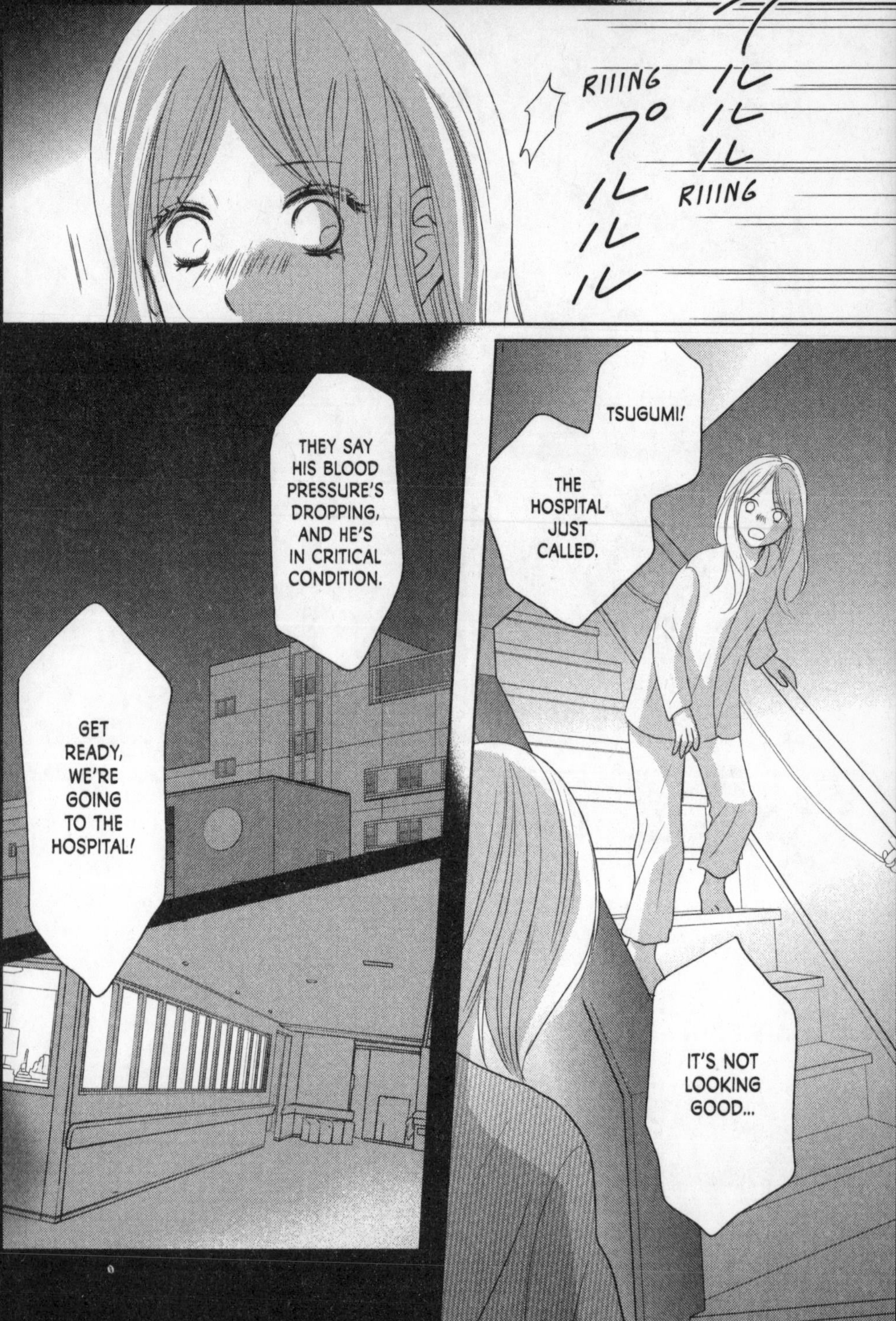
プルルル
RIIING
プルルル
RIIING
TSUGUMI!
THE HOSPITAL JUST CALLED.
IT'S NOT LOOKING GOOD...
THEY SAY HIS BLOOD PRESSURE'S DROPPING, AND HE'S IN CRITICAL CONDITION.
GET READY, WE'RE GOING TO THE HOSPITAL!

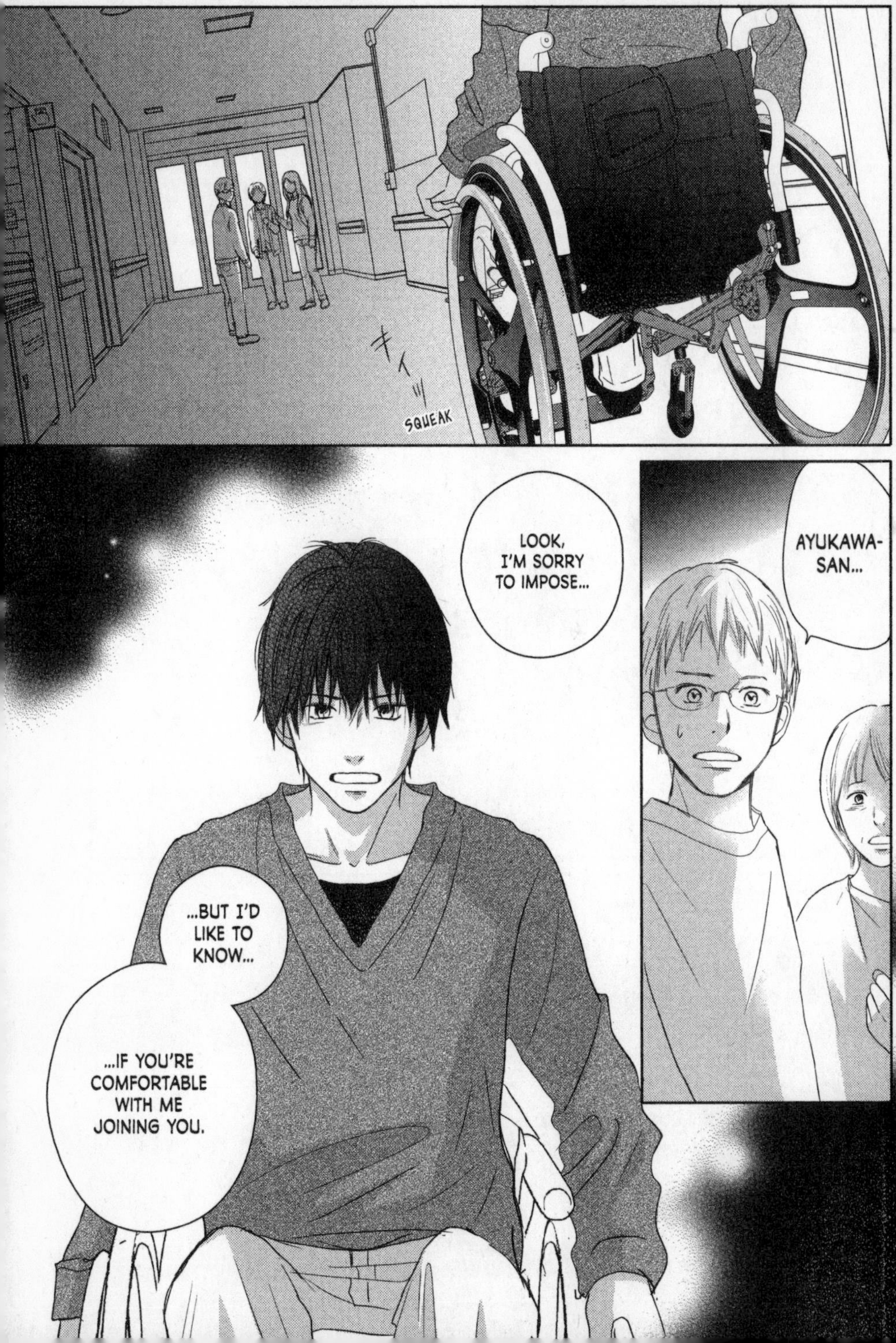
キィッ
SQUEAK
AYUKAWA-SAN...
LOOK, I'M SORRY TO IMPOSE...
...BUT I'D LIKE TO KNOW...
...IF YOU'RE COMFORTABLE WITH ME JOINING YOU.

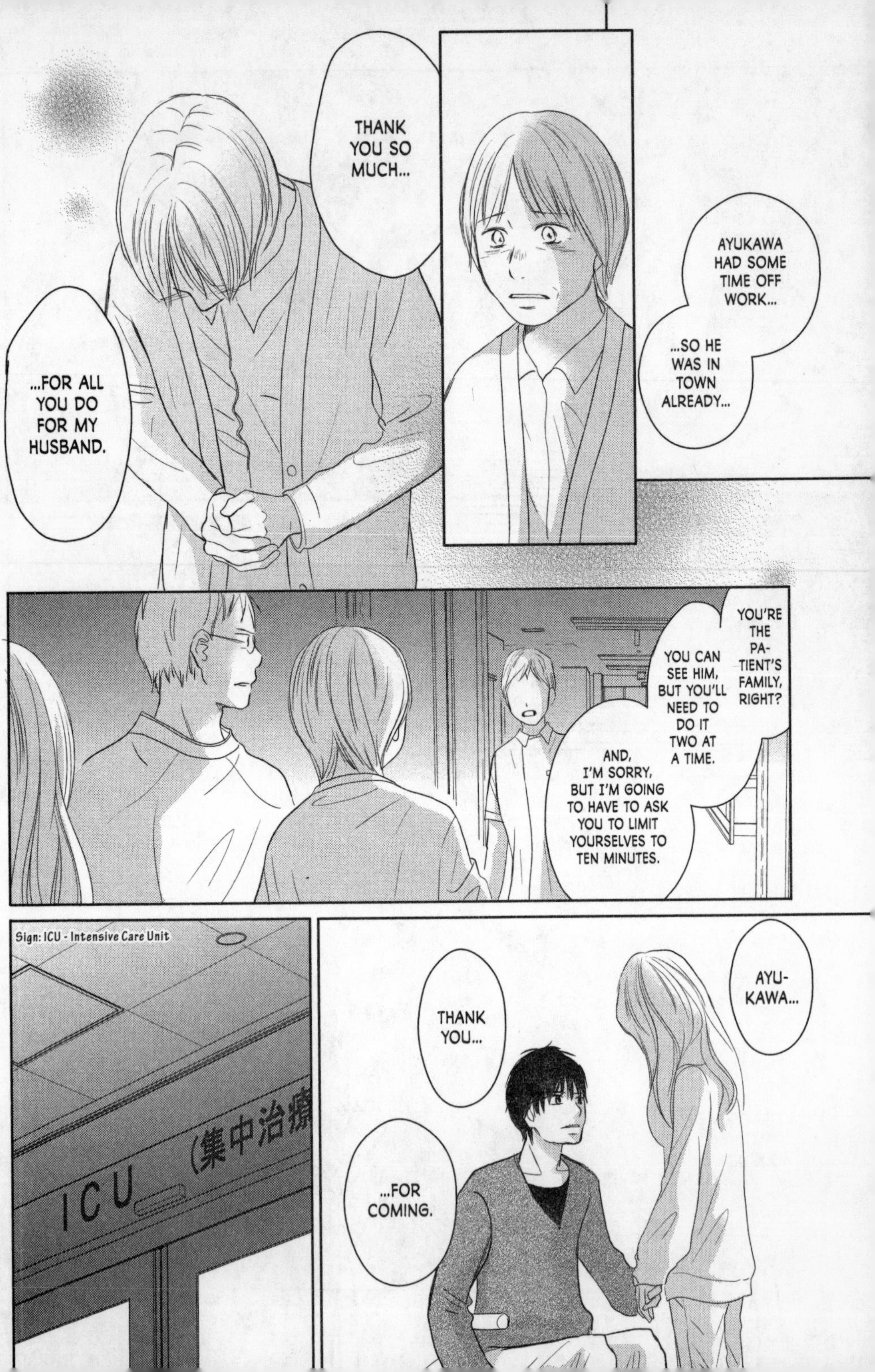
AYUKAWA HAD SOME TIME OFF WORK...
...SO HE WAS IN TOWN ALREADY...
THANK YOU SO MUCH...
...FOR ALL YOU DO FOR MY HUSBAND.
YOU'RE THE PA-TIENT'S FAMILY, RIGHT?
YOU CAN SEE HIM, BUT YOU'LL NEED TO DO IT TWO AT A TIME.
AND, I'M SORRY, BUT I'M GOING TO HAVE TO ASK YOU TO LIMIT YOURSELVES TO TEN MINUTES.
AYU-KAWA...
THANK YOU...
...FOR COMING.
Sign: ICU - Intensive Care Unit
ICU
(集中治

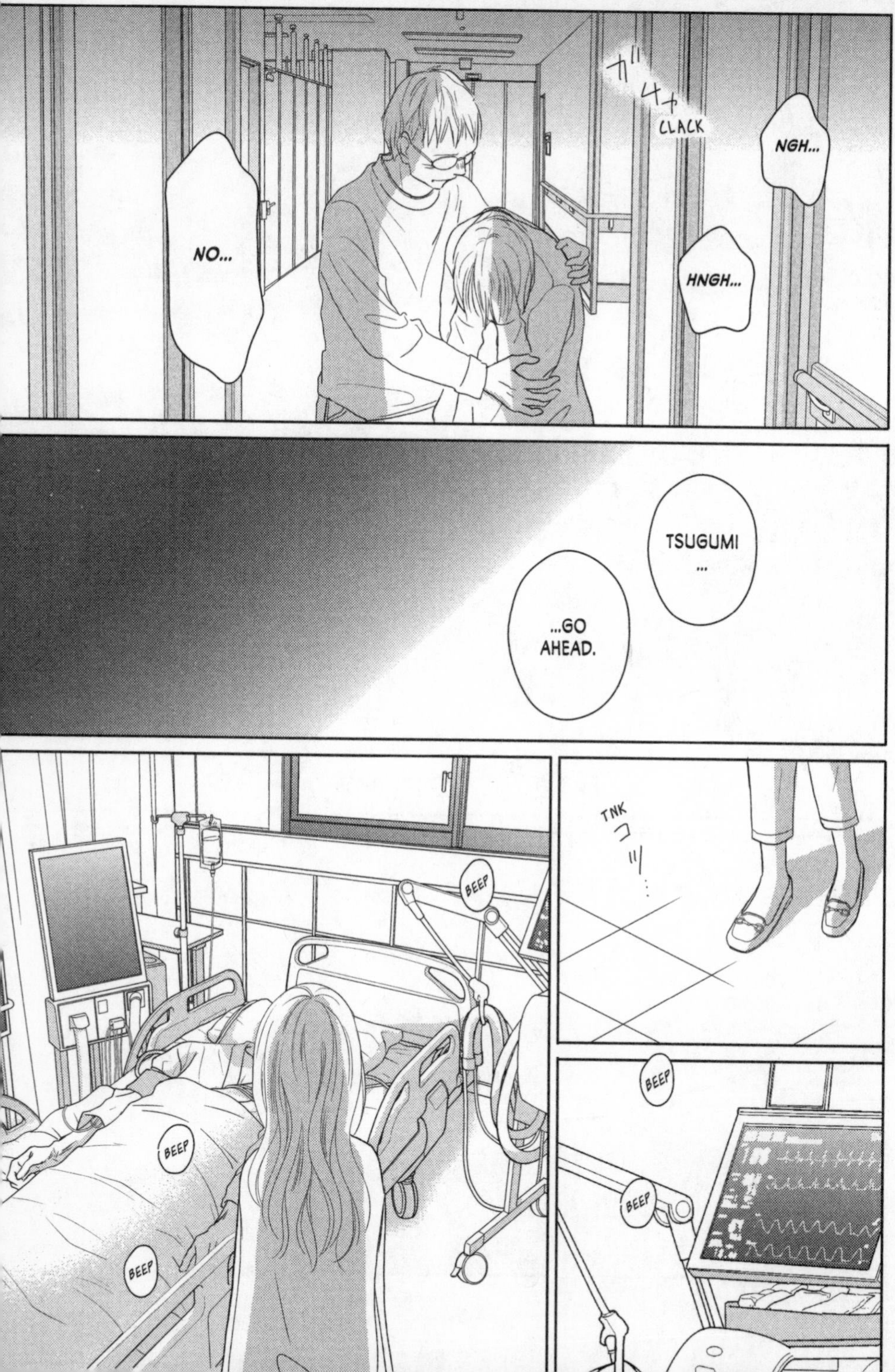

CLACK
NGH...
HNGH...
NO...
TSUGUMI ...
...GO AHEAD.
TNK
BEEP
BEEP
BEEP
BEEP
BEEP

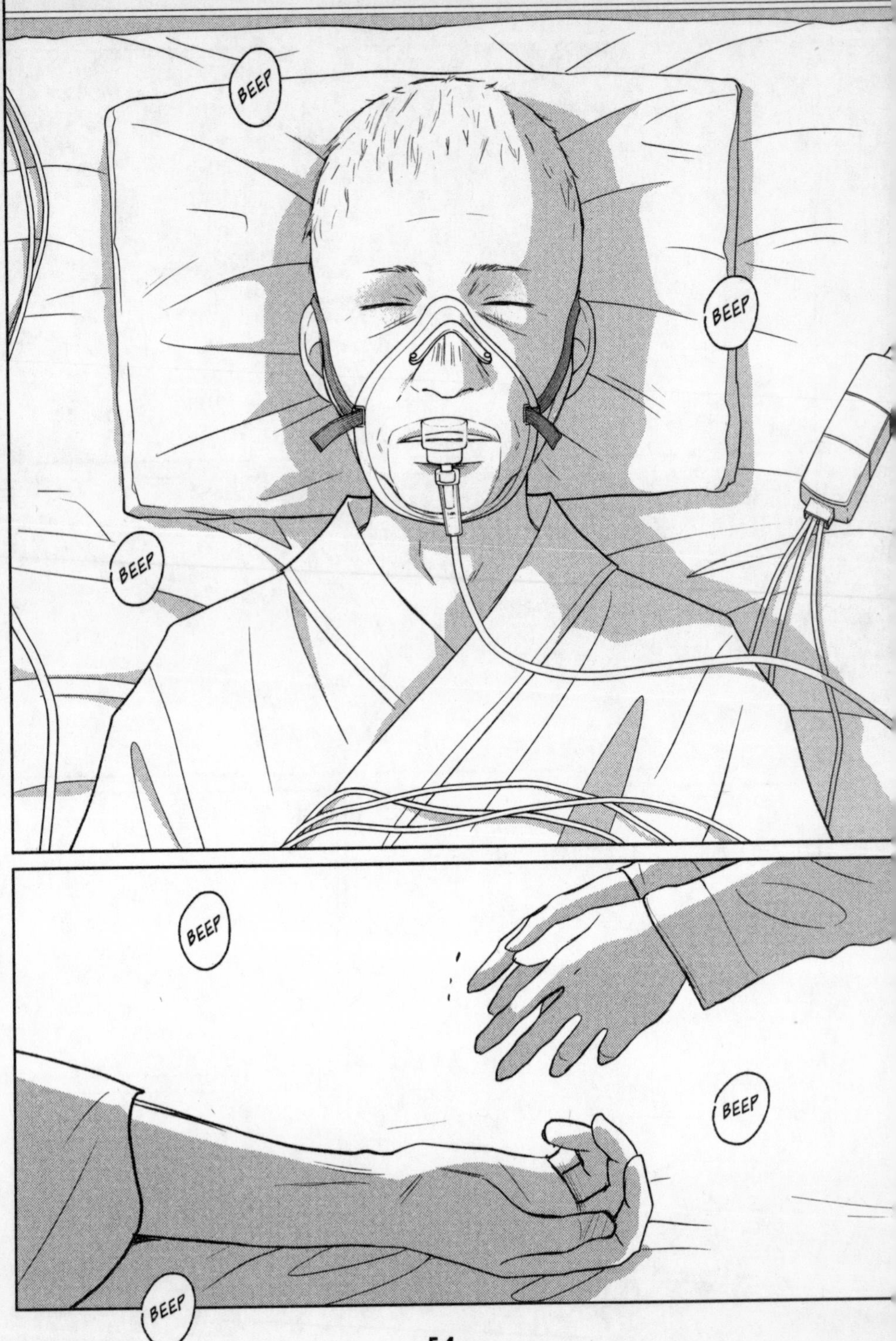
BEEP
BEEP
BEEP
BEEP
BEEP
BEEP
BEEP

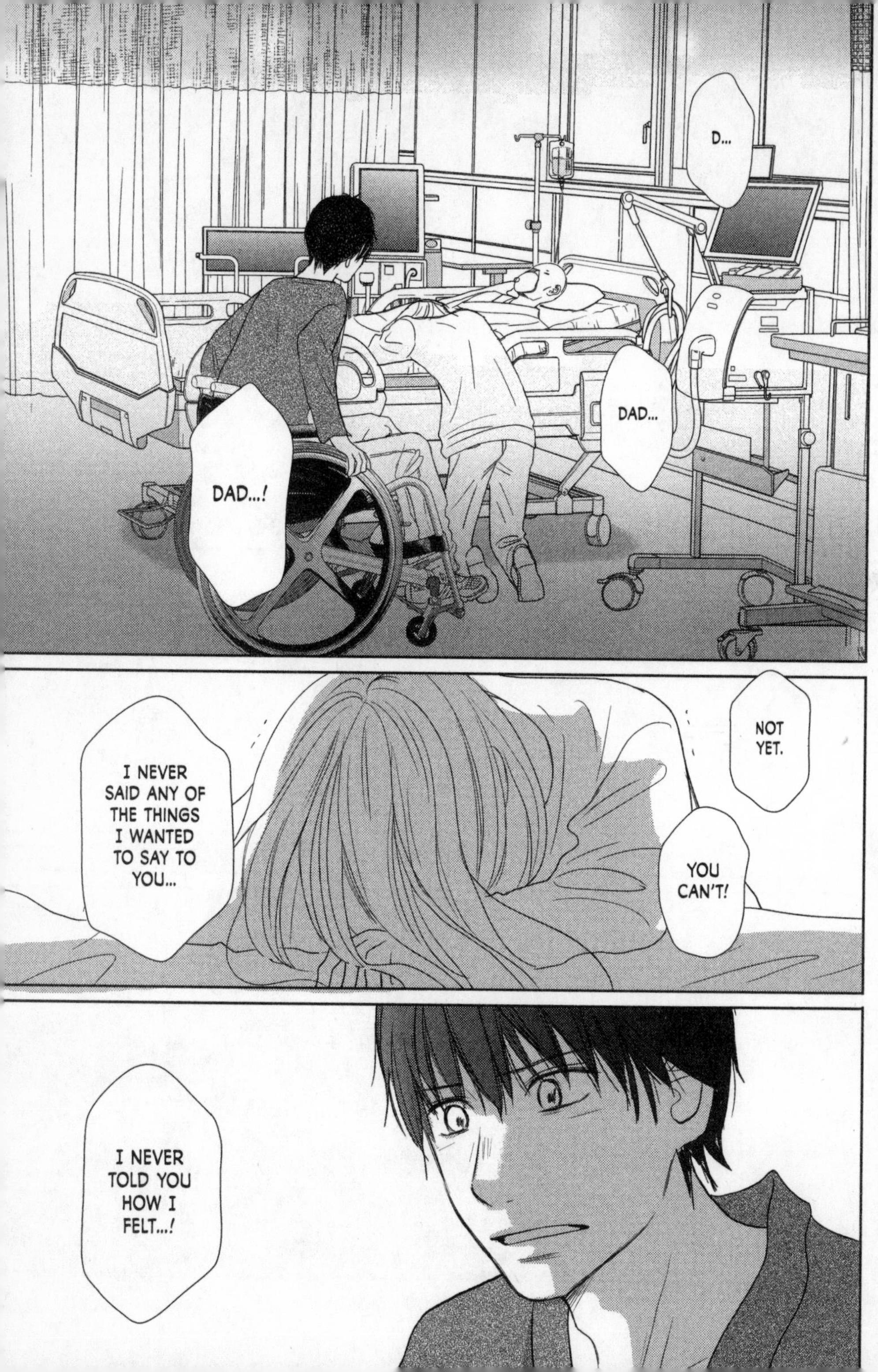
D...
DAD...
DAD...!
NOT YET.
YOU CAN'T!
I NEVER SAID ANY OF THE THINGS I WANTED TO SAY TO YOU...
I NEVER TOLD YOU HOW I FELT...!

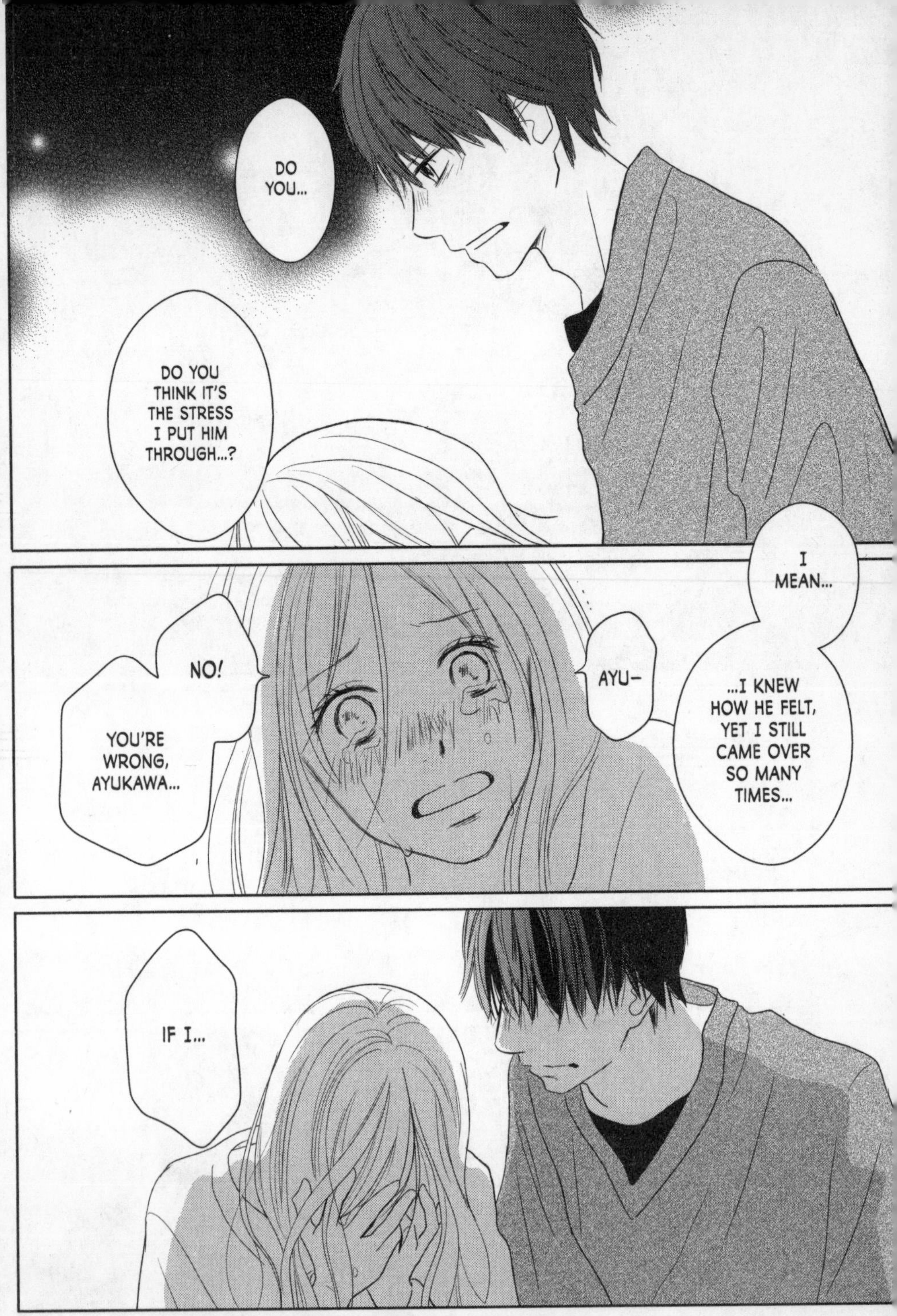
DO YOU...
DO YOU THINK IT'S THE STRESS I PUT HIM THROUGH...?
I MEAN...
...I KNEW HOW HE FELT, YET I STILL CAME OVER SO MANY TIMES...
AYU-
NO!
YOU'RE WRONG, AYUKAWA...
IF I...

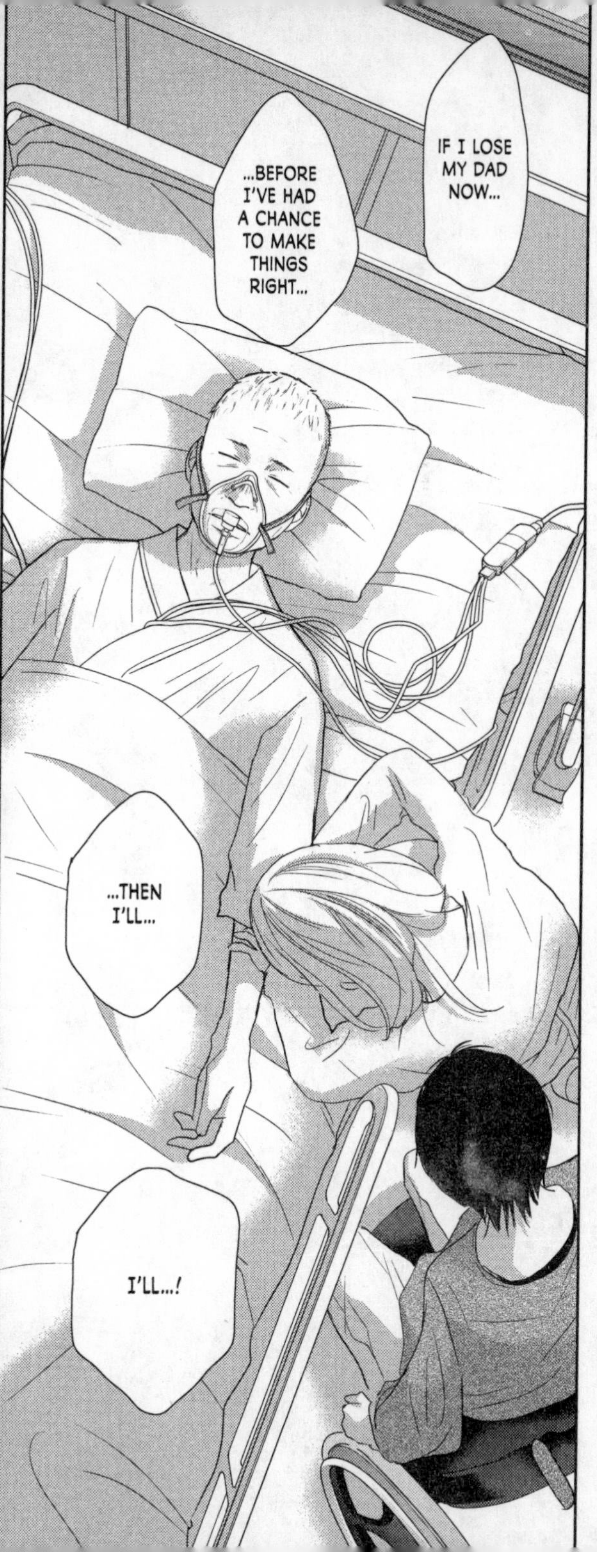
IF I LOSE MY DAD NOW...
...BEFORE I'VE HAD A CHANCE TO MAKE THINGS RIGHT...
...THEN I'LL...
I'LL...!
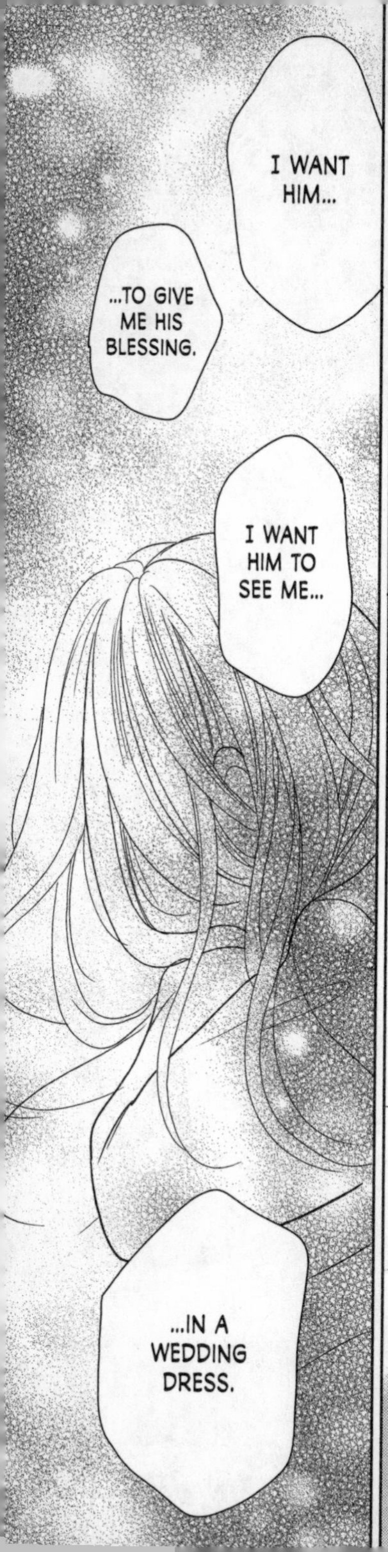
I WANT HIM...
...TO GIVE ME HIS BLESSING.
I WANT HIM TO SEE ME...
...IN A WEDDING DRESS.

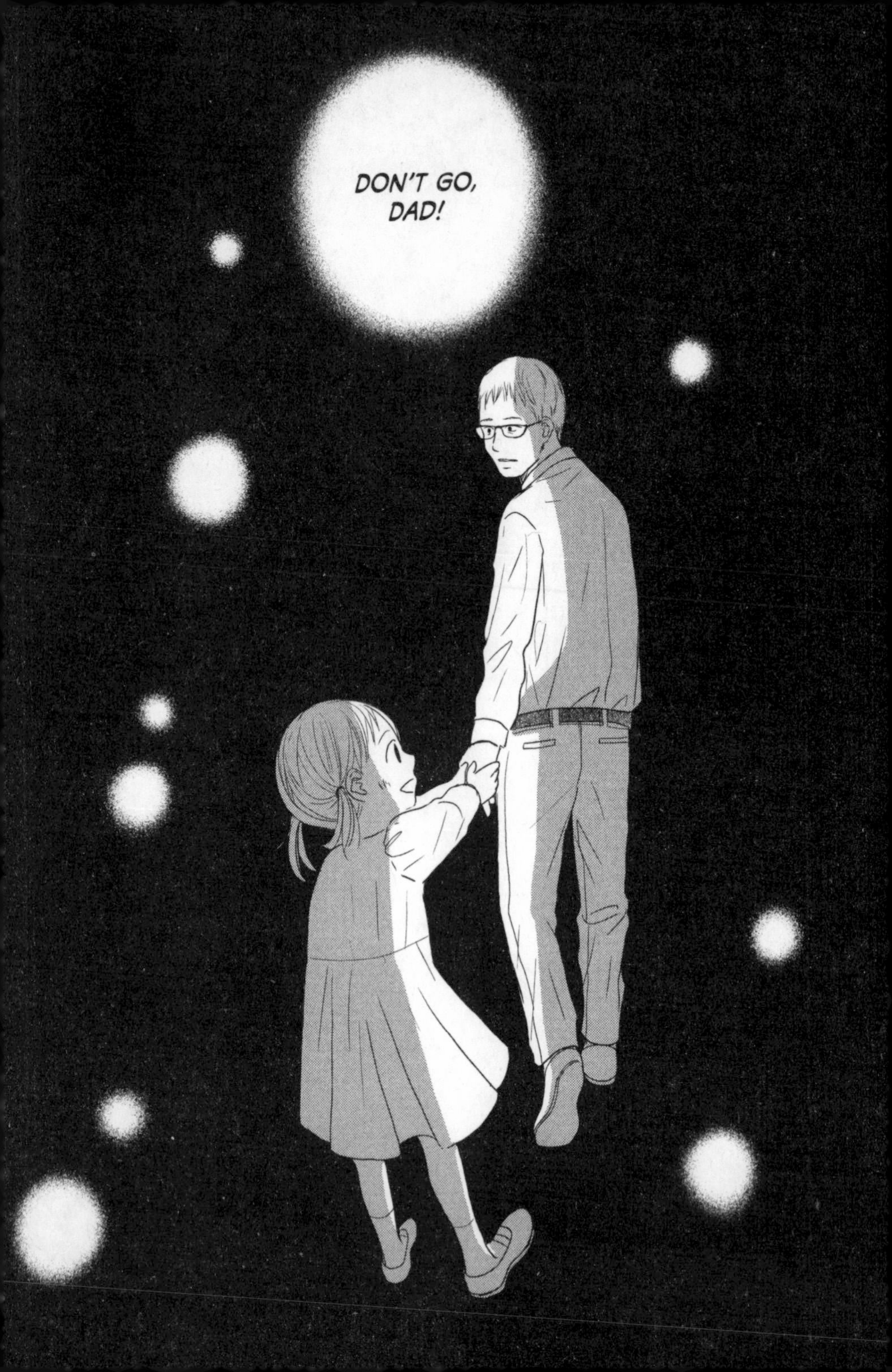
DON'T GO, DAD!

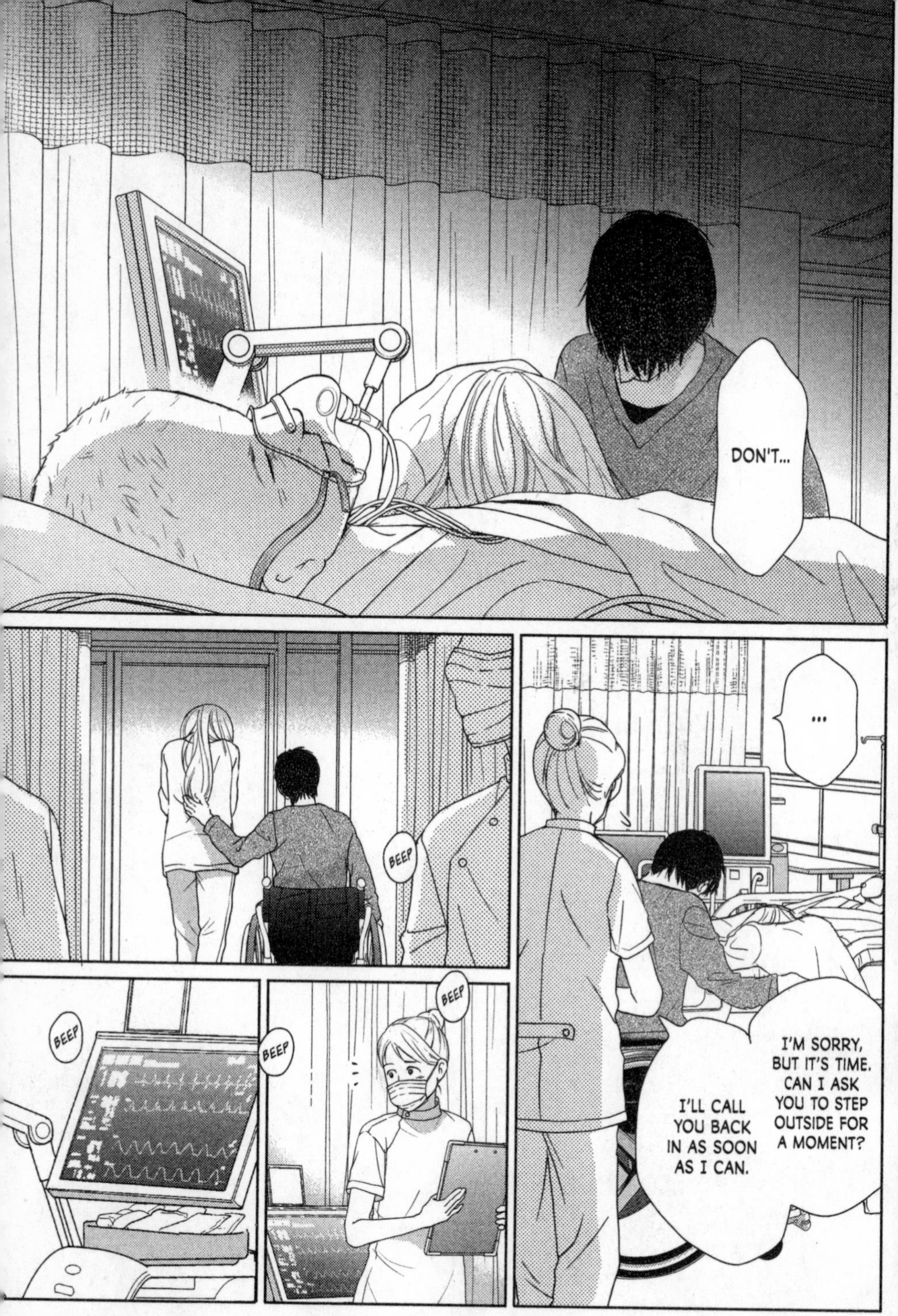
DON'T...
...
I'M SORRY, BUT IT'S TIME. CAN I ASK YOU TO STEP OUTSIDE FOR A MOMENT?
I'LL CALL YOU BACK IN AS SOON AS I CAN.
BEEP
BEEP
BEEP
BEEP

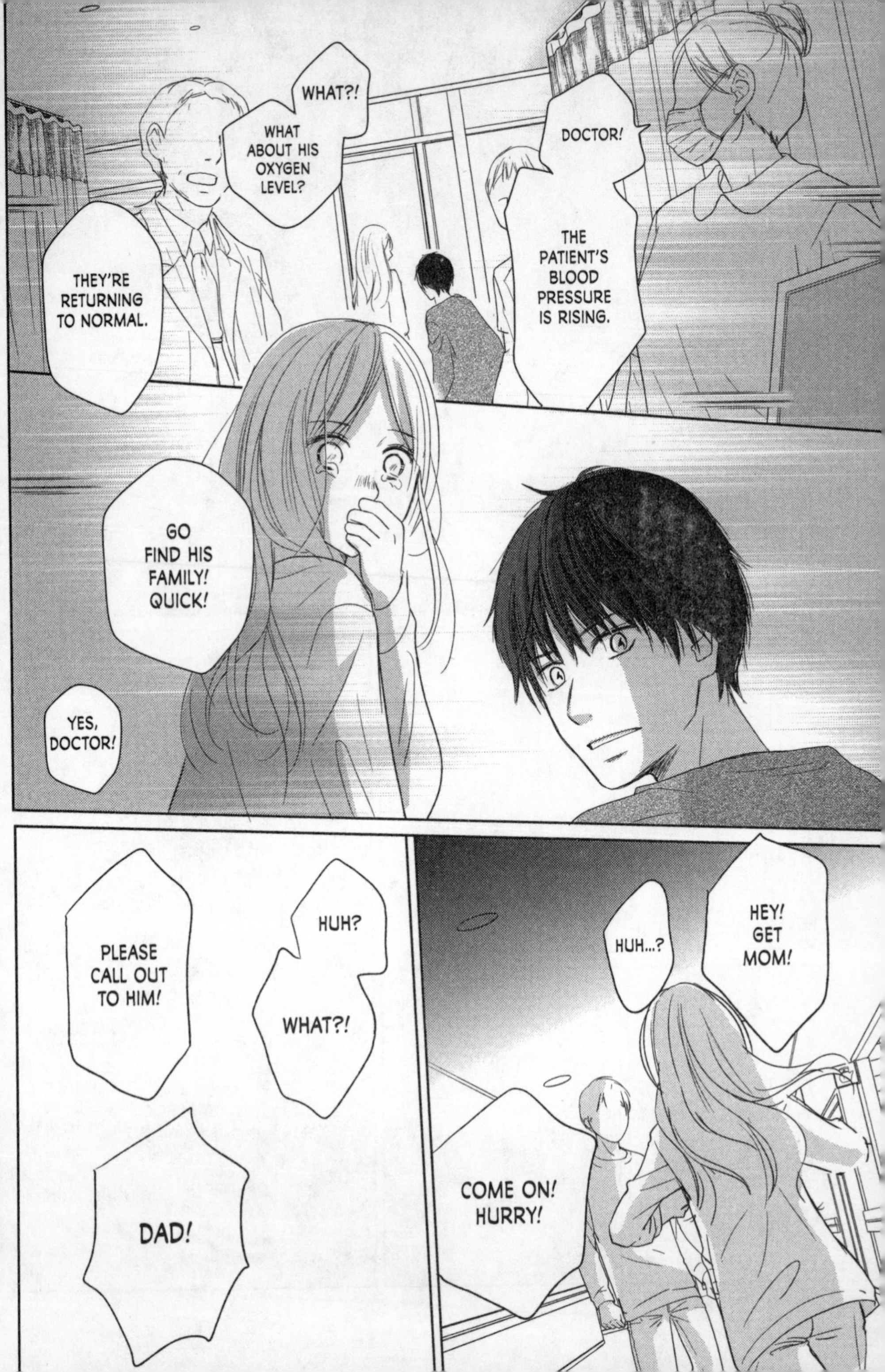
DOCTOR!
THE PATIENT'S BLOOD PRESSURE IS RISING.
WHAT?!
WHAT ABOUT HIS OXYGEN LEVEL?
THEY'RE RETURNING TO NORMAL.
GO FIND HIS FAMILY! QUICK!
YES, DOCTOR!
HEY! GET MOM!
HUH...?
COME ON! HURRY!
HUH?
WHAT?!
PLEASE CALL OUT TO HIM!
DAD!

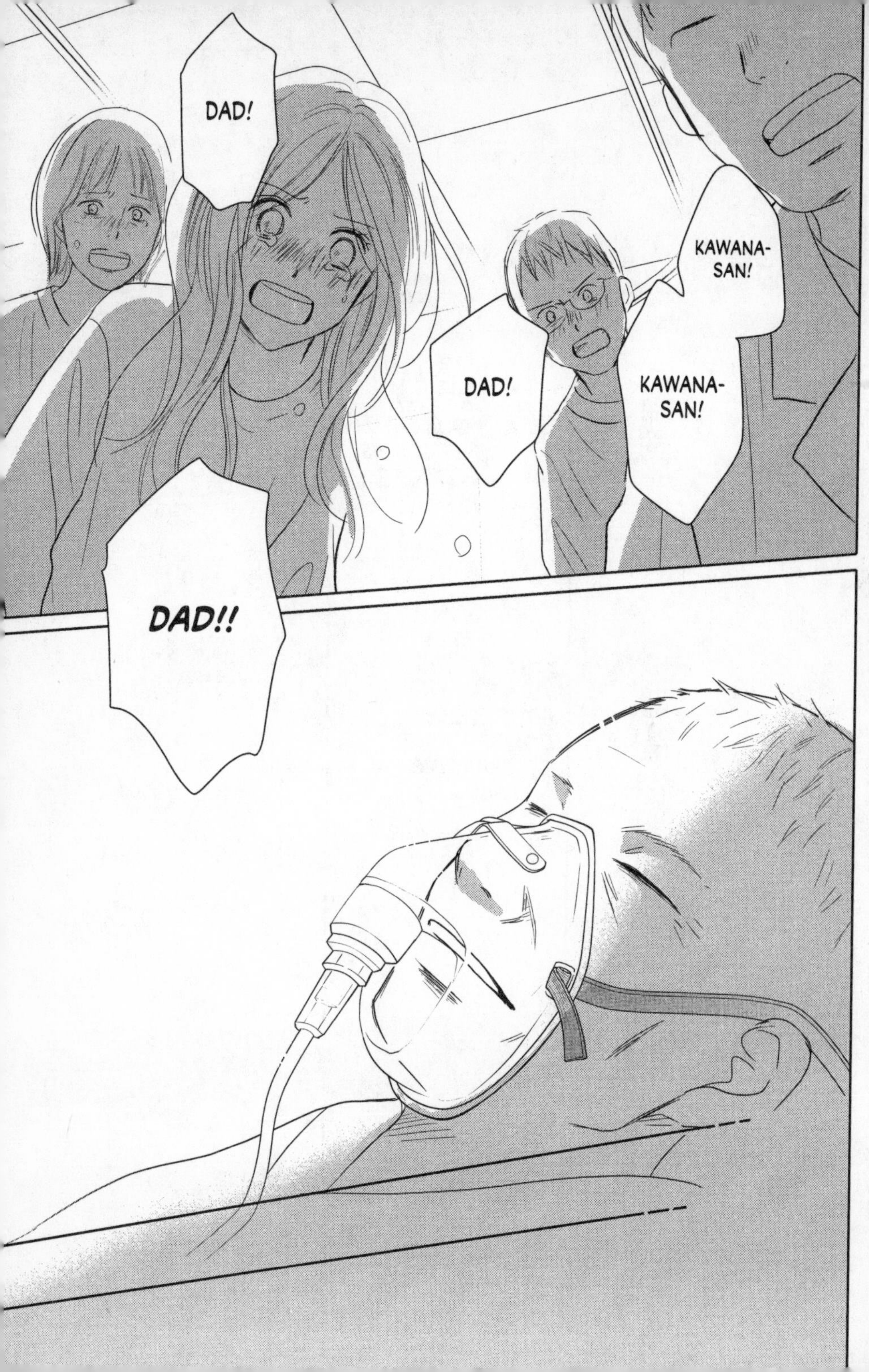
KAWANA-SAN!
KAWANA-SAN!
DAD!
DAD!
DAD!!

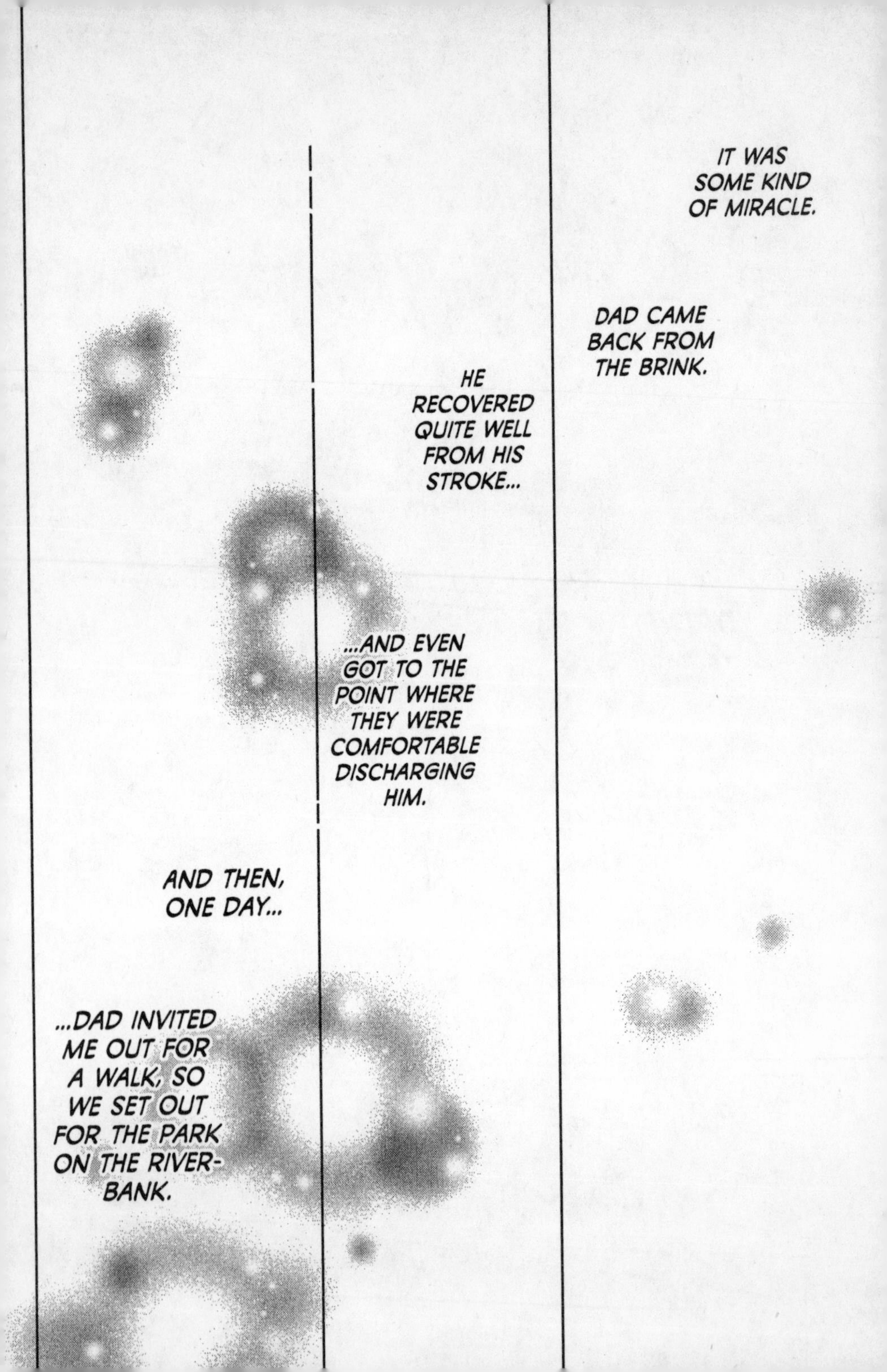
IT WAS SOME KIND OF MIRACLE.
DAD CAME BACK FROM THE BRINK.
HE RECOVERED QUITE WELL FROM HIS STROKE...
...AND EVEN GOT TO THE POINT WHERE THEY WERE COMFORTABLE DISCHARGING HIM.
AND THEN, ONE DAY...
...DAD INVITED ME OUT FOR A WALK, SO WE SET OUT FOR THE PARK ON THE RIVER-BANK.

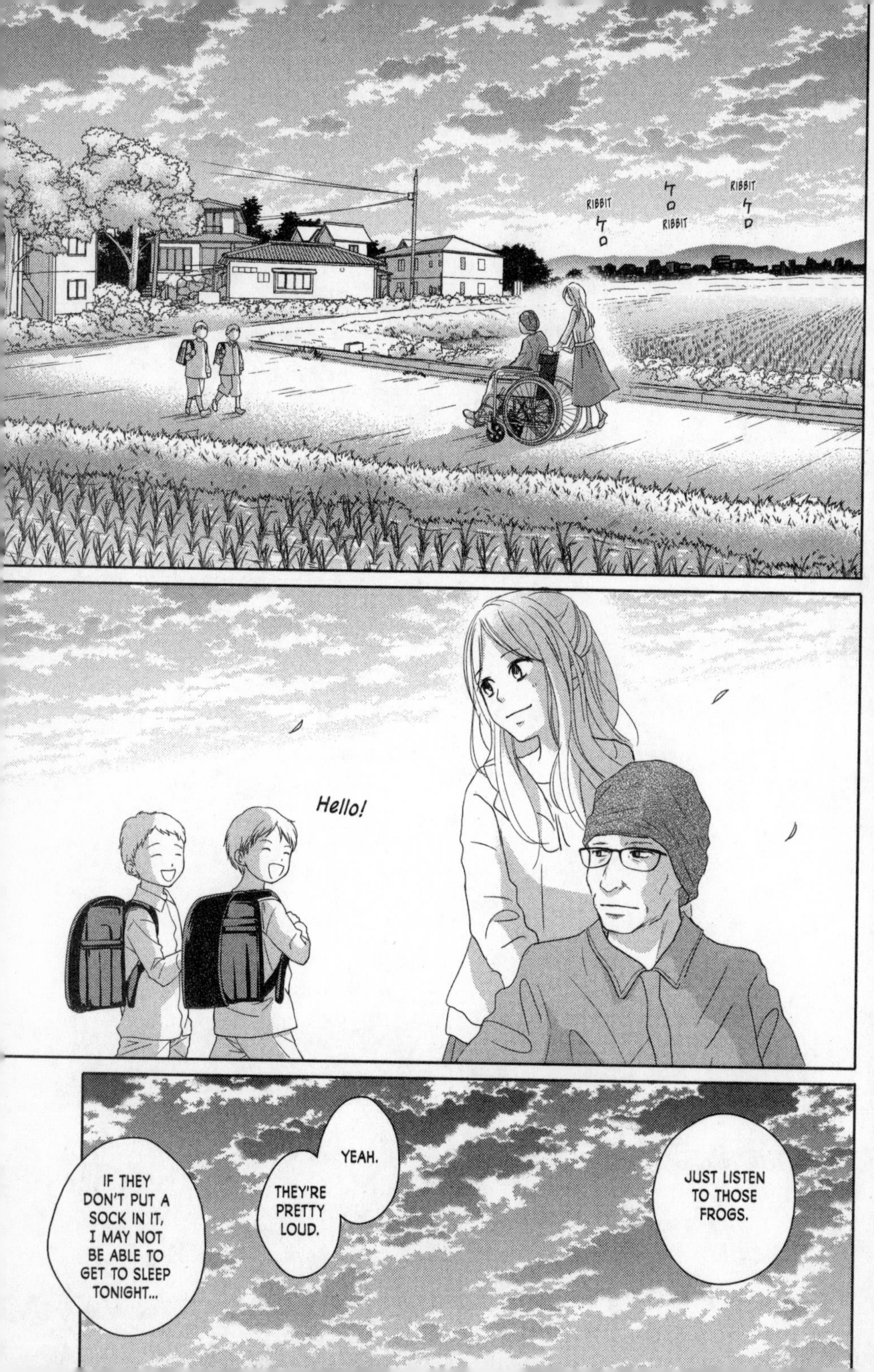
RIBBIT
ケロ
ケロ
RIBBIT
RIBBIT
ケロ
Hello!
JUST LISTEN TO THOSE FROGS.
YEAH.
THEY'RE PRETTY LOUD.
IF THEY DON'T PUT A SOCK IN IT, I MAY NOT BE ABLE TO GET TO SLEEP TONIGHT...

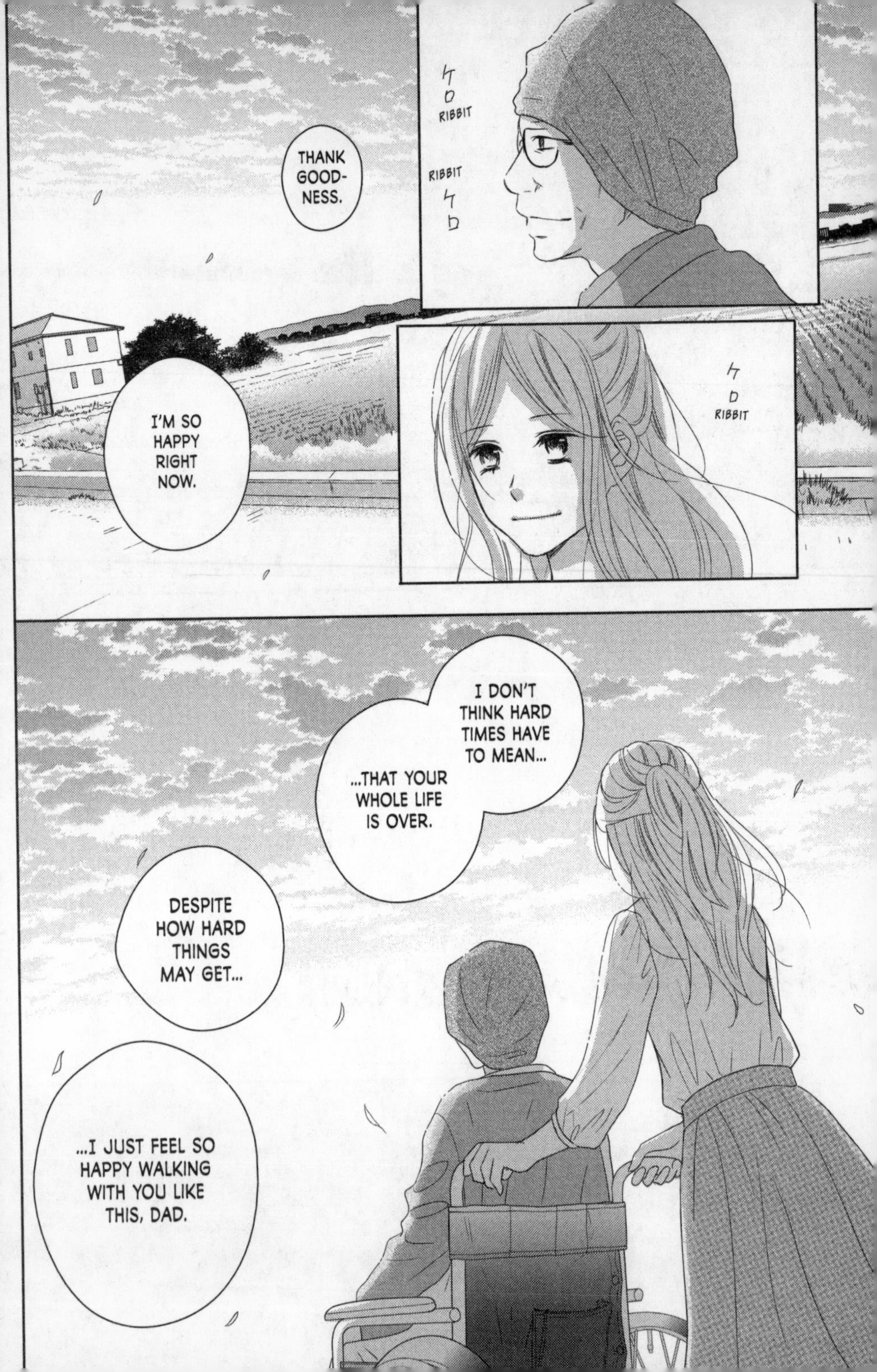
ケロ
RIBBIT
RIBBIT
ケロ
THANK GOODNESS.
ケロ
RIBBIT
I'M SO HAPPY RIGHT NOW.
I DON'T THINK HARD TIMES HAVE TO MEAN...
...THAT YOUR WHOLE LIFE IS OVER.
DESPITE HOW HARD THINGS MAY GET...
...I JUST FEEL SO HAPPY WALKING WITH YOU LIKE THIS, DAD.

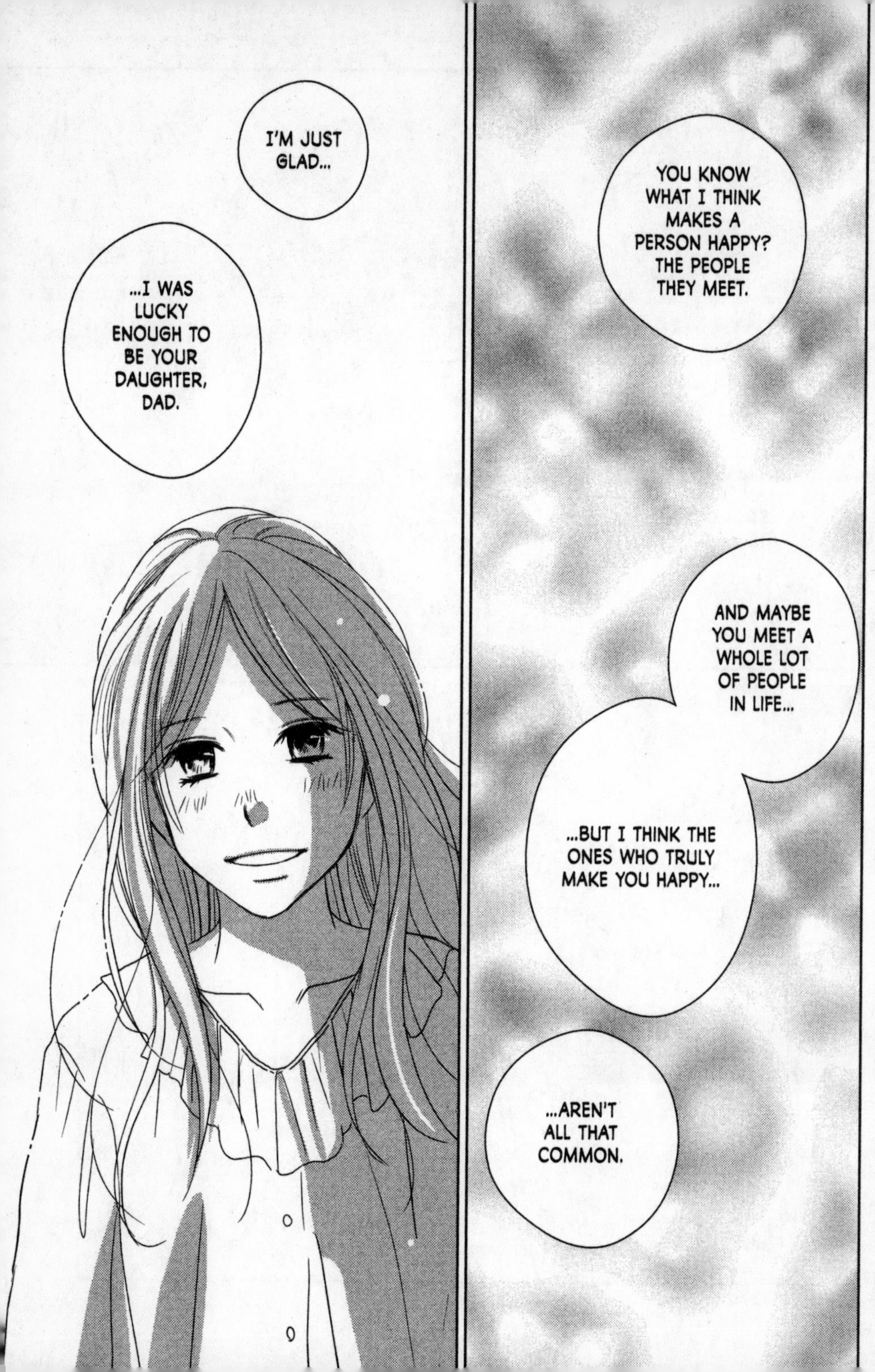
YOU KNOW WHAT I THINK MAKES A PERSON HAPPY? THE PEOPLE THEY MEET.
AND MAYBE YOU MEET A WHOLE LOT OF PEOPLE IN LIFE...
...BUT I THINK THE ONES WHO TRULY MAKE YOU HAPPY...
...AREN'T ALL THAT COMMON.
I'M JUST GLAD...
...I WAS LUCKY ENOUGH TO BE YOUR DAUGHTER, DAD.

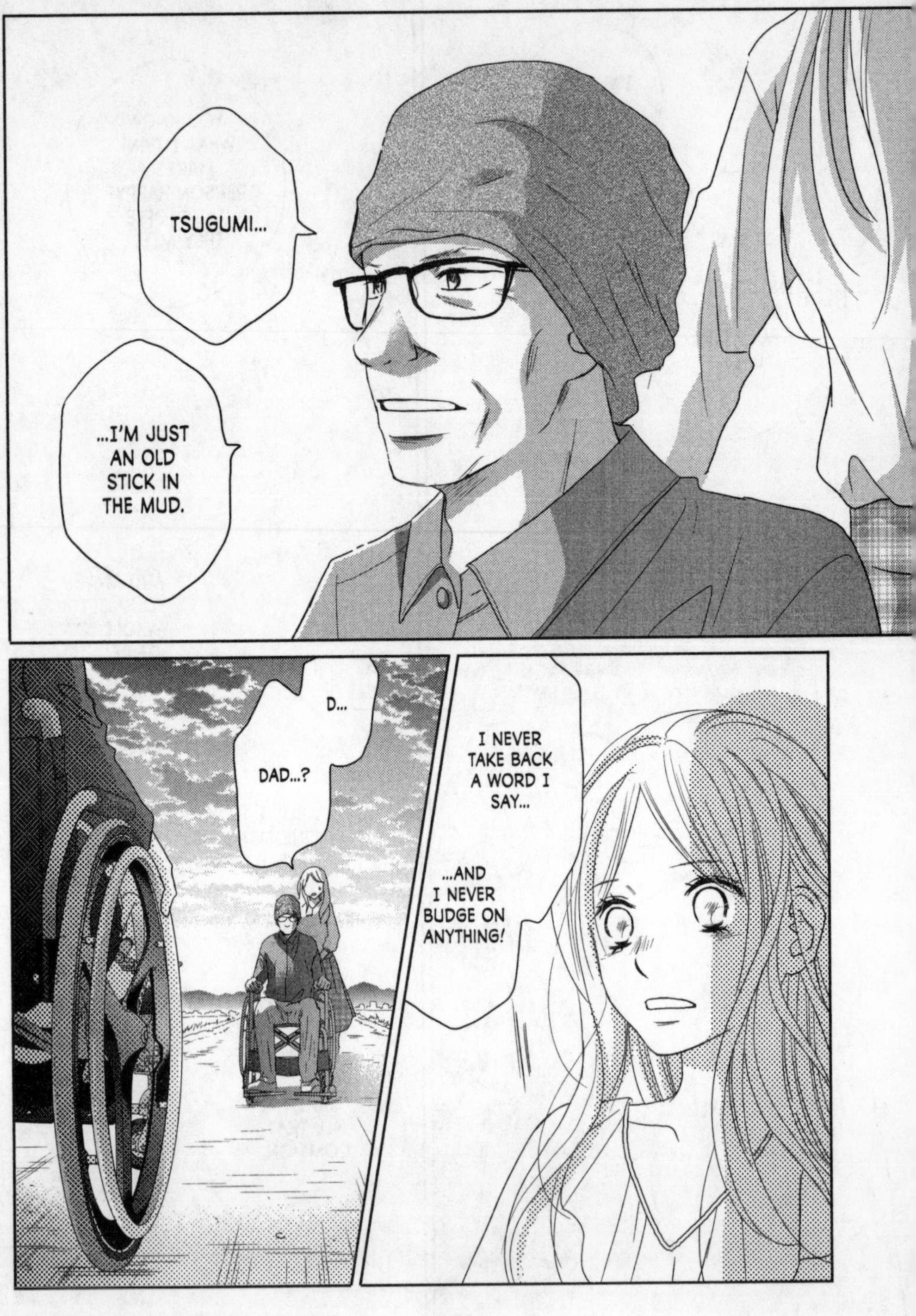
TSUGUMI...
...I'M JUST AN OLD STICK IN THE MUD.
I NEVER TAKE BACK A WORD I SAY...
...AND I NEVER BUDGE ON ANYTHING!
D...
DAD...?

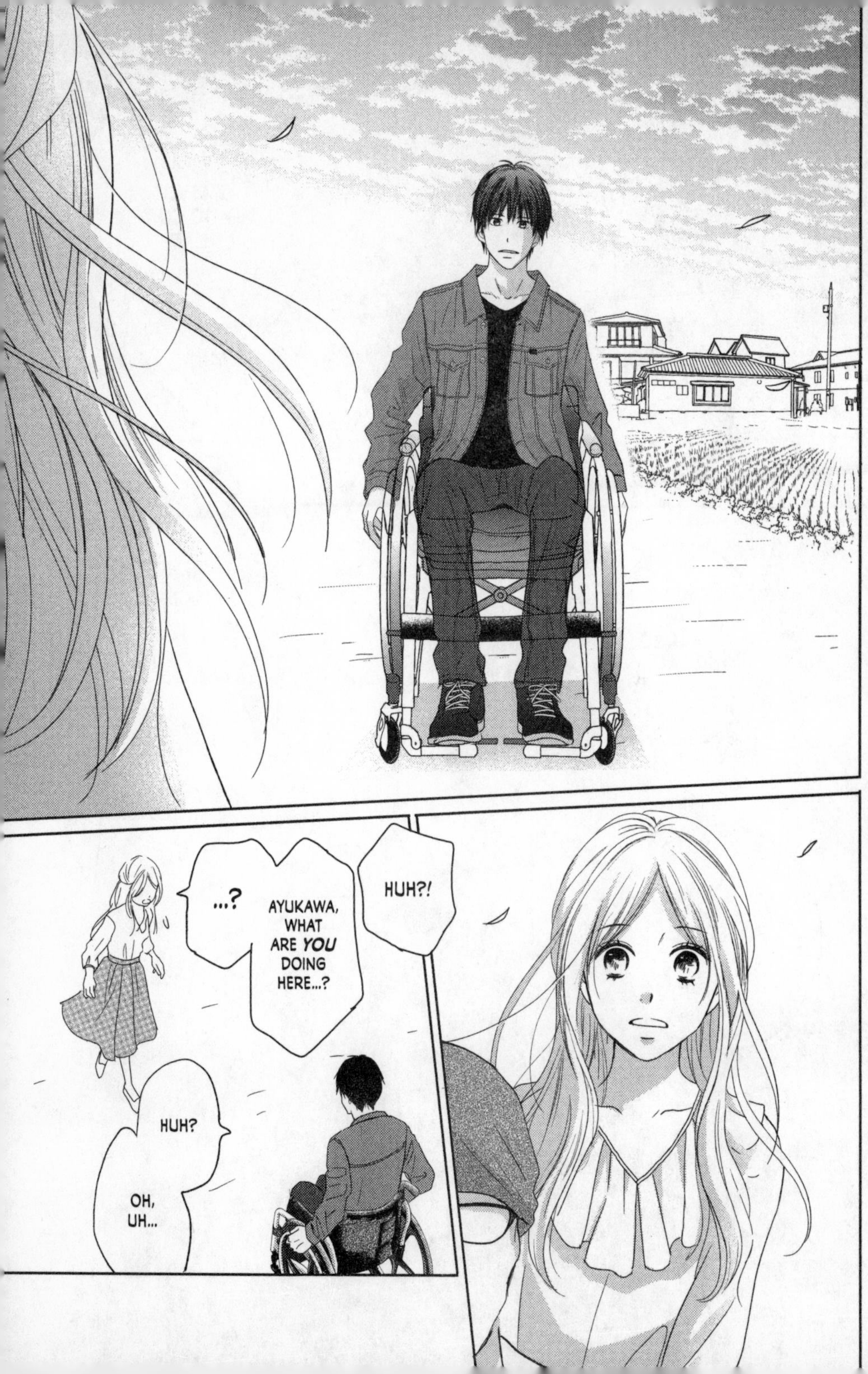
HUH?!
...?
AYUKAWA, WHAT ARE *YOU* DOING HERE...?
HUH?
OH, UH...

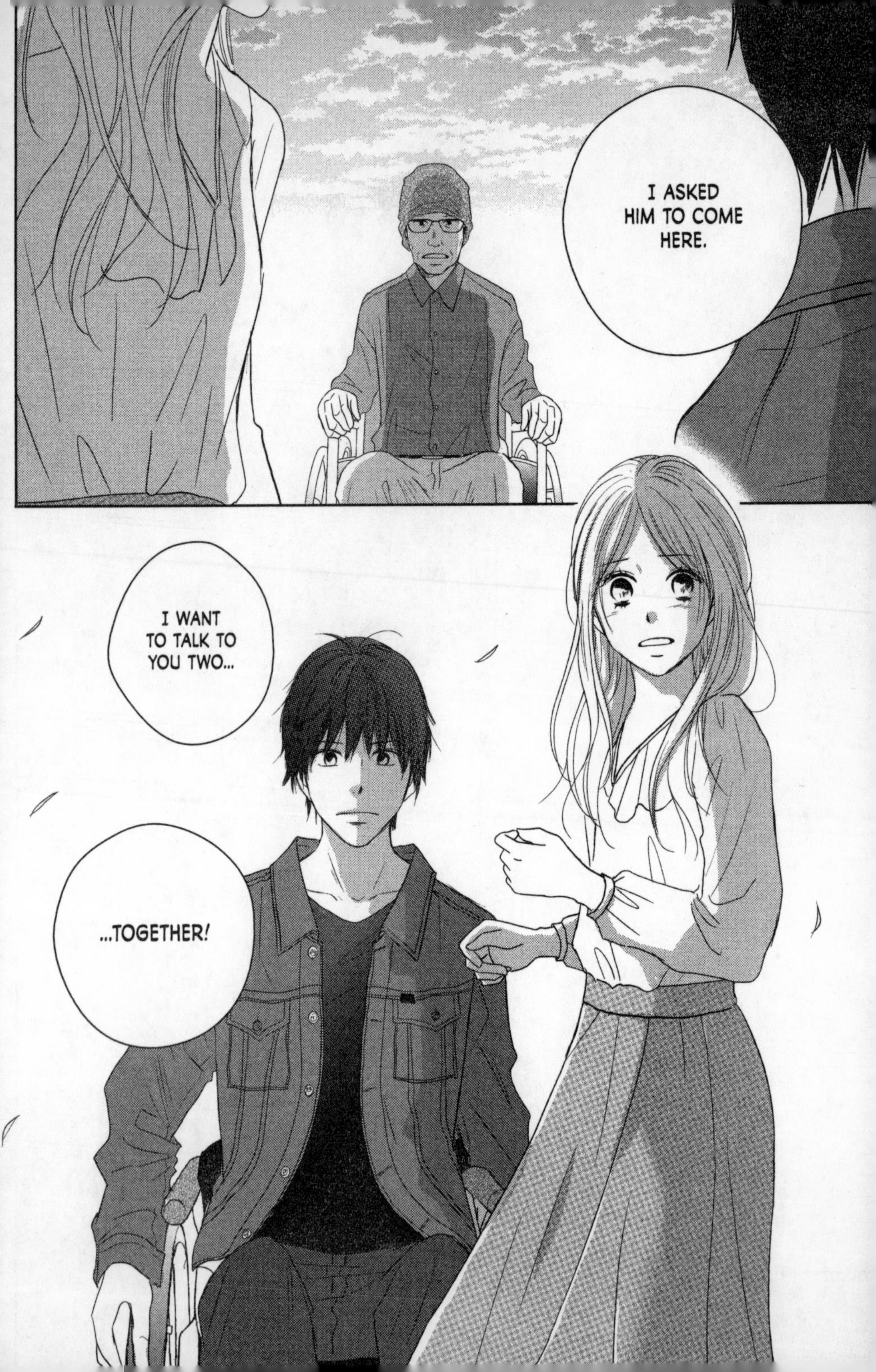
I ASKED HIM TO COME HERE.
I WANT TO TALK TO YOU TWO...
...TOGETHER!

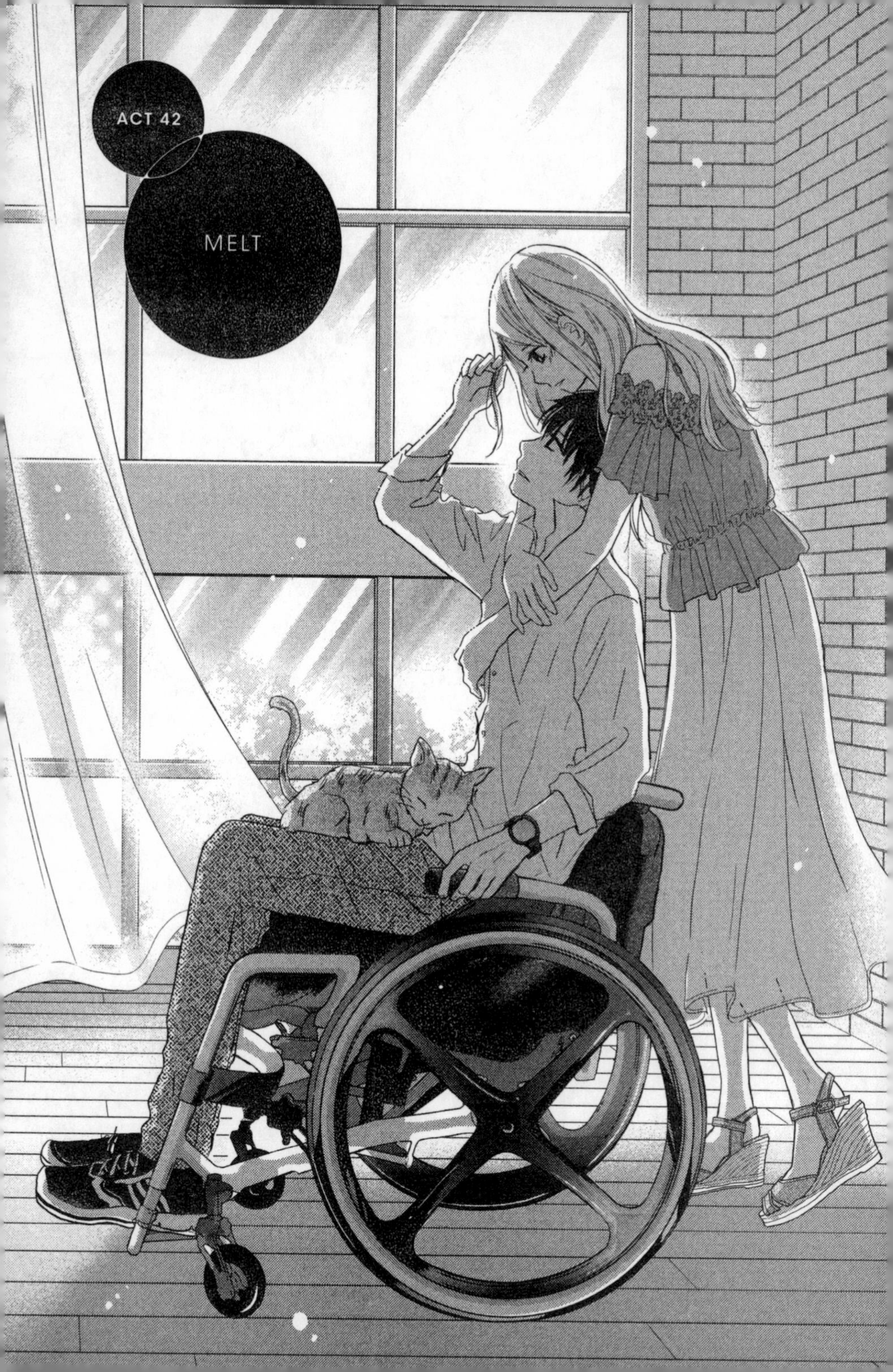
ACT 42
MELT

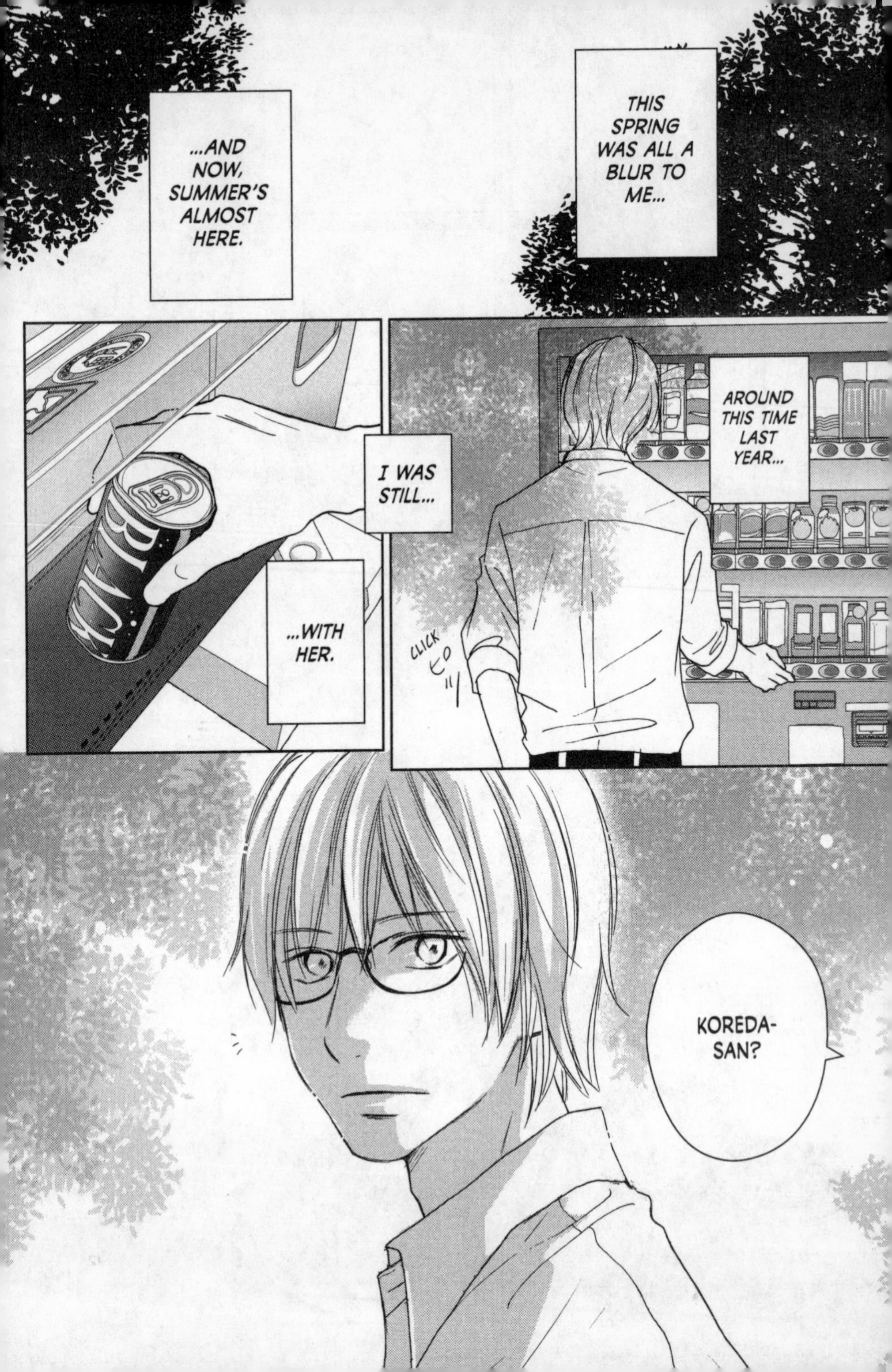
THIS SPRING WAS ALL A BLUR TO ME...
...AND NOW, SUMMER'S ALMOST HERE.
AROUND THIS TIME LAST YEAR...
CLICK
I WAS STILL...
...WITH HER.
KOREDA-SAN?

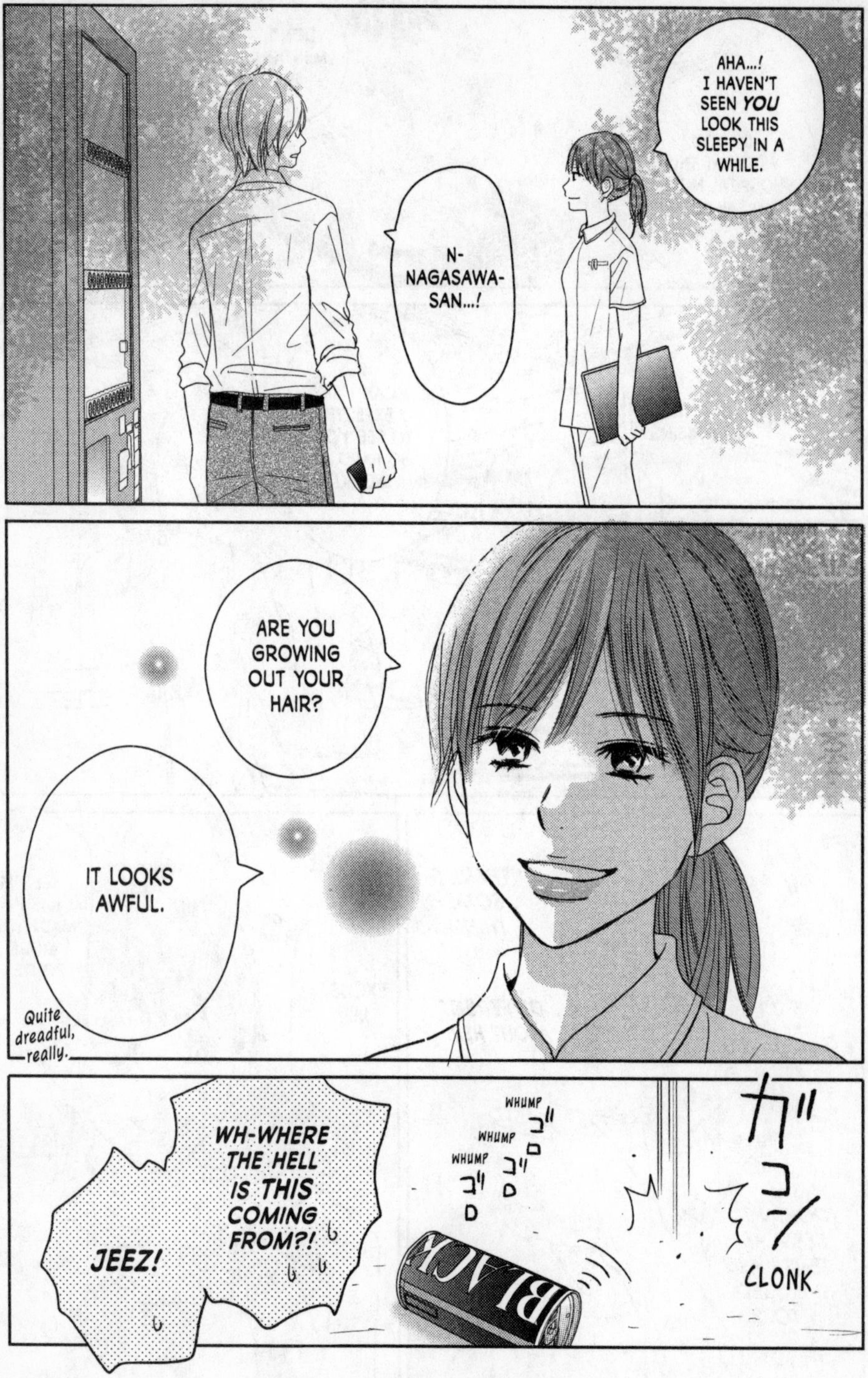
AHA...! I HAVEN'T SEEN *YOU* LOOK THIS SLEEPY IN A WHILE.
N-NAGASAWA-SAN...!
ARE YOU GROWING OUT YOUR HAIR?
IT LOOKS AWFUL.
Quite dreadful, really.
ガコー
CLONK
ゴロ
WHUMP
ゴロ
WHUMP
ゴロ
WHUMP
BLACK
WH-WHERE THE HELL IS THIS COMING FROM?!
JEEZ!

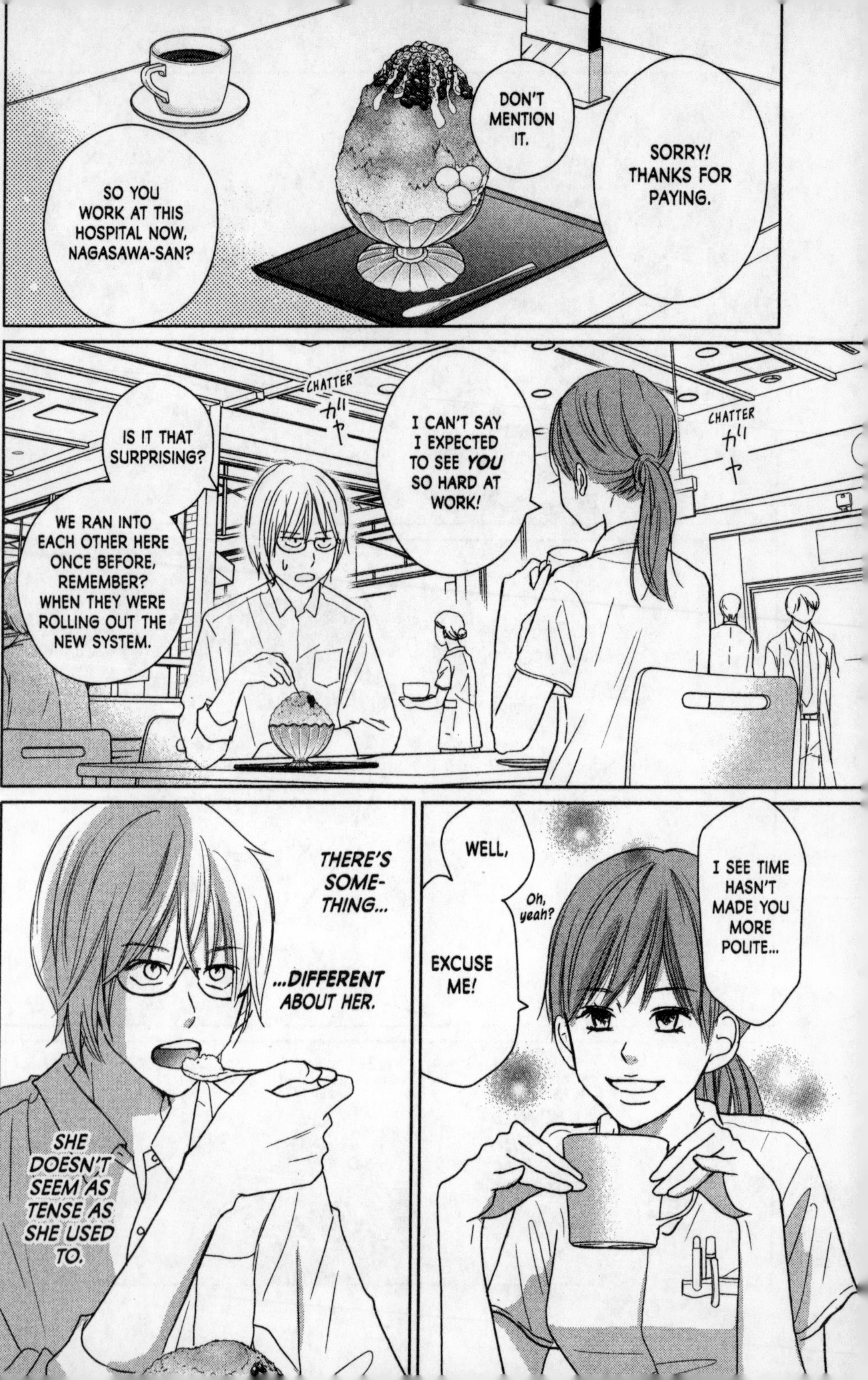
SORRY! THANKS FOR PAYING.
DON'T MENTION IT.
SO YOU WORK AT THIS HOSPITAL NOW, NAGASAWA-SAN?
CHATTER
ガヤ
I CAN'T SAY I EXPECTED TO SEE *YOU* SO HARD AT WORK!
CHATTER
ガヤ
IS IT THAT SURPRISING?
WE RAN INTO EACH OTHER HERE ONCE BEFORE, REMEMBER? WHEN THEY WERE ROLLING OUT THE NEW SYSTEM.
I SEE TIME HASN'T MADE YOU MORE POLITE...
WELL,
Oh, yeah?
EXCUSE ME!
THERE'S SOME-THING...
...DIFFERENT ABOUT HER.
SHE DOESN'T SEEM AS TENSE AS SHE USED TO.

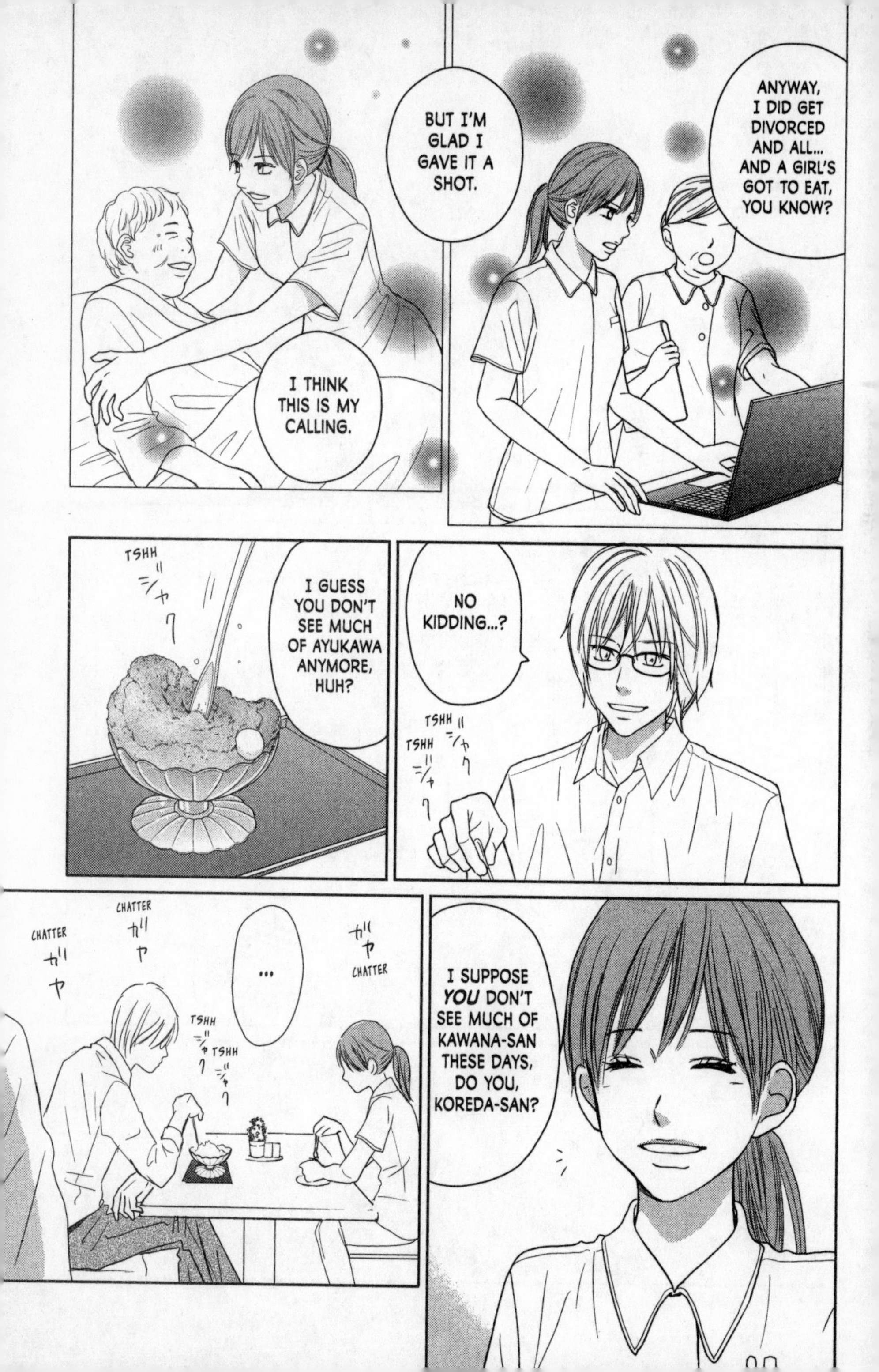
ANYWAY, I DID GET DIVORCED AND ALL... AND A GIRL'S GOT TO EAT, YOU KNOW?
BUT I'M GLAD I GAVE IT A SHOT.
I THINK THIS IS MY CALLING.
NO KIDDING...?
TSHH
TSHH
TSHH
I GUESS YOU DON'T SEE MUCH OF AYUKAWA ANYMORE, HUH?
I SUPPOSE *YOU* DON'T SEE MUCH OF KAWANA-SAN THESE DAYS, DO YOU, KOREDA-SAN?
CHATTER
...
TSHH
TSHH
CHATTER
CHATTER

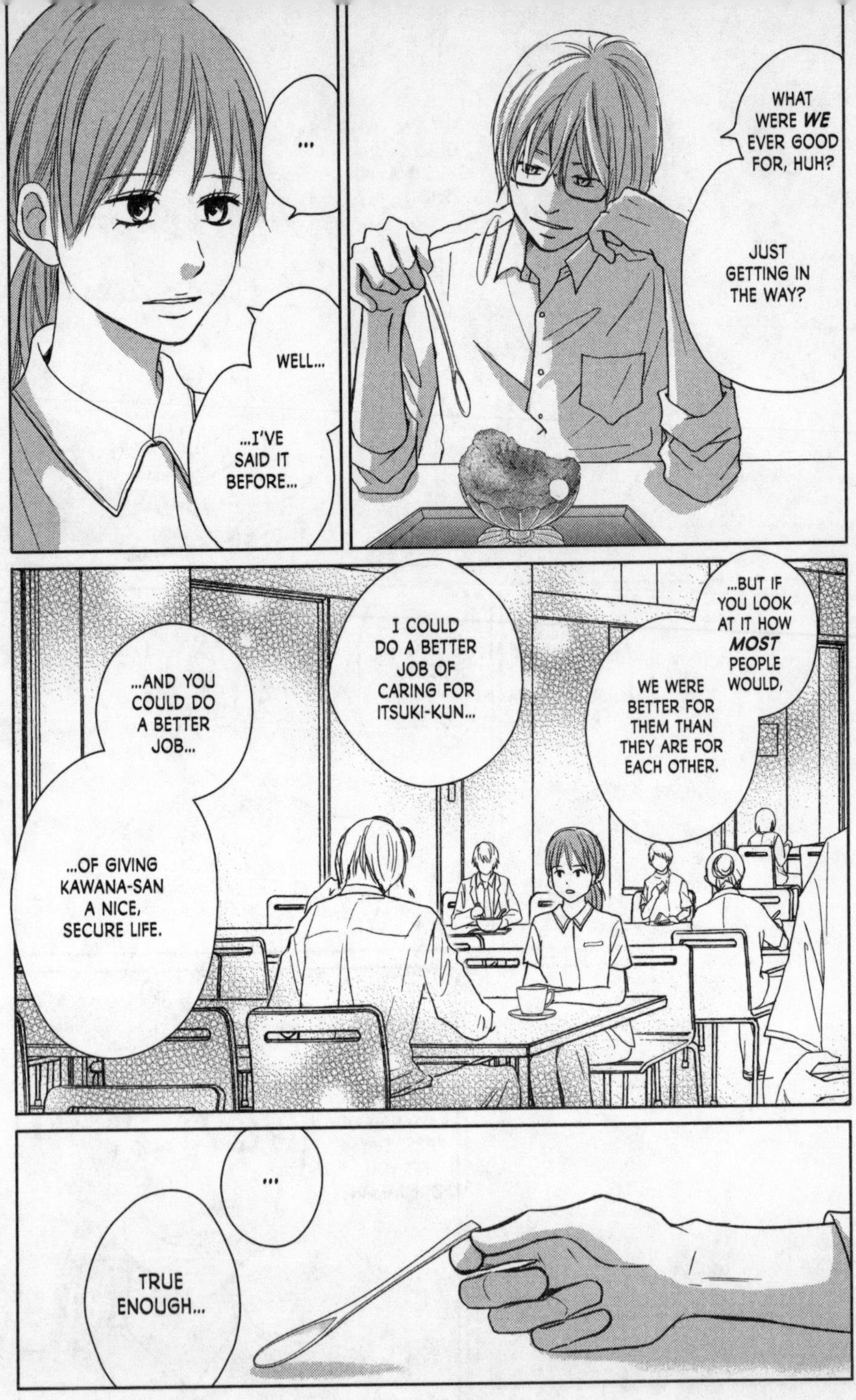
WHAT WERE *WE* EVER GOOD FOR, HUH?
JUST GETTING IN THE WAY?
...
WELL...
...I'VE SAID IT BEFORE...
...BUT IF YOU LOOK AT IT HOW *MOST* PEOPLE WOULD,
WE WERE BETTER FOR THEM THAN THEY ARE FOR EACH OTHER.
I COULD DO A BETTER JOB OF CARING FOR ITSUKI-KUN...
...AND YOU COULD DO A BETTER JOB...
...OF GIVING KAWANA-SAN A NICE, SECURE LIFE.
...
TRUE ENOUGH...

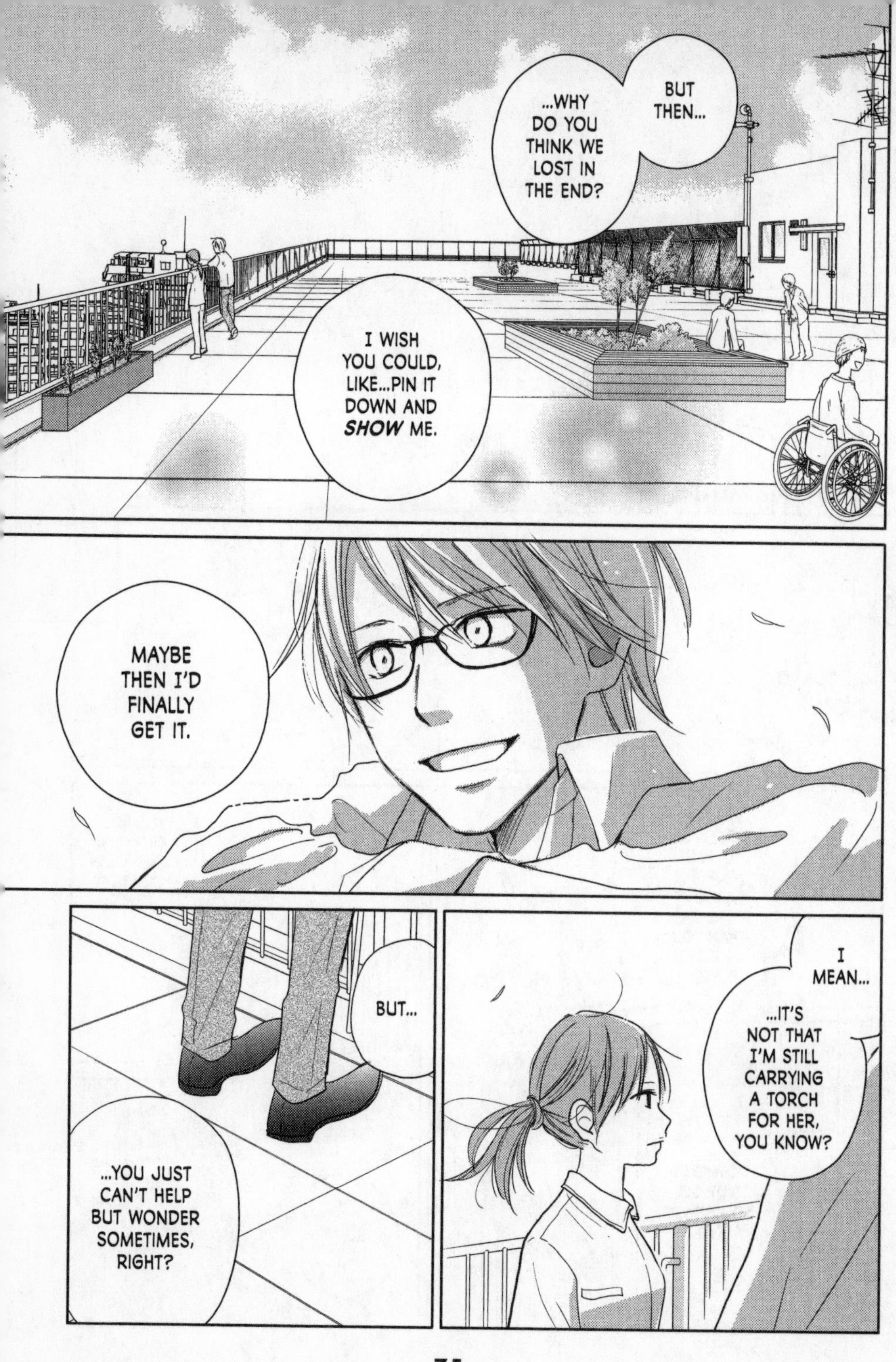
BUT THEN...
...WHY DO YOU THINK WE LOST IN THE END?
I WISH YOU COULD, LIKE...PIN IT DOWN AND *SHOW* ME.
MAYBE THEN I'D FINALLY GET IT.
I MEAN...
...IT'S NOT THAT I'M STILL CARRYING A TORCH FOR HER, YOU KNOW?
BUT...
...YOU JUST CAN'T HELP BUT WONDER SOMETIMES, RIGHT?

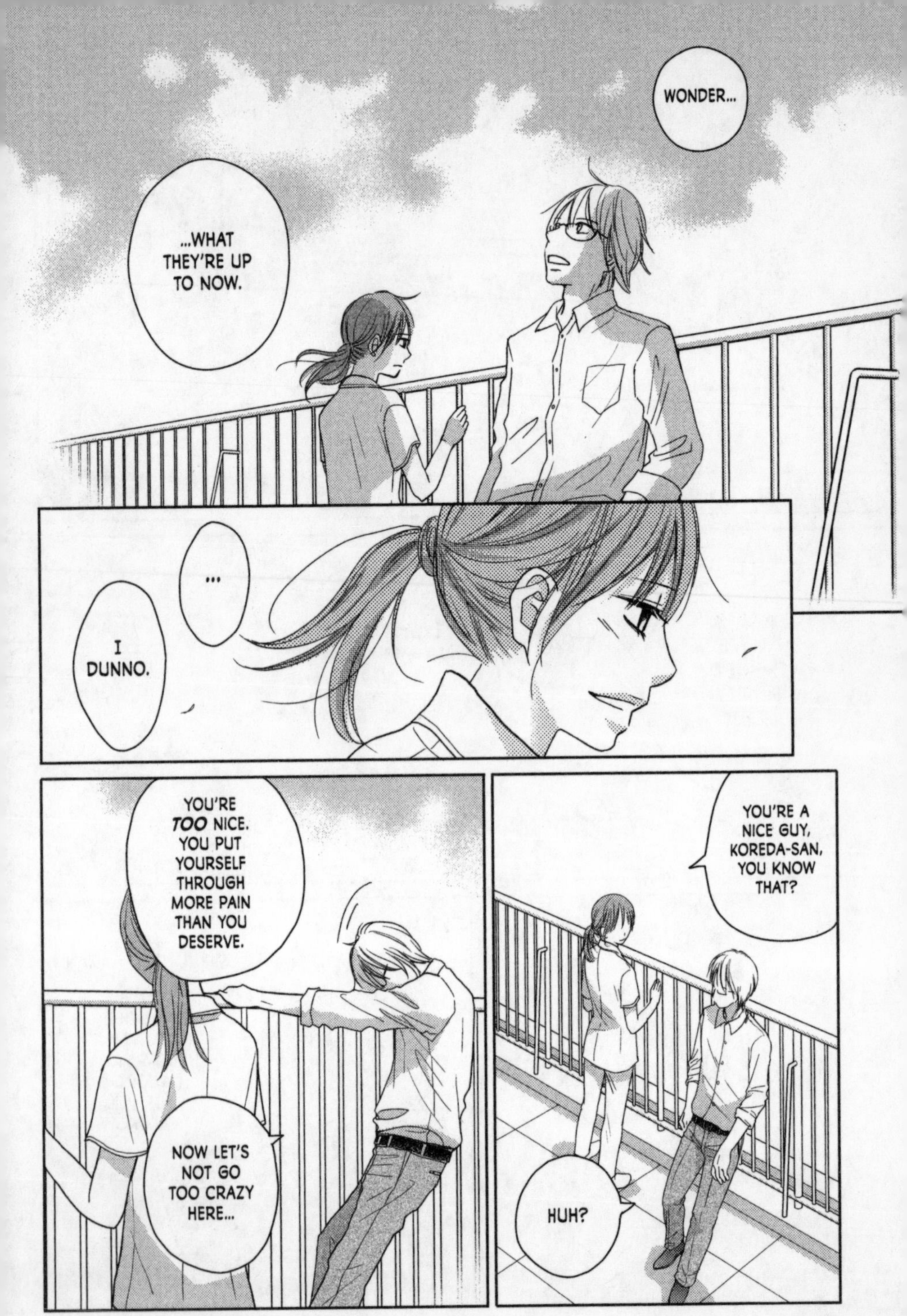
WONDER...
...WHAT THEY'RE UP TO NOW.
...
I DUNNO.
YOU'RE A NICE GUY, KOREDA-SAN, YOU KNOW THAT?
HUH?
YOU'RE *TOO* NICE. YOU PUT YOURSELF THROUGH MORE PAIN THAN YOU DESERVE.
NOW LET'S NOT GO TOO CRAZY HERE...

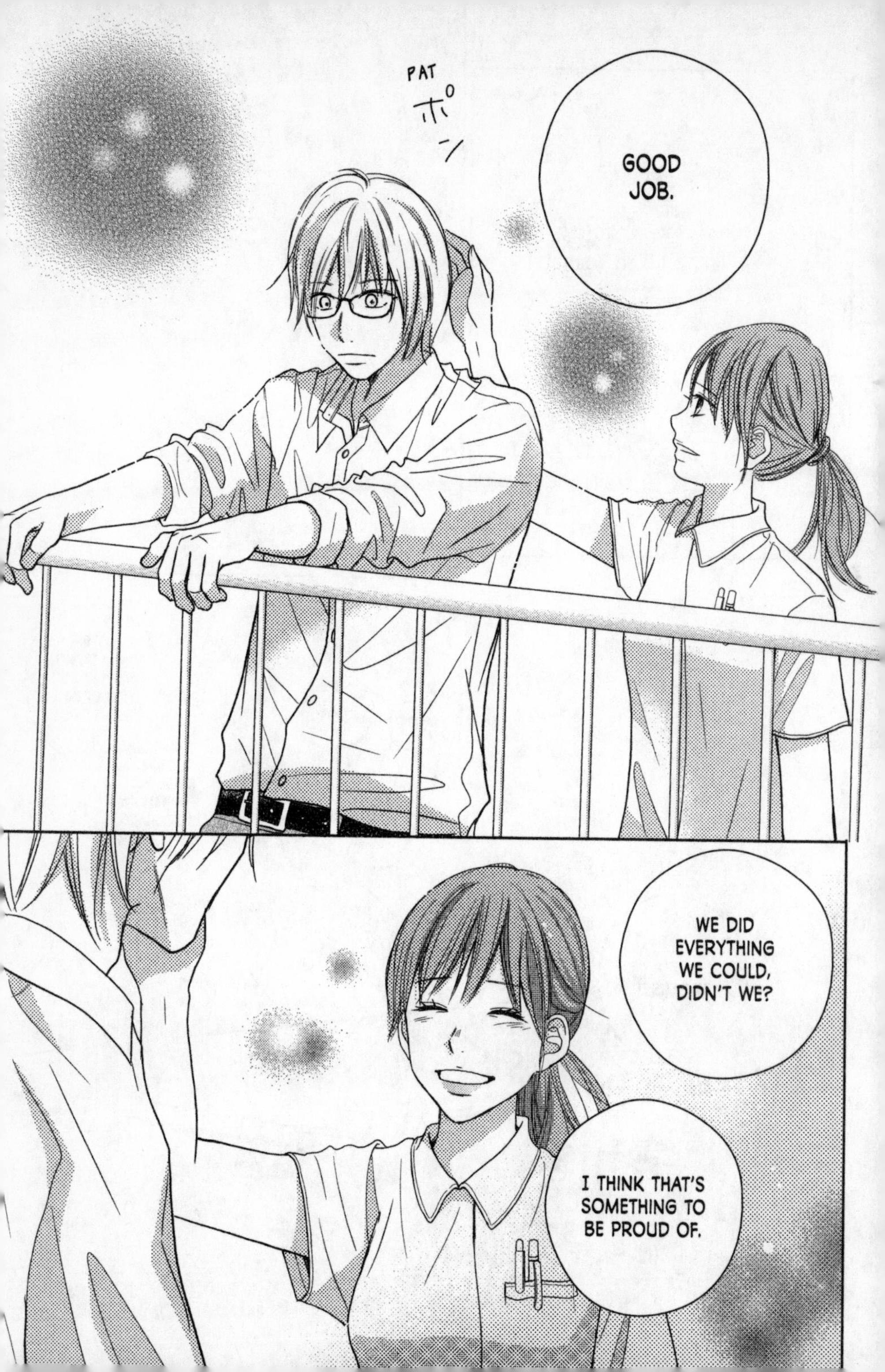

PAT
ポン
GOOD JOB.
WE DID EVERYTHING WE COULD, DIDN'T WE?
I THINK THAT'S SOMETHING TO BE PROUD OF.

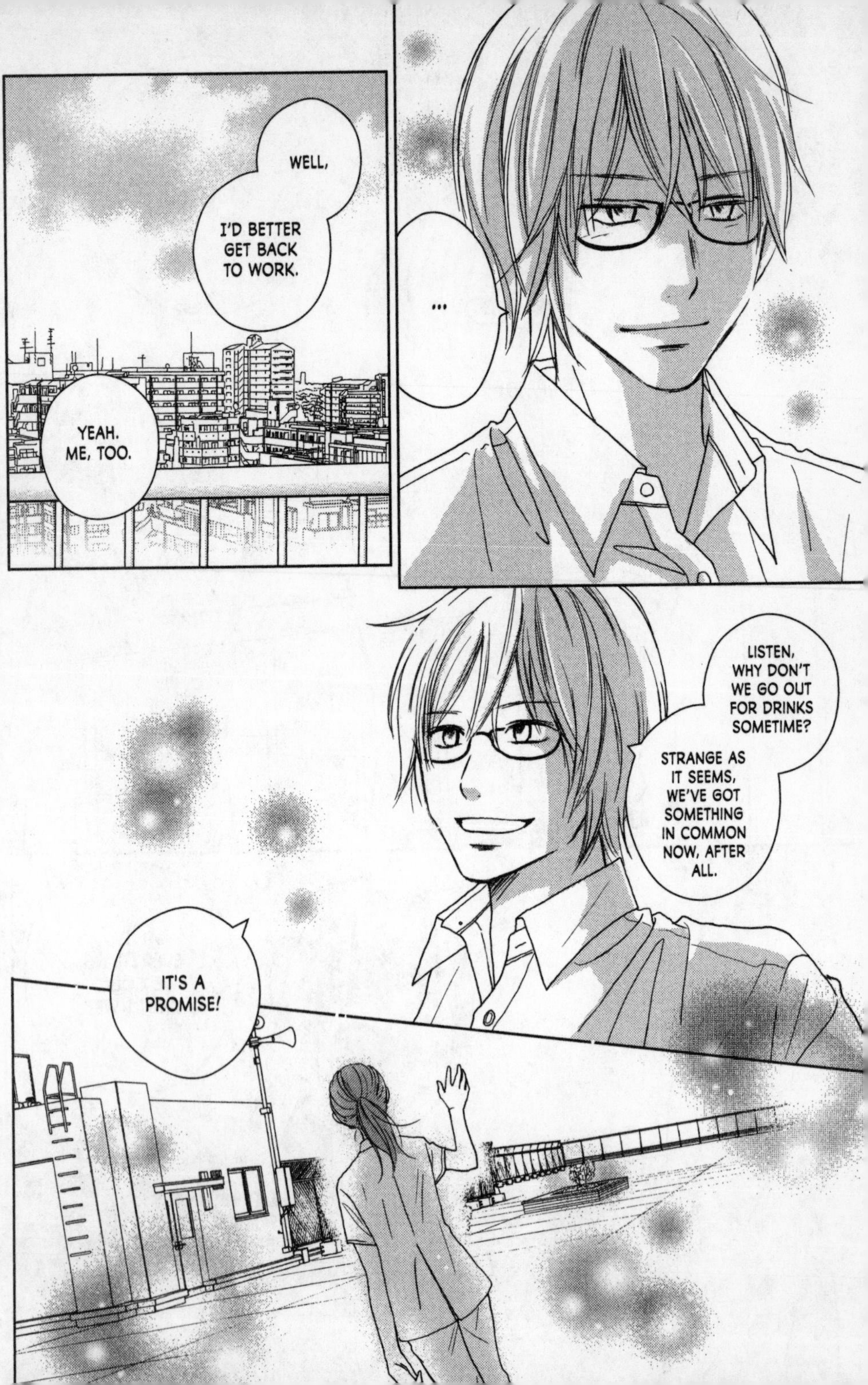
...
WELL,
I'D BETTER GET BACK TO WORK.
YEAH. ME, TOO.
LISTEN, WHY DON'T WE GO OUT FOR DRINKS SOMETIME?
STRANGE AS IT SEEMS, WE'VE GOT SOMETHING IN COMMON NOW, AFTER ALL.
IT'S A PROMISE!

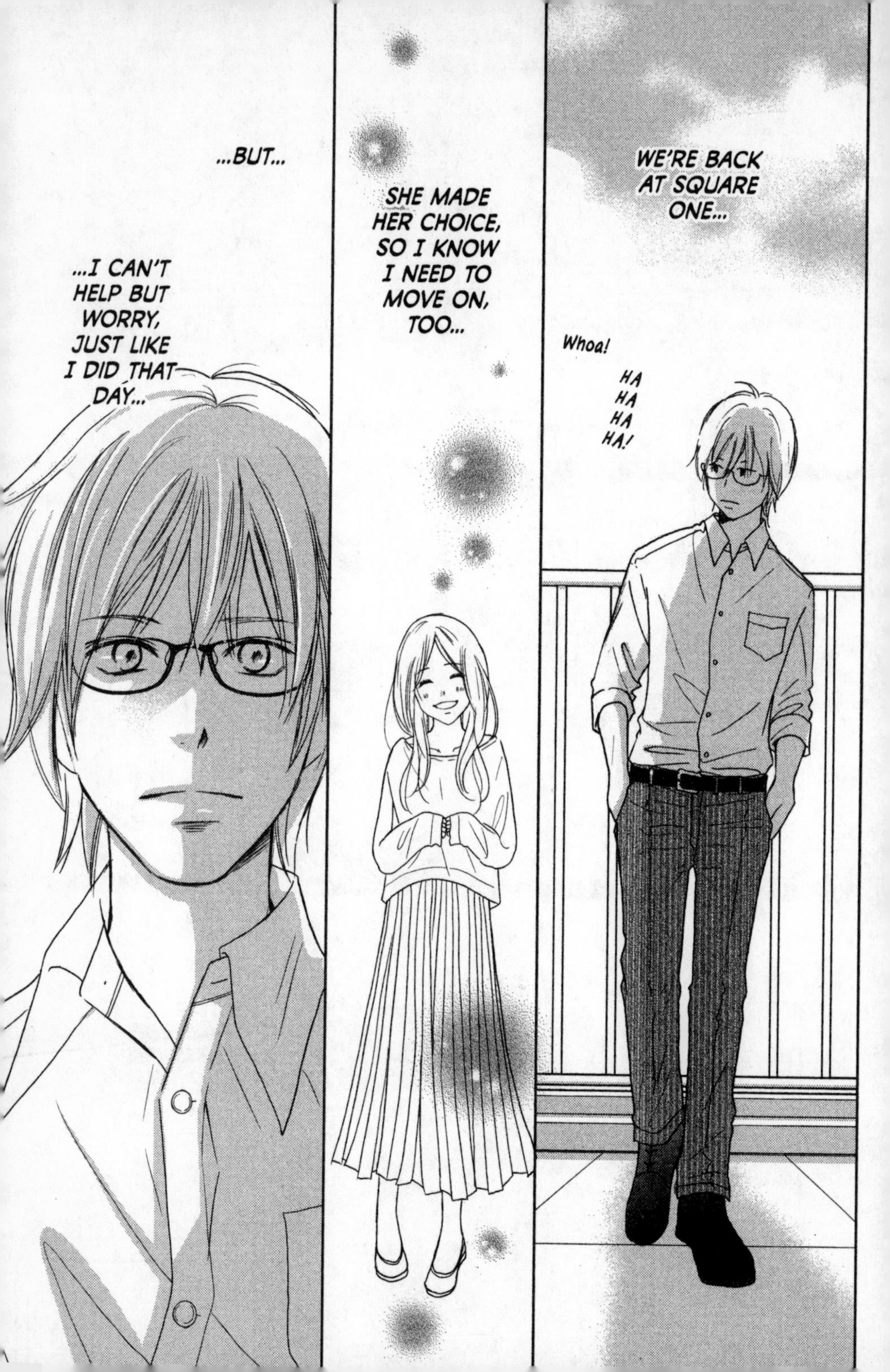
WE'RE BACK AT SQUARE ONE...
Whoa!
HA HA HA HA!
SHE MADE HER CHOICE, SO I KNOW I NEED TO MOVE ON, TOO...
...BUT...
...I CAN'T HELP BUT WORRY, JUST LIKE I DID THAT DAY...

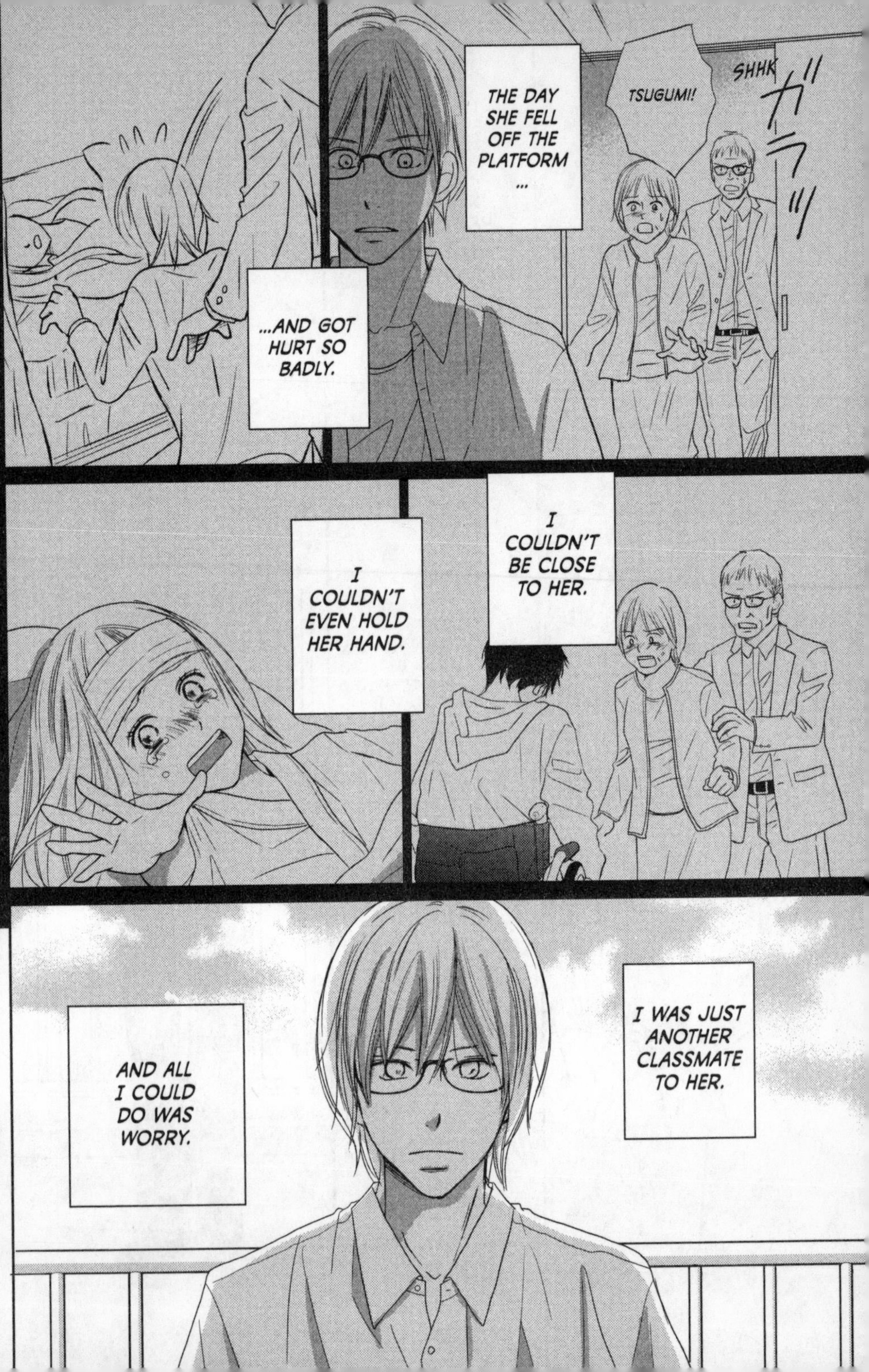
SHHK
TSUGUMI!
THE DAY SHE FELL OFF THE PLATFORM ...
...AND GOT HURT SO BADLY.
I COULDN'T BE CLOSE TO HER.
I COULDN'T EVEN HOLD HER HAND.
I WAS JUST ANOTHER CLASSMATE TO HER.
AND ALL I COULD DO WAS WORRY.

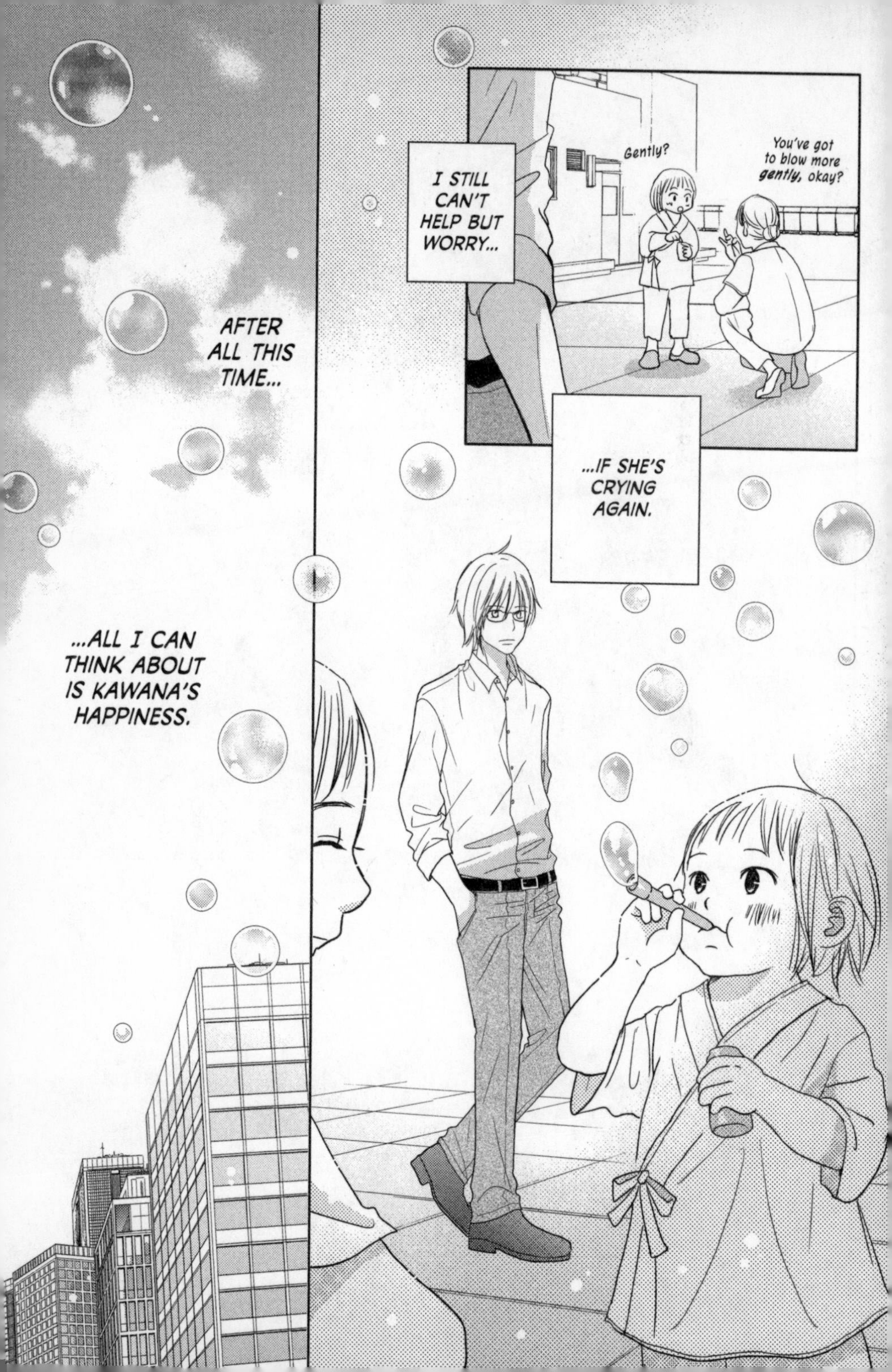
You've got to blow more *gently*, okay?
Gently?
I STILL CAN'T HELP BUT WORRY...
...IF SHE'S CRYING AGAIN.
AFTER ALL THIS TIME...
...ALL I CAN THINK ABOUT IS KAWANA'S HAPPINESS.

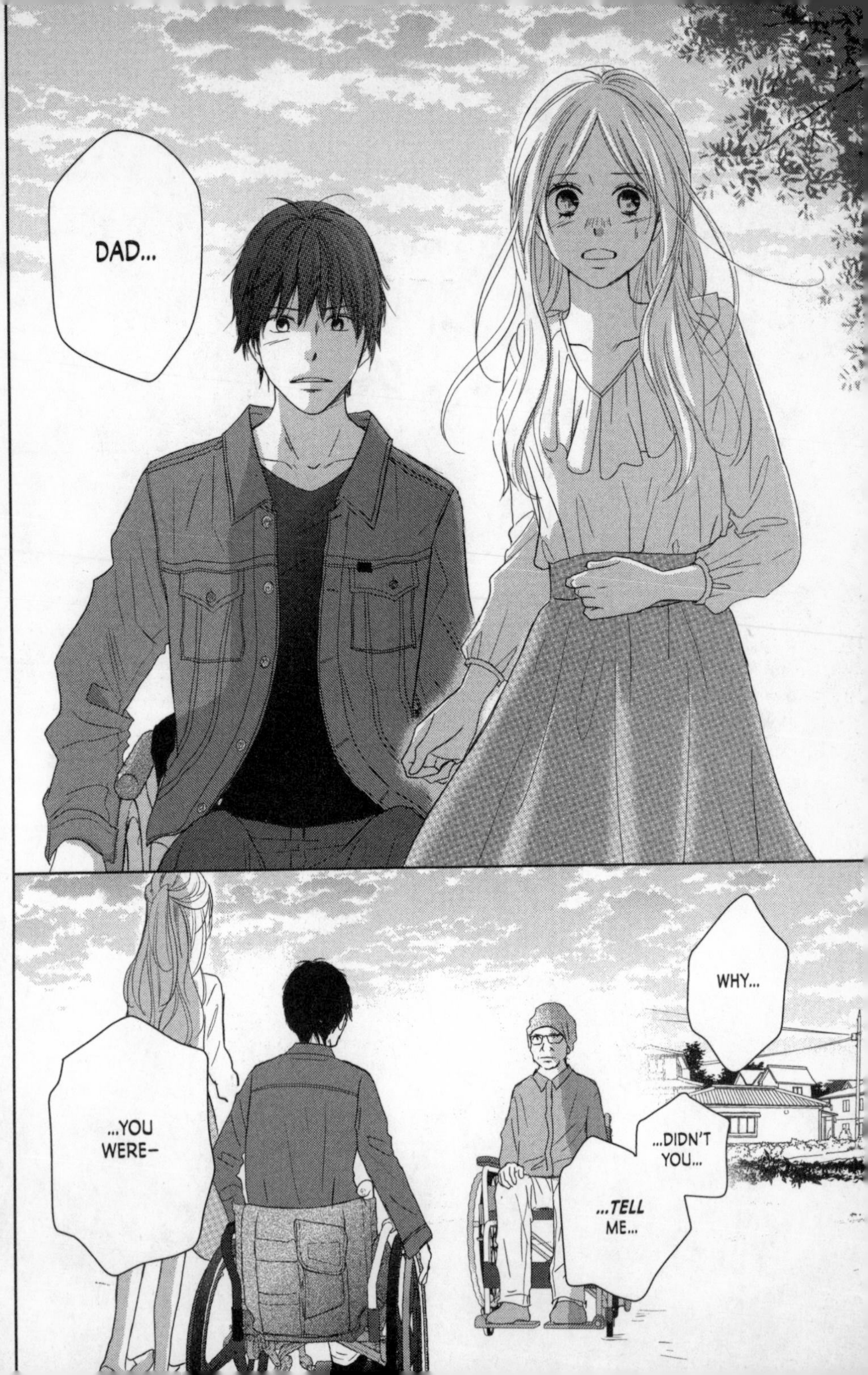
DAD...
WHY...
...DIDN'T YOU...
...TELL ME...
...YOU WERE–

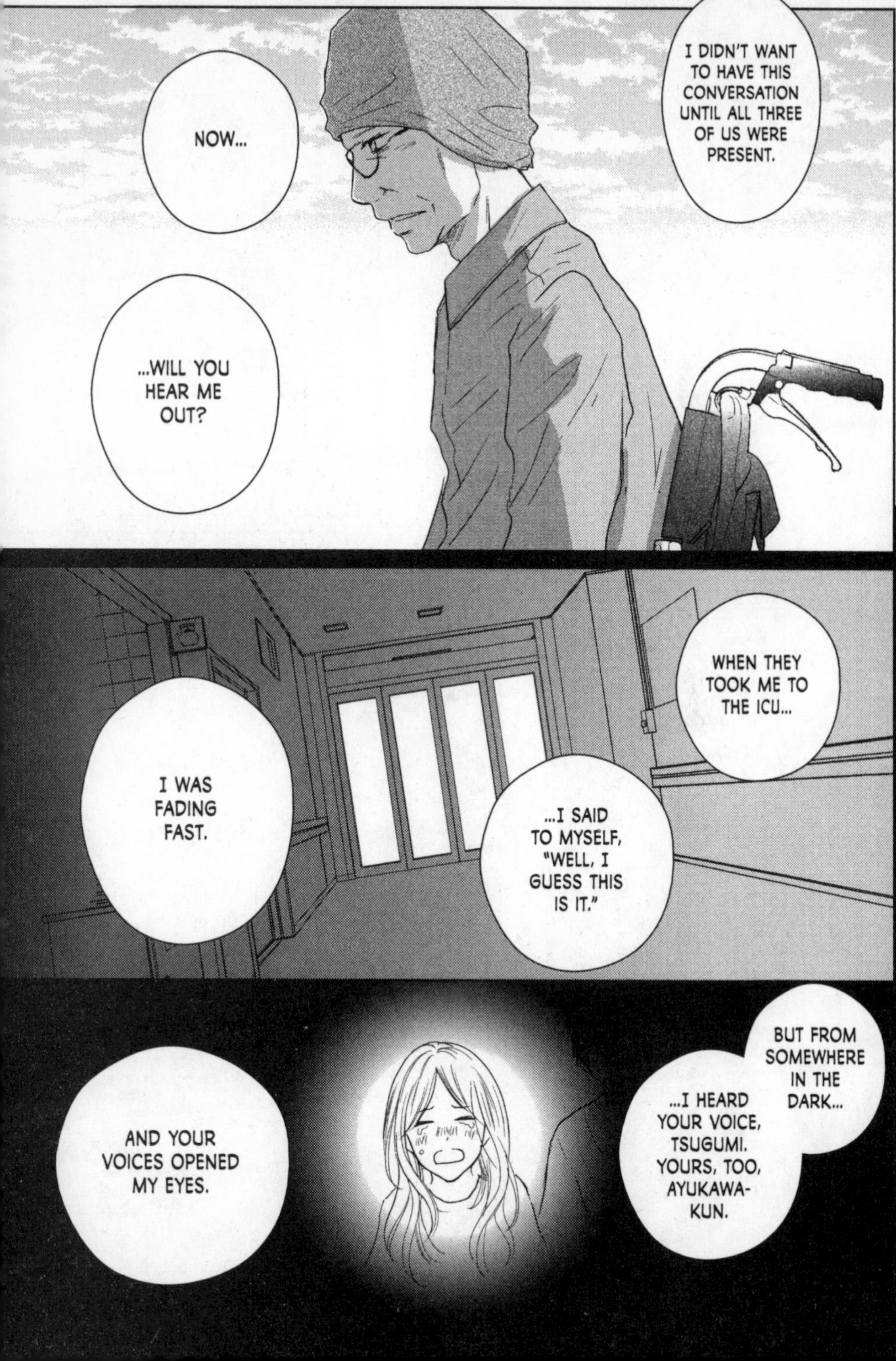
I DIDN'T WANT TO HAVE THIS CONVERSATION UNTIL ALL THREE OF US WERE PRESENT.
NOW...
...WILL YOU HEAR ME OUT?
WHEN THEY TOOK ME TO THE ICU...
...I SAID TO MYSELF, "WELL, I GUESS THIS IS IT."
I WAS FADING FAST.
BUT FROM SOMEWHERE IN THE DARK...
...I HEARD YOUR VOICE, TSUGUMI. YOURS, TOO, AYUKAWA-KUN.
AND YOUR VOICES OPENED MY EYES.

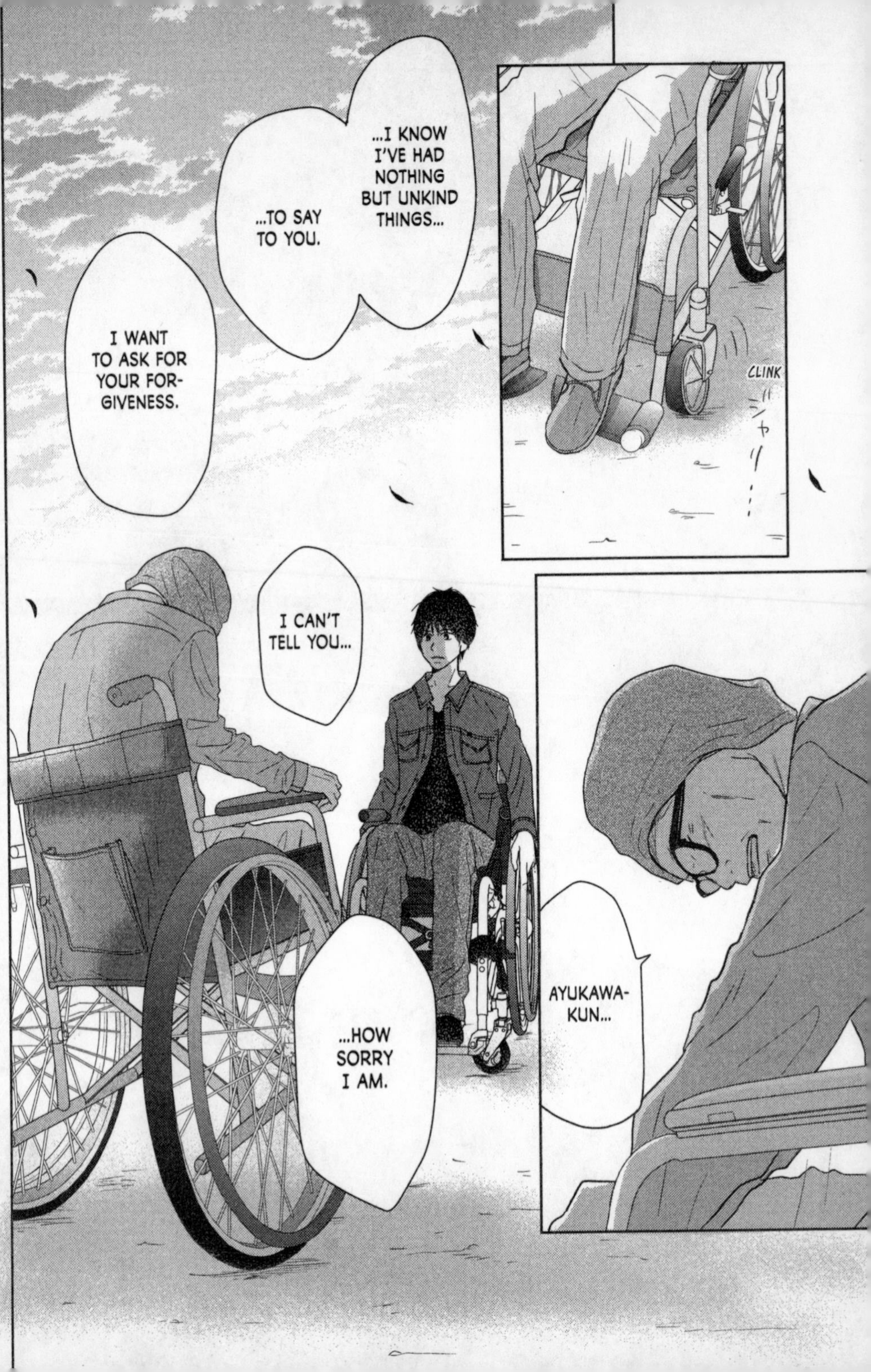
CLINK
ジャリ…
AYUKAWA-KUN...
...I KNOW I'VE HAD NOTHING BUT UNKIND THINGS...
...TO SAY TO YOU.
I WANT TO ASK FOR YOUR FOR-GIVENESS.
I CAN'T TELL YOU...
...HOW SORRY I AM.

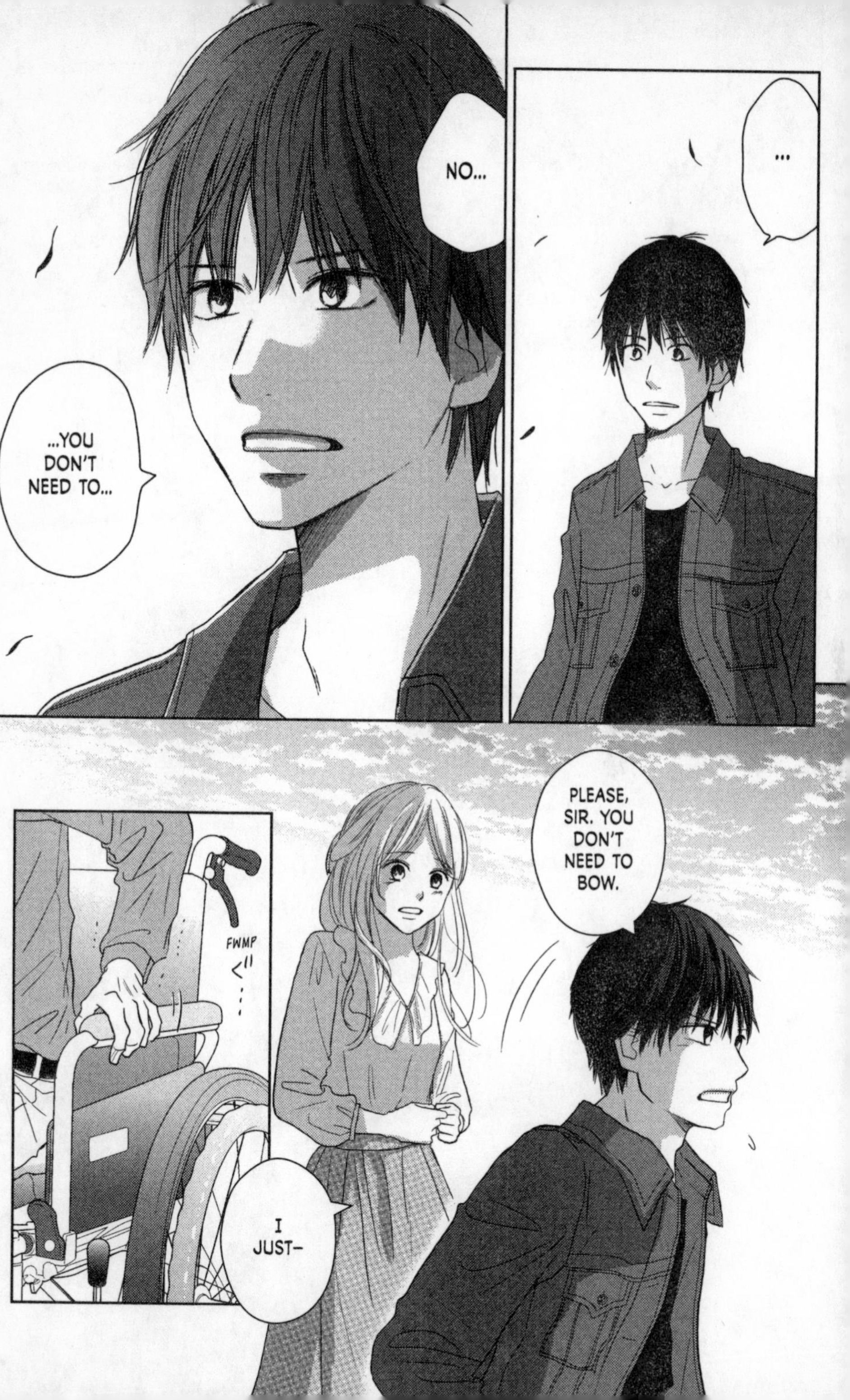
...
NO...
...YOU DON'T NEED TO...
PLEASE, SIR. YOU DON'T NEED TO BOW.
I JUST–
FWMP

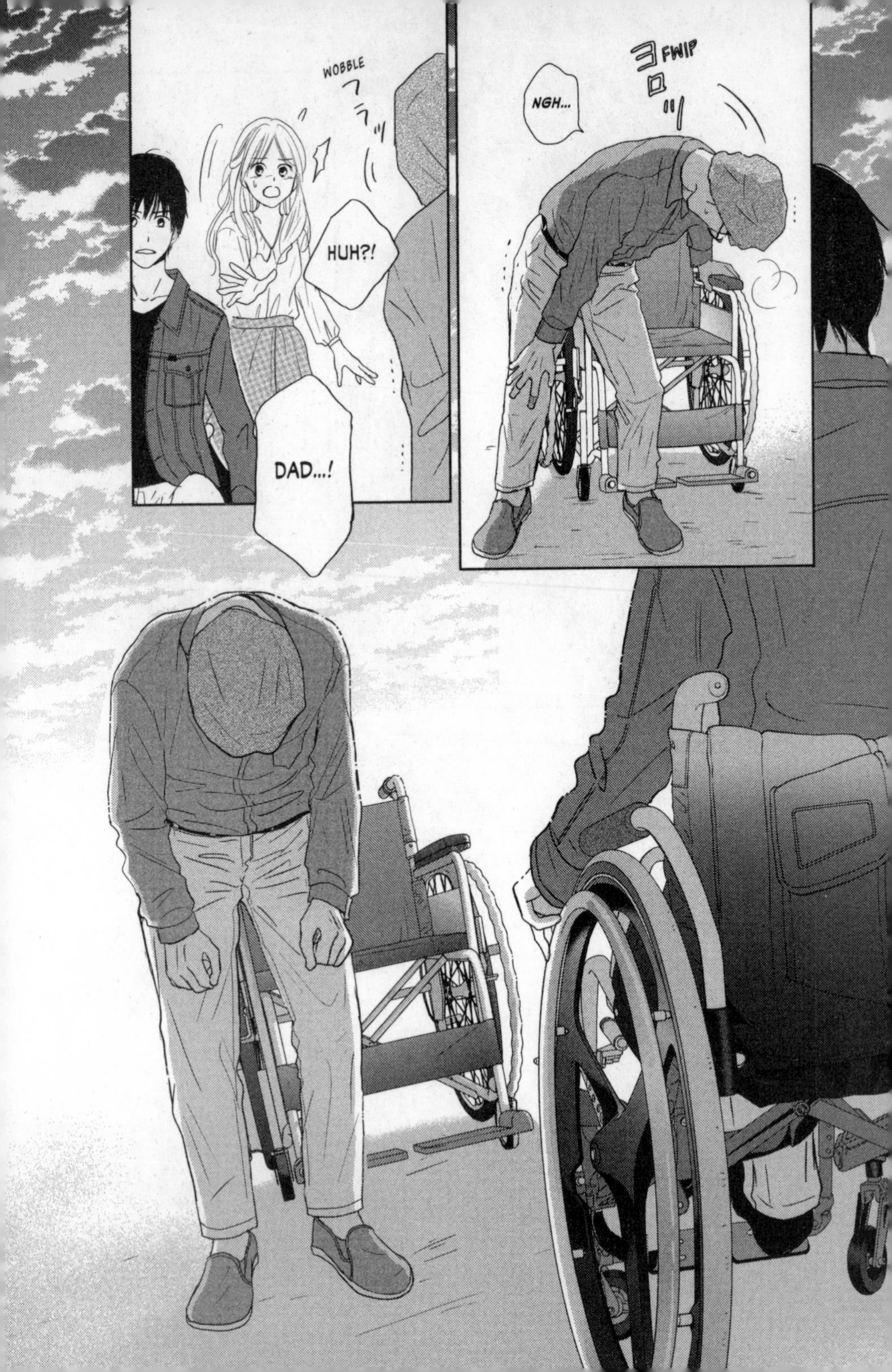
NGH...
ヨロッ FWIP
WOBBLE フラッ
HUH?!
DAD...!

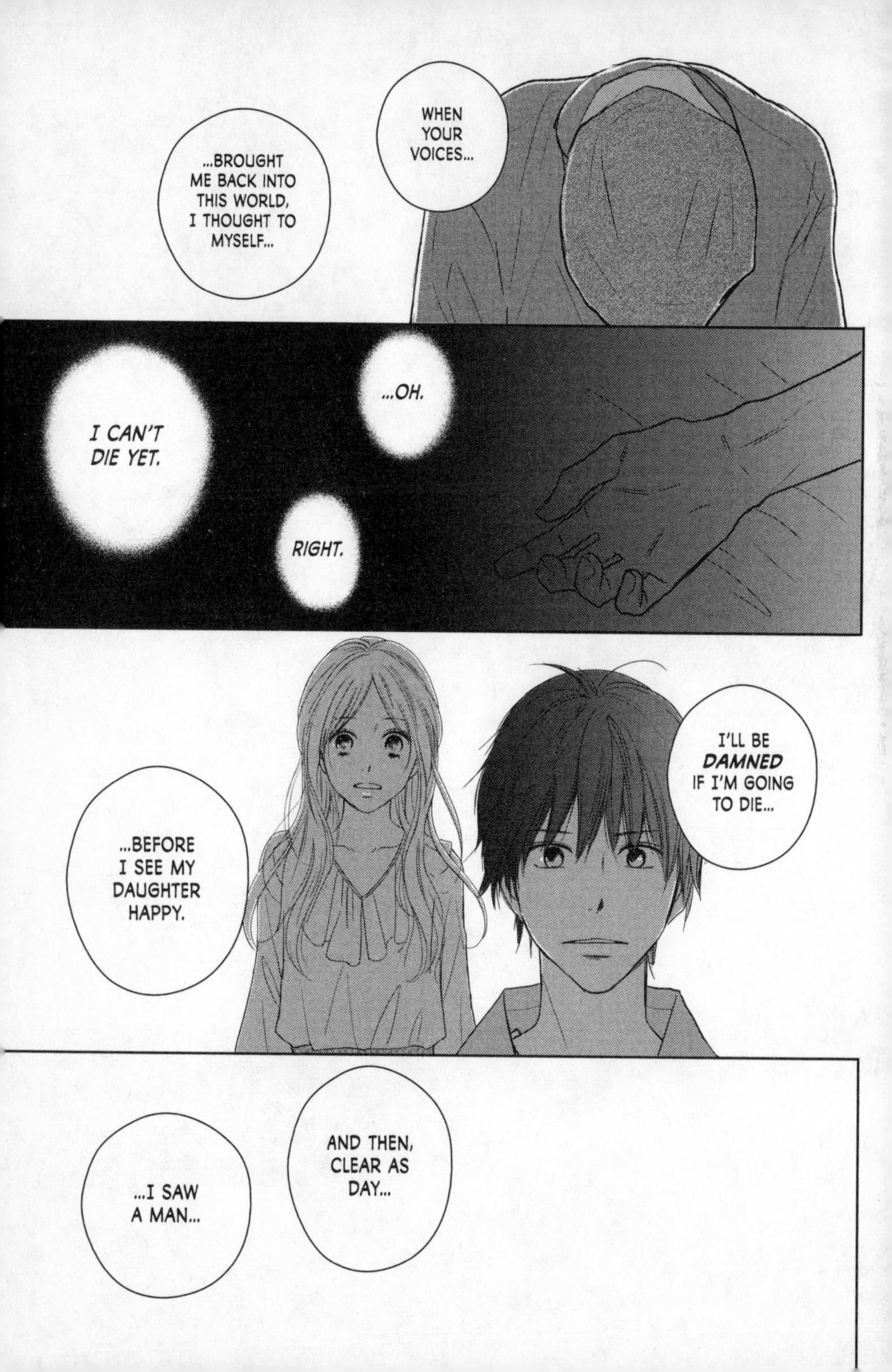
WHEN YOUR VOICES...
...BROUGHT ME BACK INTO THIS WORLD, I THOUGHT TO MYSELF...
...OH.
RIGHT.
I CAN'T DIE YET.
I'LL BE *DAMNED* IF I'M GOING TO DIE...
...BEFORE I SEE MY DAUGHTER HAPPY.
AND THEN, CLEAR AS DAY...
...I SAW A MAN...

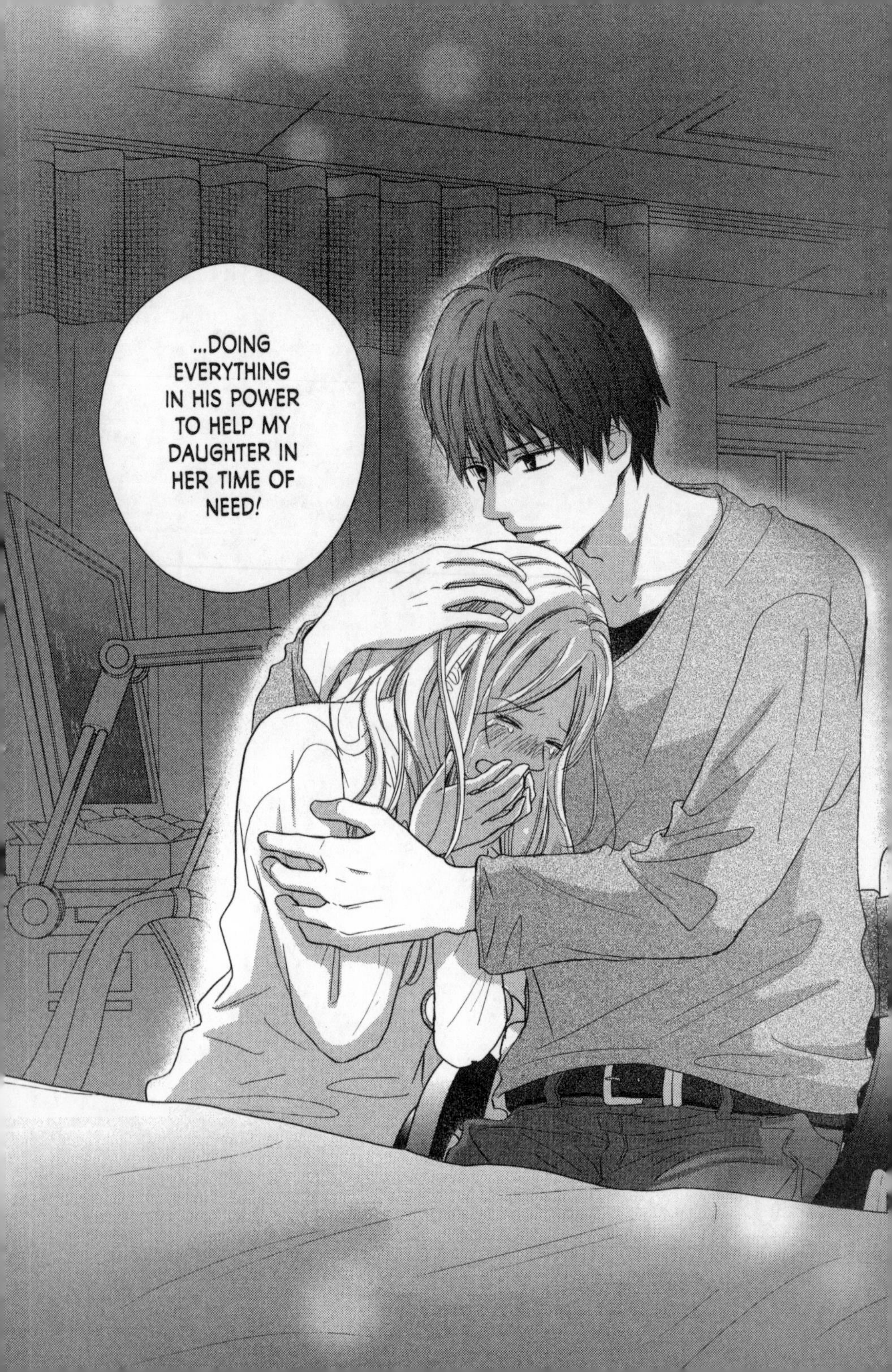
...DOING EVERYTHING IN HIS POWER TO HELP MY DAUGHTER IN HER TIME OF NEED!

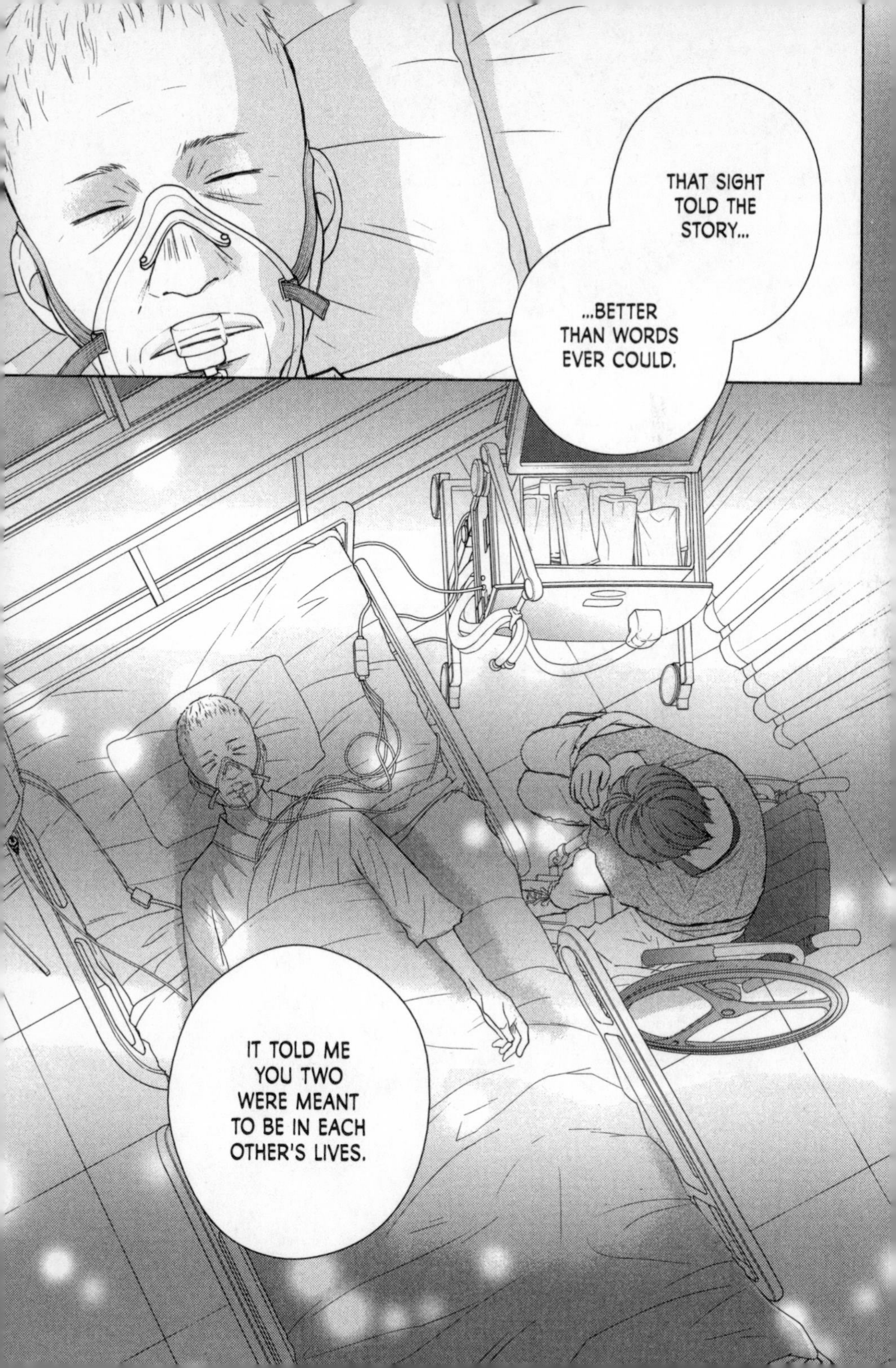
THAT SIGHT TOLD THE STORY...
...BETTER THAN WORDS EVER COULD.
IT TOLD ME YOU TWO WERE MEANT TO BE IN EACH OTHER'S LIVES.

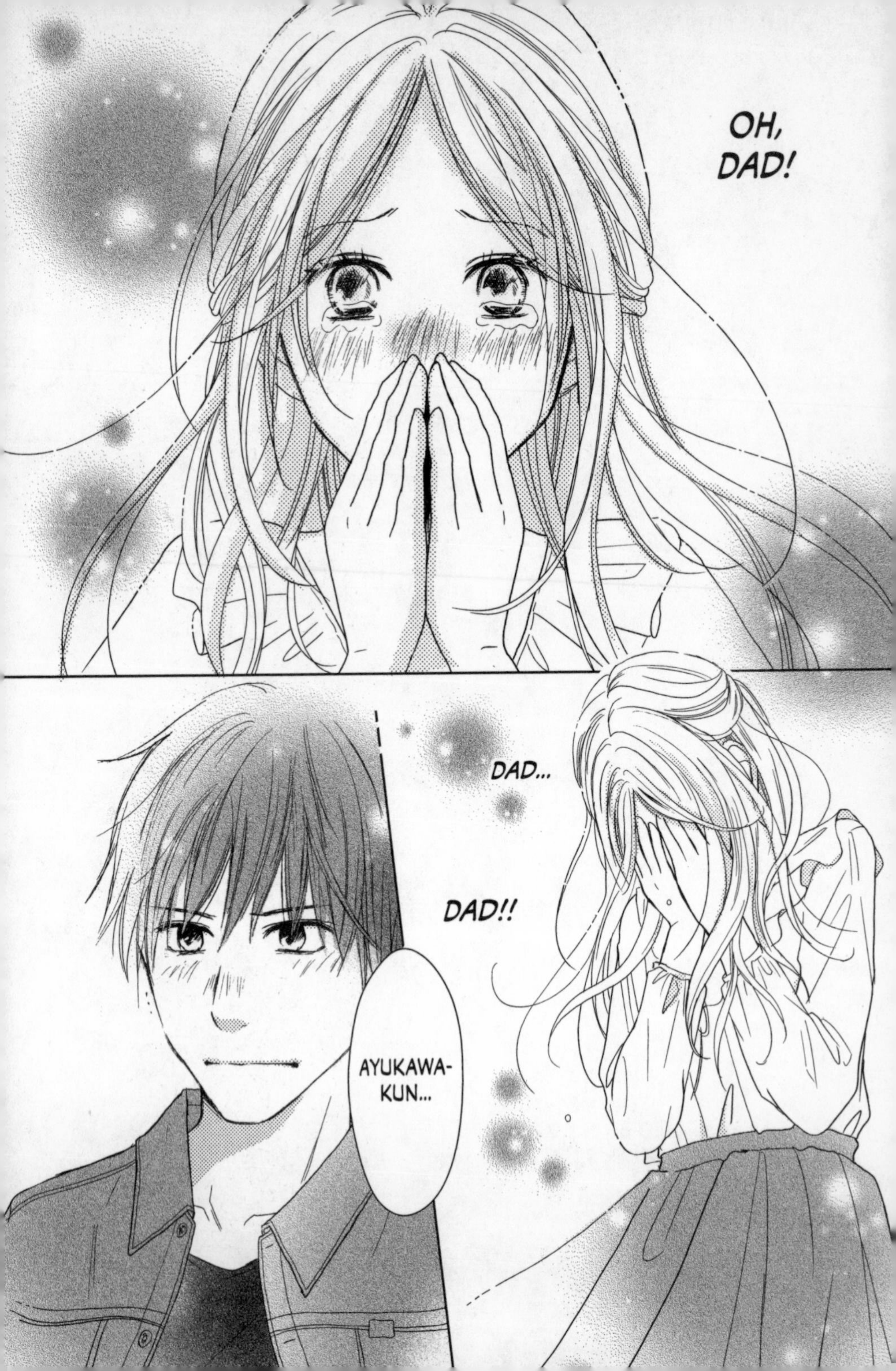
OH, DAD!
DAD...
DAD!!
AYUKAWA-KUN...

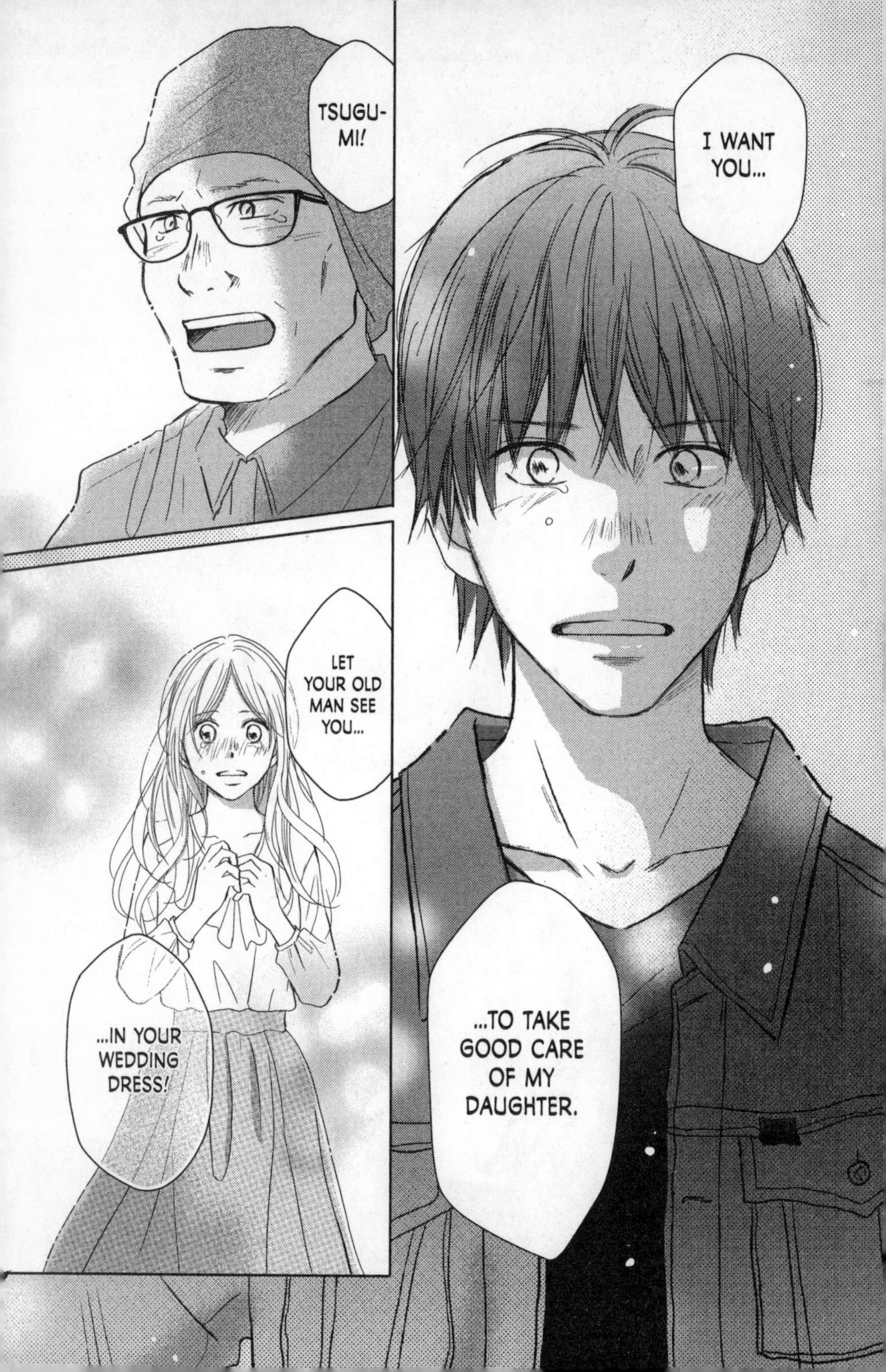
I WANT YOU...
...TO TAKE GOOD CARE OF MY DAUGHTER.
TSUGU-MI!
LET YOUR OLD MAN SEE YOU...
...IN YOUR WEDDING DRESS!

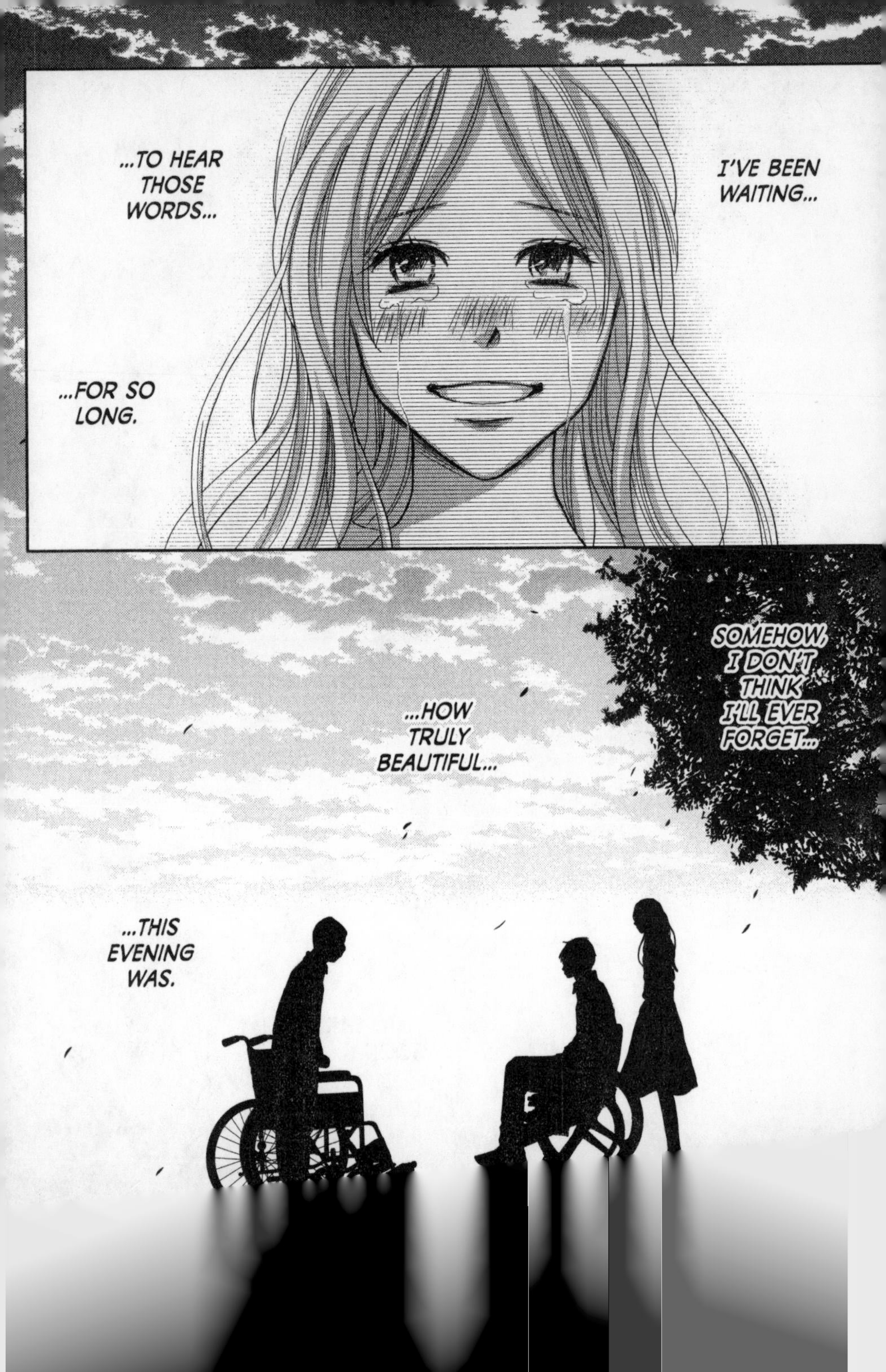
I'VE BEEN WAITING...
...TO HEAR THOSE WORDS...
...FOR SO LONG.
SOMEHOW, I DON'T THINK I'LL EVER FORGET...
...HOW TRULY BEAUTIFUL...
...THIS EVENING WAS.

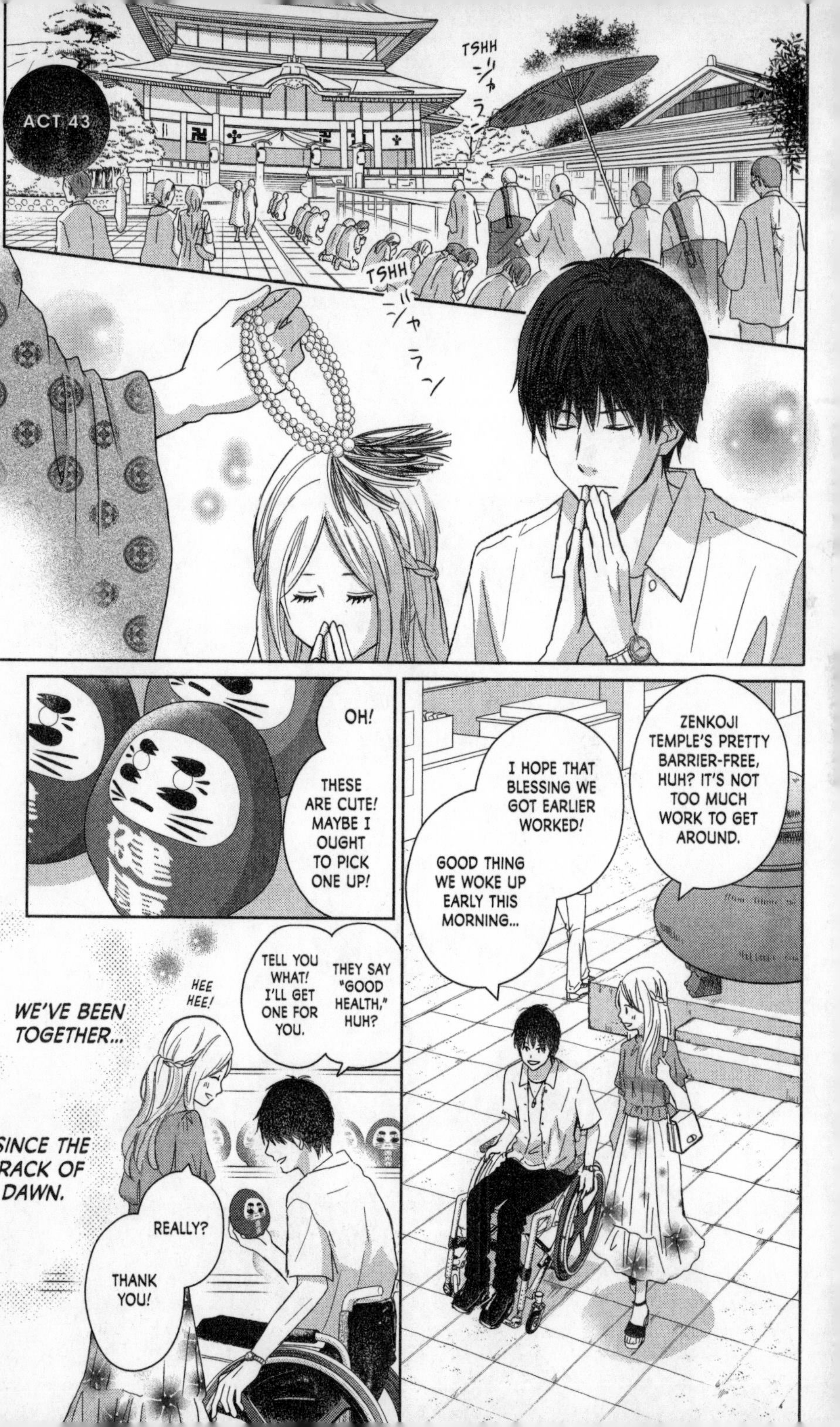
ACT 43
TSHH
ジャラン
TSHH
ジャラン
ZENKOJI TEMPLE'S PRETTY BARRIER-FREE, HUH? IT'S NOT TOO MUCH WORK TO GET AROUND.
I HOPE THAT BLESSING WE GOT EARLIER WORKED!
GOOD THING WE WOKE UP EARLY THIS MORNING...
OH!
THESE ARE CUTE! MAYBE I OUGHT TO PICK ONE UP!
THEY SAY "GOOD HEALTH," HUH?
TELL YOU WHAT! I'LL GET ONE FOR YOU.
HEE HEE!
WE'VE BEEN TOGETHER...
REALLY?
THANK YOU!
...SINCE THE CRACK OF DAWN.

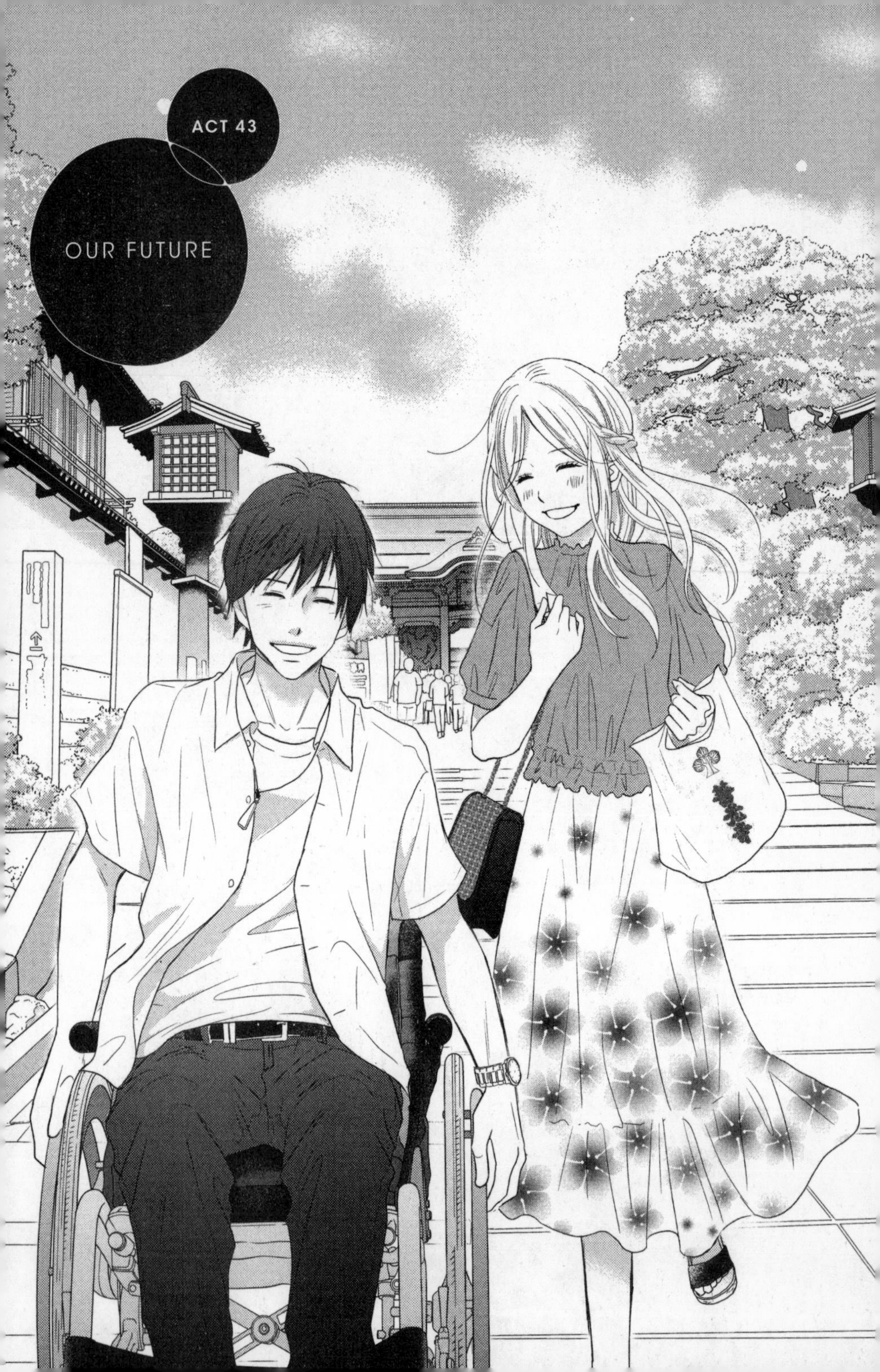
ACT 43
OUR FUTURE

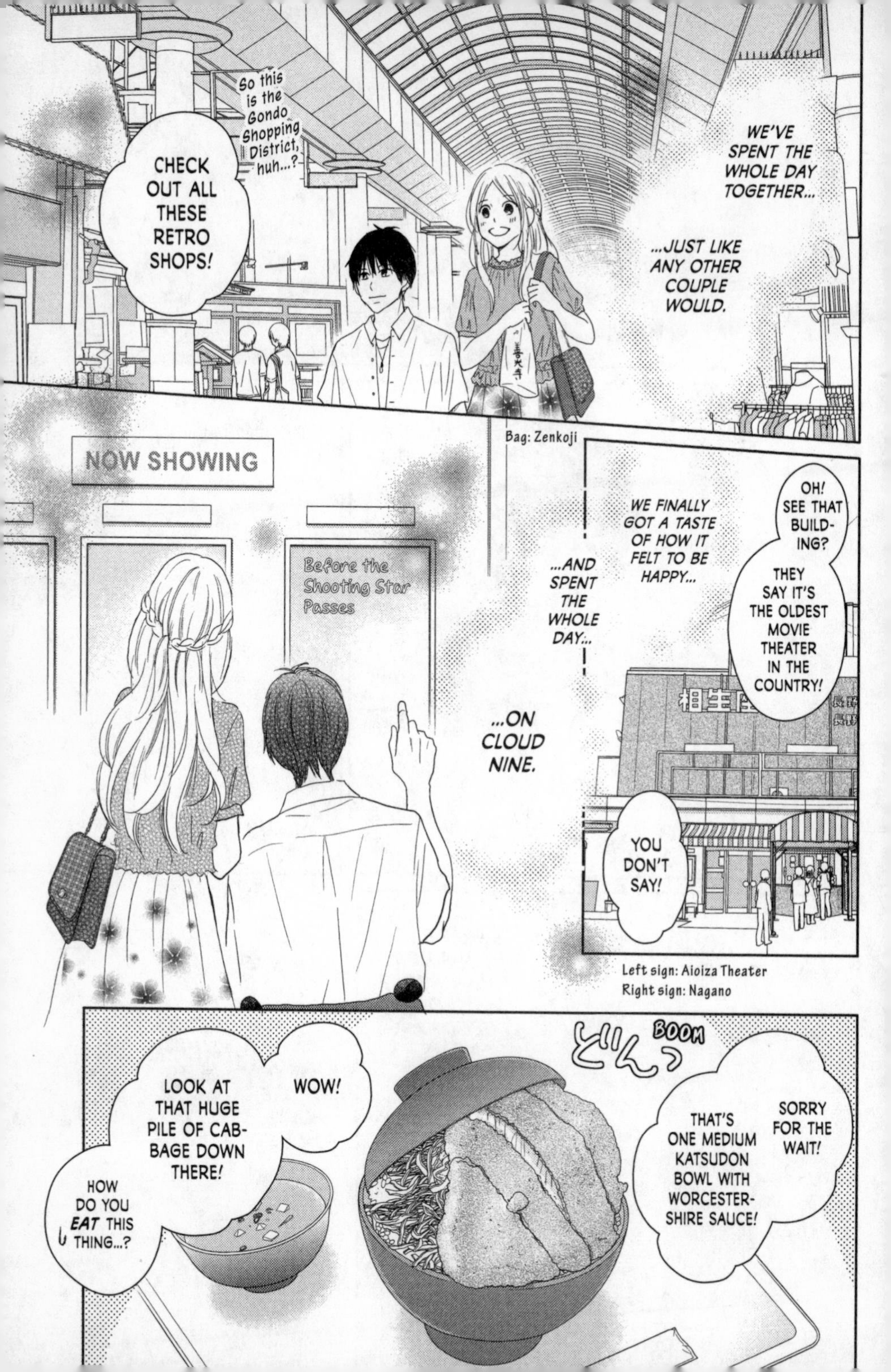
WE'VE SPENT THE WHOLE DAY TOGETHER...
...JUST LIKE ANY OTHER COUPLE WOULD.
So this is the Gondo Shopping District, huh...?
CHECK OUT ALL THESE RETRO SHOPS!
Bag: Zenkoji
OH! SEE THAT BUILDING?
THEY SAY IT'S THE OLDEST MOVIE THEATER IN THE COUNTRY!
YOU DON'T SAY!
Left sign: Aioiza Theater
Right sign: Nagano
WE FINALLY GOT A TASTE OF HOW IT FELT TO BE HAPPY...
...AND SPENT THE WHOLE DAY...
...ON CLOUD NINE.
NOW SHOWING
Before the Shooting Star Passes
BOOM
SORRY FOR THE WAIT!
THAT'S ONE MEDIUM KATSUDON BOWL WITH WORCESTERSHIRE SAUCE!
WOW!
LOOK AT THAT HUGE PILE OF CABBAGE DOWN THERE!
HOW DO YOU *EAT* THIS THING...?

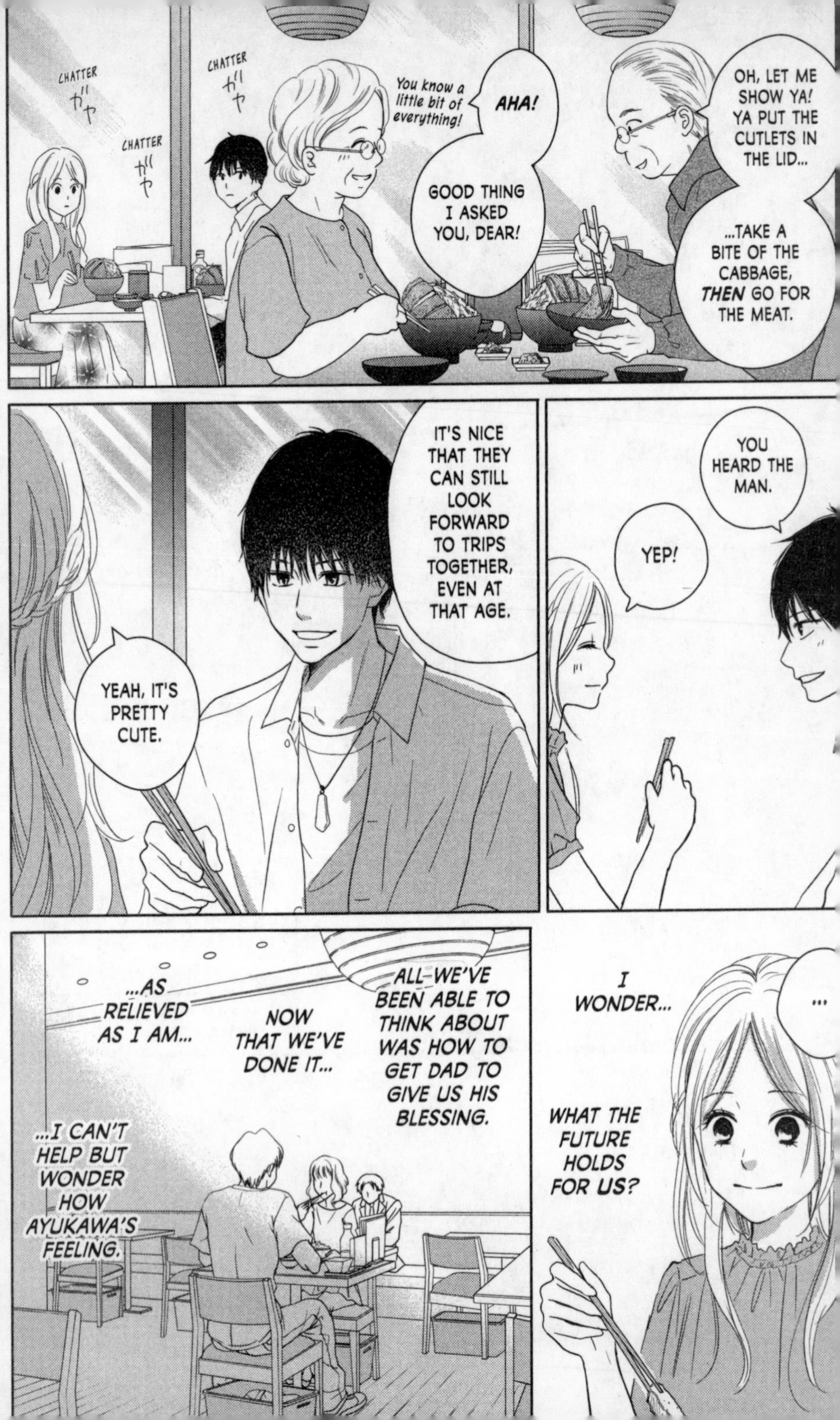
OH, LET ME SHOW YA! YA PUT THE CUTLETS IN THE LID...
...TAKE A BITE OF THE CABBAGE, THEN GO FOR THE MEAT.
AHA!
You know a little bit of everything!
GOOD THING I ASKED YOU, DEAR!
CHATTER ガヤ
CHATTER ガヤ
CHATTER ガヤ
YOU HEARD THE MAN.
YEP!
IT'S NICE THAT THEY CAN STILL LOOK FORWARD TO TRIPS TOGETHER, EVEN AT THAT AGE.
YEAH, IT'S PRETTY CUTE.
...
I WONDER...
WHAT THE FUTURE HOLDS FOR US?
ALL WE'VE BEEN ABLE TO THINK ABOUT WAS HOW TO GET DAD TO GIVE US HIS BLESSING.
NOW THAT WE'VE DONE IT...
...AS RELIEVED AS I AM...
...I CAN'T HELP BUT WONDER HOW AYUKAWA'S FEELING.

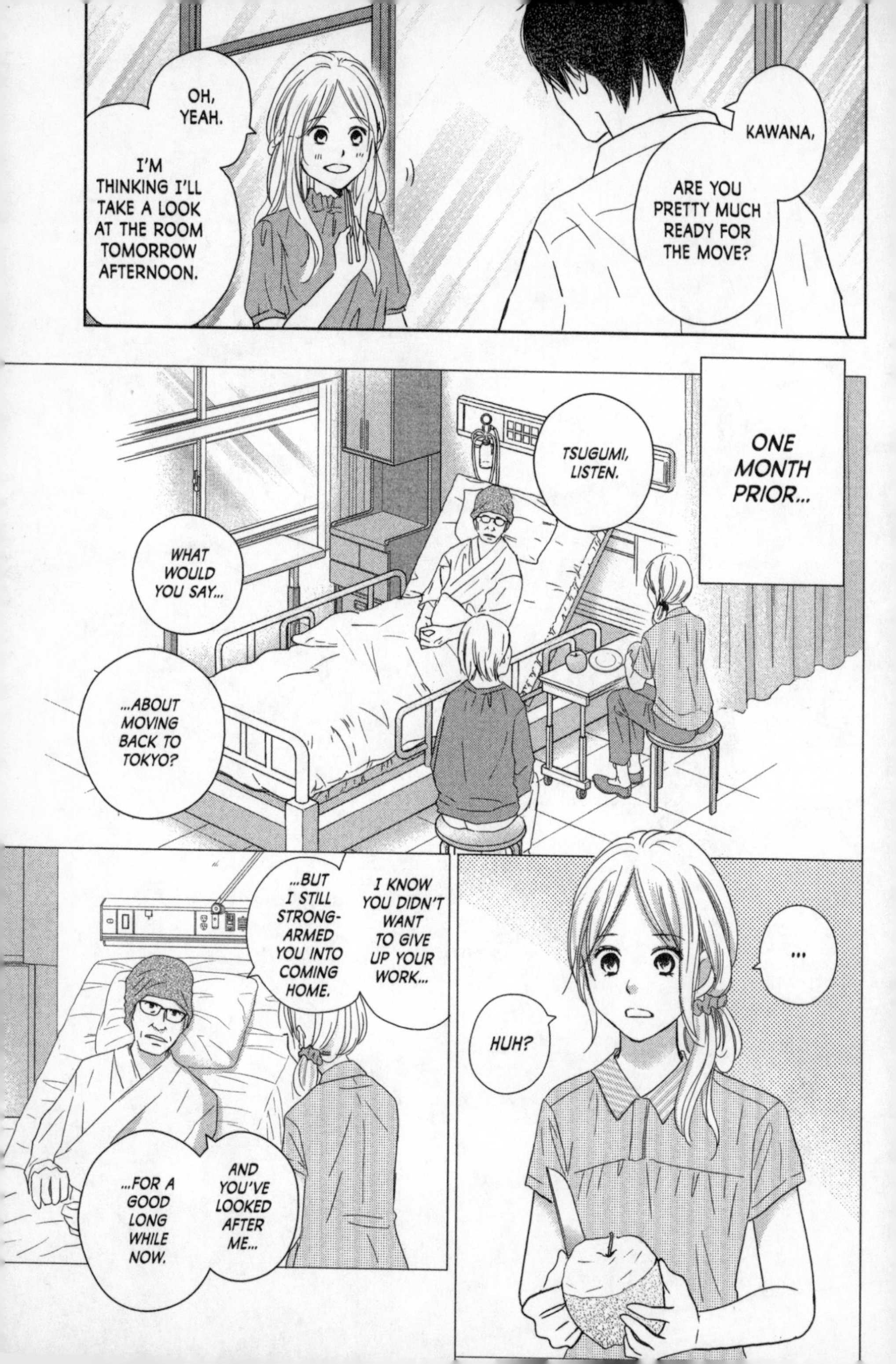
KAWANA,
ARE YOU PRETTY MUCH READY FOR THE MOVE?
OH, YEAH.
I'M THINKING I'LL TAKE A LOOK AT THE ROOM TOMORROW AFTERNOON.
ONE MONTH PRIOR...
TSUGUMI, LISTEN.
WHAT WOULD YOU SAY...
...ABOUT MOVING BACK TO TOKYO?
...
HUH?
I KNOW YOU DIDN'T WANT TO GIVE UP YOUR WORK...
...BUT I STILL STRONG-ARMED YOU INTO COMING HOME.
AND YOU'VE LOOKED AFTER ME...
...FOR A GOOD LONG WHILE NOW.

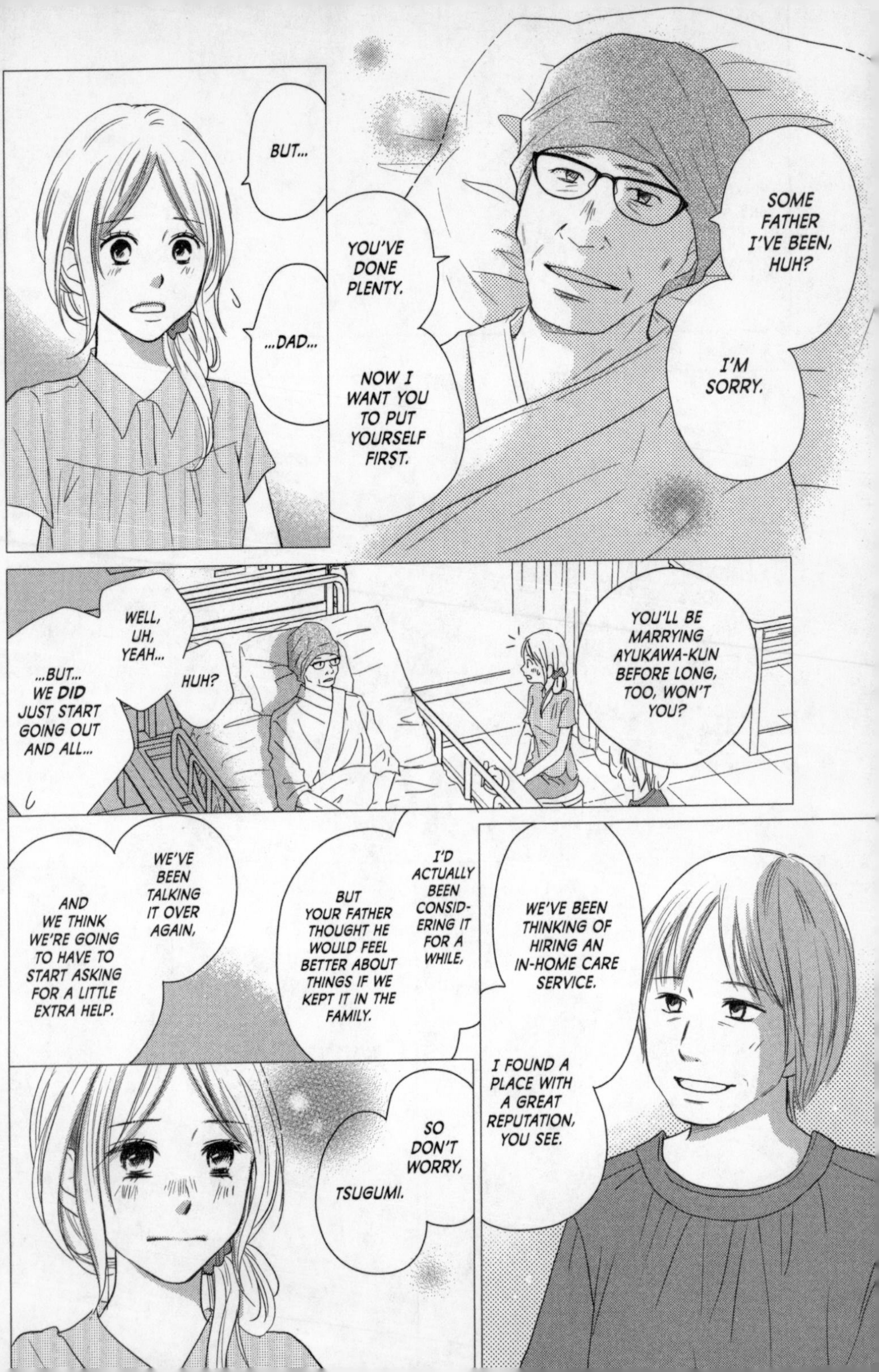
SOME FATHER I'VE BEEN, HUH?
I'M SORRY.
YOU'VE DONE PLENTY.
NOW I WANT YOU TO PUT YOURSELF FIRST.
BUT...
...DAD...
YOU'LL BE MARRYING AYUKAWA-KUN BEFORE LONG, TOO, WON'T YOU?
HUH?
WELL, UH, YEAH...
...BUT... WE **DID** JUST START GOING OUT AND ALL...
WE'VE BEEN THINKING OF HIRING AN IN-HOME CARE SERVICE.
I FOUND A PLACE WITH A GREAT REPUTATION, YOU SEE.
I'D ACTUALLY BEEN CONSIDERING IT FOR A WHILE,
BUT YOUR FATHER THOUGHT HE WOULD FEEL BETTER ABOUT THINGS IF WE KEPT IT IN THE FAMILY.
WE'VE BEEN TALKING IT OVER AGAIN,
AND WE THINK WE'RE GOING TO HAVE TO START ASKING FOR A LITTLE EXTRA HELP.
SO DON'T WORRY,
TSUGUMI.

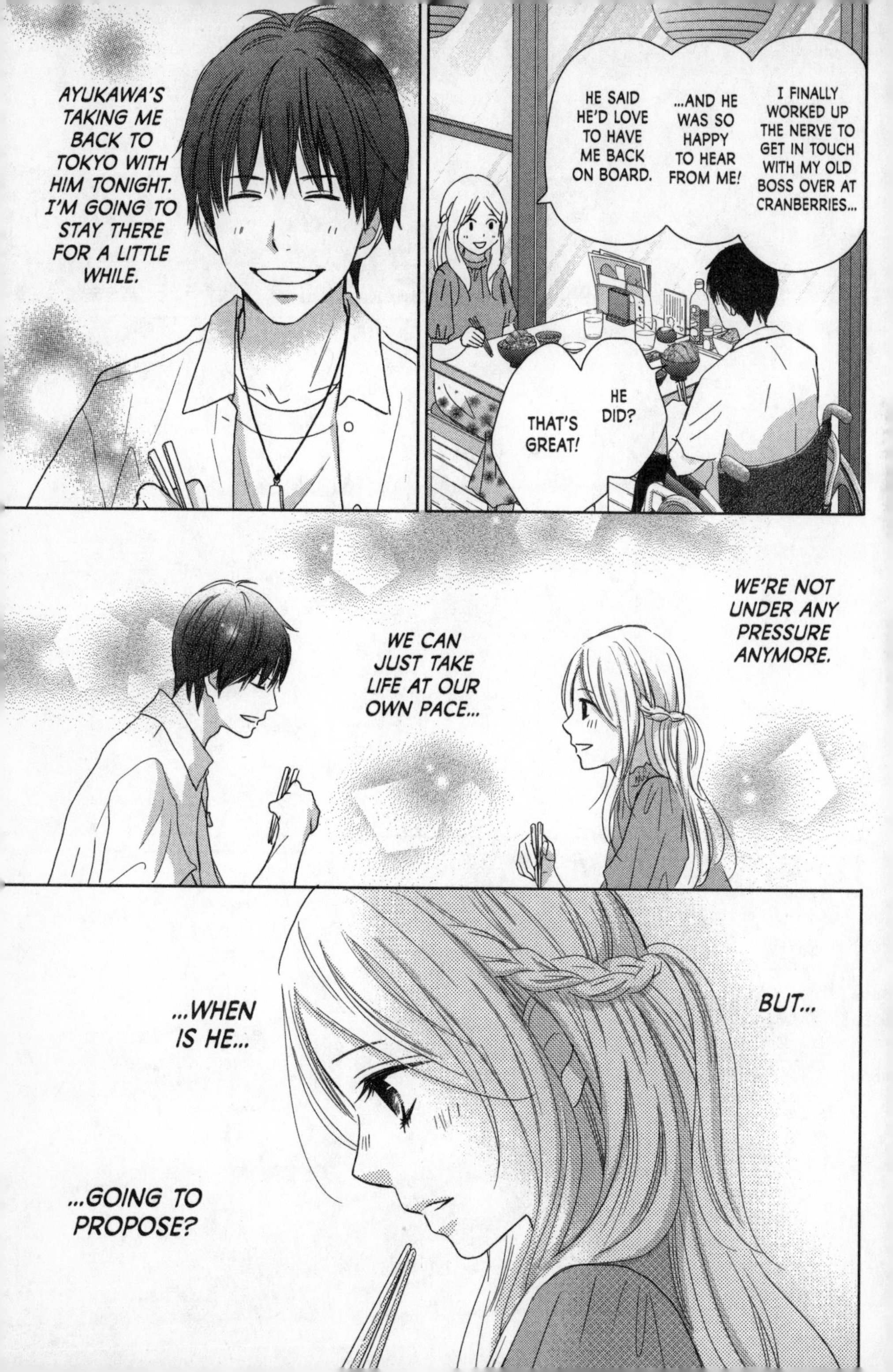
I FINALLY WORKED UP THE NERVE TO GET IN TOUCH WITH MY OLD BOSS OVER AT CRANBERRIES...
...AND HE WAS SO HAPPY TO HEAR FROM ME!
HE SAID HE'D LOVE TO HAVE ME BACK ON BOARD.
HE DID?
THAT'S GREAT!
AYUKAWA'S TAKING ME BACK TO TOKYO WITH HIM TONIGHT. I'M GOING TO STAY THERE FOR A LITTLE WHILE.
WE'RE NOT UNDER ANY PRESSURE ANYMORE.
WE CAN JUST TAKE LIFE AT OUR OWN PACE...
BUT...
...WHEN IS HE...
...GOING TO PROPOSE?

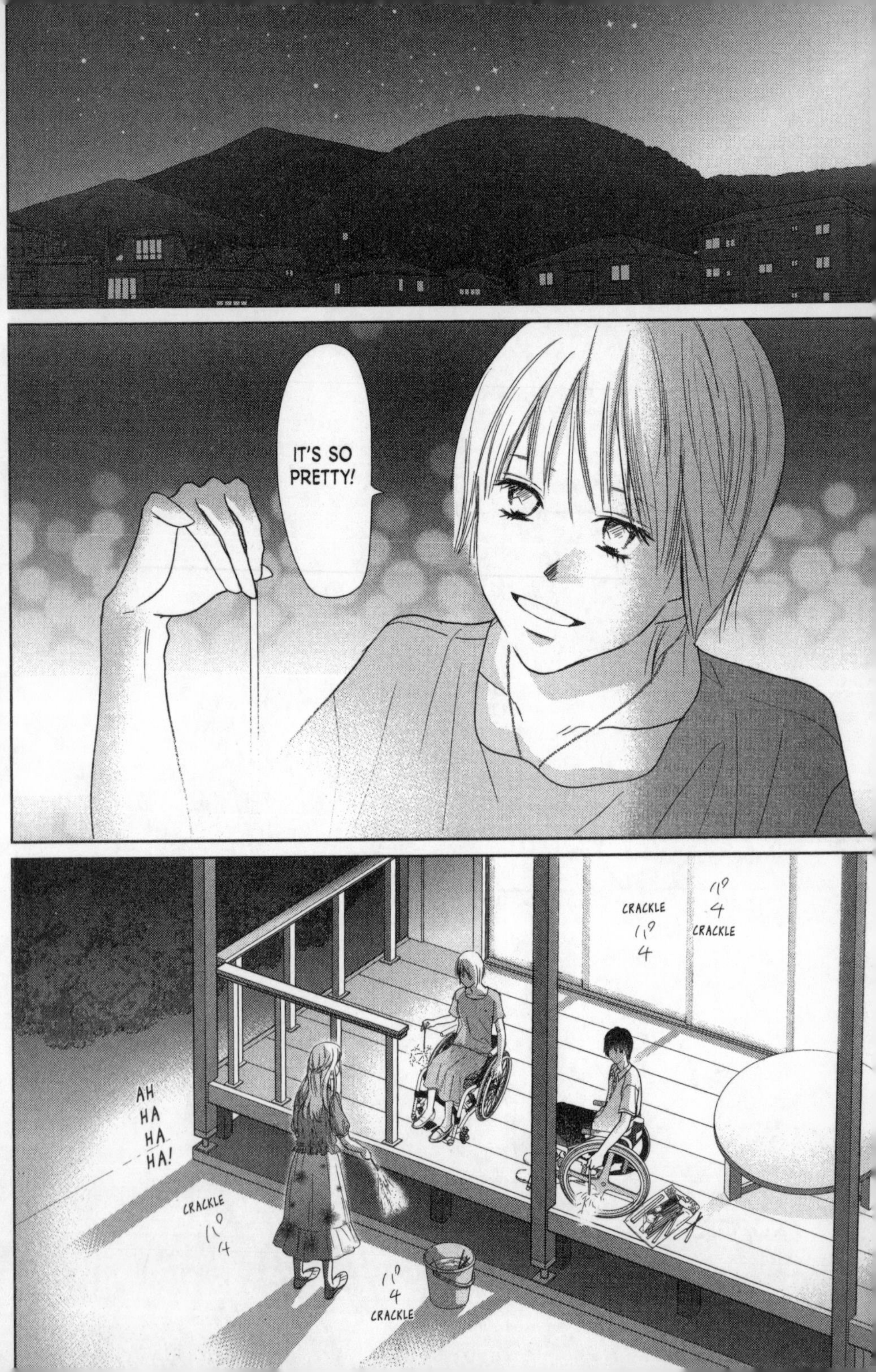
IT'S SO PRETTY!
パチ
CRACKLE
CRACKLE
パチ
AH HA HA HA!
CRACKLE
パチ
パチ
CRACKLE

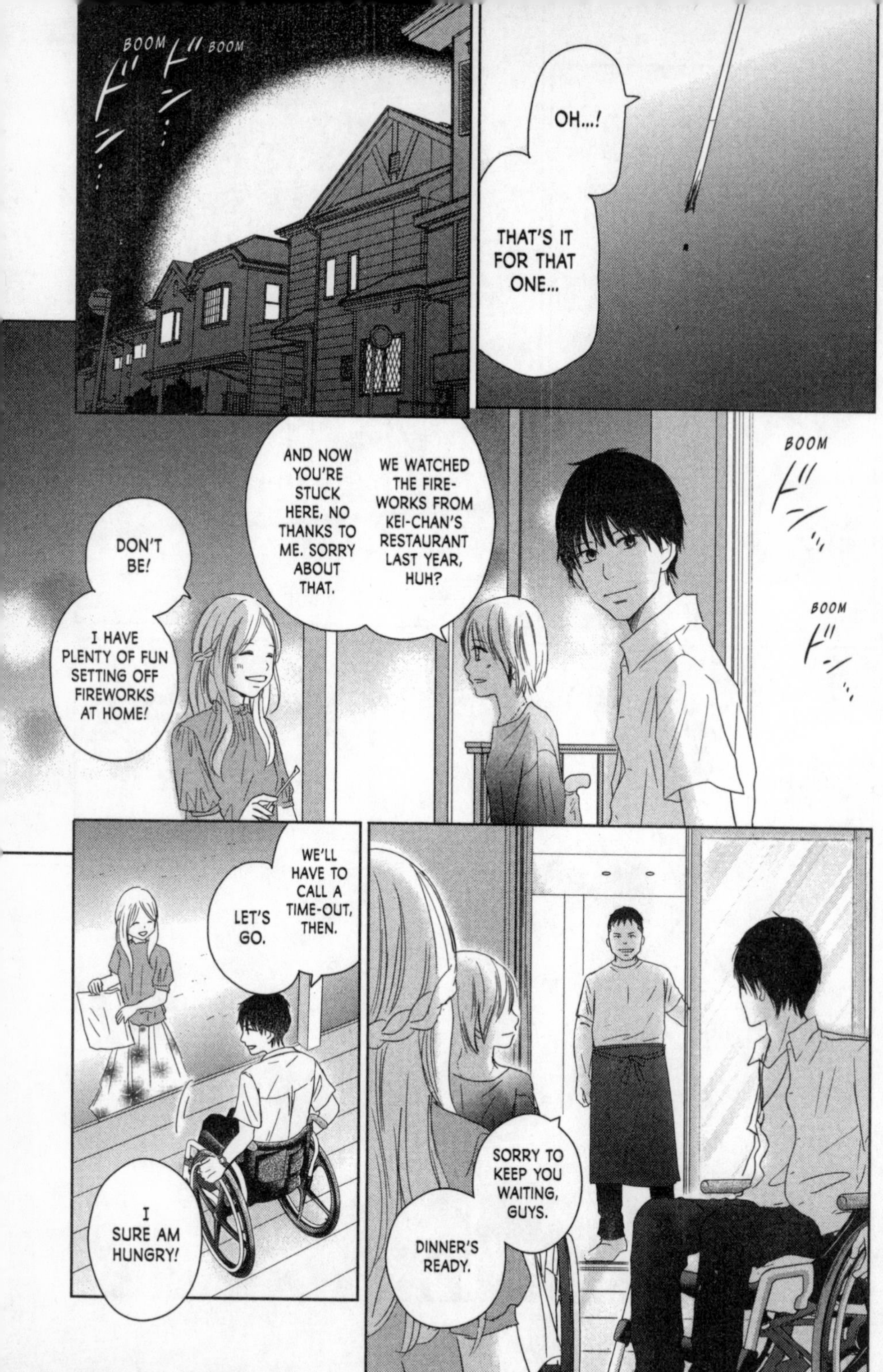
OH...!
THAT'S IT FOR THAT ONE...
BOOM BOOM
BOOM
BOOM
WE WATCHED THE FIRE-WORKS FROM KEI-CHAN'S RESTAURANT LAST YEAR, HUH?
AND NOW YOU'RE STUCK HERE, NO THANKS TO ME. SORRY ABOUT THAT.
DON'T BE!
I HAVE PLENTY OF FUN SETTING OFF FIREWORKS AT HOME!
SORRY TO KEEP YOU WAITING, GUYS.
DINNER'S READY.
WE'LL HAVE TO CALL A TIME-OUT, THEN.
LET'S GO.
I SURE AM HUNGRY!

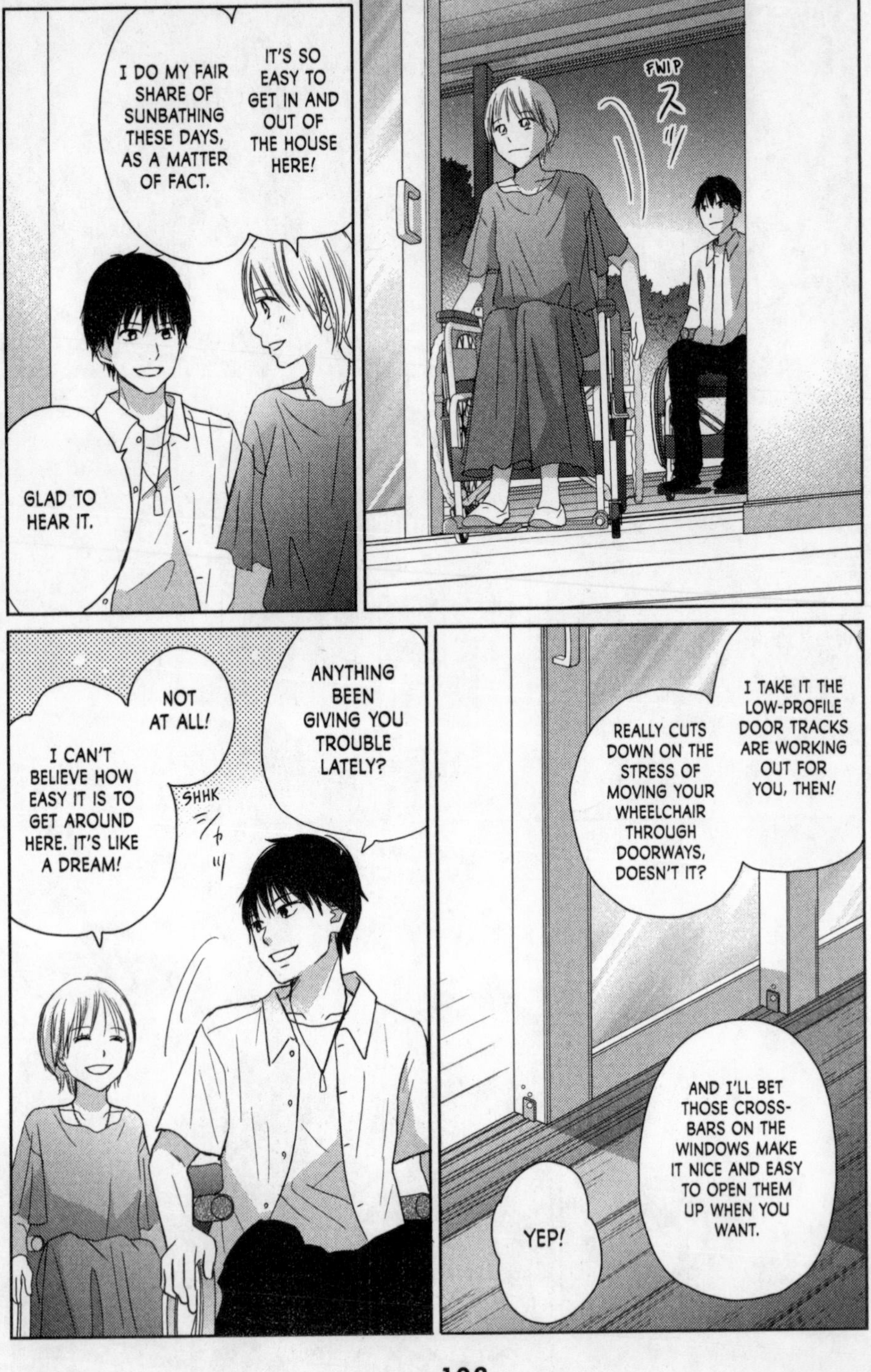
FWIP
スッ
IT'S SO EASY TO GET IN AND OUT OF THE HOUSE HERE!
I DO MY FAIR SHARE OF SUNBATHING THESE DAYS, AS A MATTER OF FACT.
GLAD TO HEAR IT.
I TAKE IT THE LOW-PROFILE DOOR TRACKS ARE WORKING OUT FOR YOU, THEN!
REALLY CUTS DOWN ON THE STRESS OF MOVING YOUR WHEELCHAIR THROUGH DOORWAYS, DOESN'T IT?
AND I'LL BET THOSE CROSS-BARS ON THE WINDOWS MAKE IT NICE AND EASY TO OPEN THEM UP WHEN YOU WANT.
YEP!
ANYTHING BEEN GIVING YOU TROUBLE LATELY?
NOT AT ALL!
I CAN'T BELIEVE HOW EASY IT IS TO GET AROUND HERE. IT'S LIKE A DREAM!
SHHK
シャッ

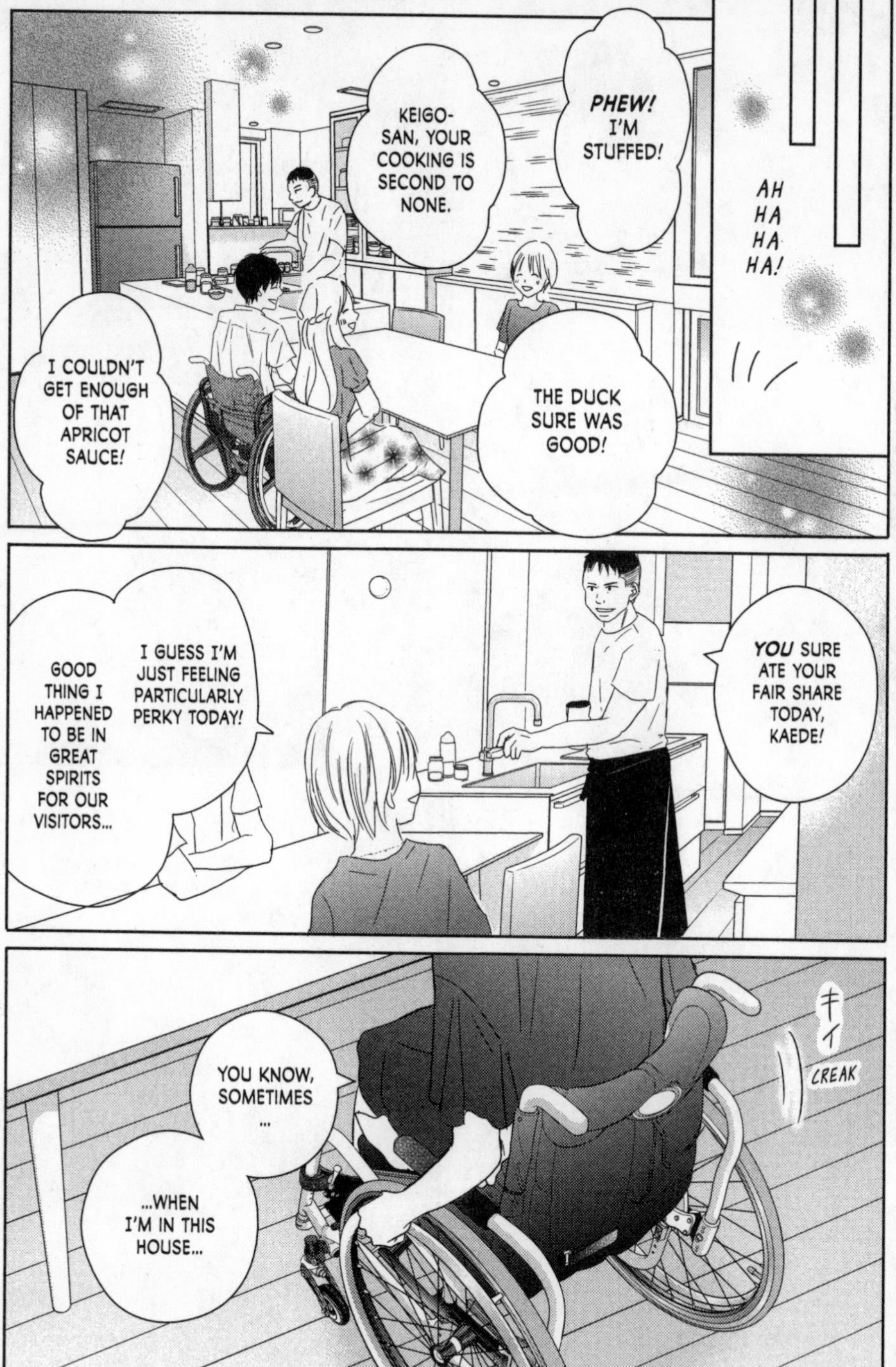
AH HA HA HA!
PHEW! I'M STUFFED!
KEIGO-SAN, YOUR COOKING IS SECOND TO NONE.
THE DUCK SURE WAS GOOD!
I COULDN'T GET ENOUGH OF THAT APRICOT SAUCE!
YOU SURE ATE YOUR FAIR SHARE TODAY, KAEDE!
I GUESS I'M JUST FEELING PARTICULARLY PERKY TODAY!
GOOD THING I HAPPENED TO BE IN GREAT SPIRITS FOR OUR VISITORS...
キイ
CREAK
YOU KNOW, SOMETIMES ...
...WHEN I'M IN THIS HOUSE...

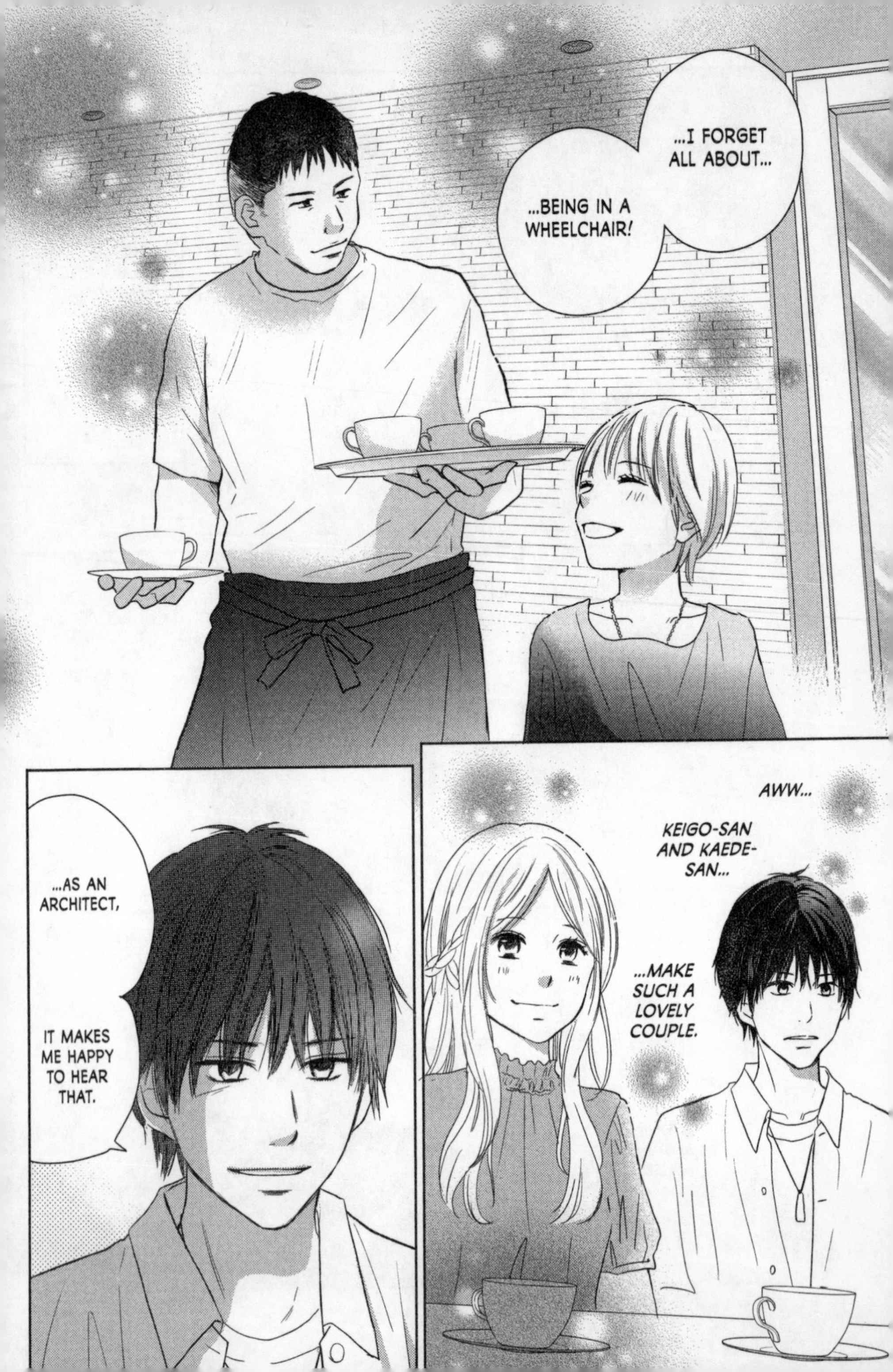
...I FORGET ALL ABOUT...
...BEING IN A WHEELCHAIR!
AWW...
KEIGO-SAN AND KAEDE-SAN...
...MAKE SUCH A LOVELY COUPLE.
...AS AN ARCHITECT,
IT MAKES ME HAPPY TO HEAR THAT.

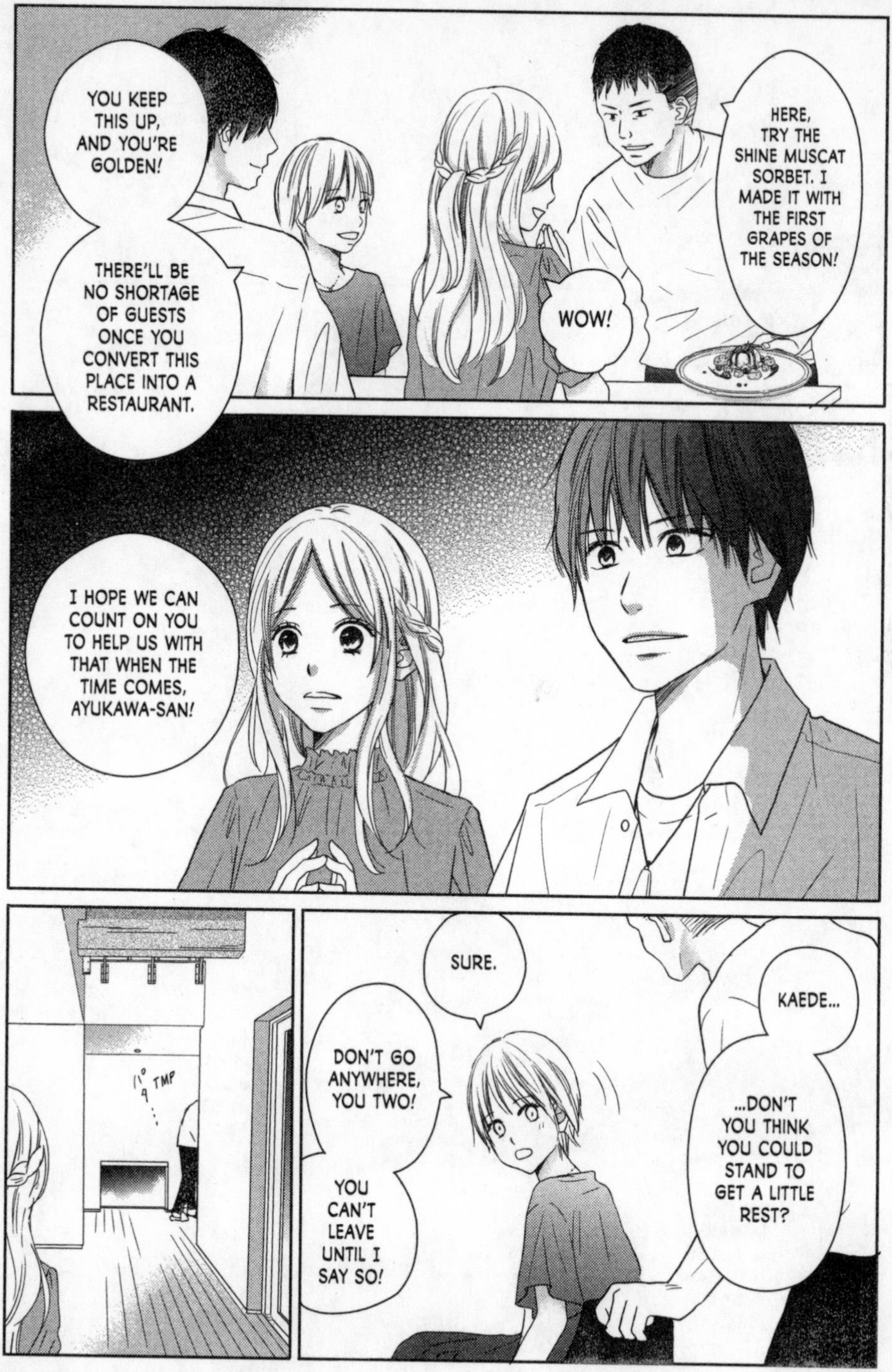
HERE, TRY THE SHINE MUSCAT SORBET. I MADE IT WITH THE FIRST GRAPES OF THE SEASON!
WOW!
YOU KEEP THIS UP, AND YOU'RE GOLDEN!
THERE'LL BE NO SHORTAGE OF GUESTS ONCE YOU CONVERT THIS PLACE INTO A RESTAURANT.
I HOPE WE CAN COUNT ON YOU TO HELP US WITH THAT WHEN THE TIME COMES, AYUKAWA-SAN!
KAEDE...
...DON'T YOU THINK YOU COULD STAND TO GET A LITTLE REST?
SURE.
DON'T GO ANYWHERE, YOU TWO!
YOU CAN'T LEAVE UNTIL I SAY SO!
TMP

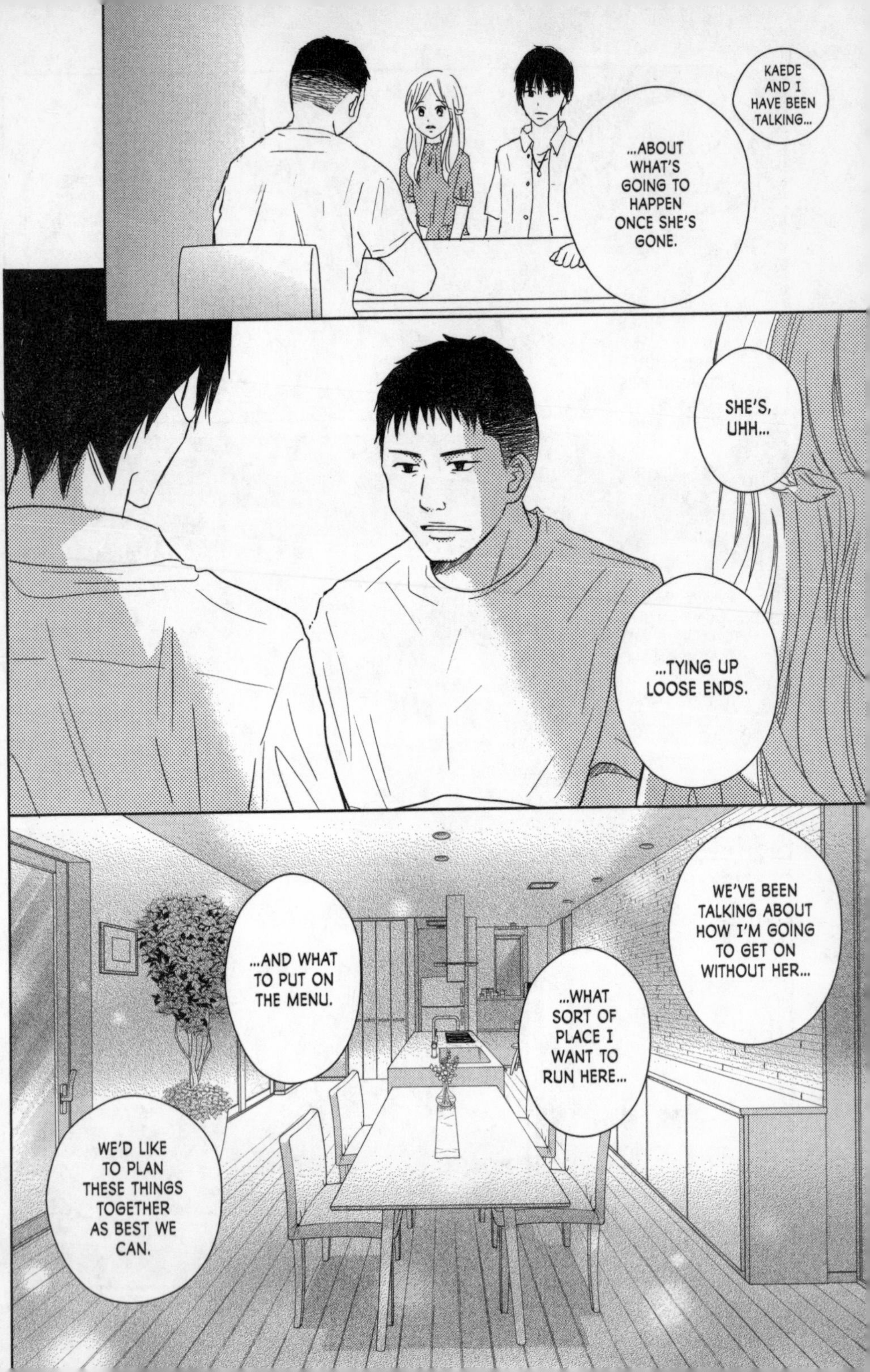
KAEDE AND I HAVE BEEN TALKING...
...ABOUT WHAT'S GOING TO HAPPEN ONCE SHE'S GONE.
SHE'S, UHH...
...TYING UP LOOSE ENDS.
WE'VE BEEN TALKING ABOUT HOW I'M GOING TO GET ON WITHOUT HER...
...WHAT SORT OF PLACE I WANT TO RUN HERE...
...AND WHAT TO PUT ON THE MENU.
WE'D LIKE TO PLAN THESE THINGS TOGETHER AS BEST WE CAN.

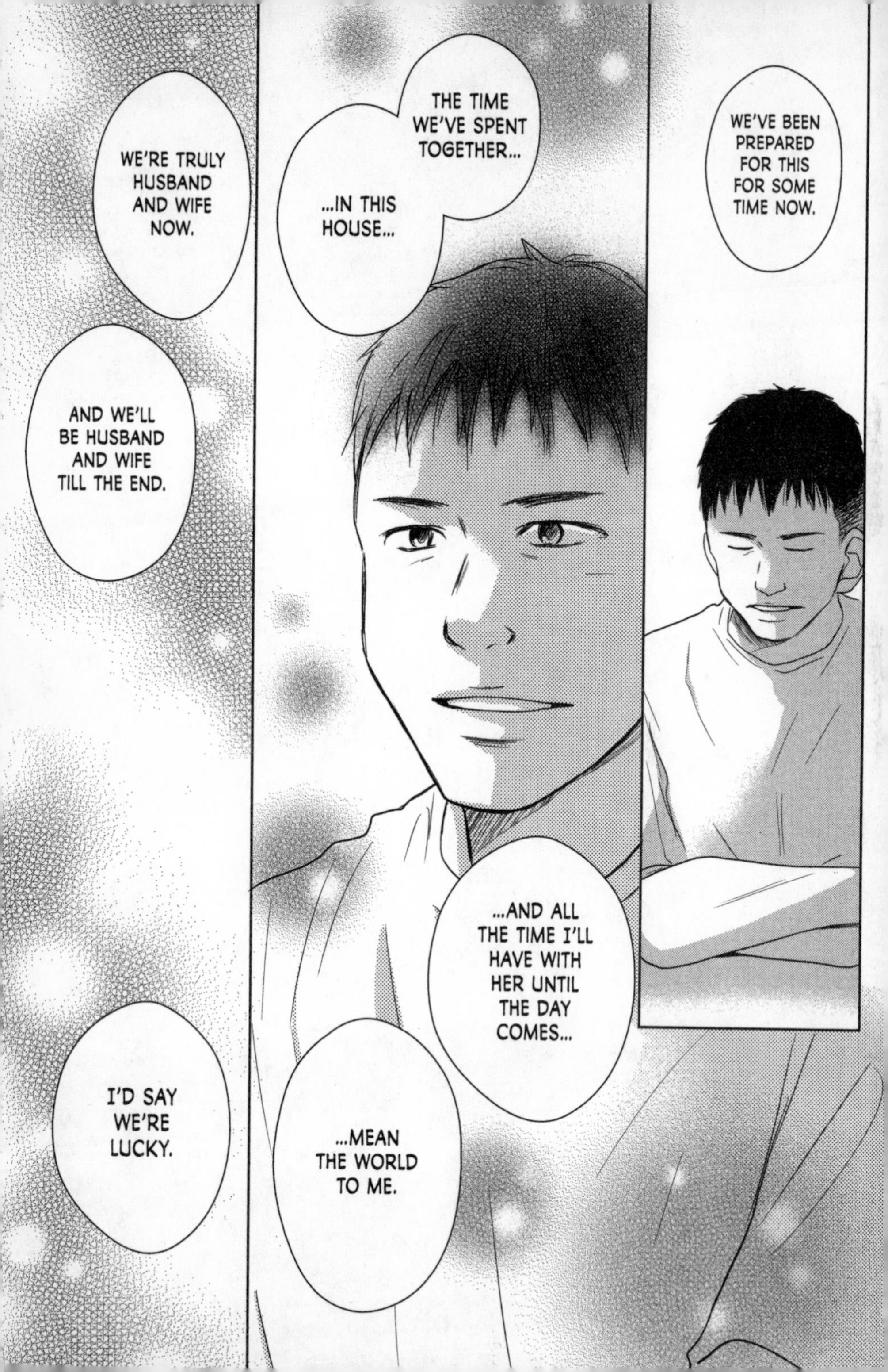
WE'VE BEEN PREPARED FOR THIS FOR SOME TIME NOW.
THE TIME WE'VE SPENT TOGETHER...
...IN THIS HOUSE...
...AND ALL THE TIME I'LL HAVE WITH HER UNTIL THE DAY COMES...
...MEAN THE WORLD TO ME.
WE'RE TRULY HUSBAND AND WIFE NOW.
AND WE'LL BE HUSBAND AND WIFE TILL THE END.
I'D SAY WE'RE LUCKY.

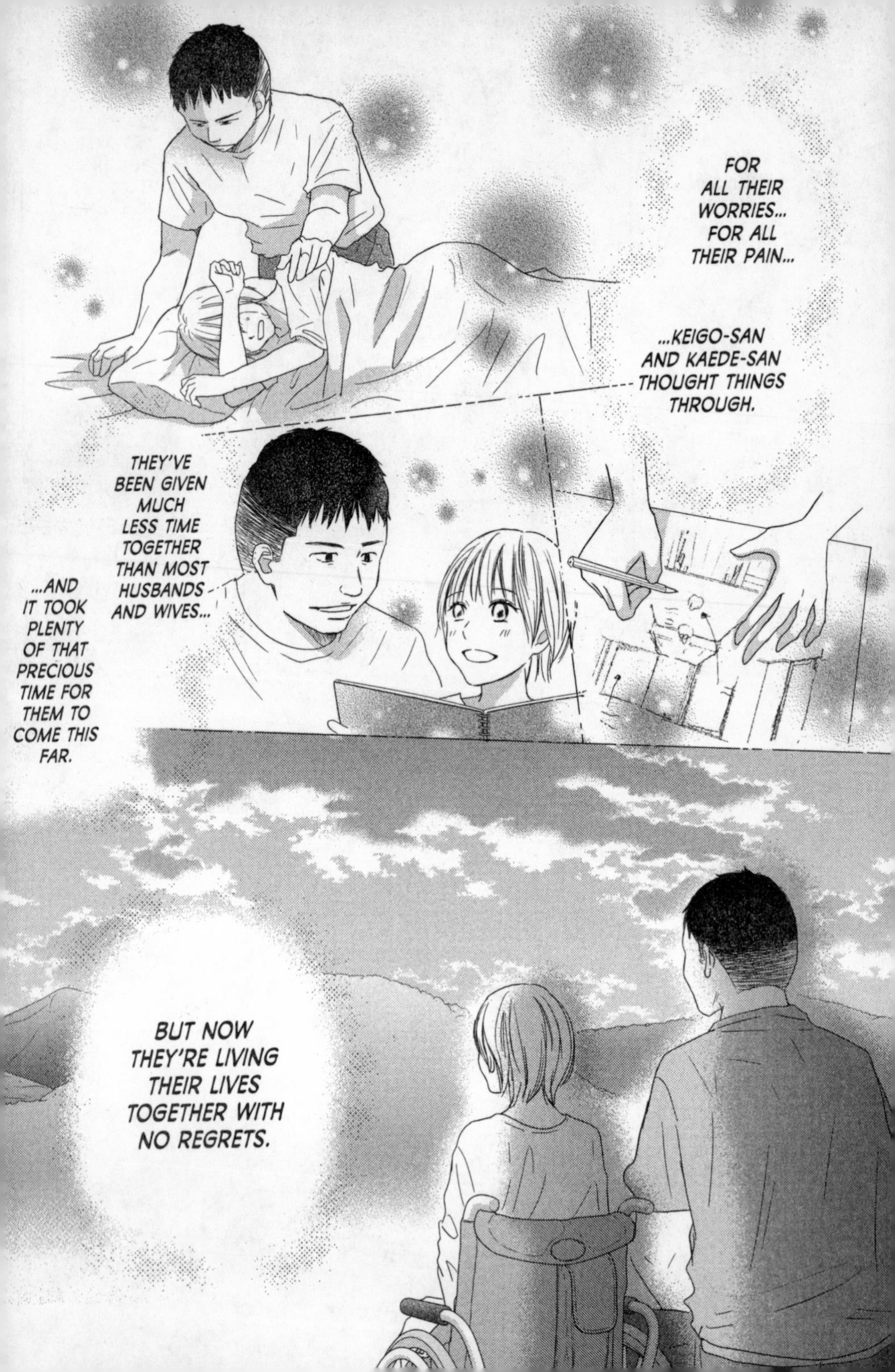
FOR ALL THEIR WORRIES... FOR ALL THEIR PAIN...
...KEIGO-SAN AND KAEDE-SAN THOUGHT THINGS THROUGH.
THEY'VE BEEN GIVEN MUCH LESS TIME TOGETHER THAN MOST HUSBANDS AND WIVES...
...AND IT TOOK PLENTY OF THAT PRECIOUS TIME FOR THEM TO COME THIS FAR.
BUT NOW THEY'RE LIVING THEIR LIVES TOGETHER WITH NO REGRETS.

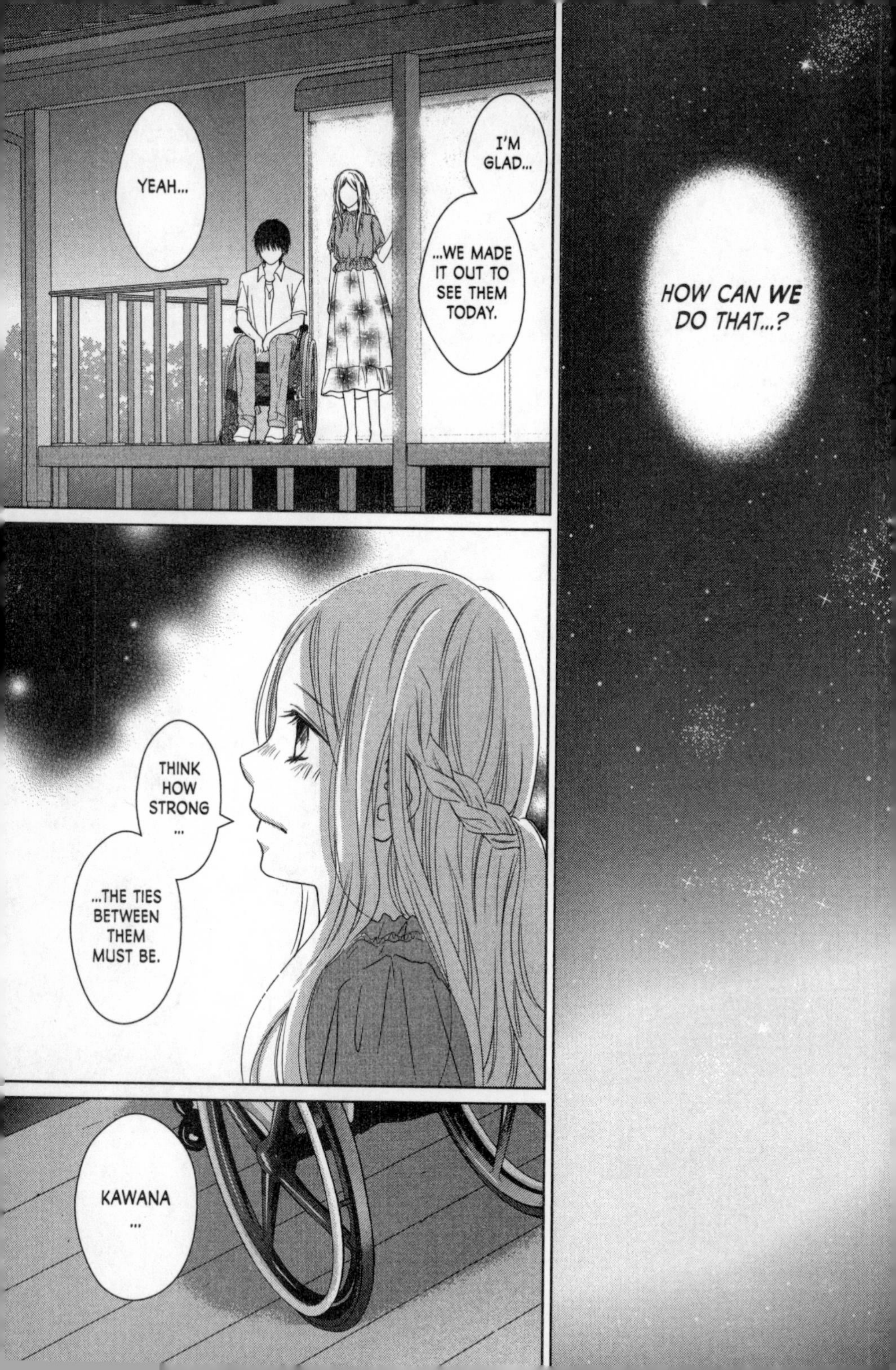
HOW CAN WE DO THAT...?
I'M GLAD...
...WE MADE IT OUT TO SEE THEM TODAY.
YEAH...
THINK HOW STRONG...
...THE TIES BETWEEN THEM MUST BE.
KAWANA...

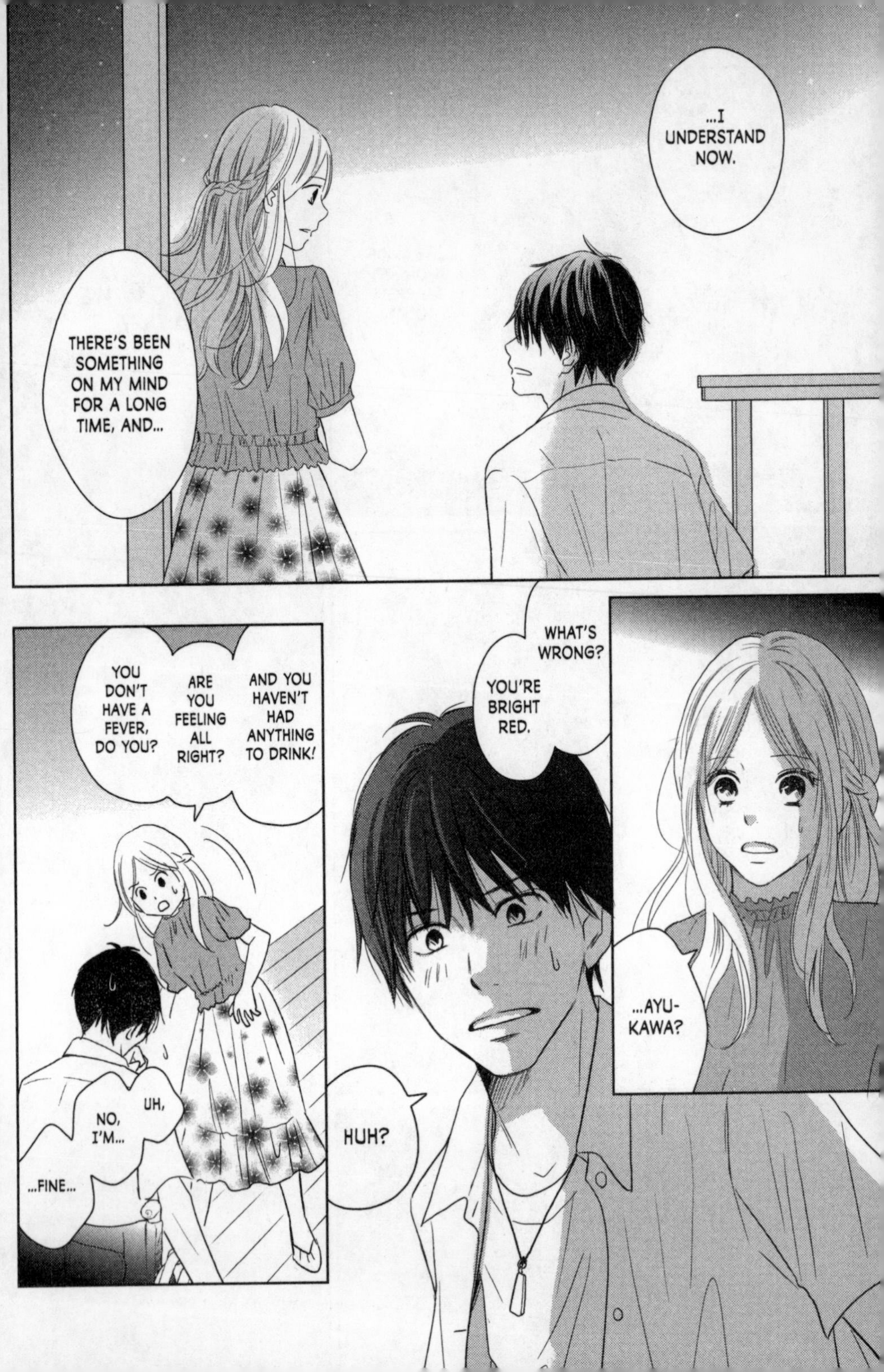
...I UNDERSTAND NOW.
THERE'S BEEN SOMETHING ON MY MIND FOR A LONG TIME, AND...
...AYU-KAWA?
HUH?
WHAT'S WRONG?
YOU'RE BRIGHT RED.
YOU DON'T HAVE A FEVER, DO YOU?
ARE YOU FEELING ALL RIGHT?
AND YOU HAVEN'T HAD ANYTHING TO DRINK!
UH,
NO, I'M...
...FINE...

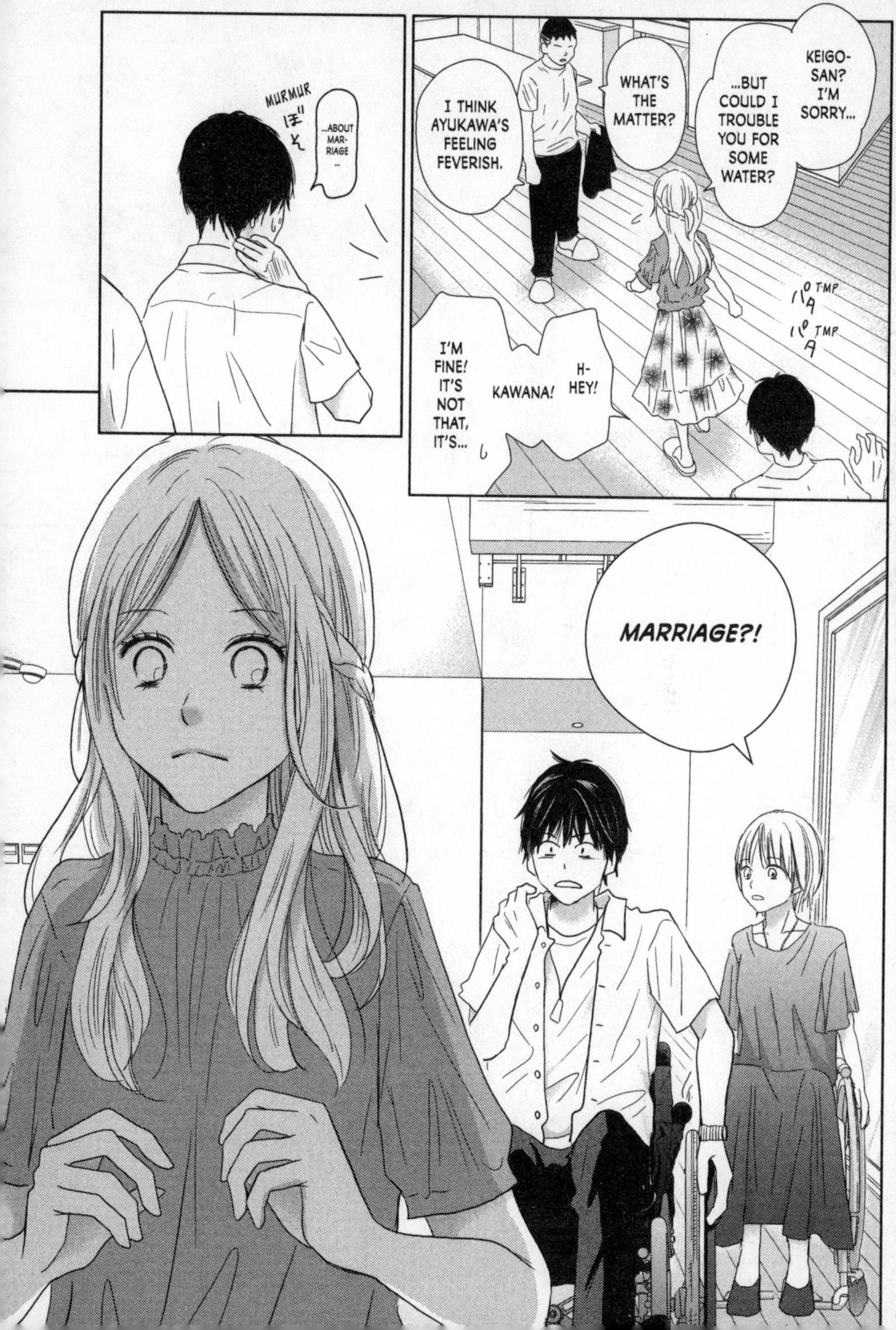
KEIGO-SAN? I'M SORRY...
...BUT COULD I TROUBLE YOU FOR SOME WATER?
WHAT'S THE MATTER?
I THINK AYUKAWA'S FEELING FEVERISH.
TMP
TMP
H-HEY!
KAWANA!
I'M FINE! IT'S NOT THAT, IT'S...
MURMUR
...ABOUT MARRIAGE...
MARRIAGE?!

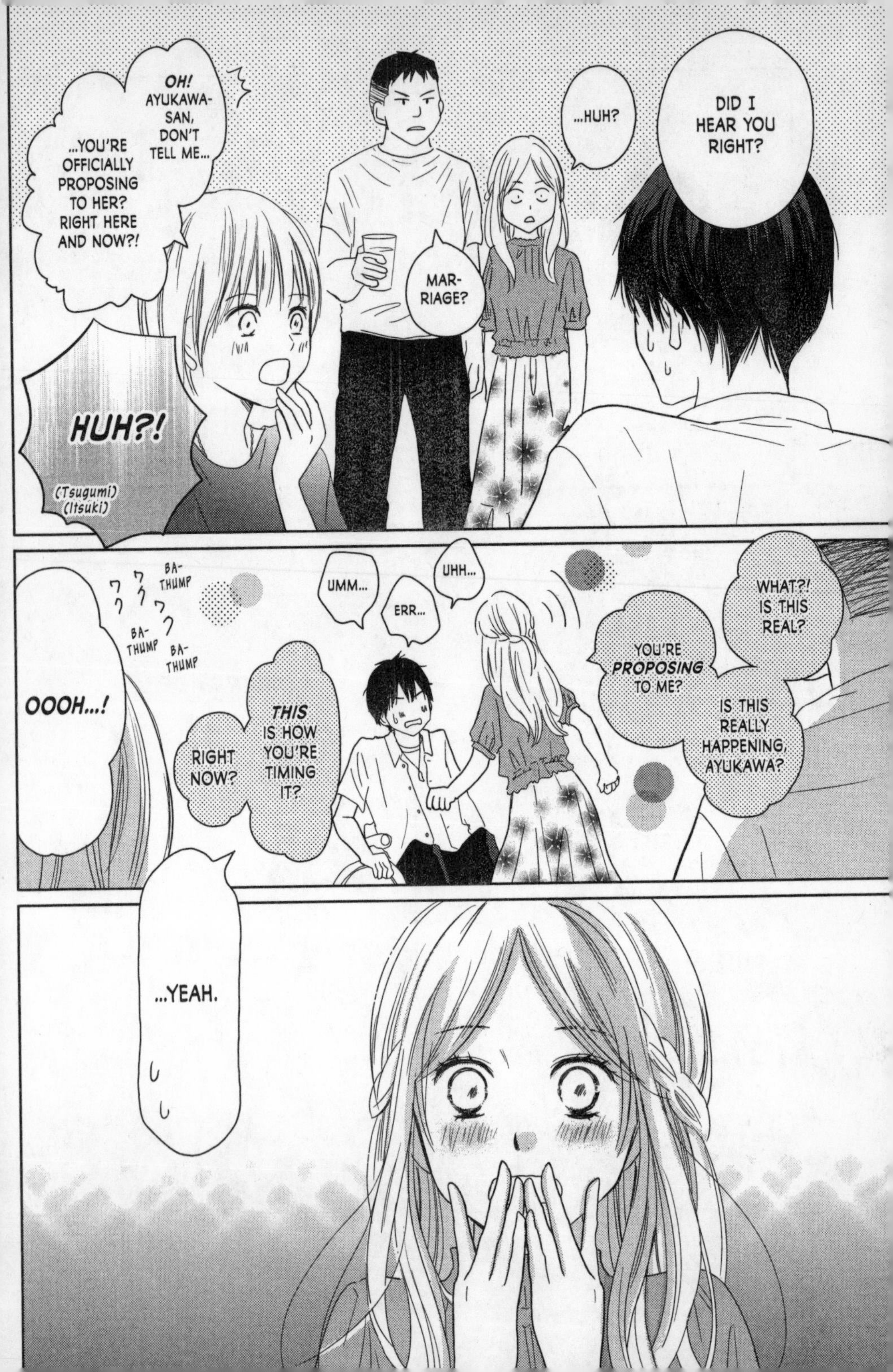
DID I HEAR YOU RIGHT?
...HUH?
MAR-RIAGE?
OH! AYUKAWA-SAN, DON'T TELL ME...
...YOU'RE OFFICIALLY PROPOSING TO HER? RIGHT HERE AND NOW?!
HUH?!
(Tsugumi) (Itsuki)
WHAT?! IS THIS REAL?
YOU'RE PROPOSING TO ME?
IS THIS REALLY HAPPENING, AYUKAWA?
UHH...
ERR...
UMM...
THIS IS HOW YOU'RE TIMING IT?
RIGHT NOW?
BA-THUMP BA-THUMP BA-THUMP
OOOH...!
...YEAH.

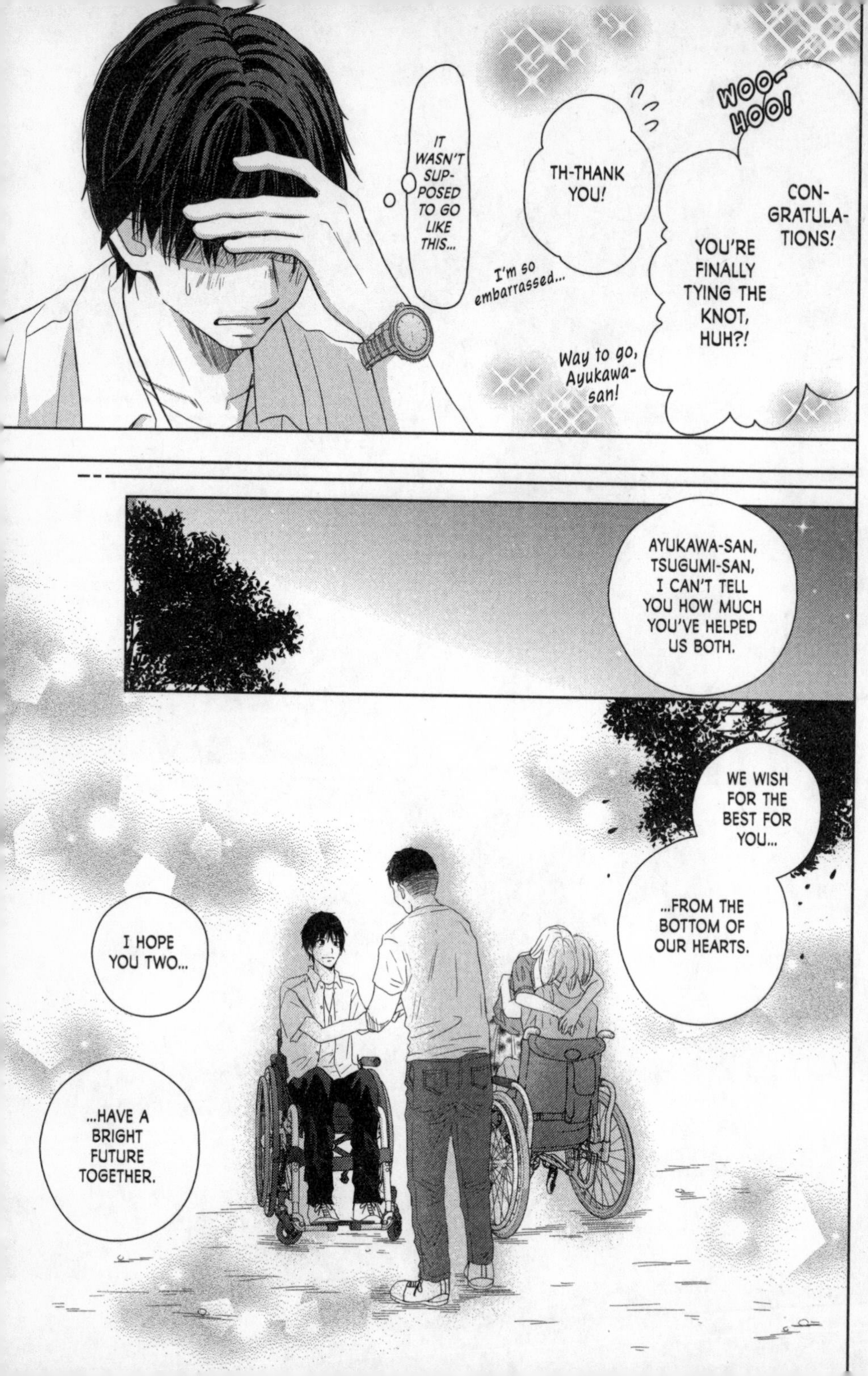
WOO-HOO!
CON-GRATULATIONS!
YOU'RE FINALLY TYING THE KNOT, HUH?!
Way to go, Ayukawa-san!
TH-THANK YOU!
I'm so embarrassed...
IT WASN'T SUP-POSED TO GO LIKE THIS...
AYUKAWA-SAN, TSUGUMI-SAN, I CAN'T TELL YOU HOW MUCH YOU'VE HELPED US BOTH.
WE WISH FOR THE BEST FOR YOU...
...FROM THE BOTTOM OF OUR HEARTS.
I HOPE YOU TWO...
...HAVE A BRIGHT FUTURE TOGETHER.

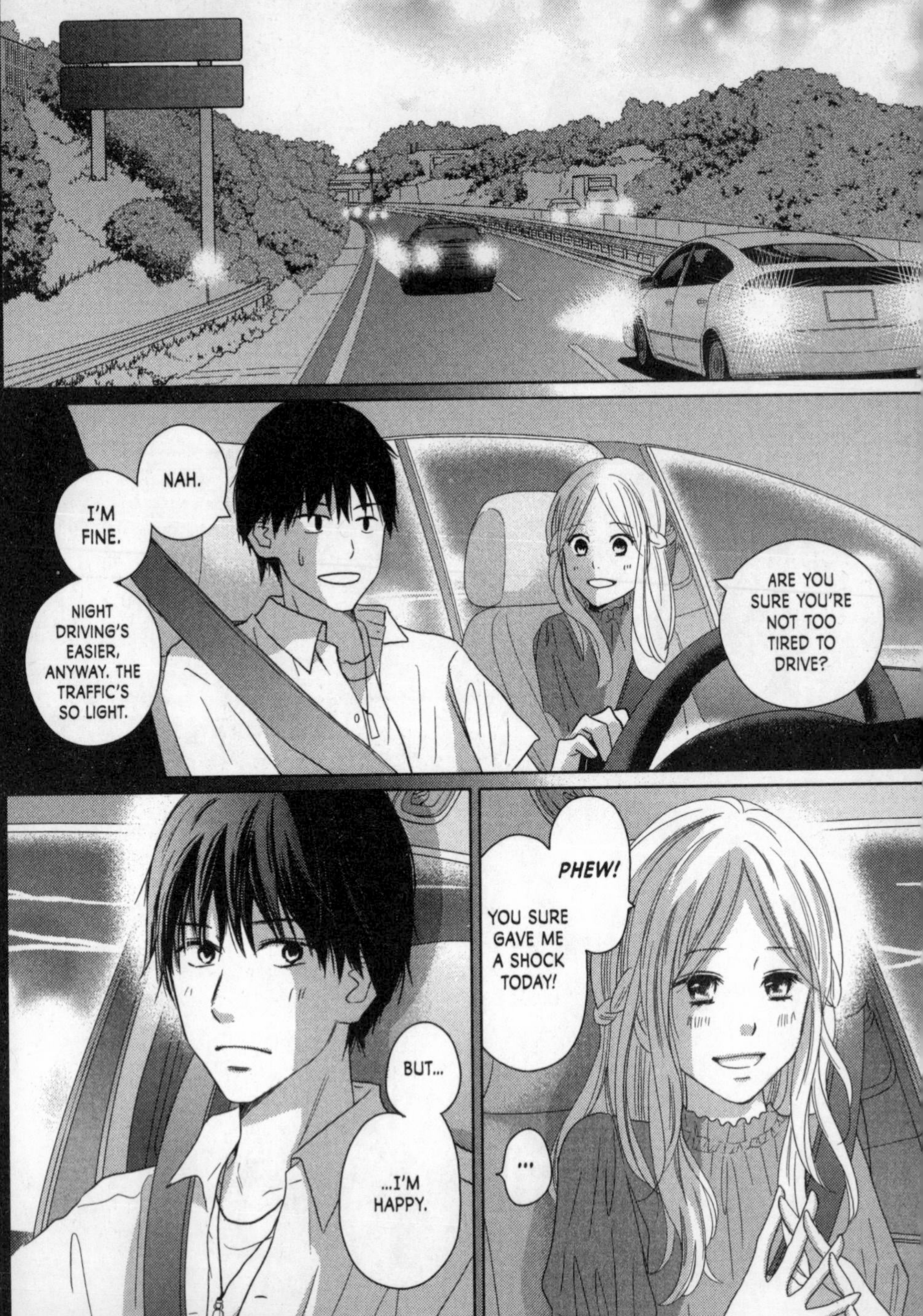
ARE YOU SURE YOU'RE NOT TOO TIRED TO DRIVE?
NAH.
I'M FINE.
NIGHT DRIVING'S EASIER, ANYWAY. THE TRAFFIC'S SO LIGHT.
PHEW!
YOU SURE GAVE ME A SHOCK TODAY!
...
BUT...
...I'M HAPPY.

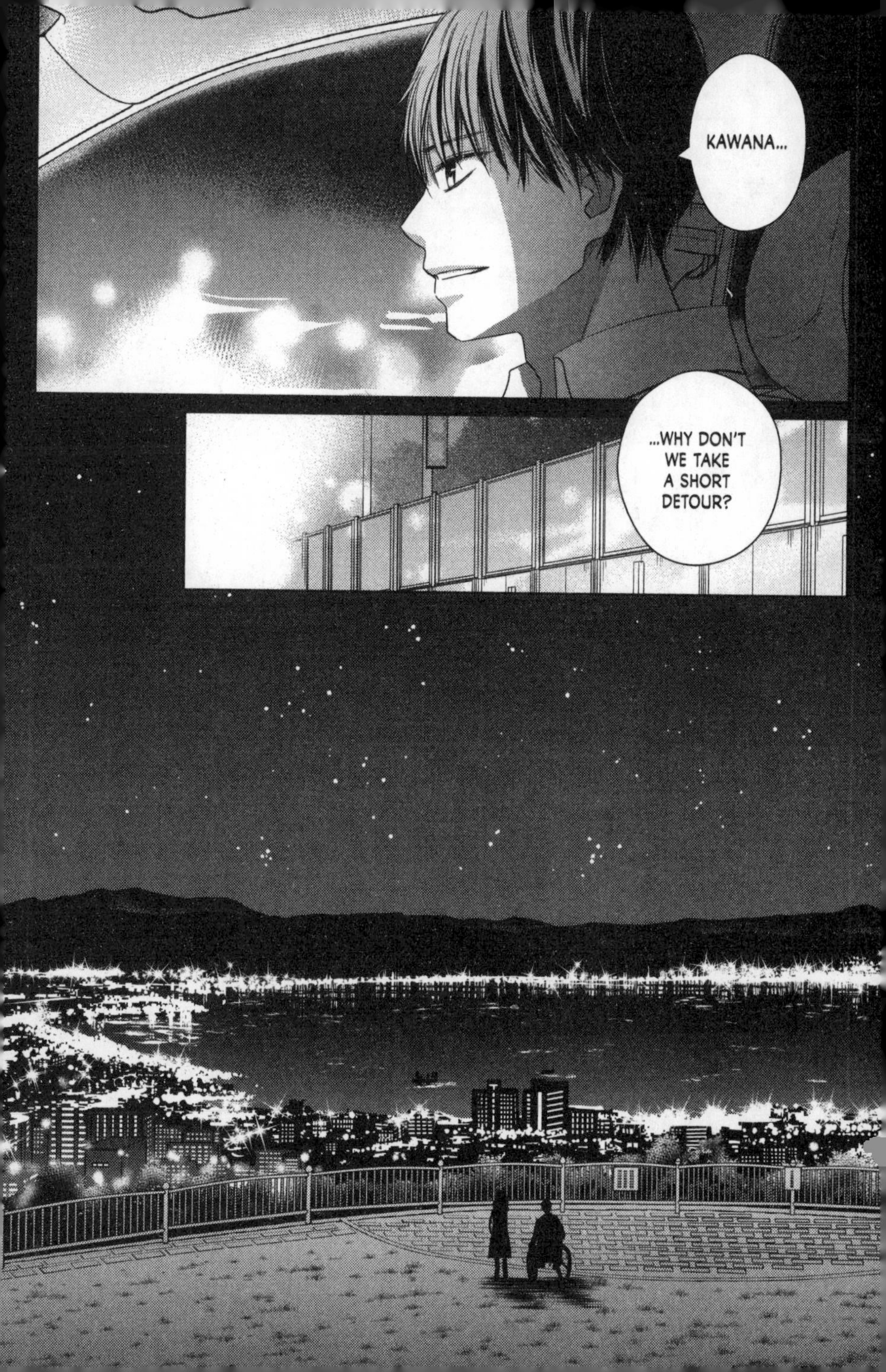
KAWANA...
...WHY DON'T WE TAKE A SHORT DETOUR?

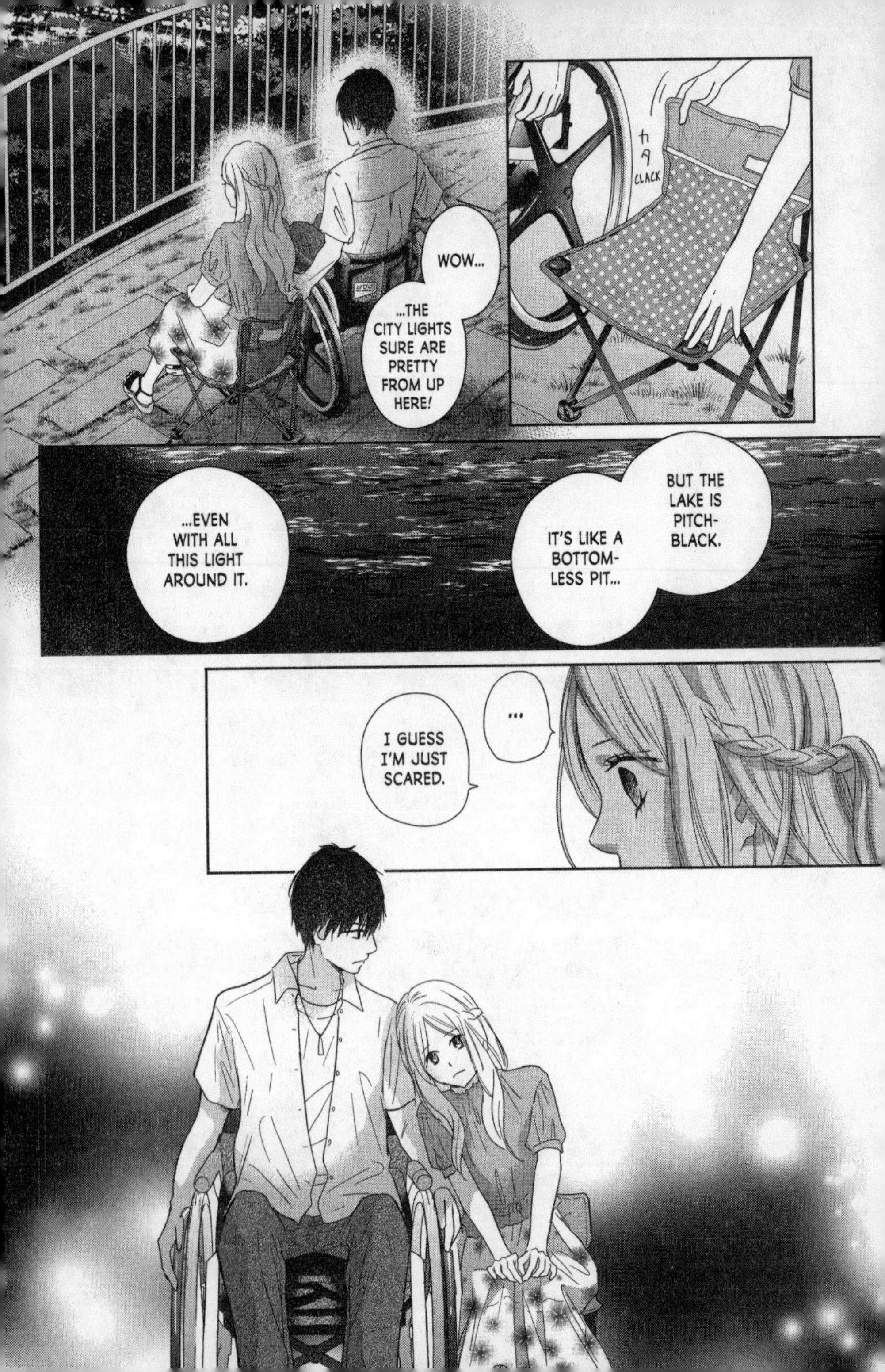
カタ
CLACK
WOW...
...THE CITY LIGHTS SURE ARE PRETTY FROM UP HERE!
BUT THE LAKE IS PITCH-BLACK.
IT'S LIKE A BOTTOMLESS PIT...
...EVEN WITH ALL THIS LIGHT AROUND IT.
...
I GUESS I'M JUST SCARED.

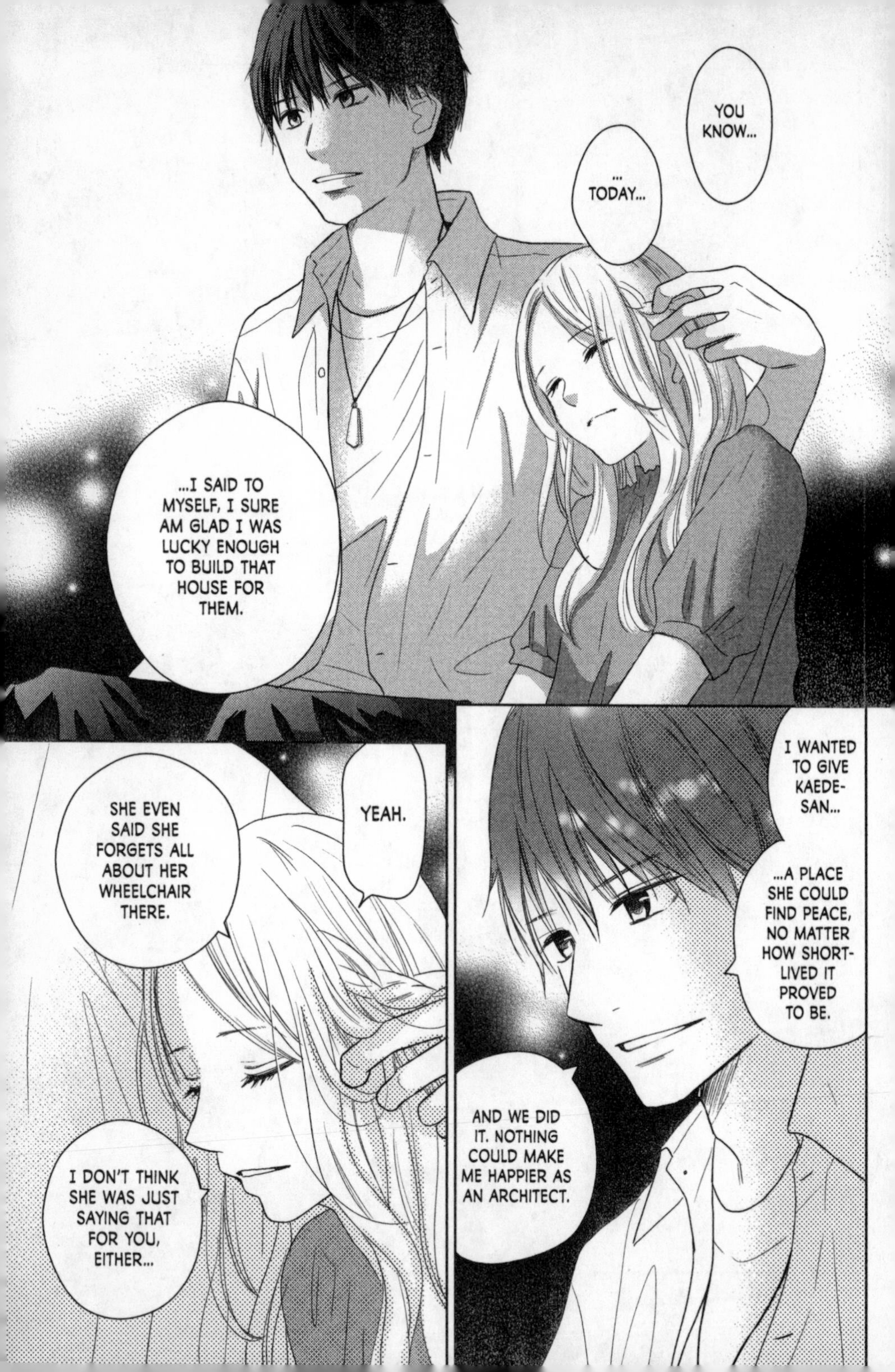
YOU KNOW...
... TODAY...
...I SAID TO MYSELF, I SURE AM GLAD I WAS LUCKY ENOUGH TO BUILD THAT HOUSE FOR THEM.
I WANTED TO GIVE KAEDE-SAN...
...A PLACE SHE COULD FIND PEACE, NO MATTER HOW SHORT-LIVED IT PROVED TO BE.
AND WE DID IT. NOTHING COULD MAKE ME HAPPIER AS AN ARCHITECT.
YEAH.
SHE EVEN SAID SHE FORGETS ALL ABOUT HER WHEELCHAIR THERE.
I DON'T THINK SHE WAS JUST SAYING THAT FOR YOU, EITHER...

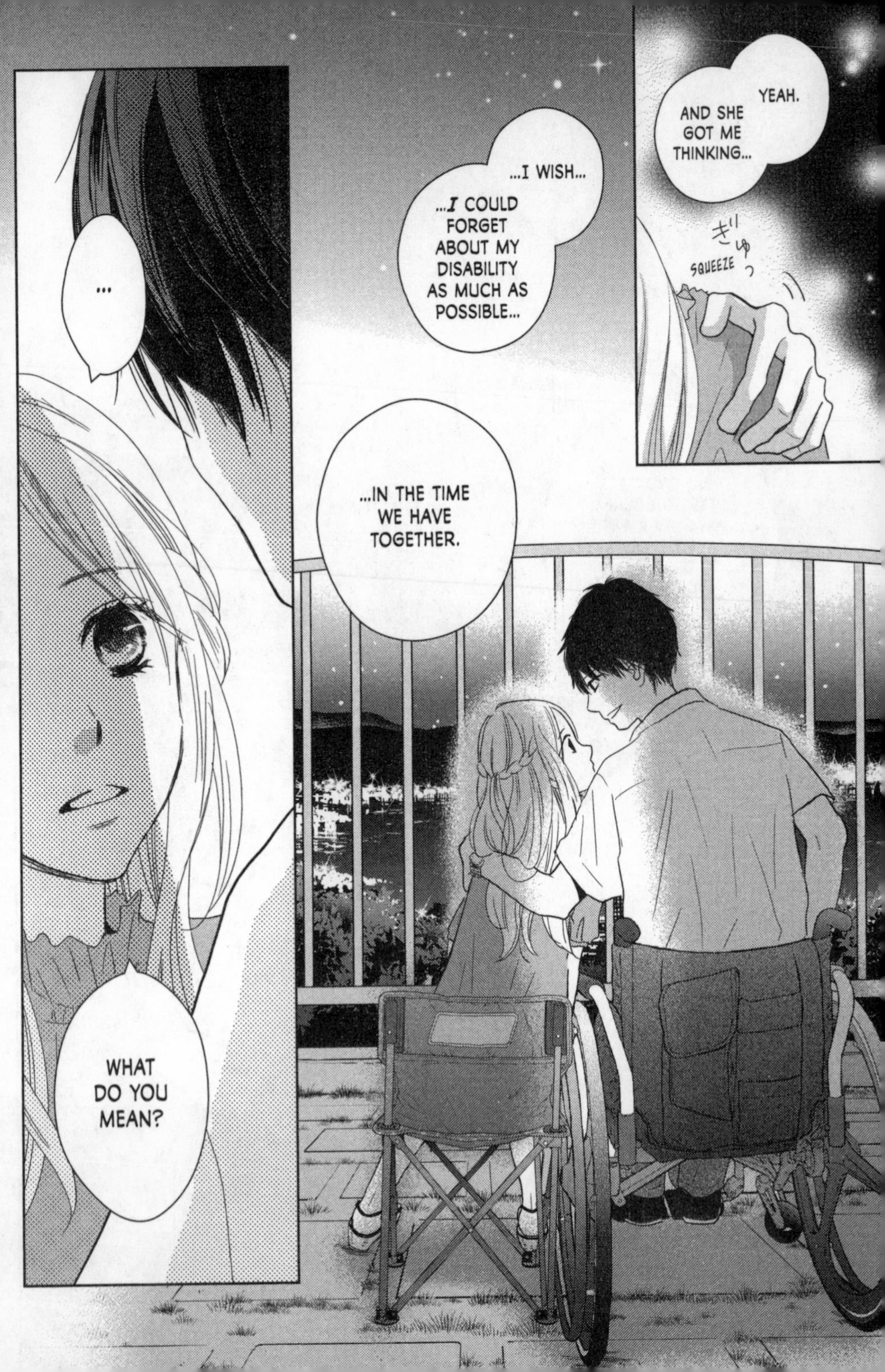
YEAH.
AND SHE GOT ME THINKING...
ぎゅっ
SQUEEZE
...I WISH...
...*I* COULD FORGET ABOUT MY DISABILITY AS MUCH AS POSSIBLE...
...IN THE TIME WE HAVE TOGETHER.
...
WHAT DO YOU MEAN?

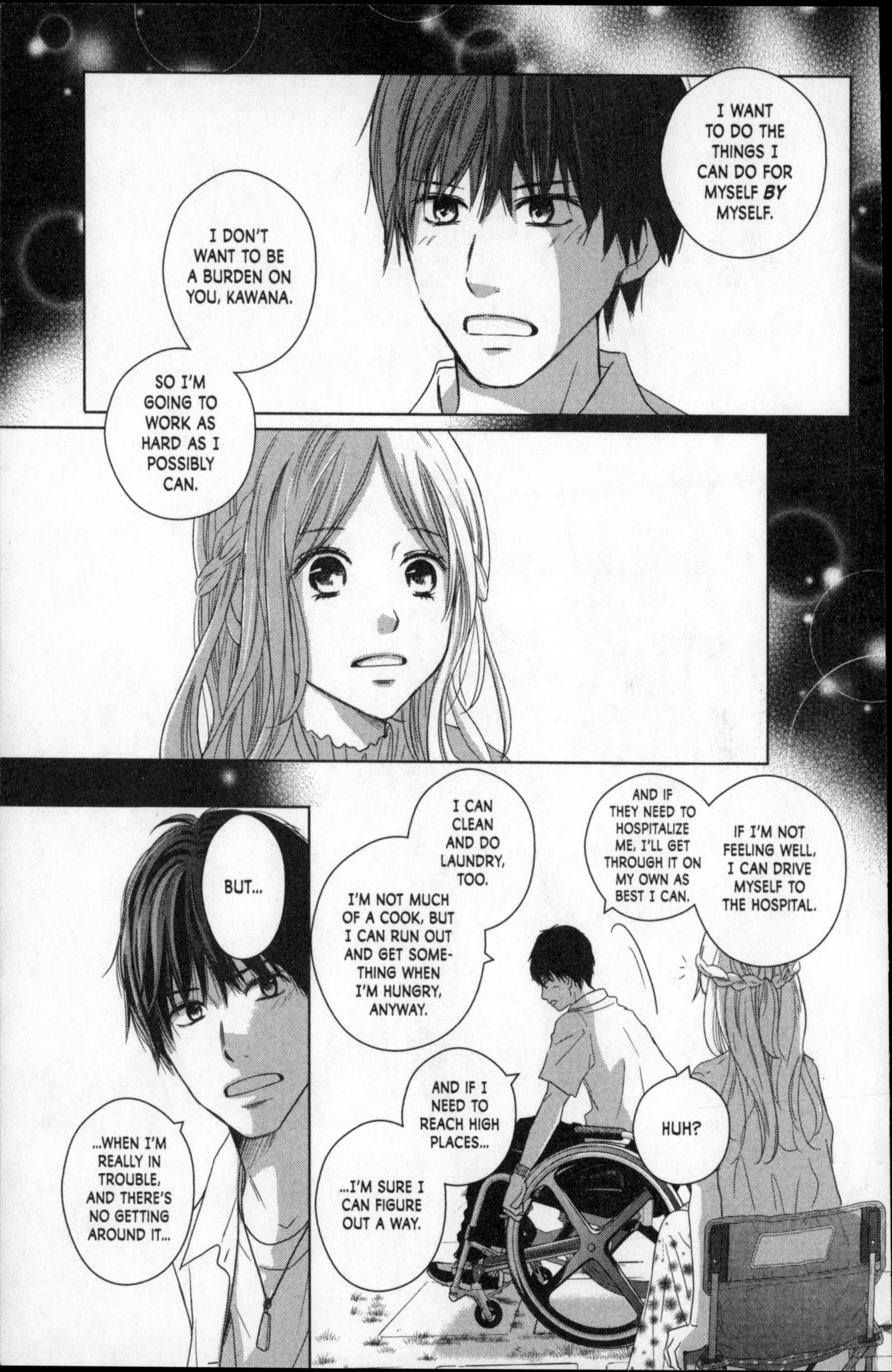

I WANT TO DO THE THINGS I CAN DO FOR MYSELF *BY* MYSELF.
I DON'T WANT TO BE A BURDEN ON YOU, KAWANA.
SO I'M GOING TO WORK AS HARD AS I POSSIBLY CAN.
IF I'M NOT FEELING WELL, I CAN DRIVE MYSELF TO THE HOSPITAL.
AND IF THEY NEED TO HOSPITALIZE ME, I'LL GET THROUGH IT ON MY OWN AS BEST I CAN.
I CAN CLEAN AND DO LAUNDRY, TOO.
I'M NOT MUCH OF A COOK, BUT I CAN RUN OUT AND GET SOME-THING WHEN I'M HUNGRY, ANYWAY.
HUH?
AND IF I NEED TO REACH HIGH PLACES...
...I'M SURE I CAN FIGURE OUT A WAY.
BUT...
...WHEN I'M REALLY IN TROUBLE, AND THERE'S NO GETTING AROUND IT...

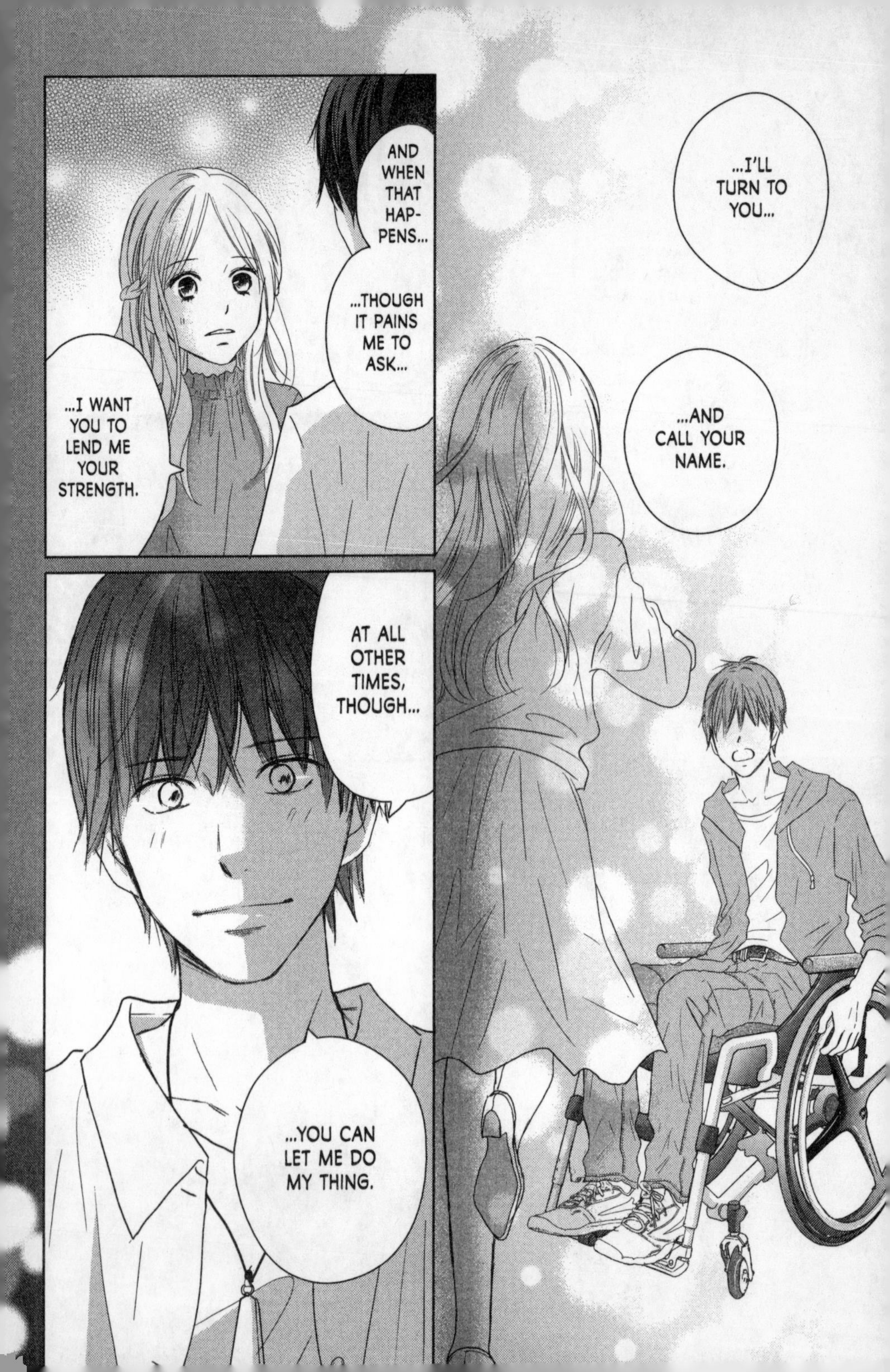
...I'LL TURN TO YOU...
...AND CALL YOUR NAME.
AND WHEN THAT HAP-PENS...
...THOUGH IT PAINS ME TO ASK...
...I WANT YOU TO LEND ME YOUR STRENGTH.
AT ALL OTHER TIMES, THOUGH...
...YOU CAN LET ME DO MY THING.

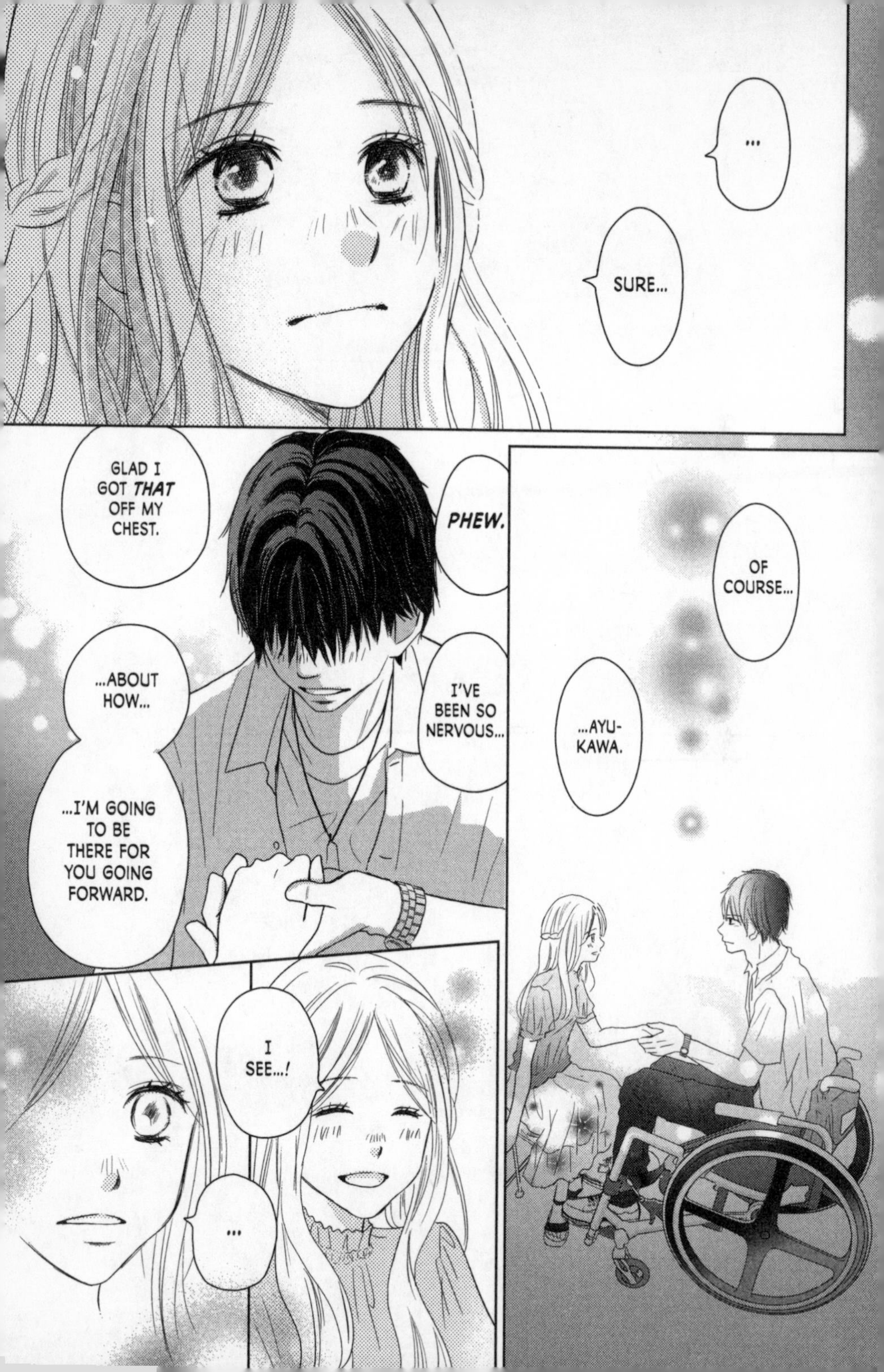
...
SURE...
OF COURSE...
...AYU-KAWA.
PHEW.
GLAD I GOT *THAT* OFF MY CHEST.
I'VE BEEN SO NERVOUS...
...ABOUT HOW...
...I'M GOING TO BE THERE FOR YOU GOING FORWARD.
I SEE...!
...

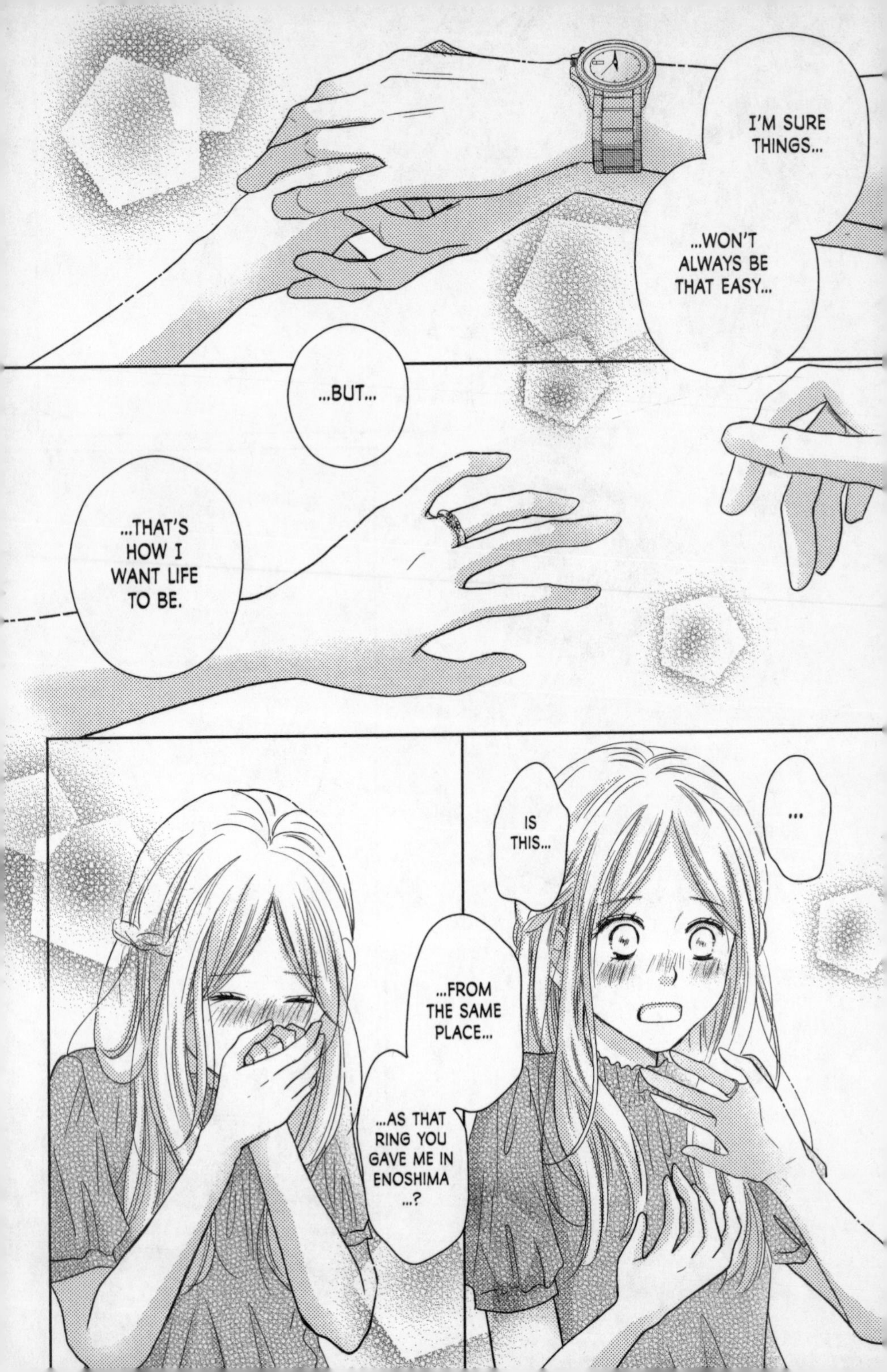
I'M SURE THINGS...
...WON'T ALWAYS BE THAT EASY...
...BUT...
...THAT'S HOW I WANT LIFE TO BE.
...
IS THIS...
...FROM THE SAME PLACE...
...AS THAT RING YOU GAVE ME IN ENOSHIMA ...?

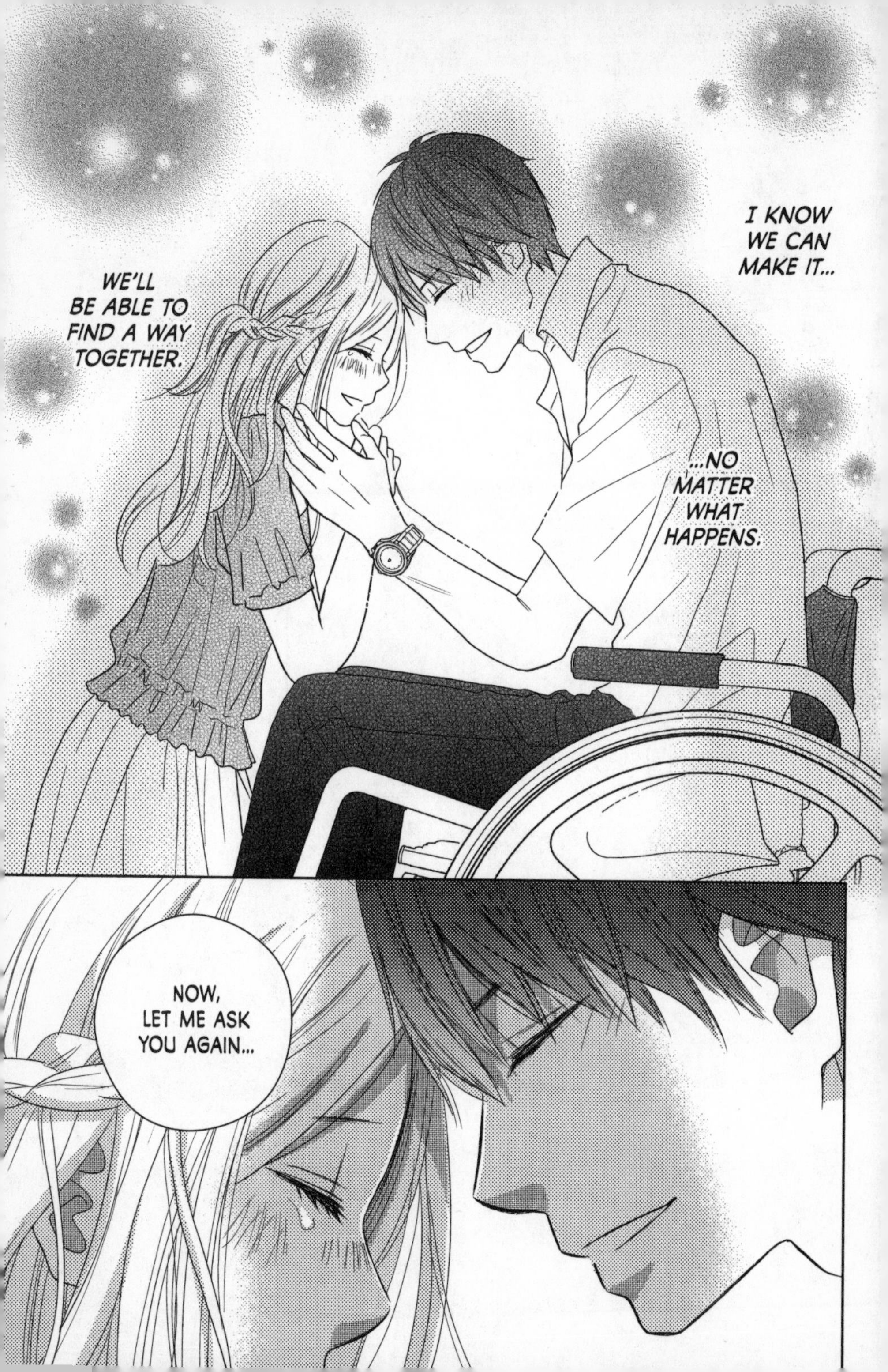
I KNOW WE CAN MAKE IT...
...NO MATTER WHAT HAPPENS.
WE'LL BE ABLE TO FIND A WAY TOGETHER.
NOW, LET ME ASK YOU AGAIN...

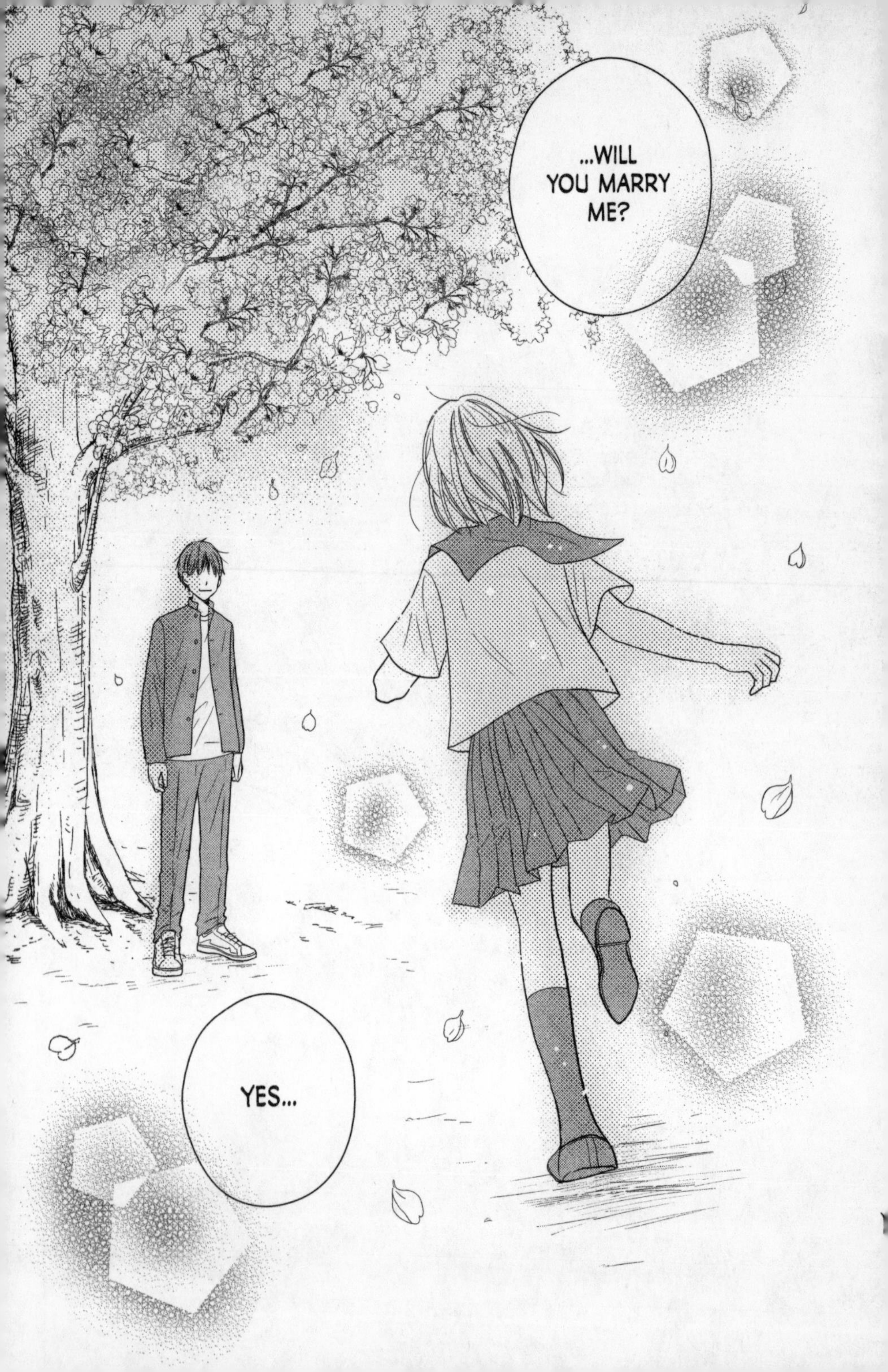
...WILL YOU MARRY ME?
YES...

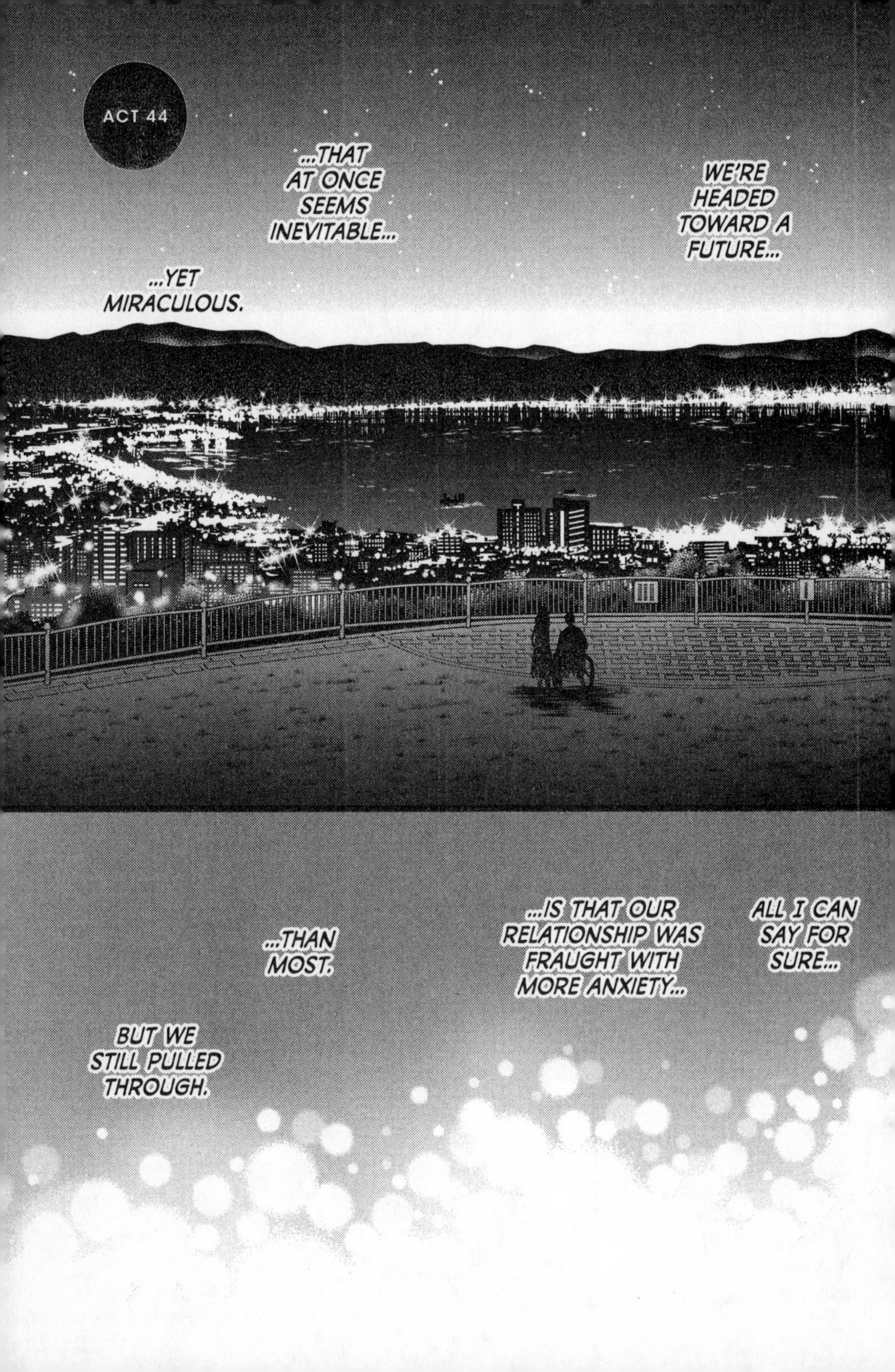
ACT 44
WE'RE HEADED TOWARD A FUTURE...
...THAT AT ONCE SEEMS INEVITABLE...
...YET MIRACULOUS.
ALL I CAN SAY FOR SURE...
...IS THAT OUR RELATIONSHIP WAS FRAUGHT WITH MORE ANXIETY...
...THAN MOST.
BUT WE STILL PULLED THROUGH.

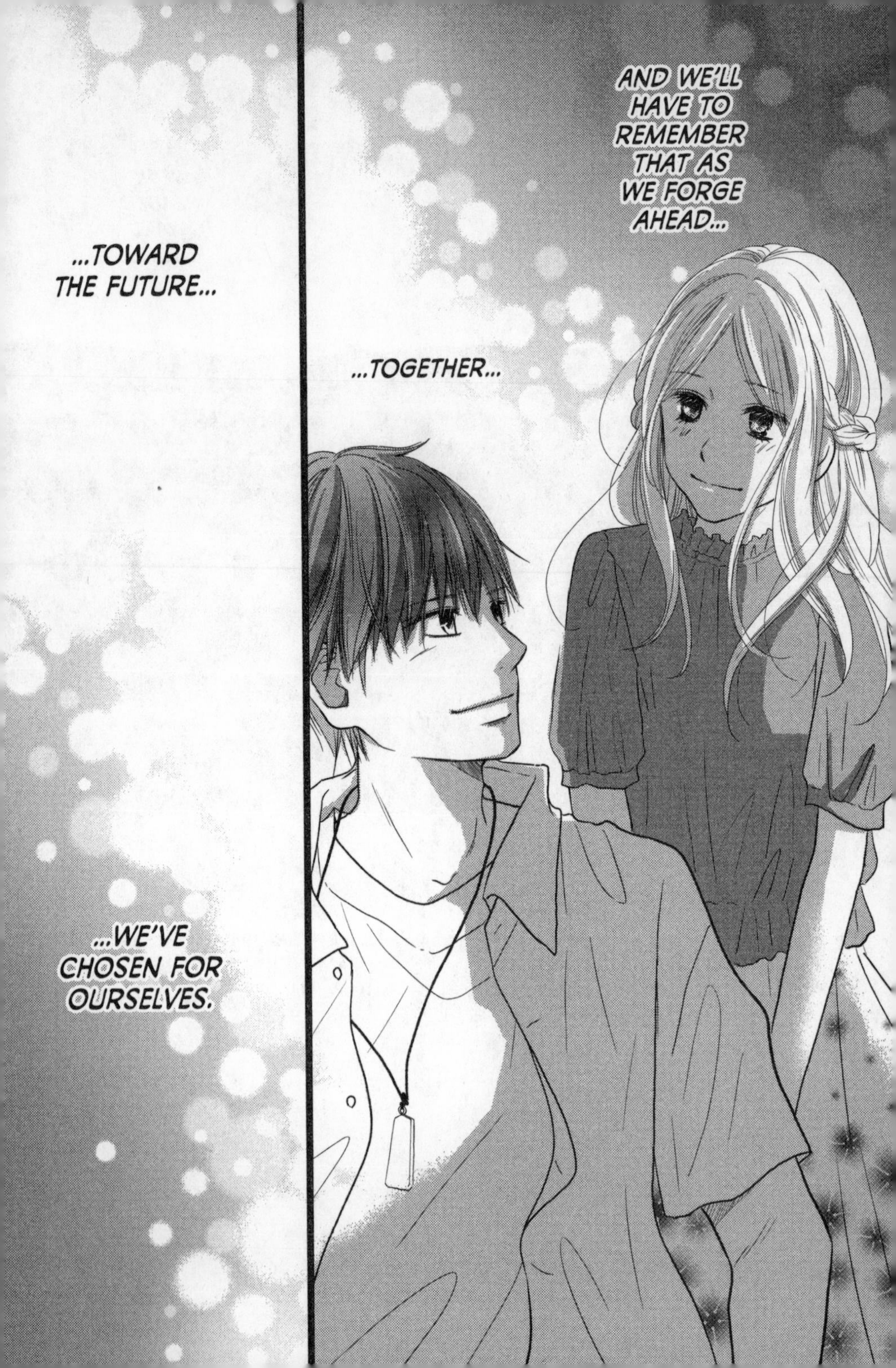
AND WE'LL HAVE TO REMEMBER THAT AS WE FORGE AHEAD...
...TOGETHER...
...TOWARD THE FUTURE...
...WE'VE CHOSEN FOR OURSELVES.

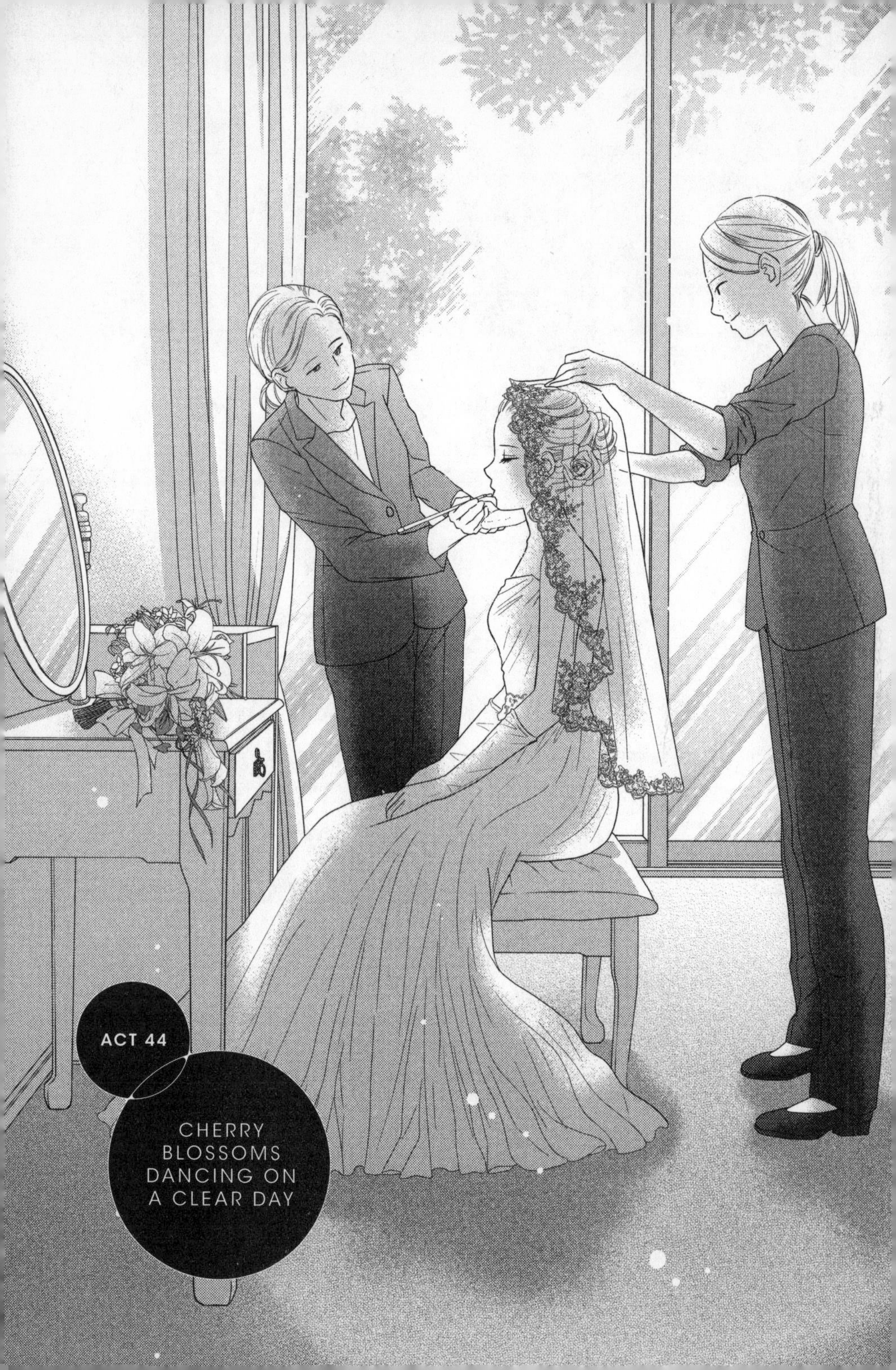
ACT 44
CHERRY BLOSSOMS DANCING ON A CLEAR DAY

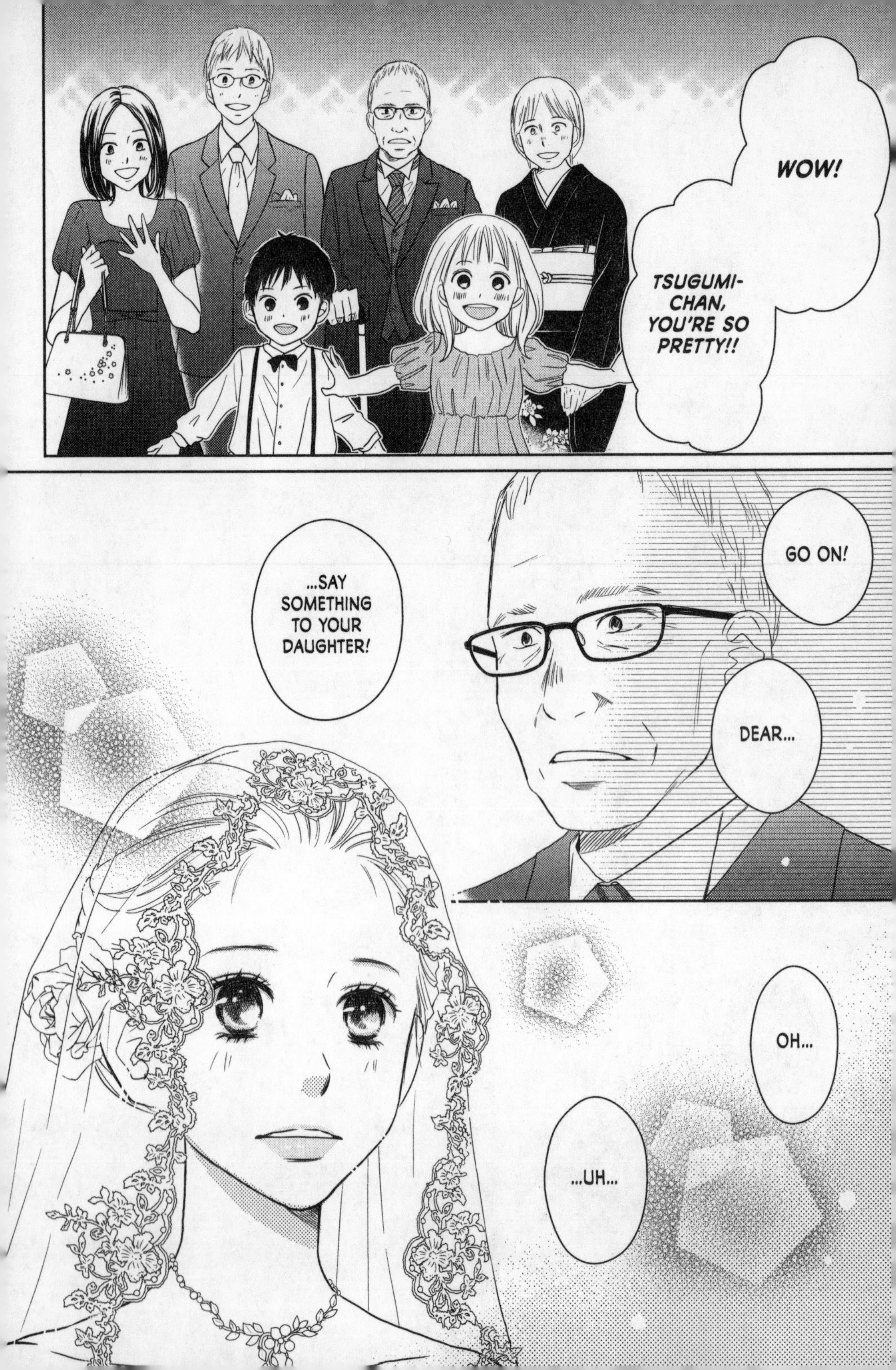
WOW!
TSUGUMI-CHAN, YOU'RE SO PRETTY!!
GO ON!
DEAR...
...SAY SOMETHING TO YOUR DAUGHTER!
OH...
...UH...

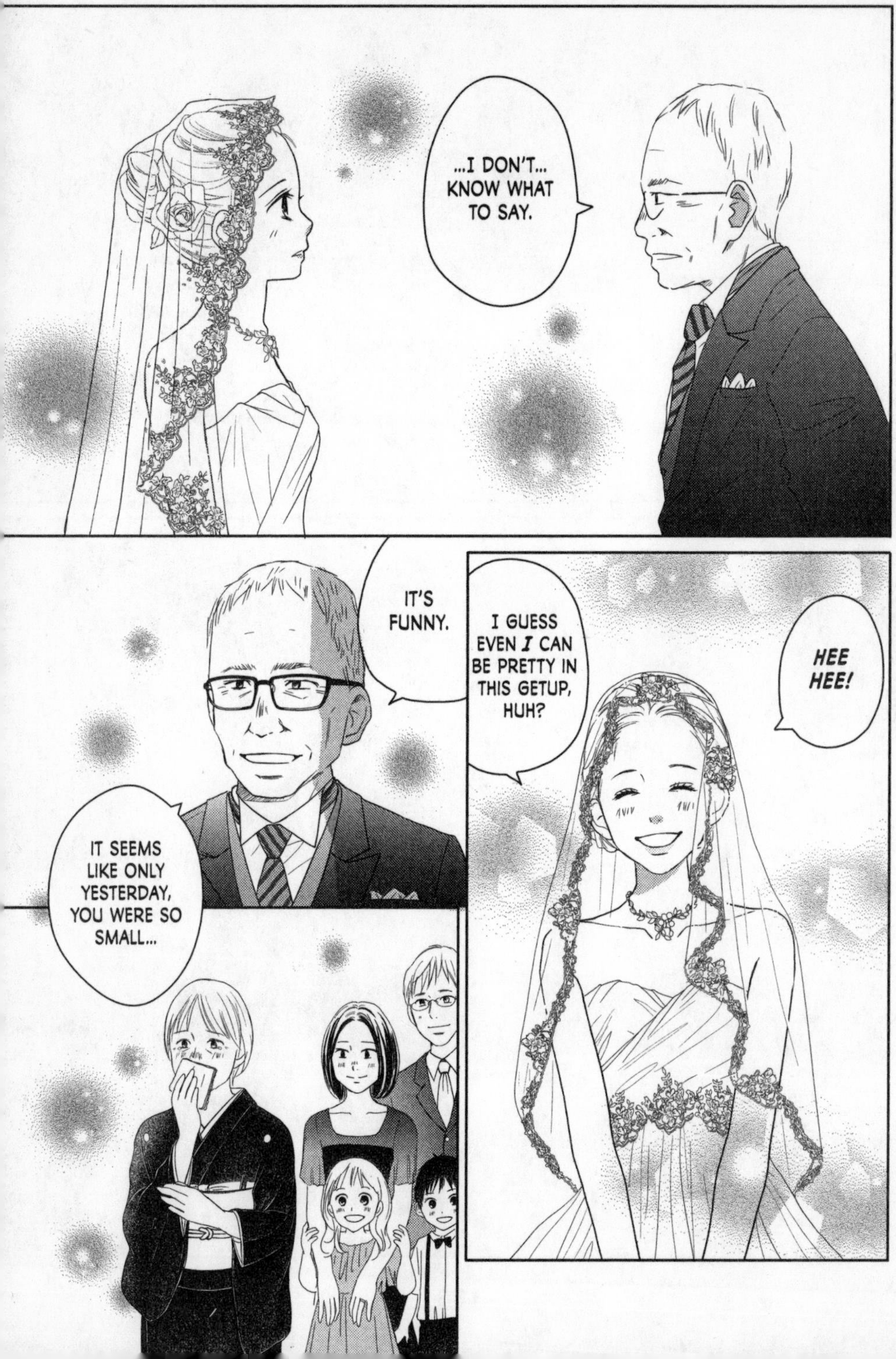
...I DON'T... KNOW WHAT TO SAY.
I GUESS EVEN *I* CAN BE PRETTY IN THIS GETUP, HUH?
HEE HEE!
IT'S FUNNY.
IT SEEMS LIKE ONLY YESTERDAY, YOU WERE SO SMALL...

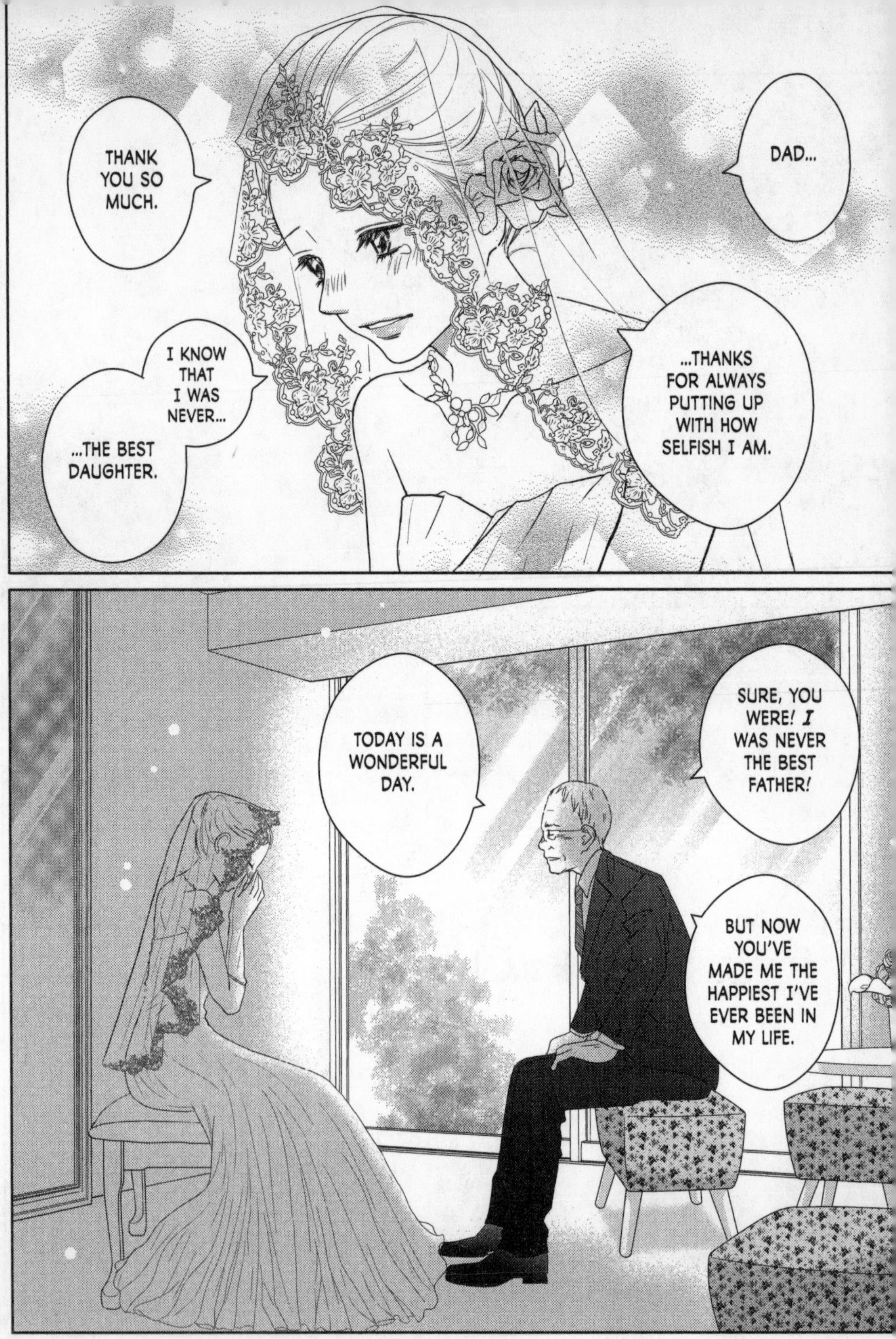
DAD...
...THANKS FOR ALWAYS PUTTING UP WITH HOW SELFISH I AM.
THANK YOU SO MUCH.
I KNOW THAT I WAS NEVER...
...THE BEST DAUGHTER.
SURE, YOU WERE! *I* WAS NEVER THE BEST FATHER!
BUT NOW YOU'VE MADE ME THE HAPPIEST I'VE EVER BEEN IN MY LIFE.
TODAY IS A WONDERFUL DAY.

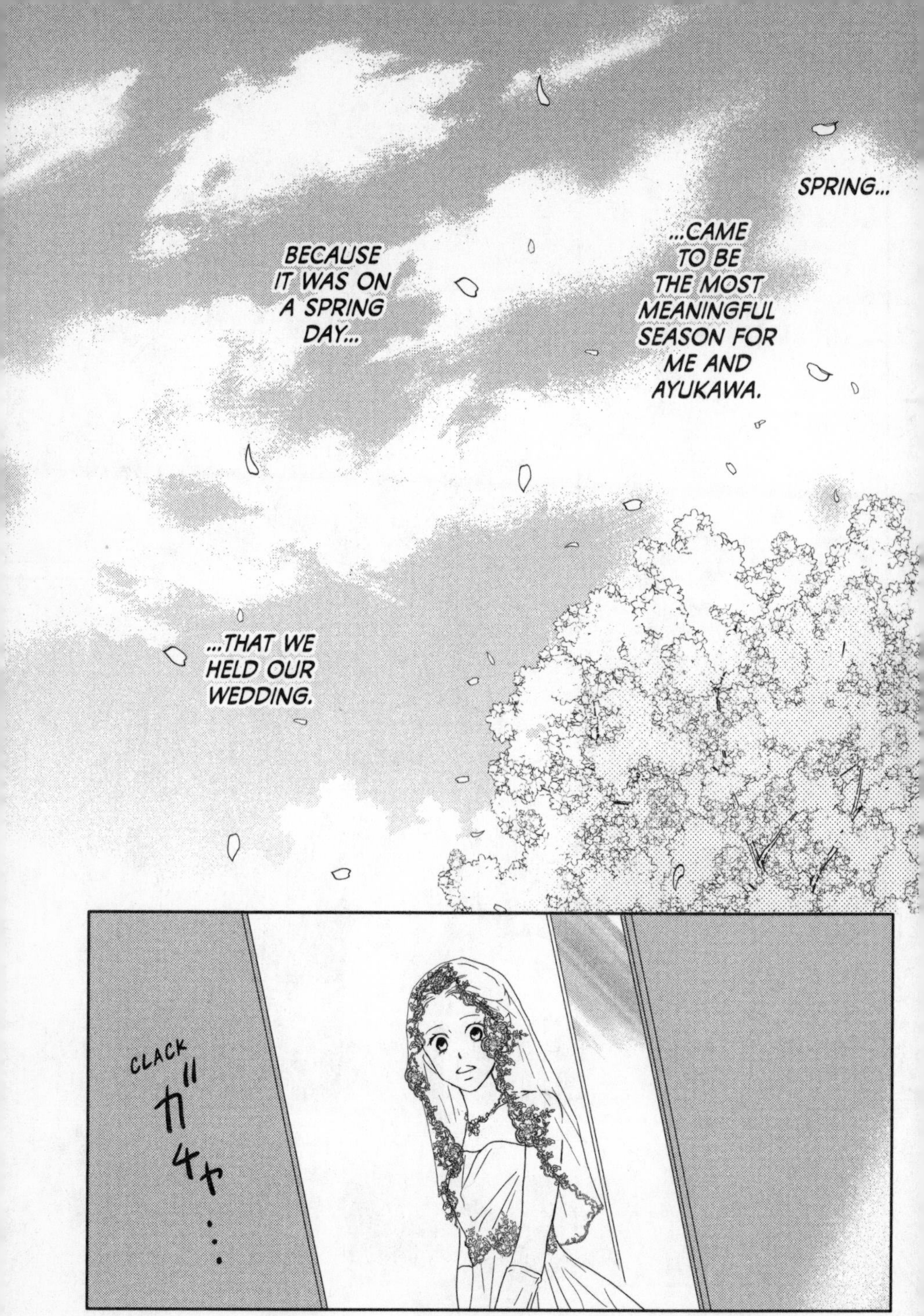
SPRING...
...CAME TO BE THE MOST MEANINGFUL SEASON FOR ME AND AYUKAWA.
BECAUSE IT WAS ON A SPRING DAY...
...THAT WE HELD OUR WEDDING.
CLACK
ガチャ...

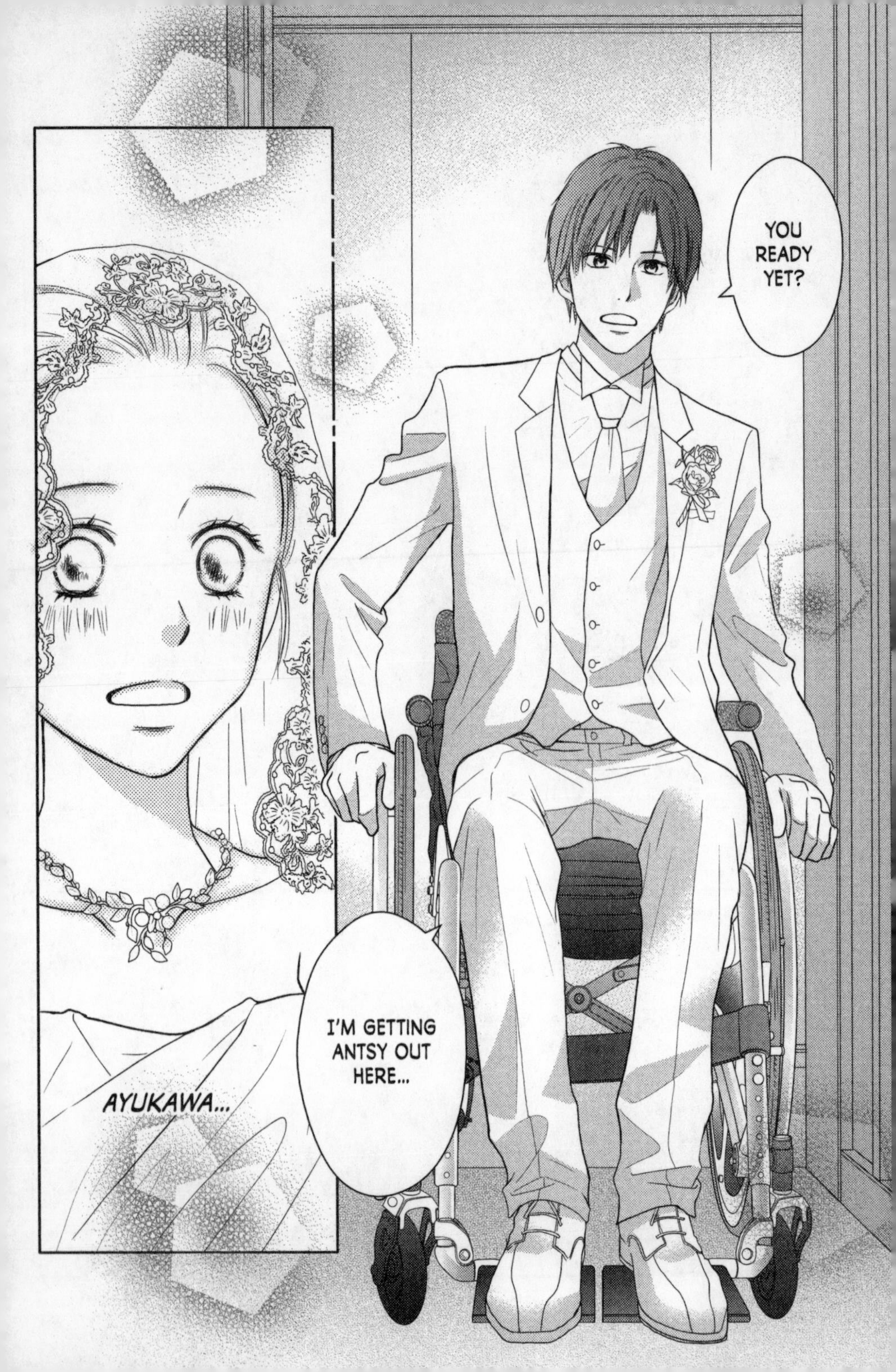
YOU READY YET?
I'M GETTING ANTSY OUT HERE...
AYUKAWA...

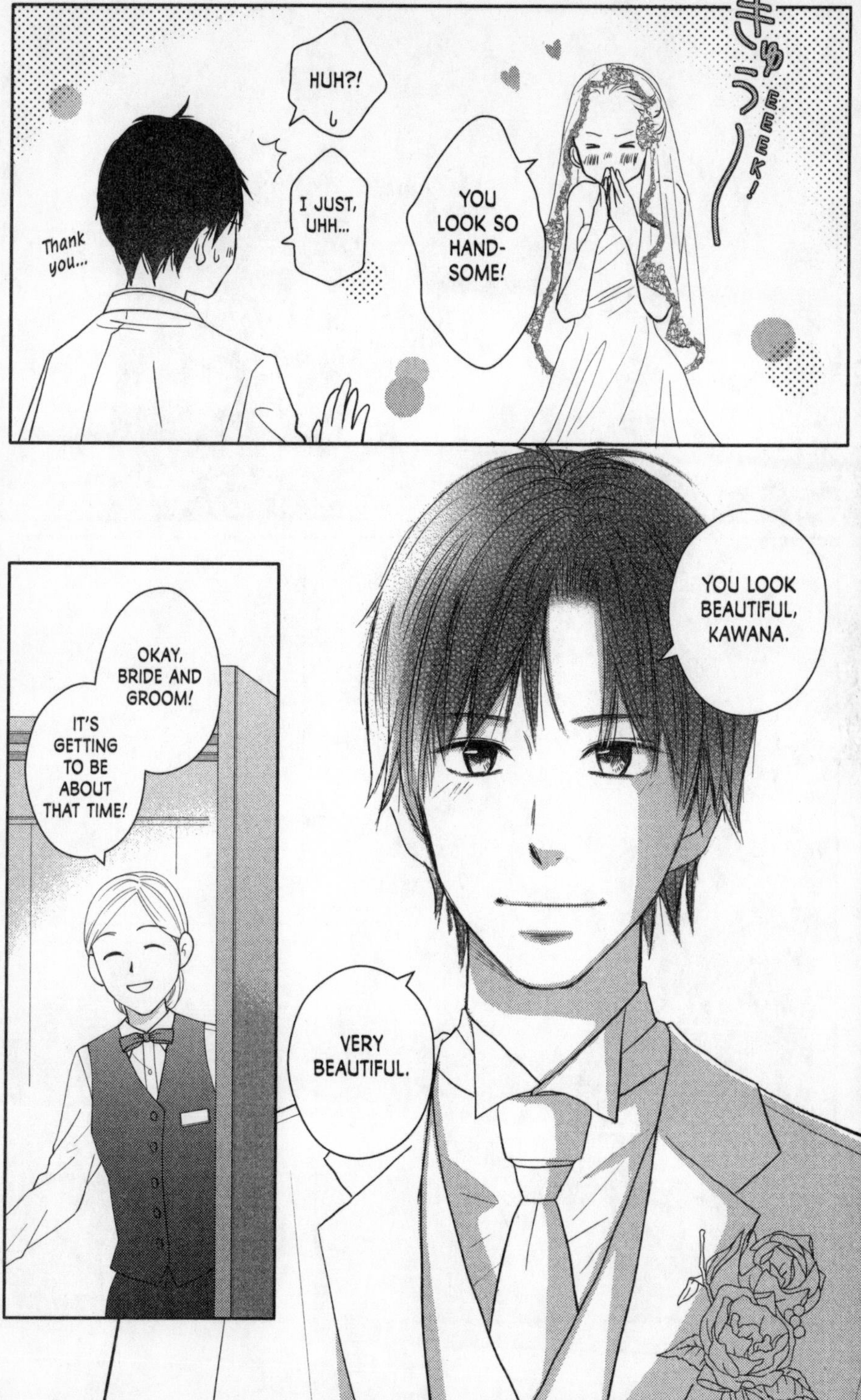
きゅう～
EEEEK!
YOU LOOK SO HAND-SOME!
HUH?!
I JUST, UHH...
Thank you...
YOU LOOK BEAUTIFUL, KAWANA.
VERY BEAUTIFUL.
OKAY, BRIDE AND GROOM!
IT'S GETTING TO BE ABOUT THAT TIME!

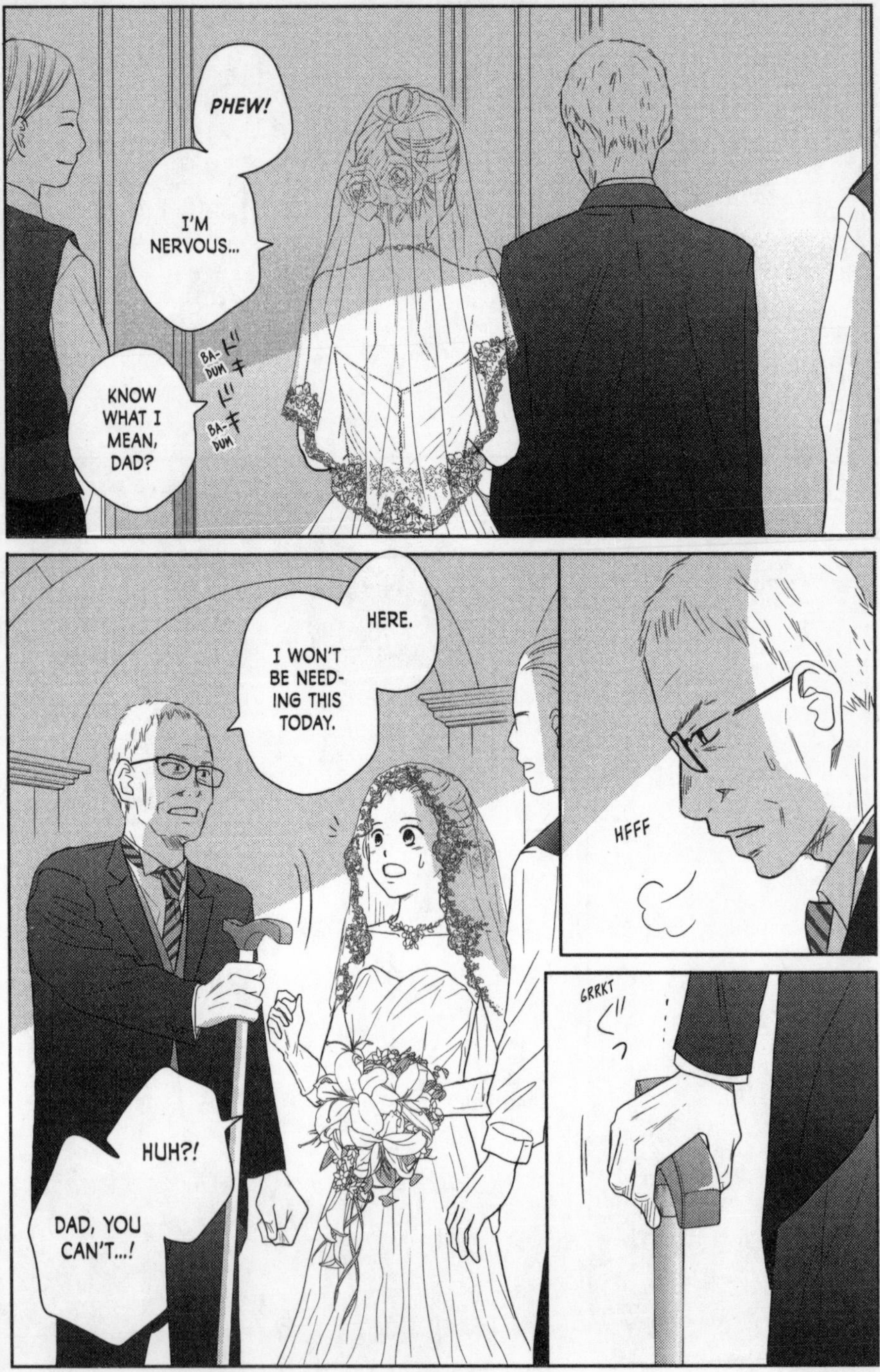
PHEW!
I'M NERVOUS...
BA-DUM ドキ
BA-DUM ドキ
KNOW WHAT I MEAN, DAD?
HFFF
GRRKT ぐっ
...
HERE.
I WON'T BE NEEDING THIS TODAY.
HUH?!
DAD, YOU CAN'T...!

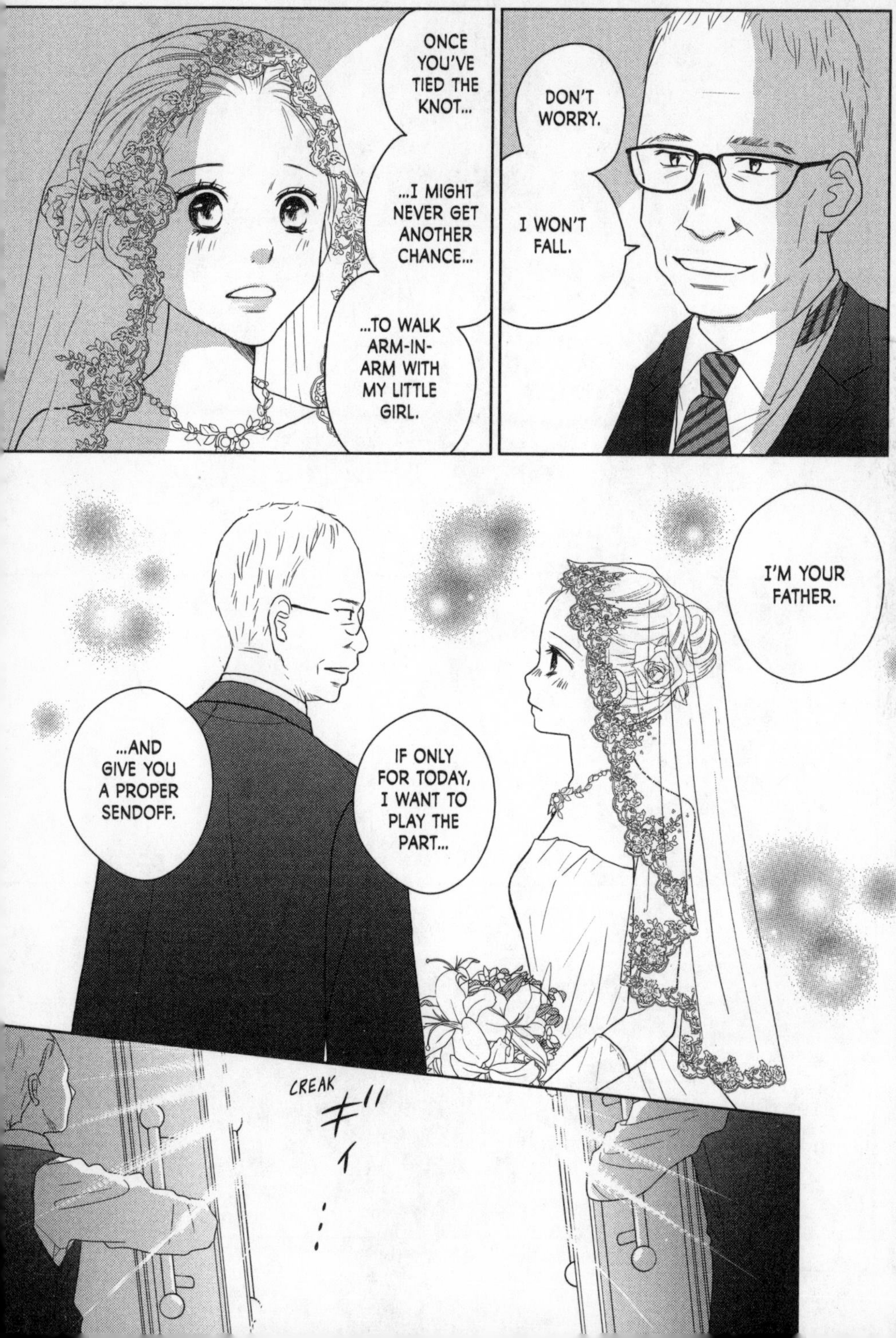

DON'T WORRY.
I WON'T FALL.
ONCE YOU'VE TIED THE KNOT...
...I MIGHT NEVER GET ANOTHER CHANCE...
...TO WALK ARM-IN-ARM WITH MY LITTLE GIRL.
I'M YOUR FATHER.
IF ONLY FOR TODAY, I WANT TO PLAY THE PART...
...AND GIVE YOU A PROPER SENDOFF.
CREAK
ギイ
...

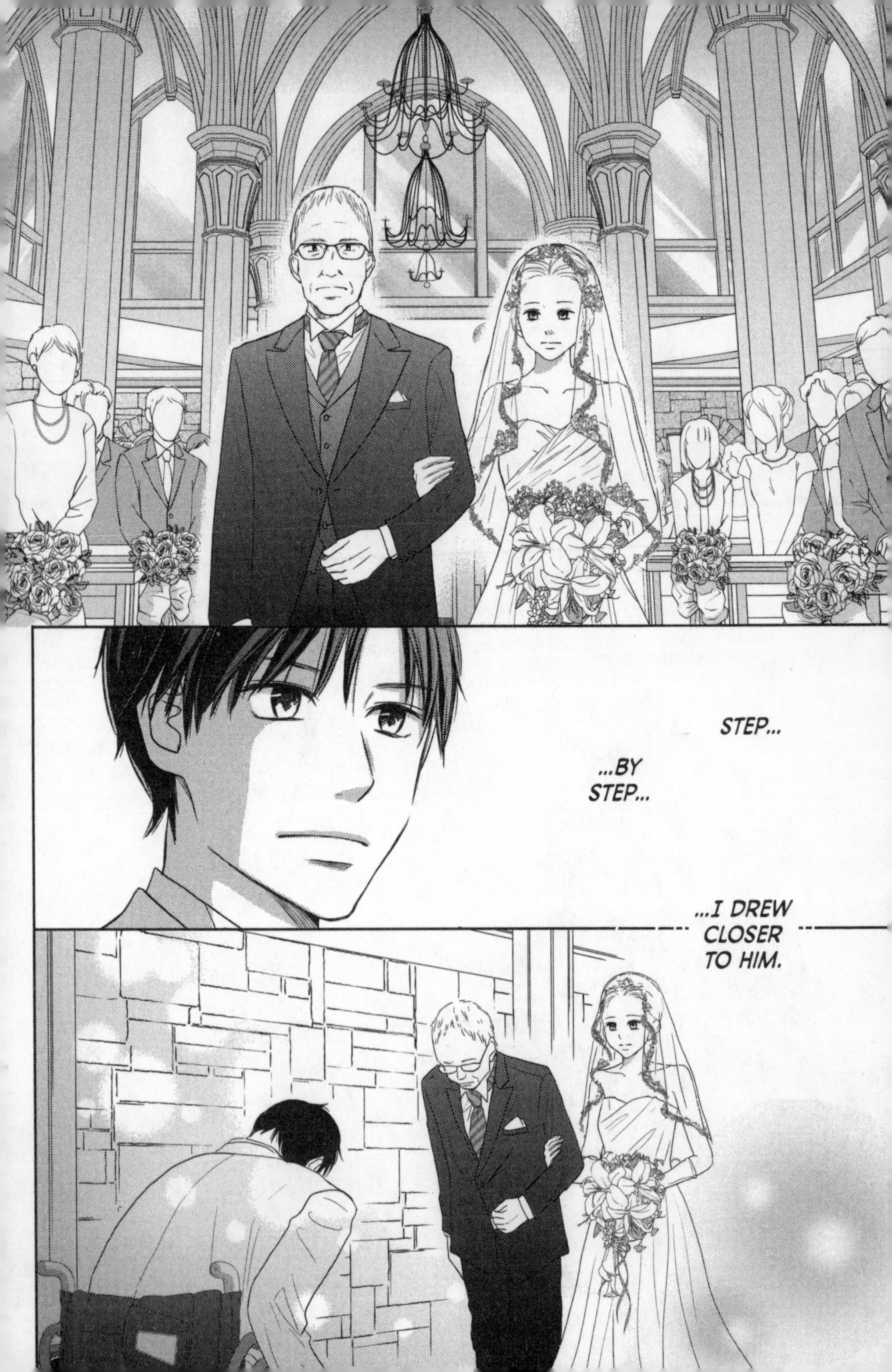
STEP...
...BY STEP...
...I DREW CLOSER TO HIM.

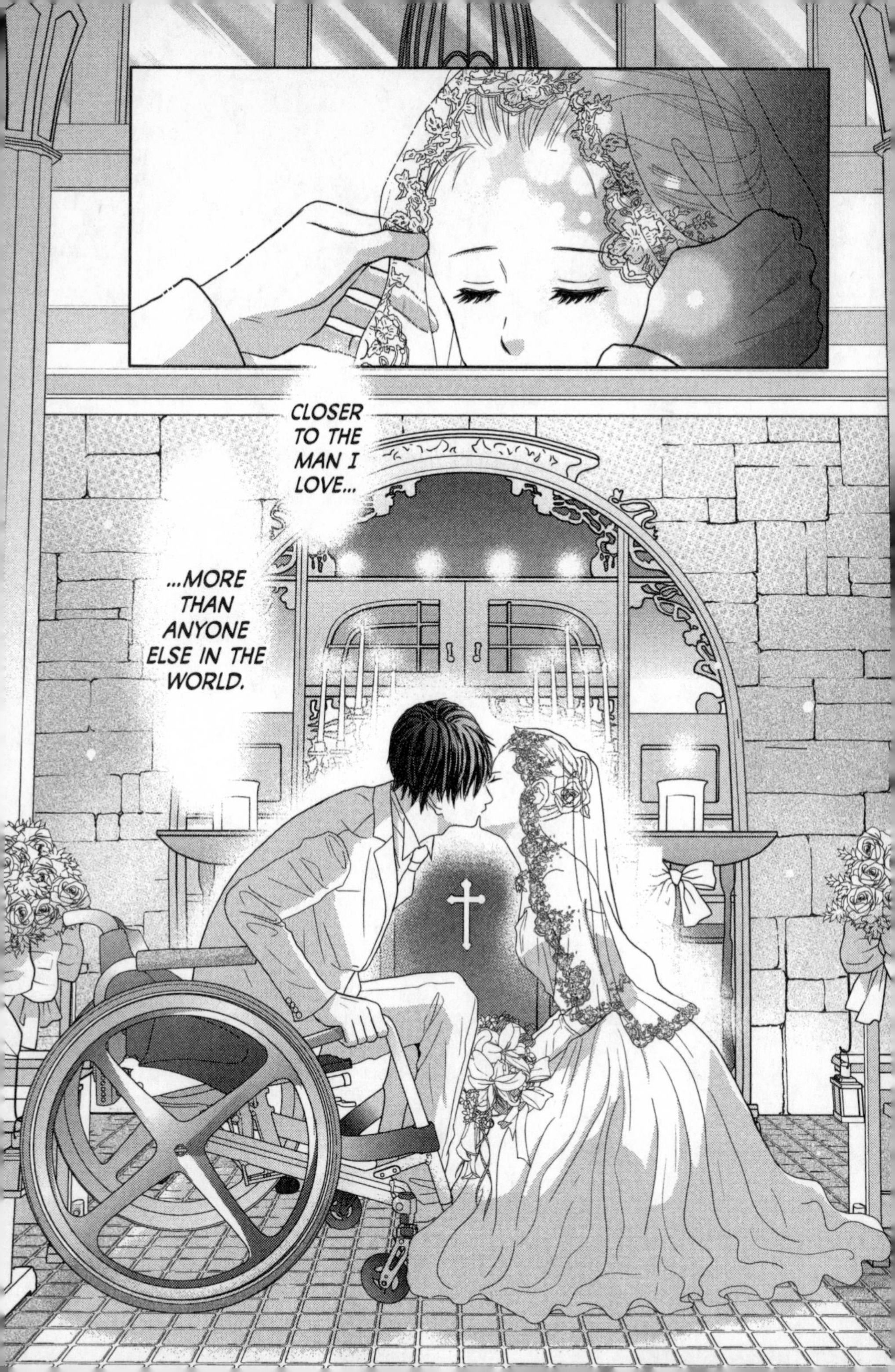
CLOSER TO THE MAN I LOVE...
...MORE THAN ANYONE ELSE IN THE WORLD.

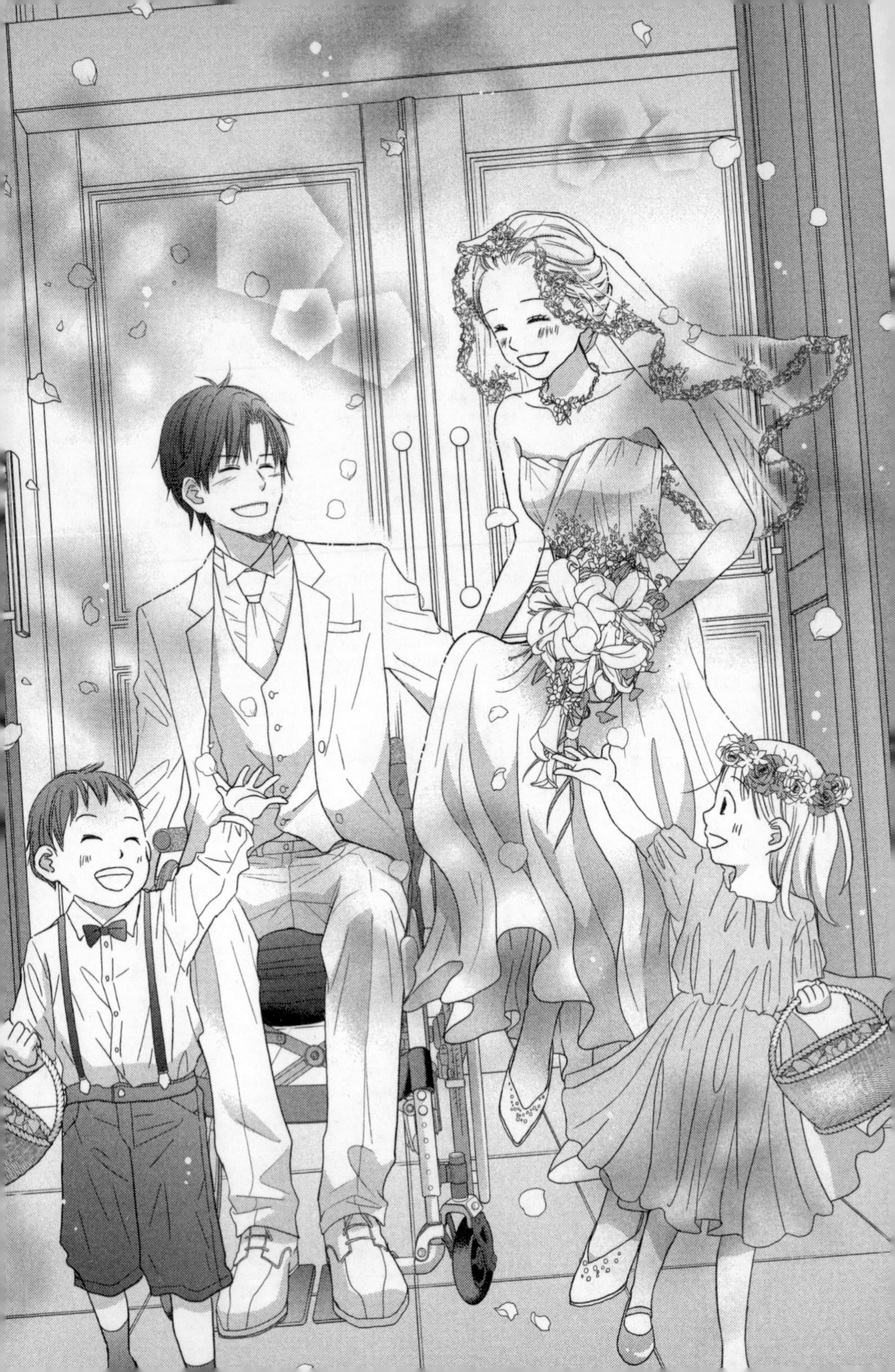

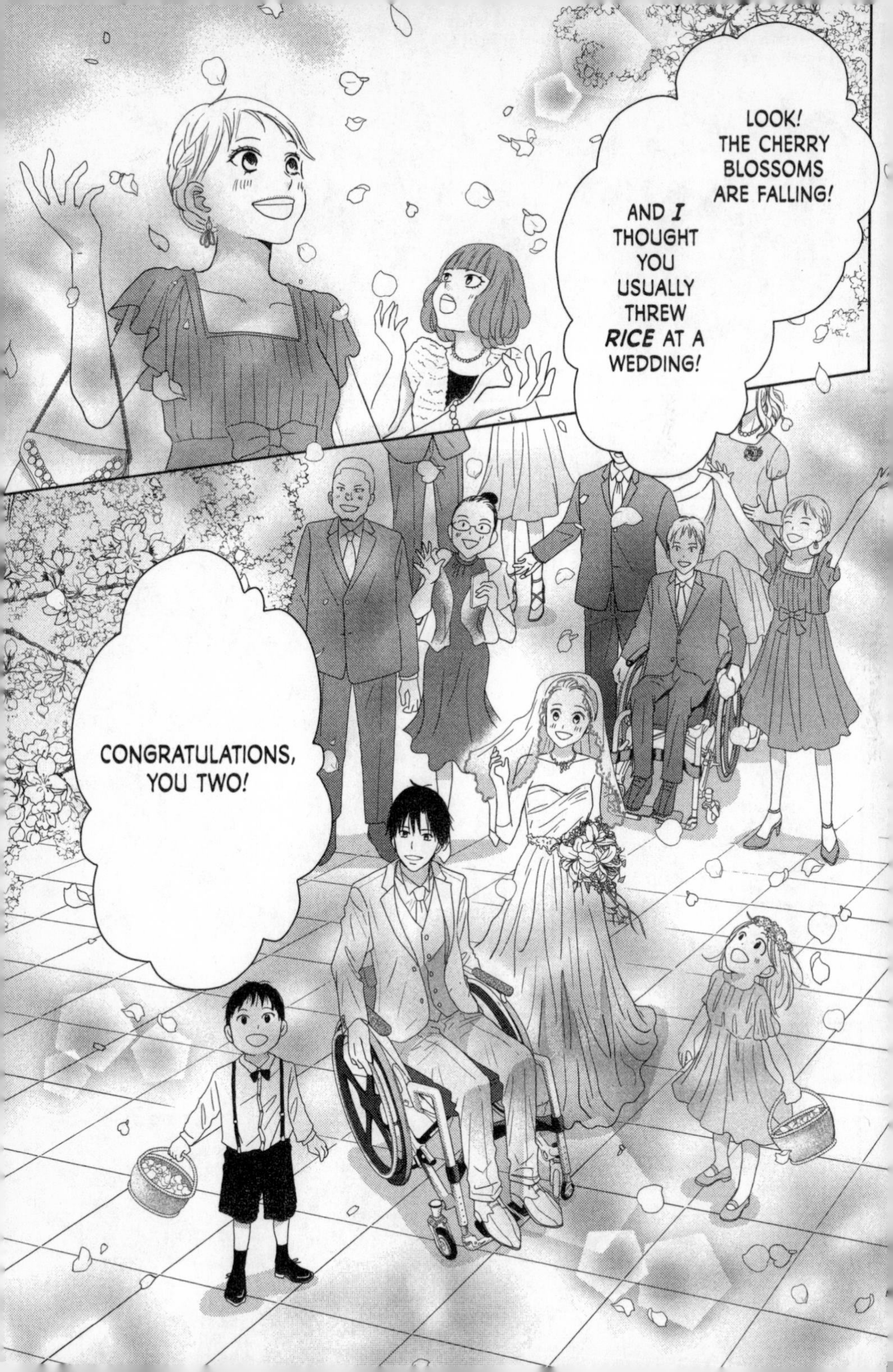
LOOK! THE CHERRY BLOSSOMS ARE FALLING!
AND *I* THOUGHT YOU USUALLY THREW *RICE* AT A WEDDING!
CONGRATULATIONS, YOU TWO!

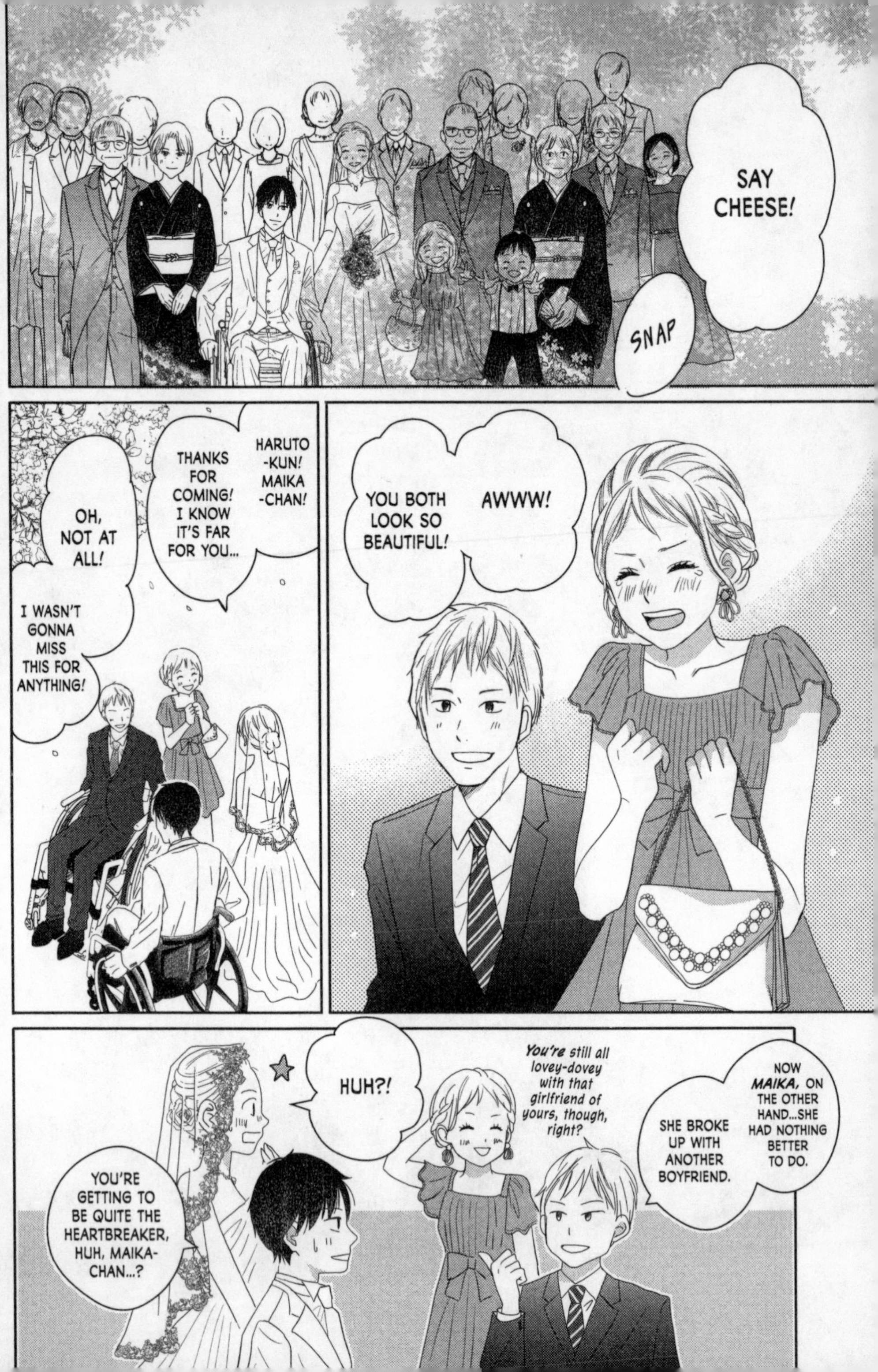
SAY CHEESE!
SNAP
AWWW!
YOU BOTH LOOK SO BEAUTIFUL!
HARUTO-KUN! MAIKA-CHAN!
THANKS FOR COMING! I KNOW IT'S FAR FOR YOU...
OH, NOT AT ALL!
I WASN'T GONNA MISS THIS FOR ANYTHING!
NOW *MAIKA,* ON THE OTHER HAND...SHE HAD NOTHING BETTER TO DO.
SHE BROKE UP WITH ANOTHER BOYFRIEND.
You're still all lovey-dovey with that girlfriend of yours, though, right?
HUH?!
YOU'RE GETTING TO BE QUITE THE HEARTBREAKER, HUH, MAIKA-CHAN...?

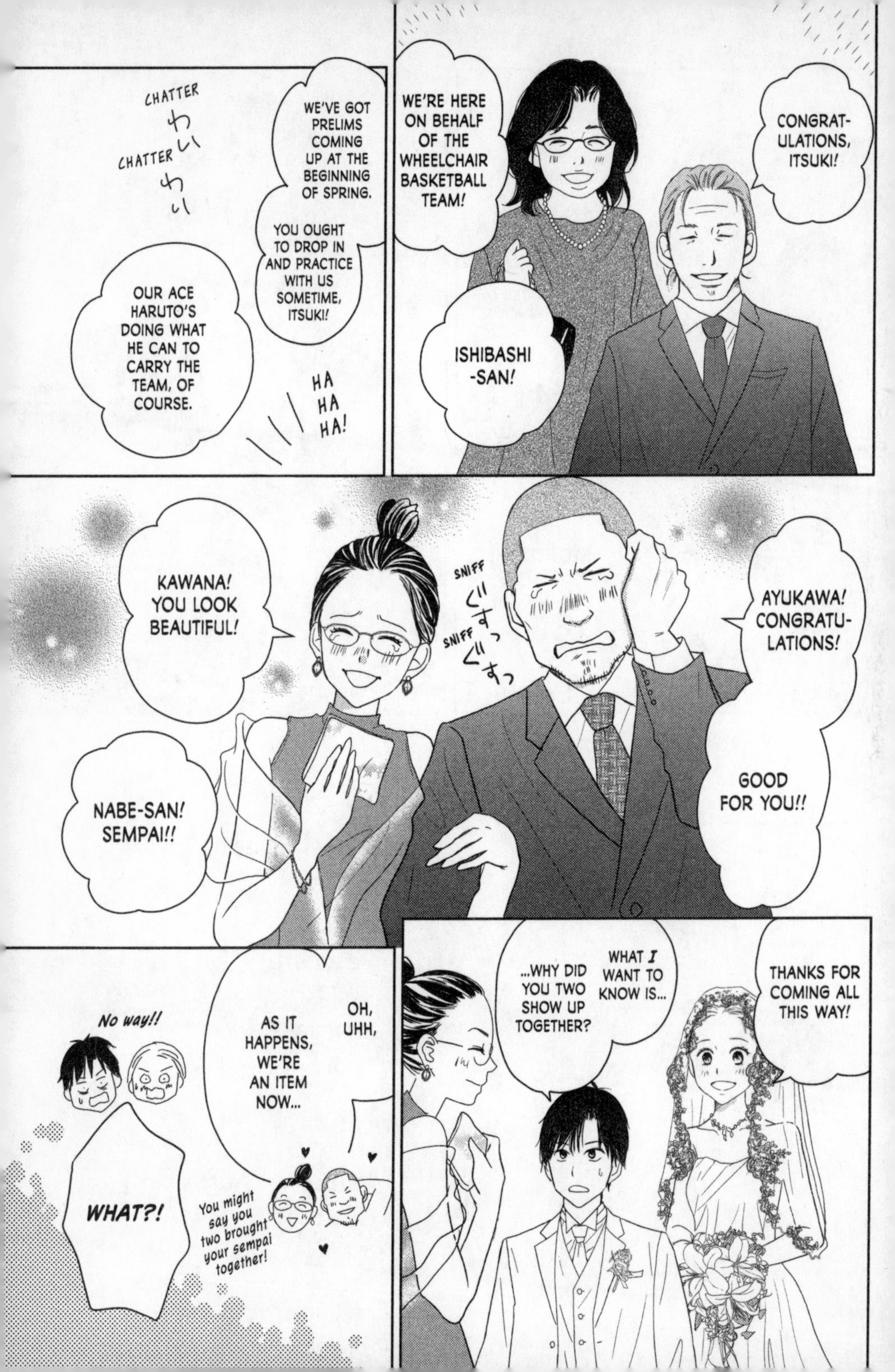
CONGRATULATIONS, ITSUKI!
WE'RE HERE ON BEHALF OF THE WHEELCHAIR BASKETBALL TEAM!
ISHIBASHI-SAN!
WE'VE GOT PRELIMS COMING UP AT THE BEGINNING OF SPRING.
YOU OUGHT TO DROP IN AND PRACTICE WITH US SOMETIME, ITSUKI!
CHATTER わい
CHATTER わい
OUR ACE HARUTO'S DOING WHAT HE CAN TO CARRY THE TEAM, OF COURSE.
HA HA HA!
AYUKAWA! CONGRATULATIONS!
GOOD FOR YOU!!
SNIFF ぐすっ
SNIFF ぐすっ
KAWANA! YOU LOOK BEAUTIFUL!
NABE-SAN! SEMPAI!!
THANKS FOR COMING ALL THIS WAY!
WHAT I WANT TO KNOW IS...
...WHY DID YOU TWO SHOW UP TOGETHER?
OH, UHH,
AS IT HAPPENS, WE'RE AN ITEM NOW...
You might say you two brought your sempai together!
No way!!
WHAT?!

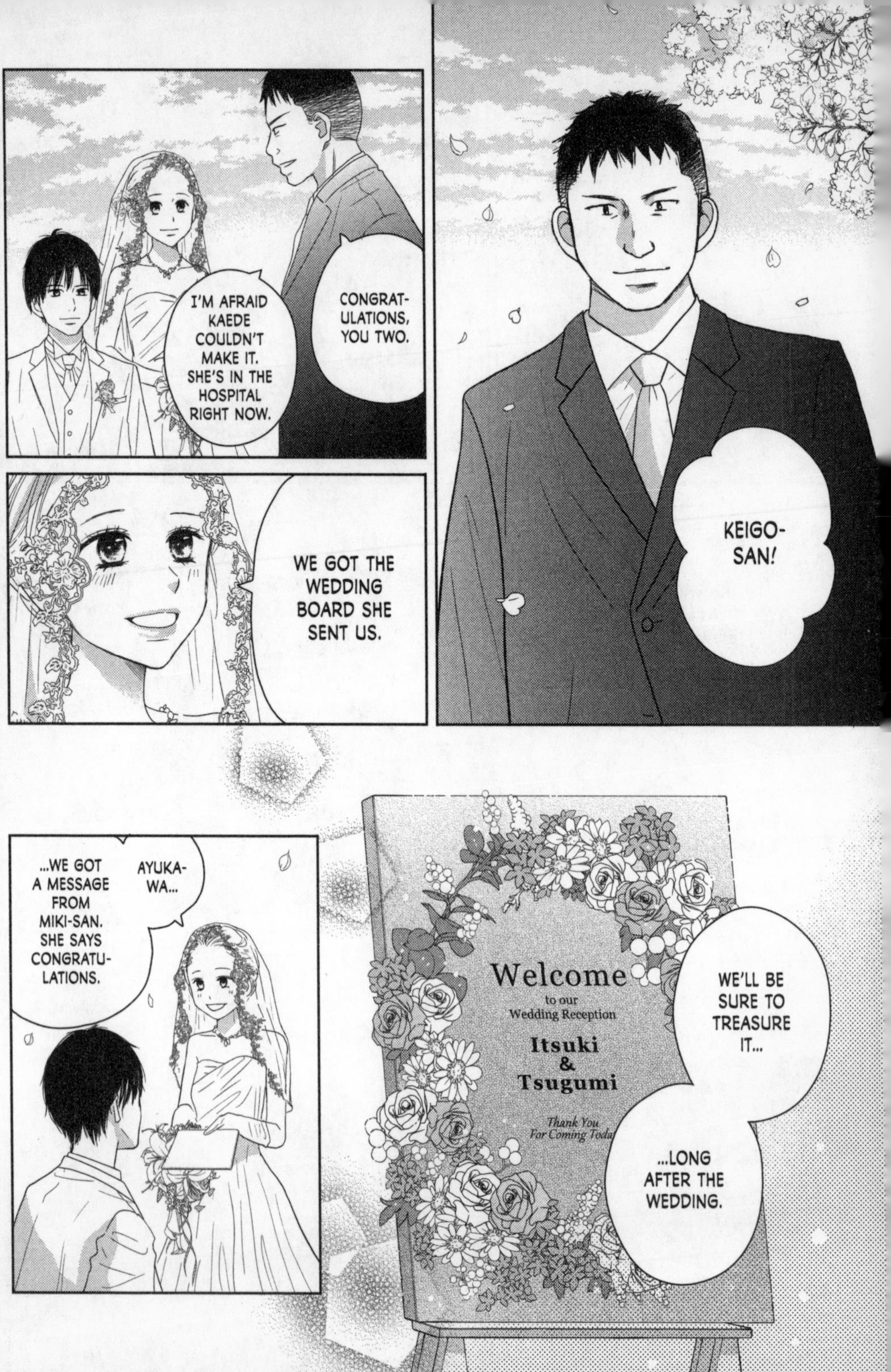
KEIGO-SAN!
CONGRAT-ULATIONS, YOU TWO.
I'M AFRAID KAEDE COULDN'T MAKE IT. SHE'S IN THE HOSPITAL RIGHT NOW.
WE GOT THE WEDDING BOARD SHE SENT US.
Welcome
to our
Wedding Reception
Itsuki
&
Tsugumi
Thank You
For Coming Toda
WE'LL BE SURE TO TREASURE IT...
...LONG AFTER THE WEDDING.
AYUKA-WA...
...WE GOT A MESSAGE FROM MIKI-SAN. SHE SAYS CONGRATU-LATIONS.

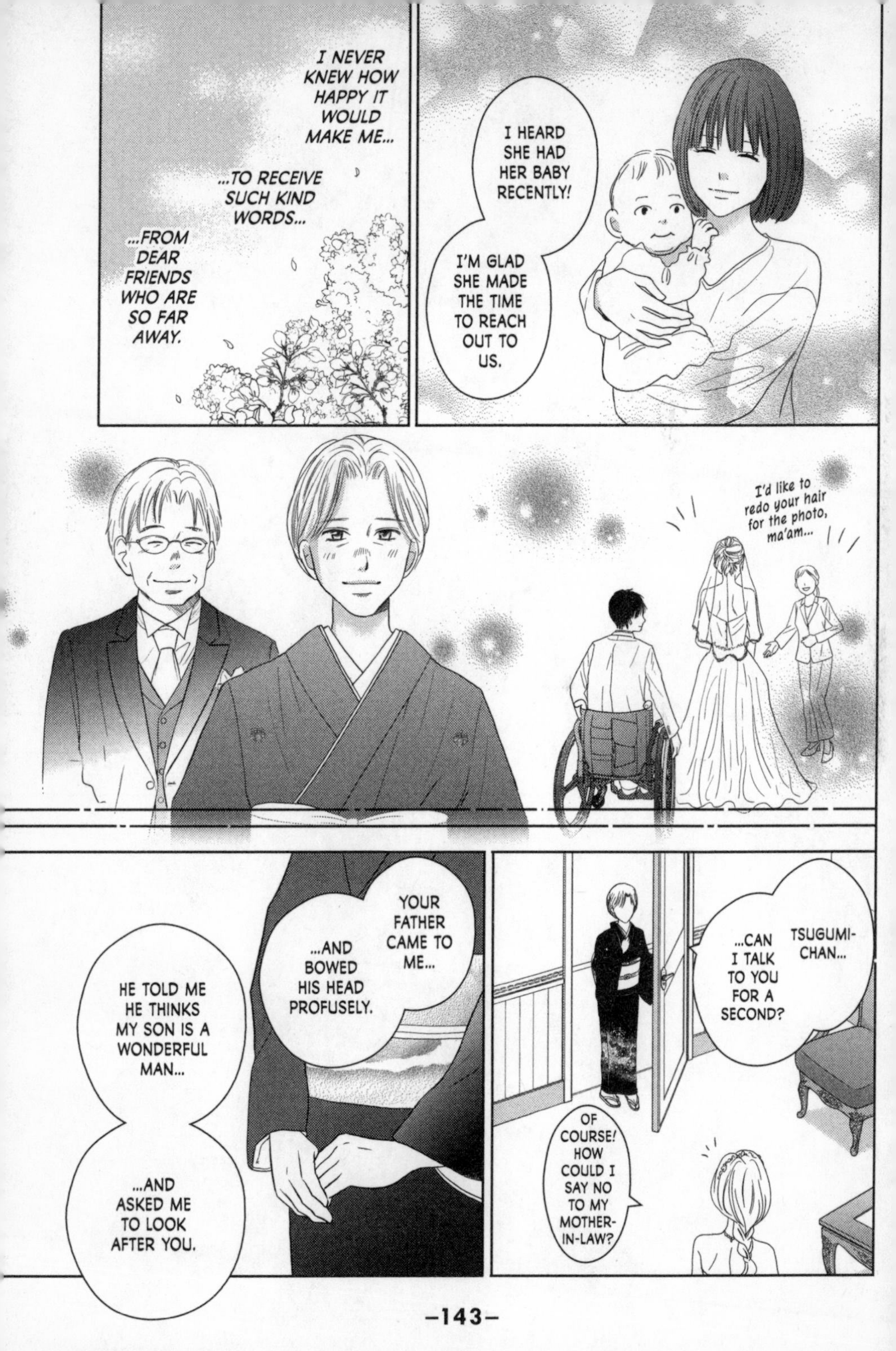
I HEARD SHE HAD HER BABY RECENTLY!
I'M GLAD SHE MADE THE TIME TO REACH OUT TO US.
I NEVER KNEW HOW HAPPY IT WOULD MAKE ME...
...TO RECEIVE SUCH KIND WORDS...
...FROM DEAR FRIENDS WHO ARE SO FAR AWAY.
I'd like to redo your hair for the photo, ma'am...
TSUGUMI-CHAN...
...CAN I TALK TO YOU FOR A SECOND?
OF COURSE! HOW COULD I SAY NO TO MY MOTHER-IN-LAW?
YOUR FATHER CAME TO ME...
...AND BOWED HIS HEAD PROFUSELY.
HE TOLD ME HE THINKS MY SON IS A WONDERFUL MAN...
...AND ASKED ME TO LOOK AFTER YOU.

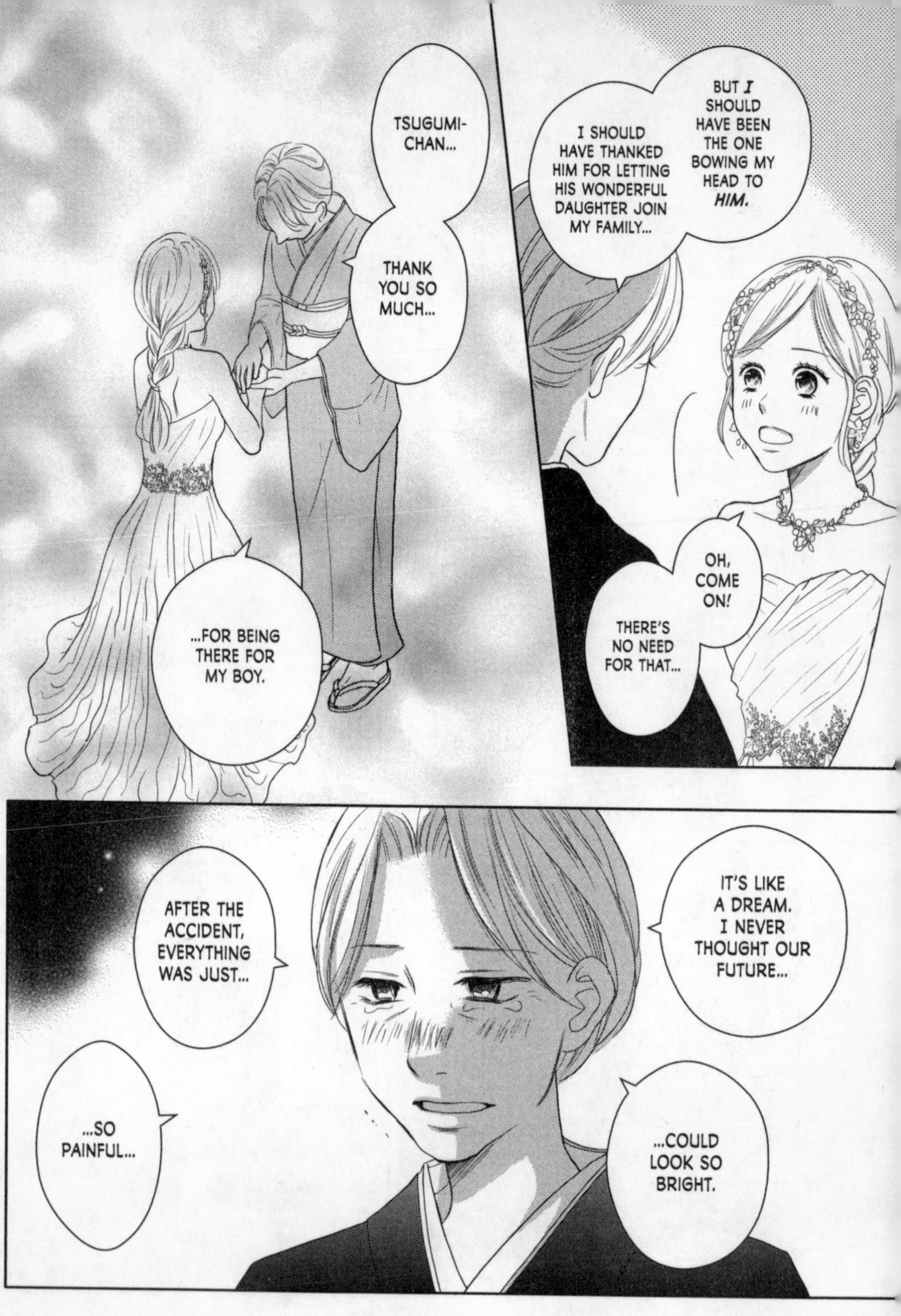

BUT *I* SHOULD HAVE BEEN THE ONE BOWING MY HEAD TO ***HIM.***
I SHOULD HAVE THANKED HIM FOR LETTING HIS WONDERFUL DAUGHTER JOIN MY FAMILY...
OH, COME ON!
THERE'S NO NEED FOR THAT...
TSUGUMI-CHAN...
THANK YOU SO MUCH...
...FOR BEING THERE FOR MY BOY.
IT'S LIKE A DREAM. I NEVER THOUGHT OUR FUTURE...
AFTER THE ACCIDENT, EVERYTHING WAS JUST...
...COULD LOOK SO BRIGHT.
...SO PAINFUL...

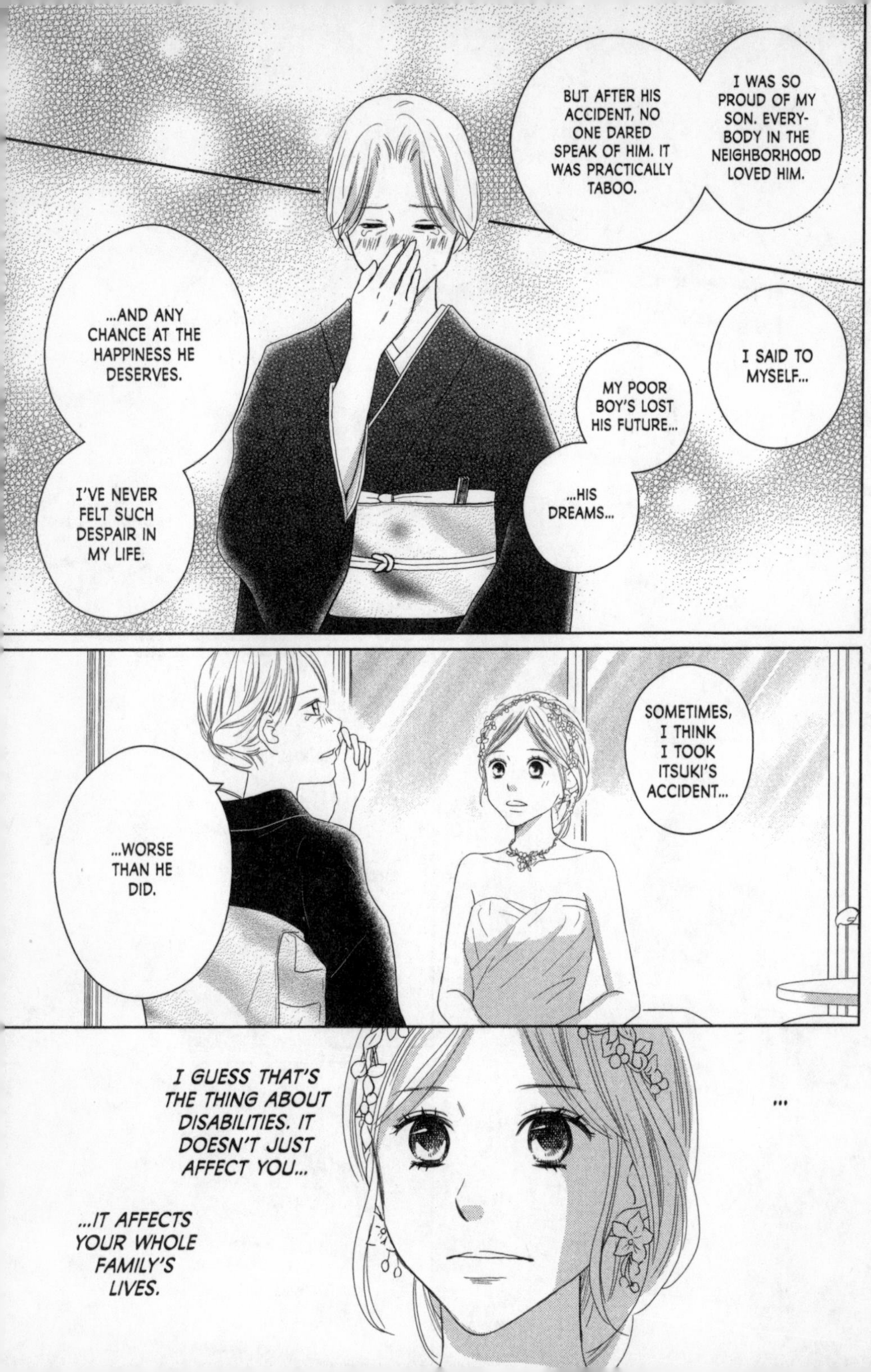
I WAS SO PROUD OF MY SON. EVERYBODY IN THE NEIGHBORHOOD LOVED HIM.
BUT AFTER HIS ACCIDENT, NO ONE DARED SPEAK OF HIM. IT WAS PRACTICALLY TABOO.
I SAID TO MYSELF...
MY POOR BOY'S LOST HIS FUTURE...
...HIS DREAMS...
...AND ANY CHANCE AT THE HAPPINESS HE DESERVES.
I'VE NEVER FELT SUCH DESPAIR IN MY LIFE.
SOMETIMES, I THINK I TOOK ITSUKI'S ACCIDENT...
...WORSE THAN HE DID.
...
I GUESS THAT'S THE THING ABOUT DISABILITIES. IT DOESN'T JUST AFFECT YOU...
...IT AFFECTS YOUR WHOLE FAMILY'S LIVES.

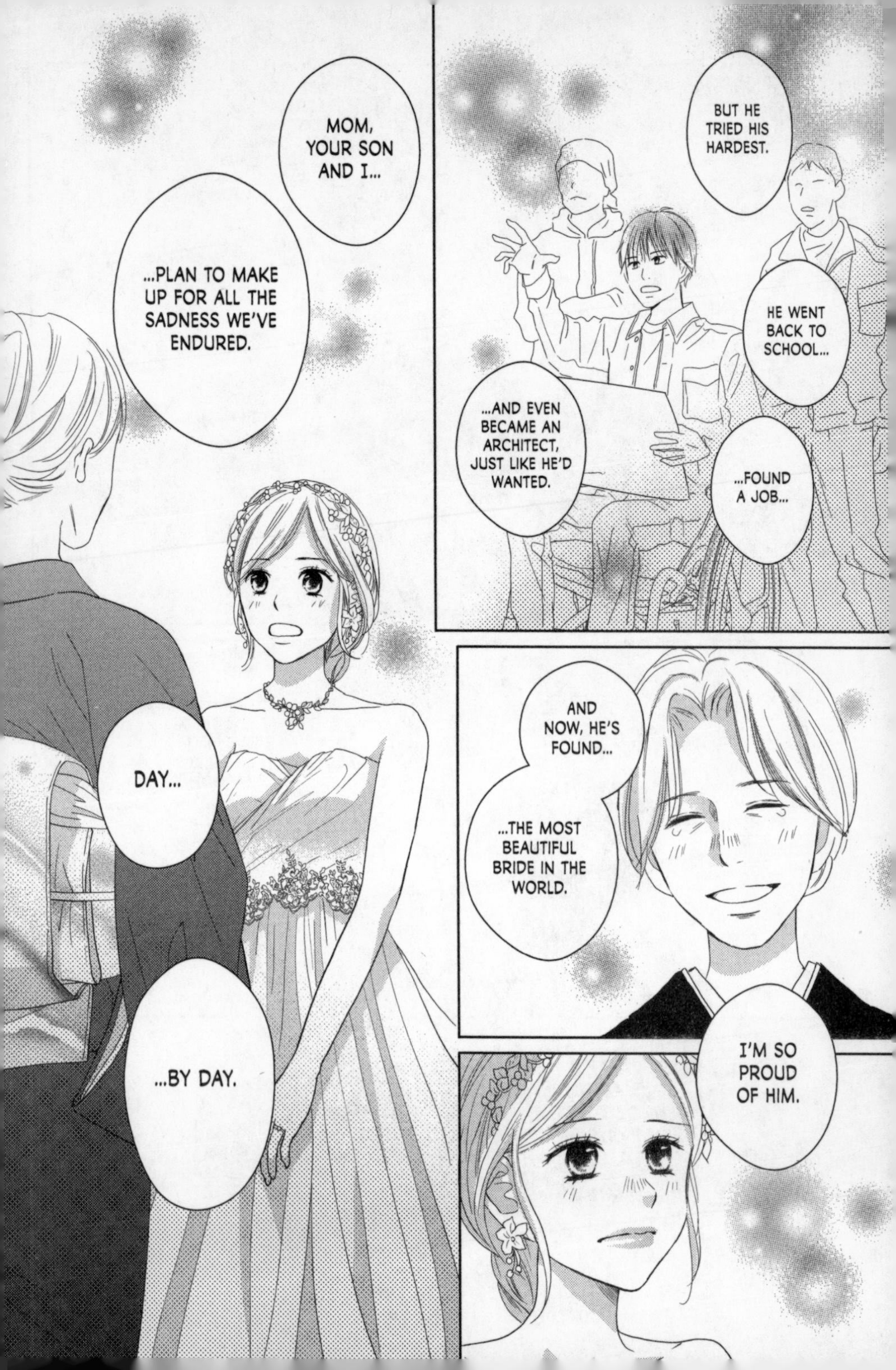
BUT HE TRIED HIS HARDEST.
HE WENT BACK TO SCHOOL...
...FOUND A JOB...
...AND EVEN BECAME AN ARCHITECT, JUST LIKE HE'D WANTED.
AND NOW, HE'S FOUND...
...THE MOST BEAUTIFUL BRIDE IN THE WORLD.
I'M SO PROUD OF HIM.
MOM, YOUR SON AND I...
...PLAN TO MAKE UP FOR ALL THE SADNESS WE'VE ENDURED.
DAY...
...BY DAY.

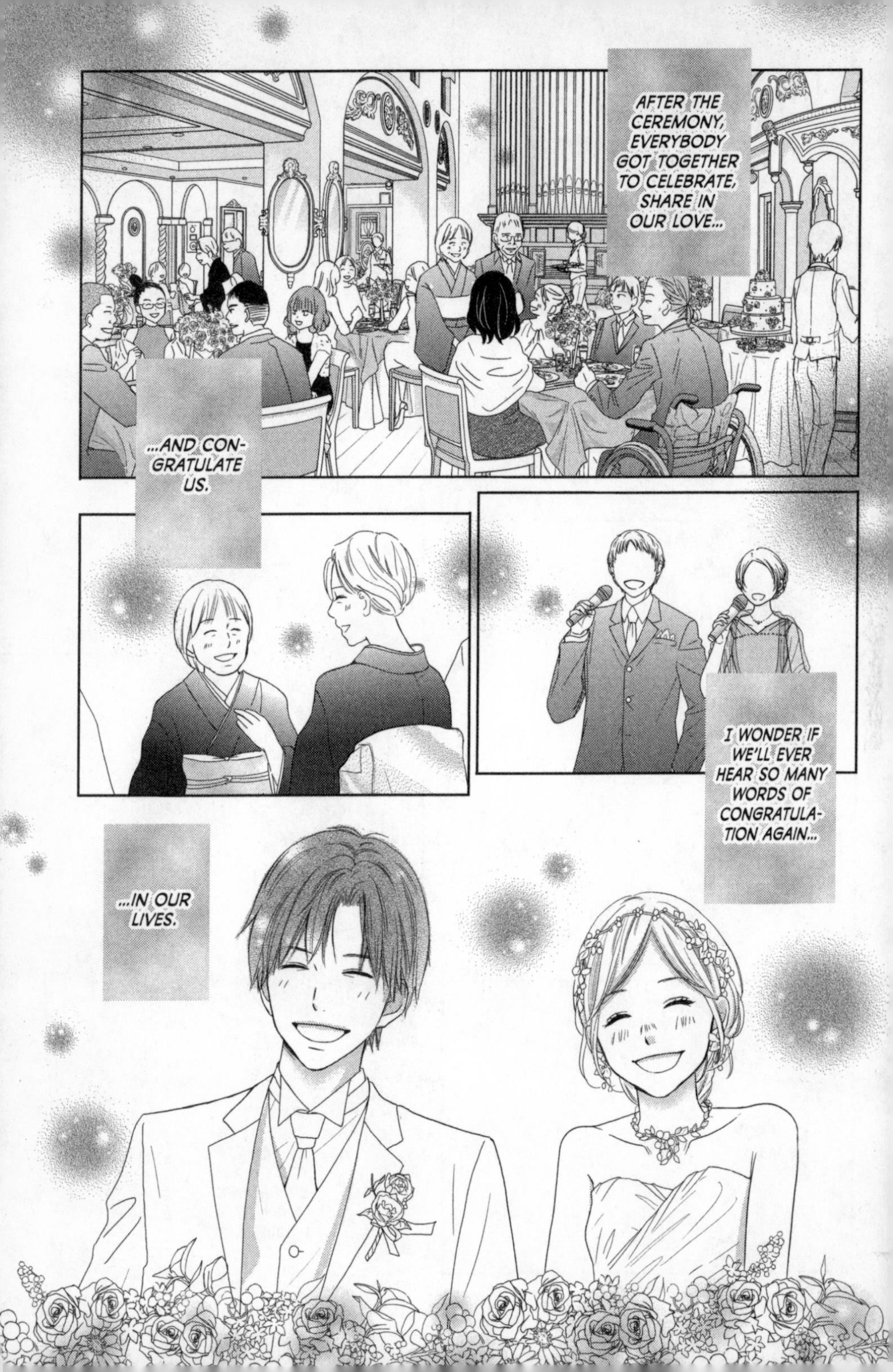
AFTER THE CEREMONY, EVERYBODY GOT TOGETHER TO CELEBRATE, SHARE IN OUR LOVE...
...AND CON-GRATULATE US.
I WONDER IF WE'LL EVER HEAR SO MANY WORDS OF CONGRATULA-TION AGAIN...
...IN OUR LIVES.

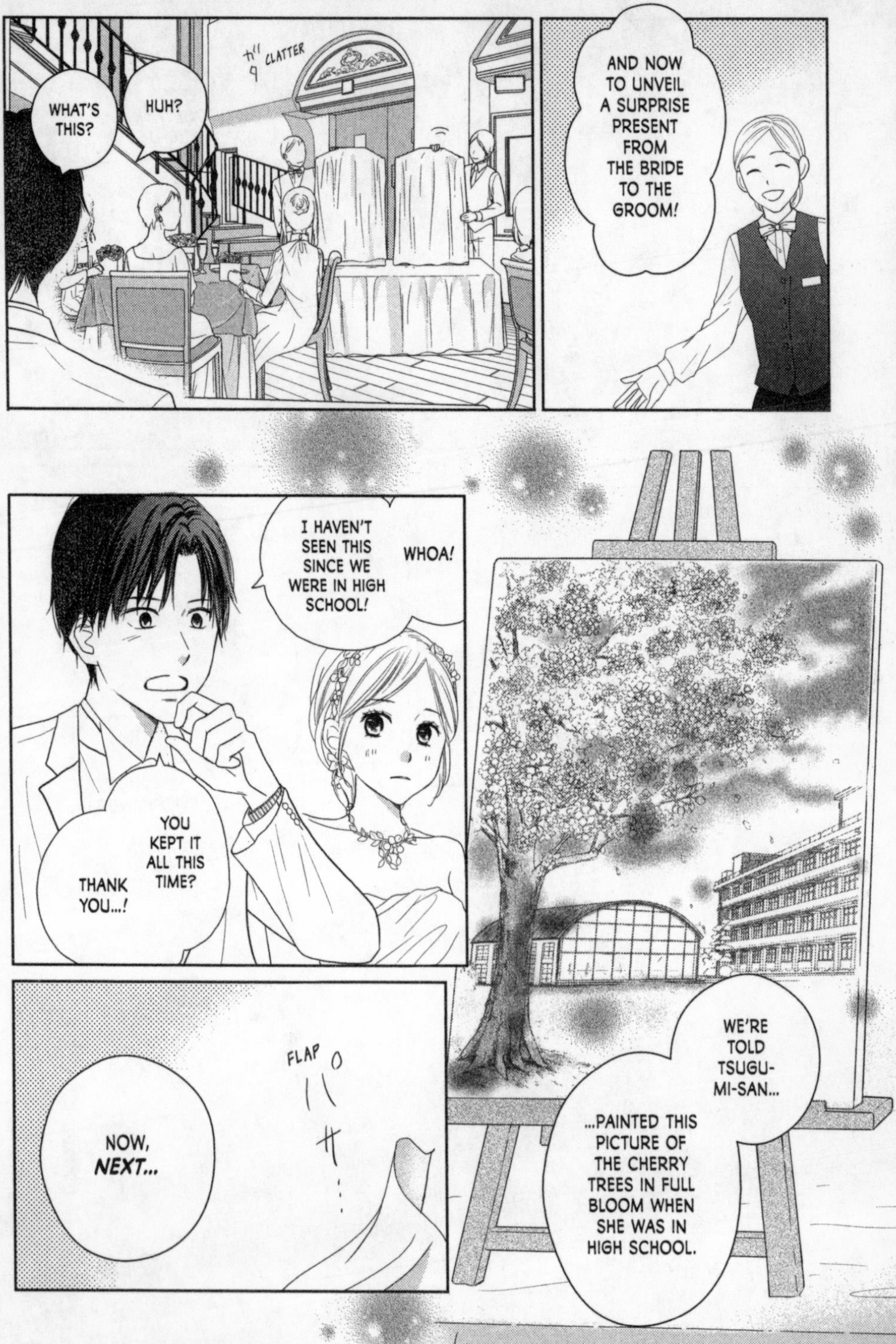
AND NOW TO UNVEIL A SURPRISE PRESENT FROM THE BRIDE TO THE GROOM!
CLATTER
HUH?
WHAT'S THIS?
WE'RE TOLD TSUGU-MI-SAN...
...PAINTED THIS PICTURE OF THE CHERRY TREES IN FULL BLOOM WHEN SHE WAS IN HIGH SCHOOL.
WHOA!
I HAVEN'T SEEN THIS SINCE WE WERE IN HIGH SCHOOL!
YOU KEPT IT ALL THIS TIME?
THANK YOU...!
FLAP
NOW, ***NEXT...***

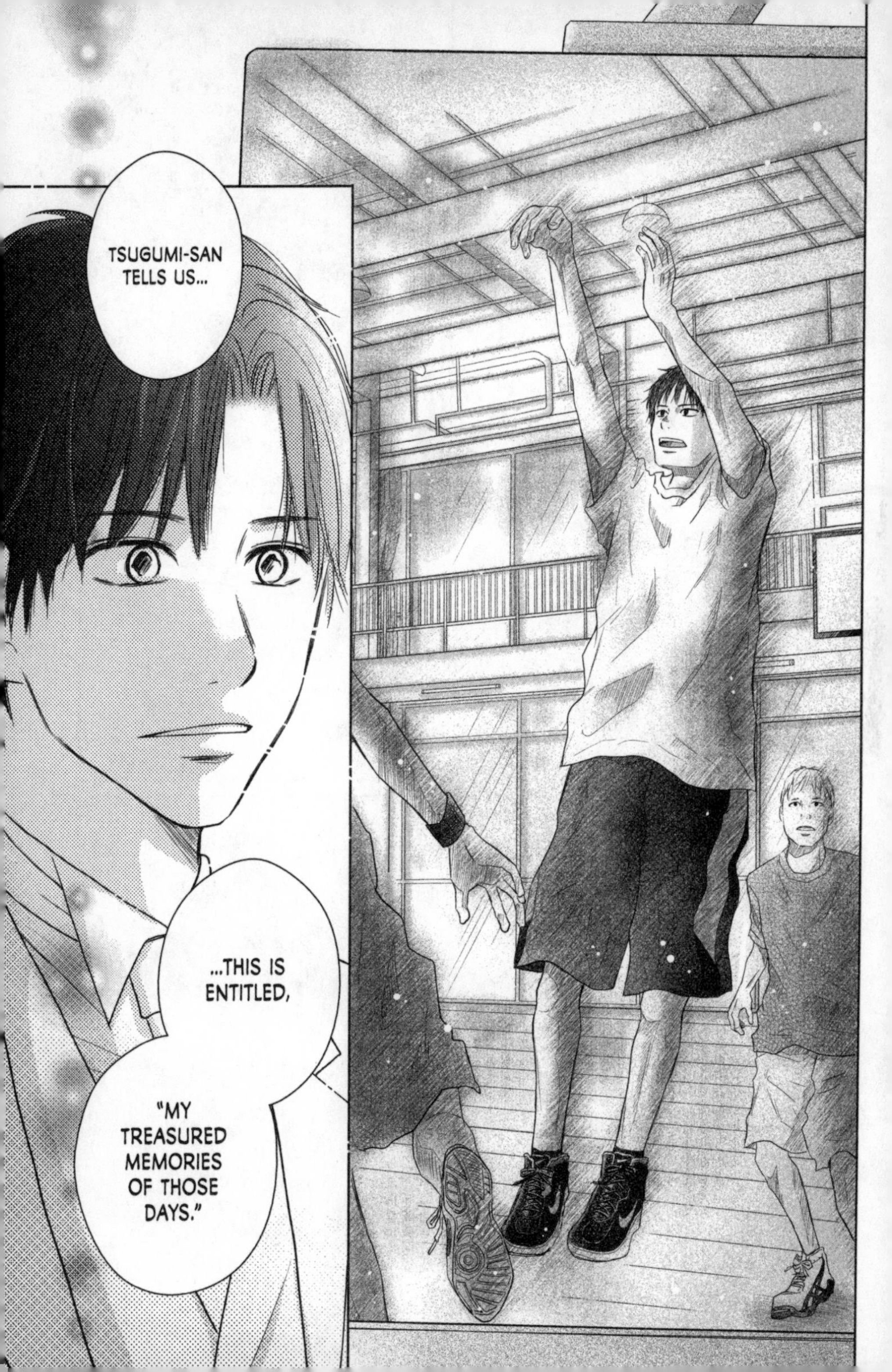
TSUGUMI-SAN TELLS US...
...THIS IS ENTITLED,
"MY TREASURED MEMORIES OF THOSE DAYS."

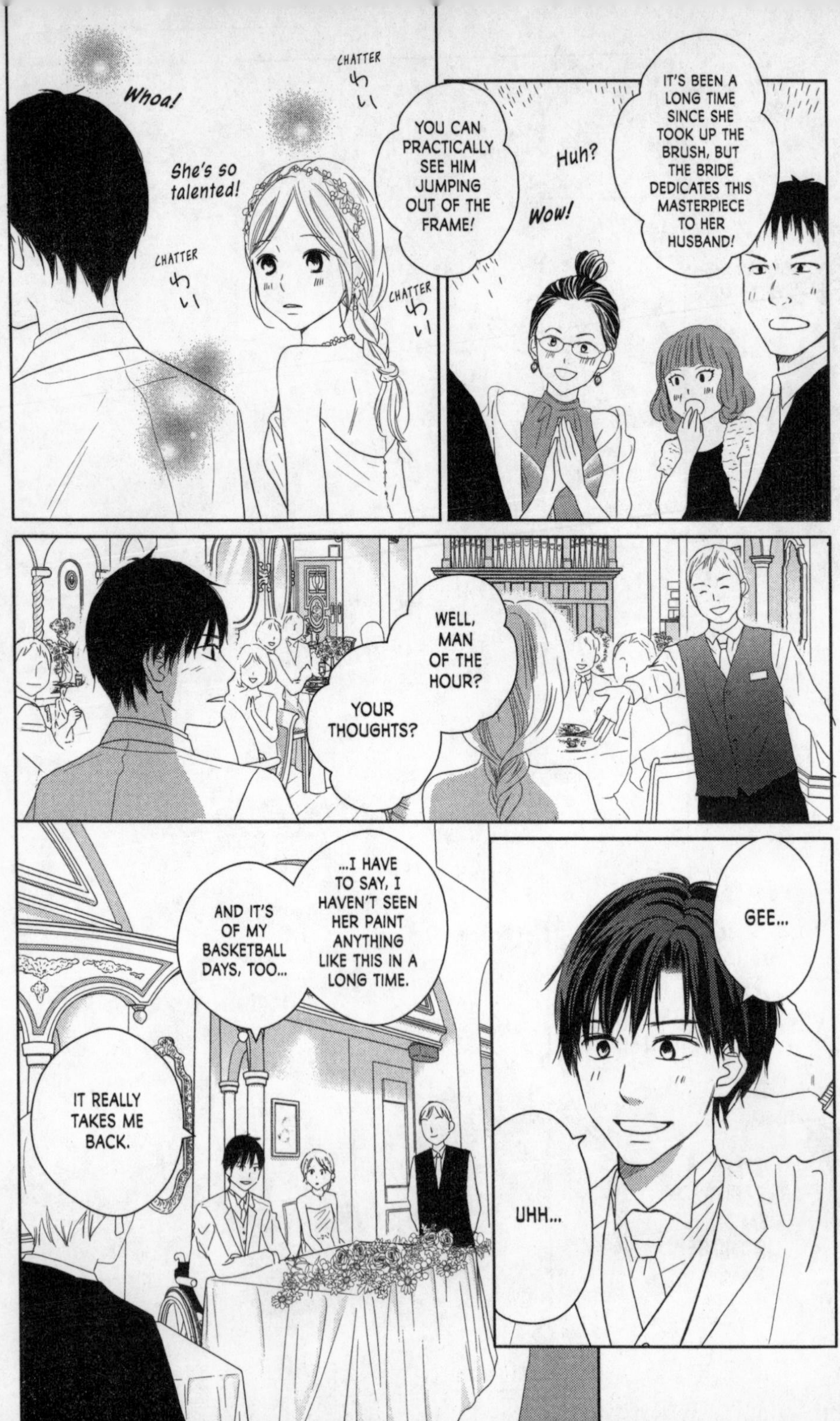
IT'S BEEN A LONG TIME SINCE SHE TOOK UP THE BRUSH, BUT THE BRIDE DEDICATES THIS MASTERPIECE TO HER HUSBAND!
Huh?
Wow!
YOU CAN PRACTICALLY SEE HIM JUMPING OUT OF THE FRAME!
CHATTER
わい
Whoa!
She's so talented!
CHATTER
わい
CHATTER
わい
WELL, MAN OF THE HOUR?
YOUR THOUGHTS?
GEE...
UHH...
...I HAVE TO SAY, I HAVEN'T SEEN HER PAINT ANYTHING LIKE THIS IN A LONG TIME.
AND IT'S OF MY BASKETBALL DAYS, TOO...
IT REALLY TAKES ME BACK.

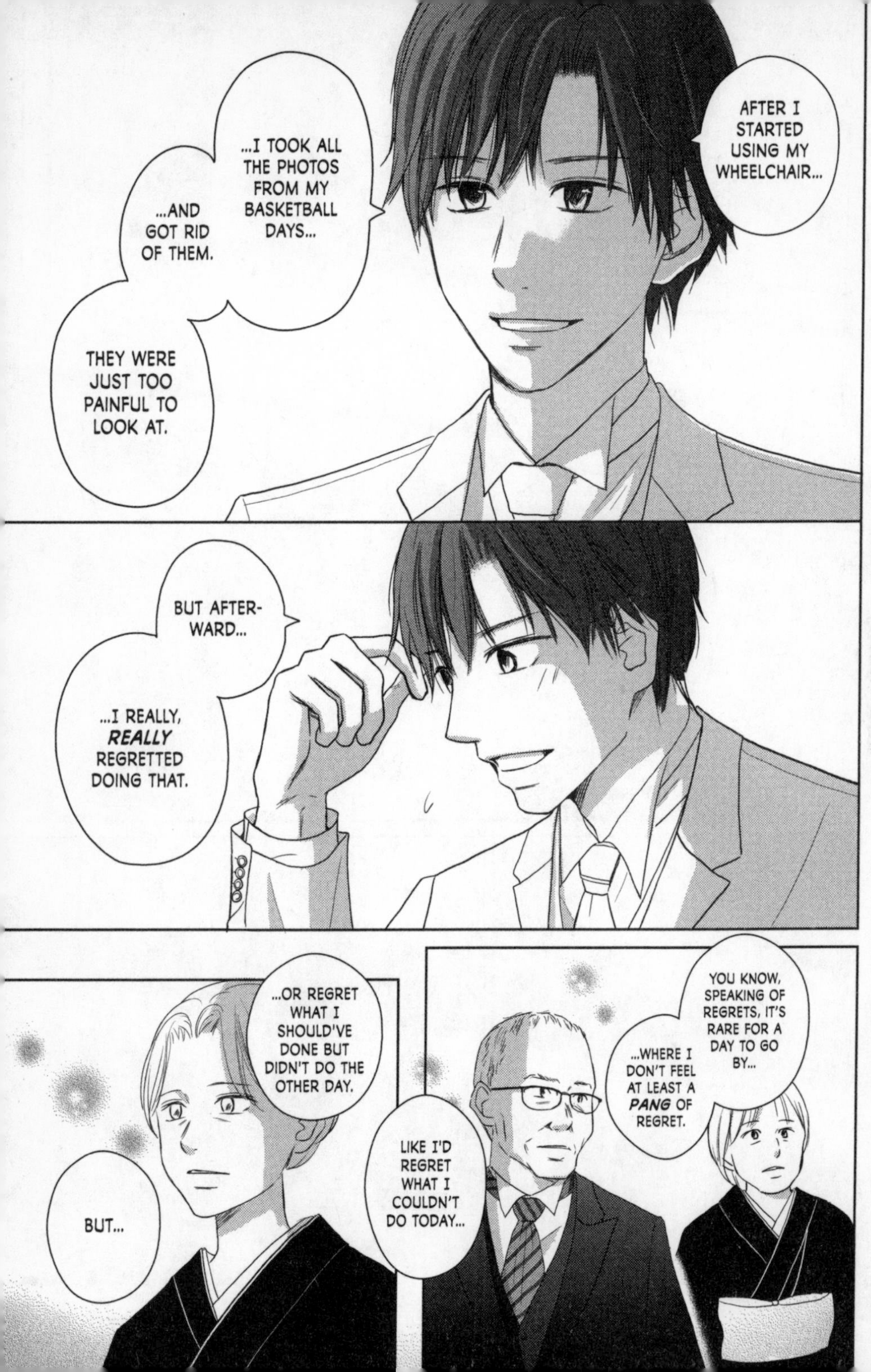
AFTER I STARTED USING MY WHEELCHAIR...
...I TOOK ALL THE PHOTOS FROM MY BASKETBALL DAYS...
...AND GOT RID OF THEM.
THEY WERE JUST TOO PAINFUL TO LOOK AT.
BUT AFTER-WARD...
...I REALLY, ***REALLY*** REGRETTED DOING THAT.
YOU KNOW, SPEAKING OF REGRETS, IT'S RARE FOR A DAY TO GO BY...
...WHERE I DON'T FEEL AT LEAST A ***PANG*** OF REGRET.
LIKE I'D REGRET WHAT I COULDN'T DO TODAY...
...OR REGRET WHAT I SHOULD'VE DONE BUT DIDN'T DO THE OTHER DAY.
BUT...

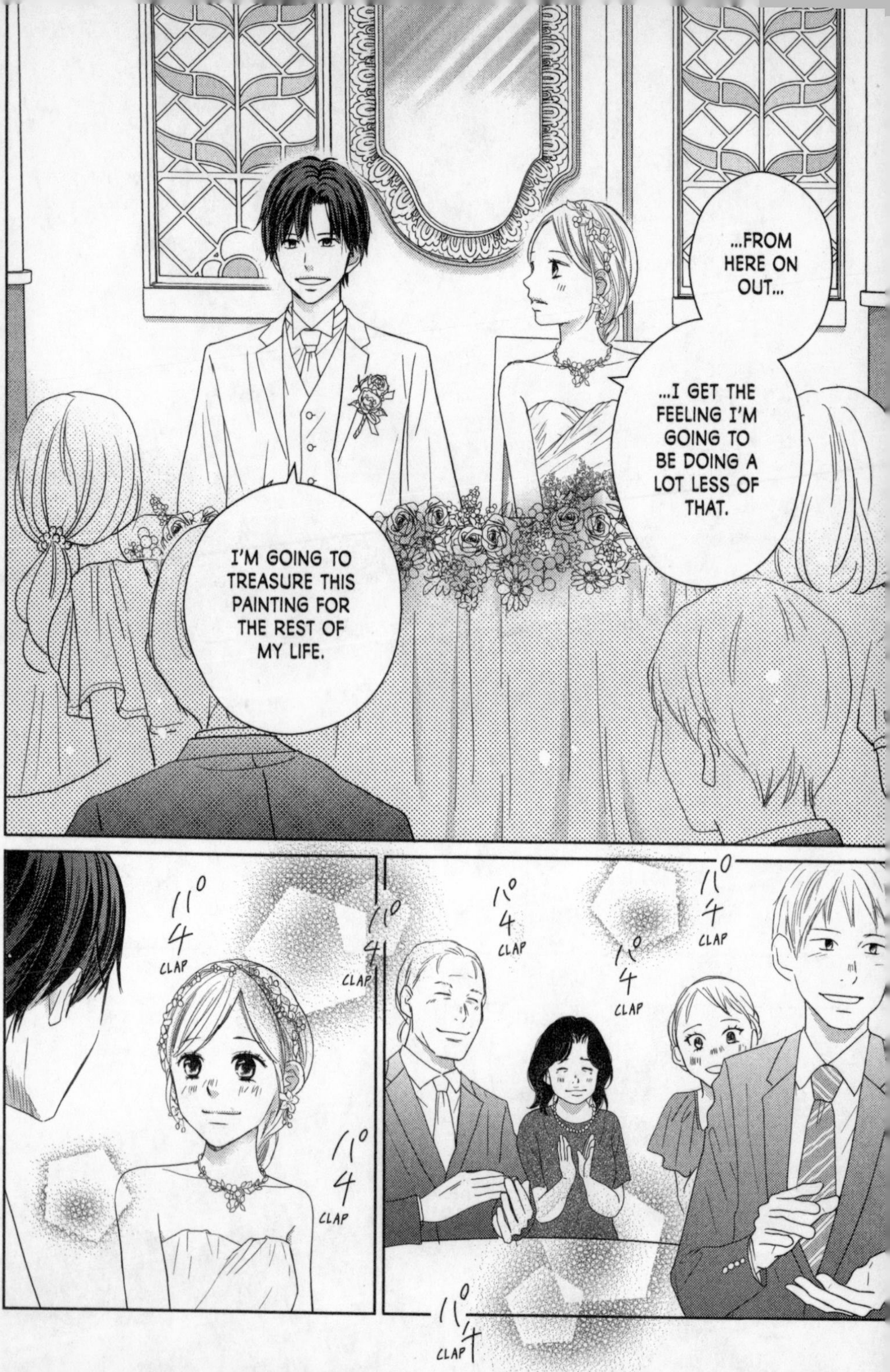
...FROM HERE ON OUT...
...I GET THE FEELING I'M GOING TO BE DOING A LOT LESS OF THAT.
I'M GOING TO TREASURE THIS PAINTING FOR THE REST OF MY LIFE.
パチ CLAP
パチ CLAP
パチ CLAP
パチ CLAP
パチ CLAP
パチ CLAP
パチ CLAP

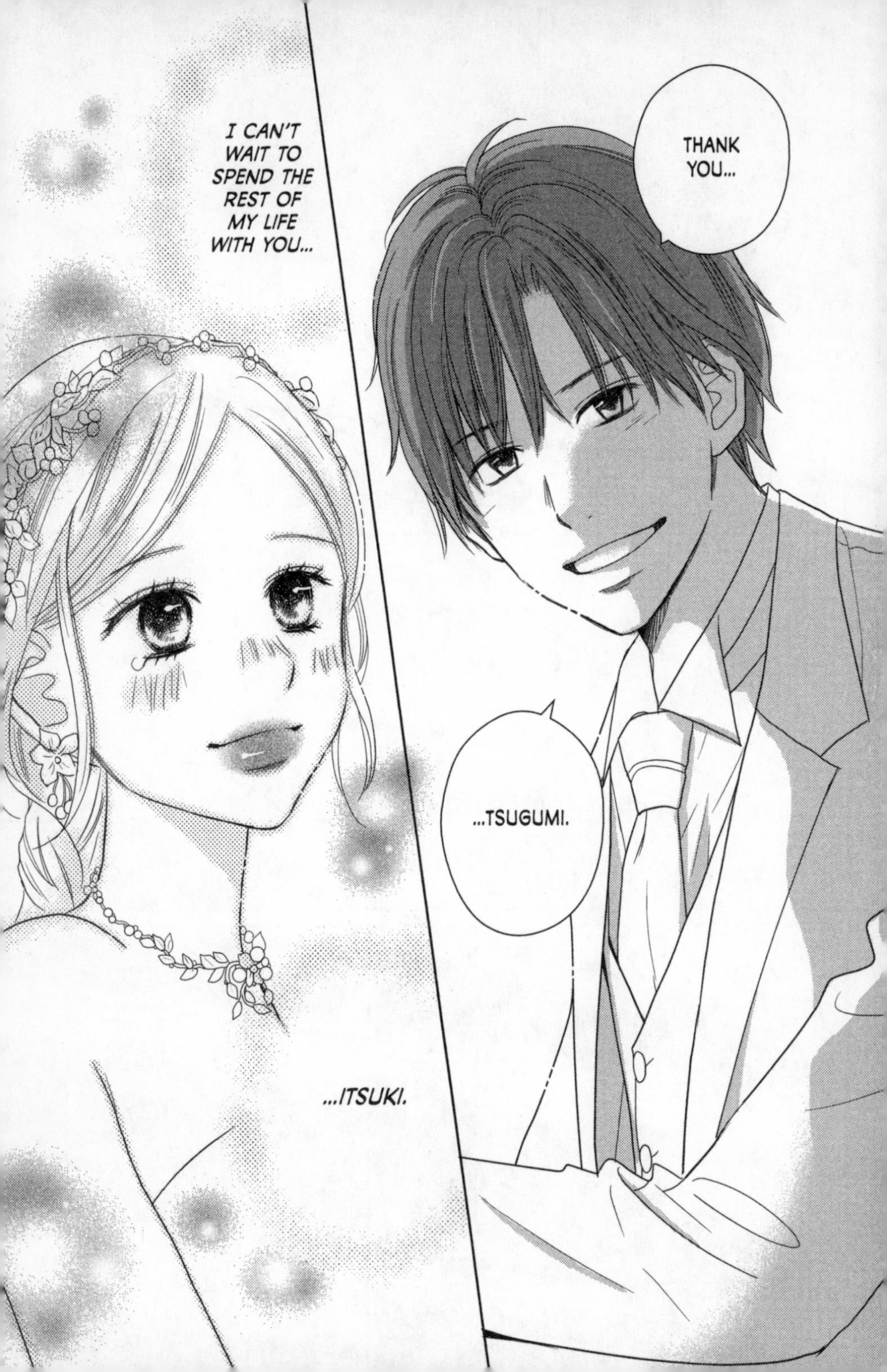
THANK YOU...
...TSUGUMI.
I CAN'T WAIT TO SPEND THE REST OF MY LIFE WITH YOU...
...ITSUKI.

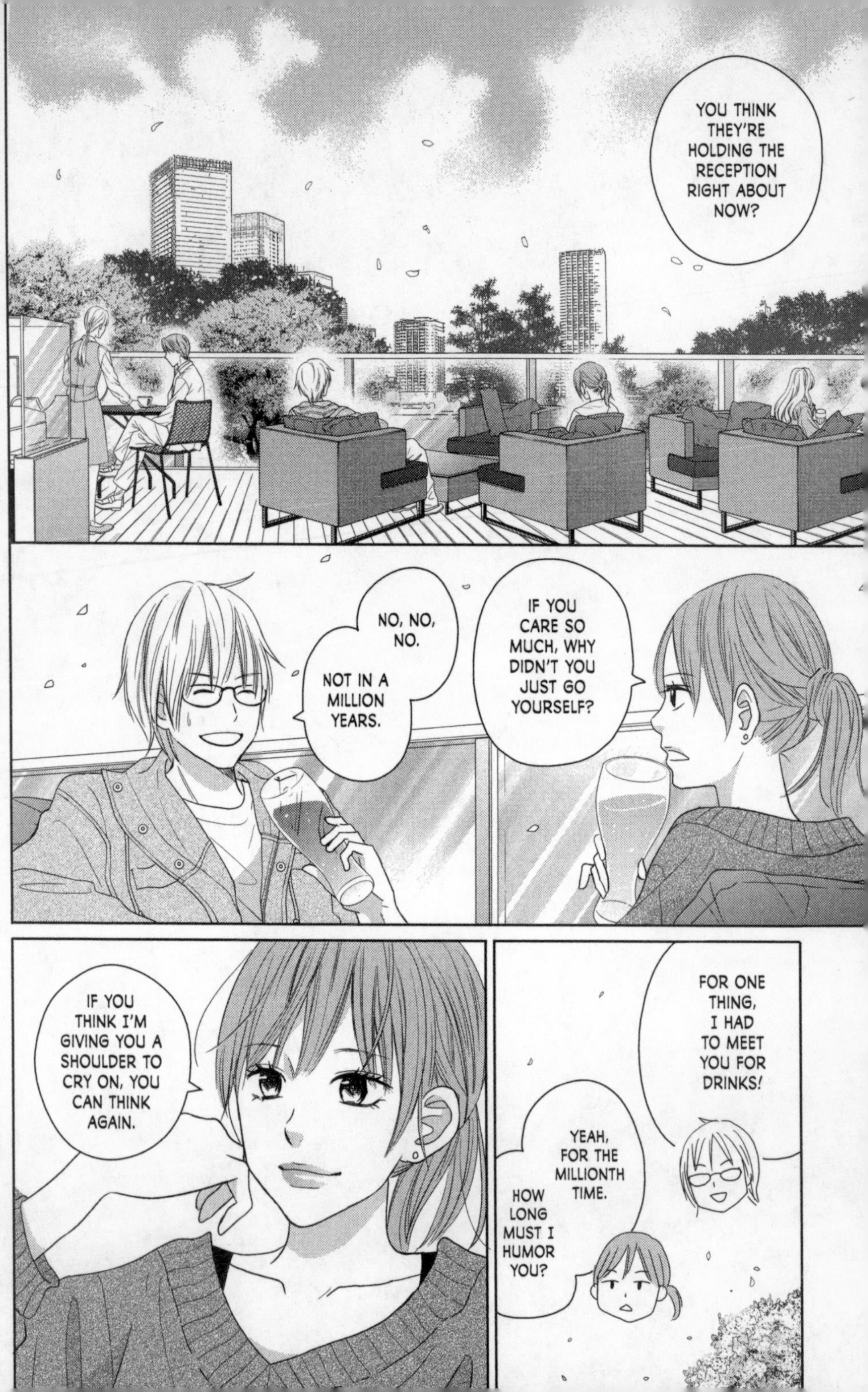
YOU THINK THEY'RE HOLDING THE RECEPTION RIGHT ABOUT NOW?
IF YOU CARE SO MUCH, WHY DIDN'T YOU JUST GO YOURSELF?
NO, NO, NO.
NOT IN A MILLION YEARS.
FOR ONE THING, I HAD TO MEET YOU FOR DRINKS!
YEAH, FOR THE MILLIONTH TIME.
HOW LONG MUST I HUMOR YOU?
IF YOU THINK I'M GIVING YOU A SHOULDER TO CRY ON, YOU CAN THINK AGAIN.

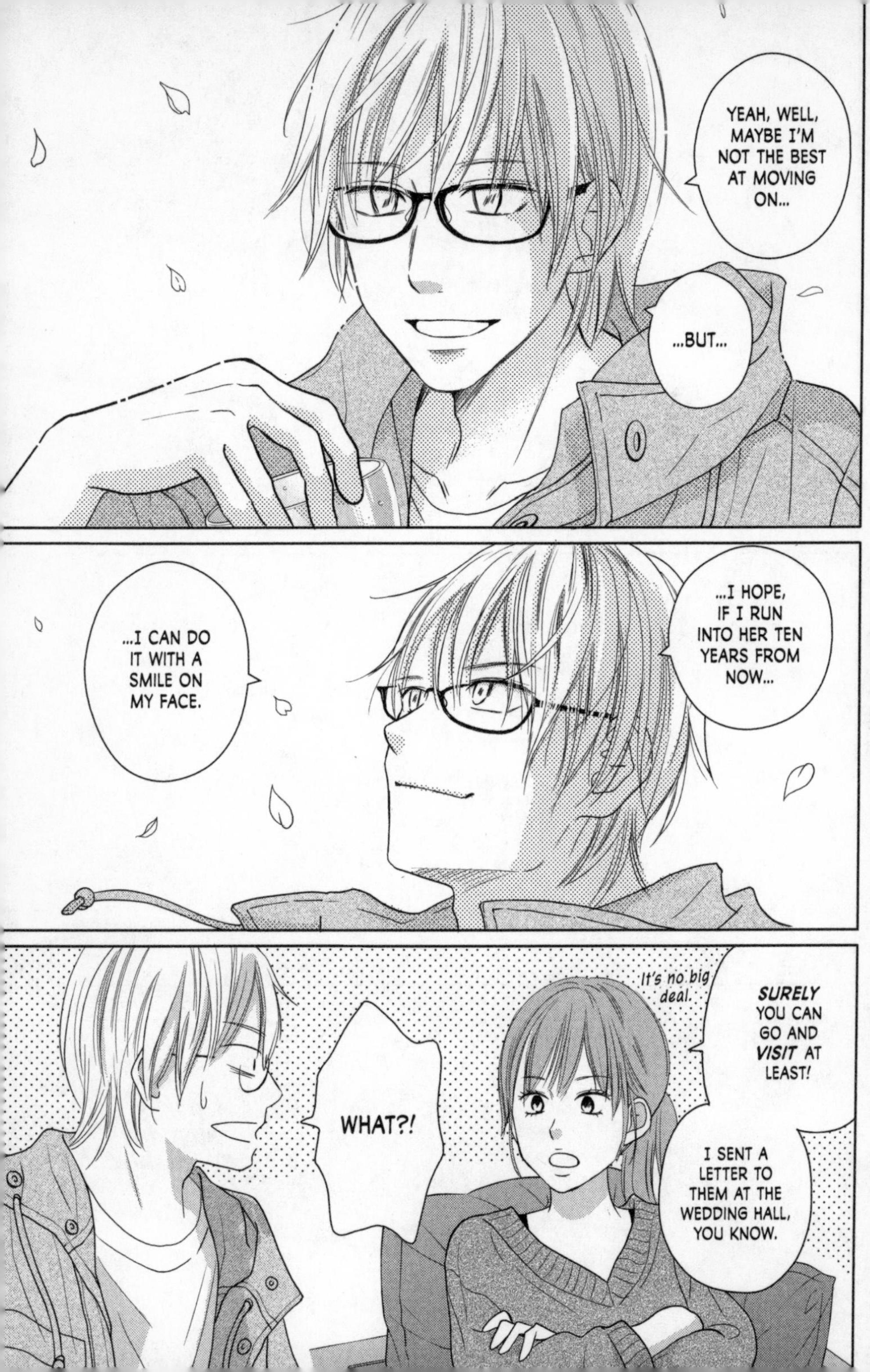
YEAH, WELL, MAYBE I'M NOT THE BEST AT MOVING ON...
...BUT...
...I HOPE, IF I RUN INTO HER TEN YEARS FROM NOW...
...I CAN DO IT WITH A SMILE ON MY FACE.
SURELY YOU CAN GO AND VISIT AT LEAST!
It's no big deal.
I SENT A LETTER TO THEM AT THE WEDDING HALL, YOU KNOW.
WHAT?!

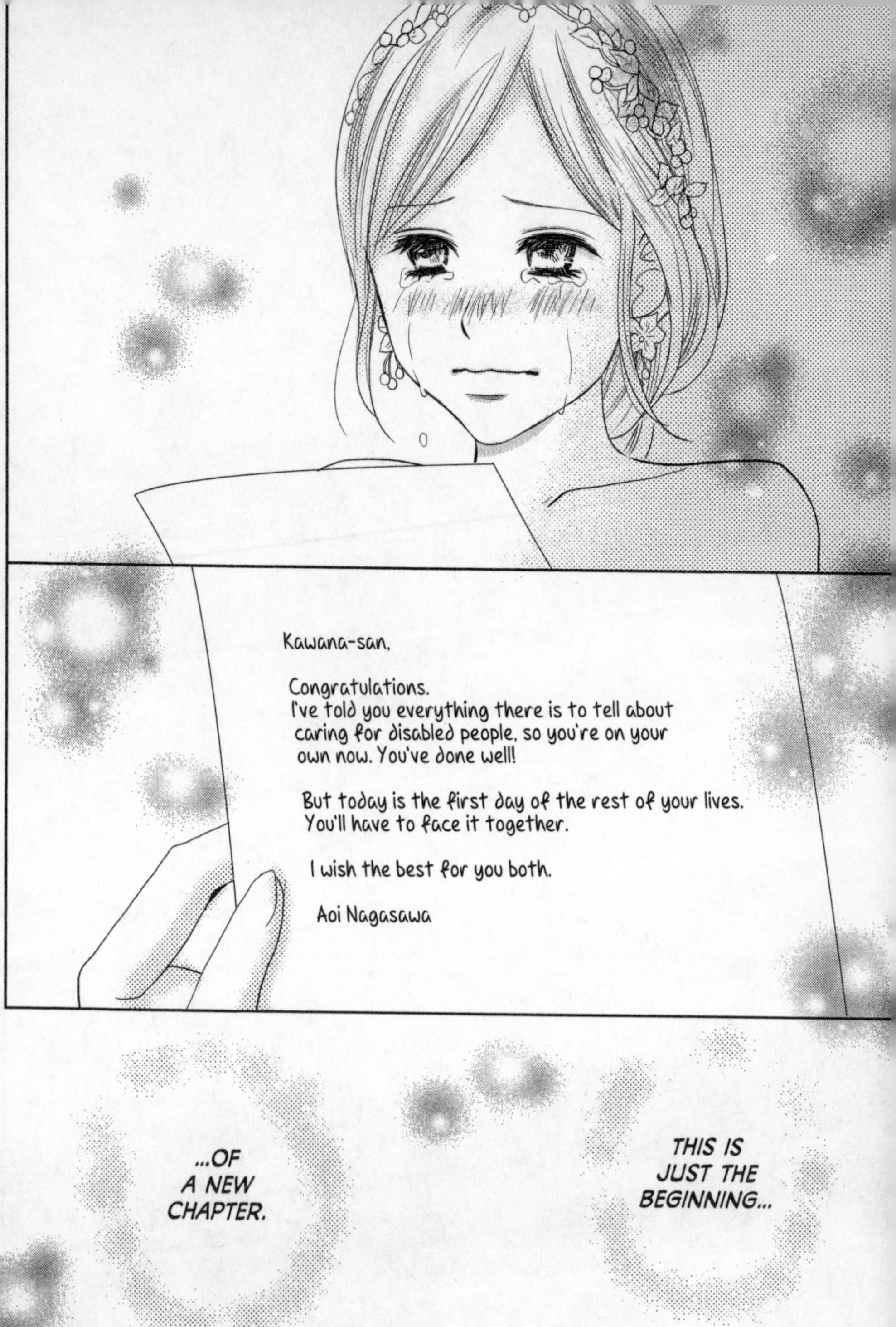
Kawana-san,
Congratulations.
I've told you everything there is to tell about caring for disabled people, so you're on your own now. You've done well!
But today is the first day of the rest of your lives. You'll have to face it together.
I wish the best for you both.
Aoi Nagasawa
THIS IS JUST THE BEGINNING...
...OF A NEW CHAPTER.

PERFECT WORLD 9 / THE END

~ BONUS MANGA ~

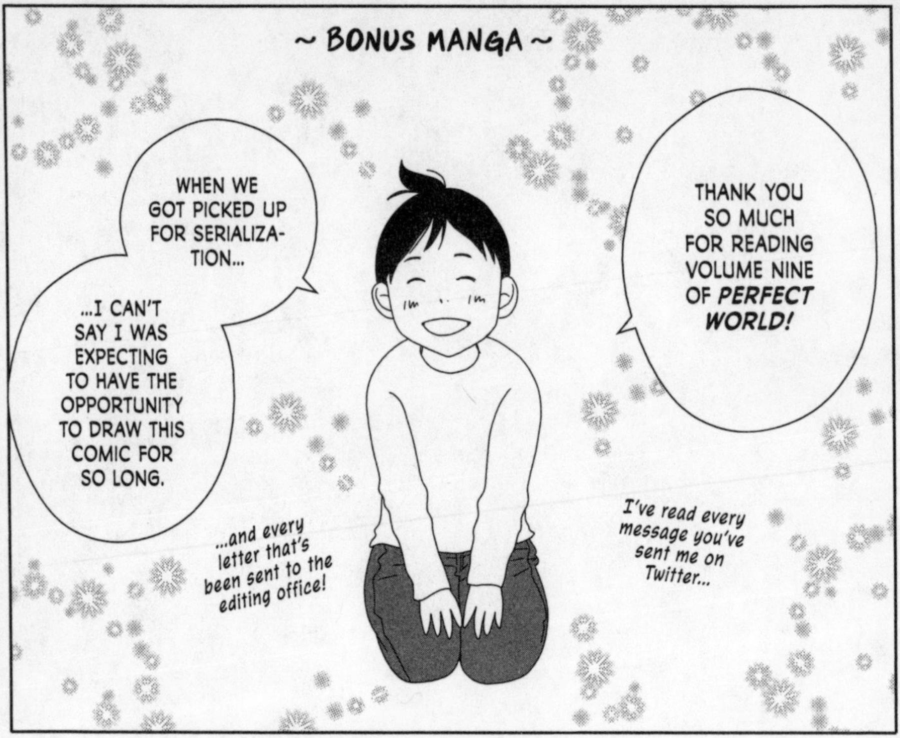
THANK YOU SO MUCH FOR READING VOLUME NINE OF *PERFECT WORLD!*
WHEN WE GOT PICKED UP FOR SERIALIZA-TION...
...I CAN'T SAY I WAS EXPECTING TO HAVE THE OPPORTUNITY TO DRAW THIS COMIC FOR SO LONG.
I've read every message you've sent me on Twitter...
...and every letter that's been sent to the editing office!

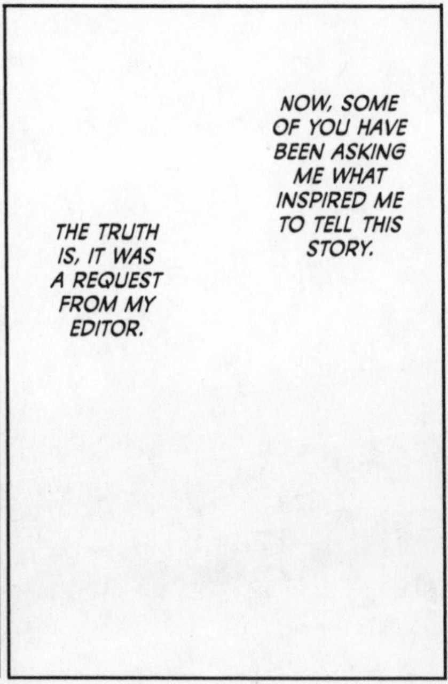
NOW, SOME OF YOU HAVE BEEN ASKING ME WHAT INSPIRED ME TO TELL THIS STORY.
THE TRUTH IS, IT WAS A REQUEST FROM MY EDITOR.

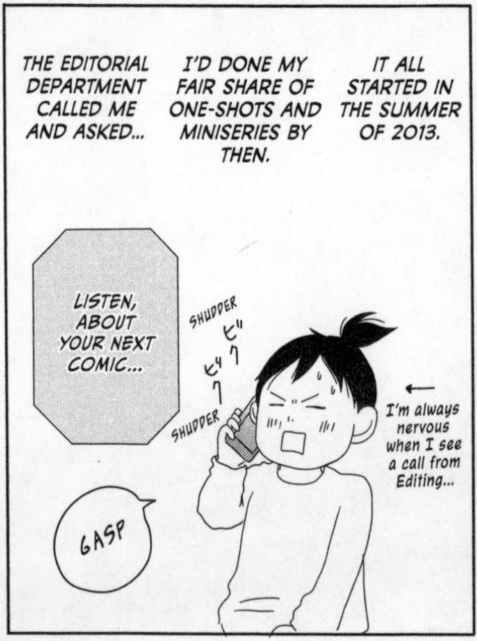
IT ALL STARTED IN THE SUMMER OF 2013.
I'D DONE MY FAIR SHARE OF ONE-SHOTS AND MINISERIES BY THEN.
THE EDITORIAL DEPARTMENT CALLED ME AND ASKED...
SHUDDER ビク
I'm always nervous when I see a call from Editing...
LISTEN, ABOUT YOUR NEXT COMIC...
SHUDDER ビック
GASP

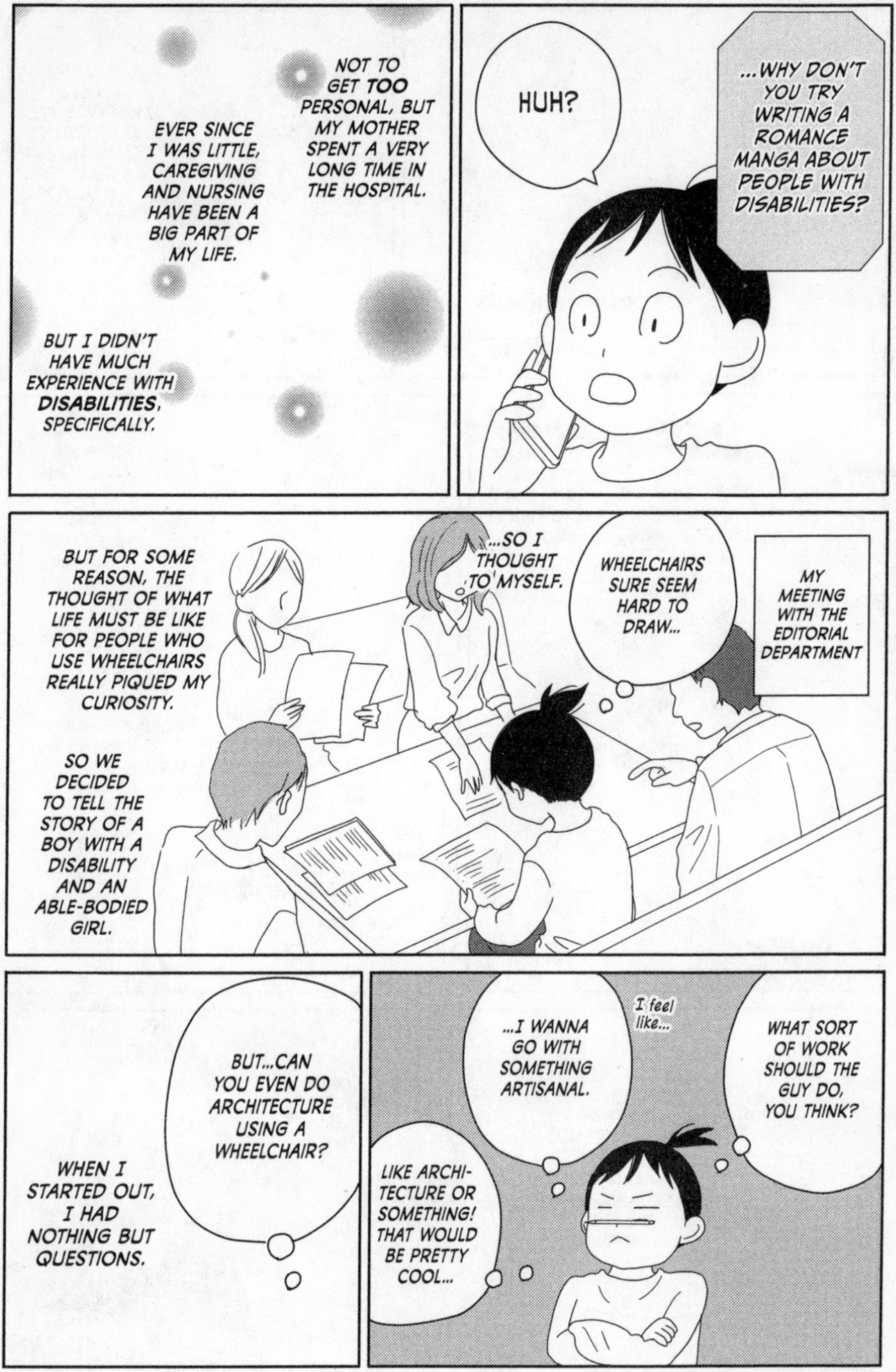
...WHY DON'T YOU TRY WRITING A ROMANCE MANGA ABOUT PEOPLE WITH DISABILITIES?
HUH?
NOT TO GET TOO PERSONAL, BUT MY MOTHER SPENT A VERY LONG TIME IN THE HOSPITAL.
EVER SINCE I WAS LITTLE, CAREGIVING AND NURSING HAVE BEEN A BIG PART OF MY LIFE.
BUT I DIDN'T HAVE MUCH EXPERIENCE WITH DISABILITIES, SPECIFICALLY.
MY MEETING WITH THE EDITORIAL DEPARTMENT
WHEELCHAIRS SURE SEEM HARD TO DRAW...
...SO I THOUGHT TO MYSELF.
BUT FOR SOME REASON, THE THOUGHT OF WHAT LIFE MUST BE LIKE FOR PEOPLE WHO USE WHEELCHAIRS REALLY PIQUED MY CURIOSITY.
SO WE DECIDED TO TELL THE STORY OF A BOY WITH A DISABILITY AND AN ABLE-BODIED GIRL.
WHAT SORT OF WORK SHOULD THE GUY DO, YOU THINK?
I feel like...
...I WANNA GO WITH SOMETHING ARTISANAL.
LIKE ARCHITECTURE OR SOMETHING! THAT WOULD BE PRETTY COOL...
BUT...CAN YOU EVEN DO ARCHITECTURE USING A WHEELCHAIR?
WHEN I STARTED OUT, I HAD NOTHING BUT QUESTIONS.

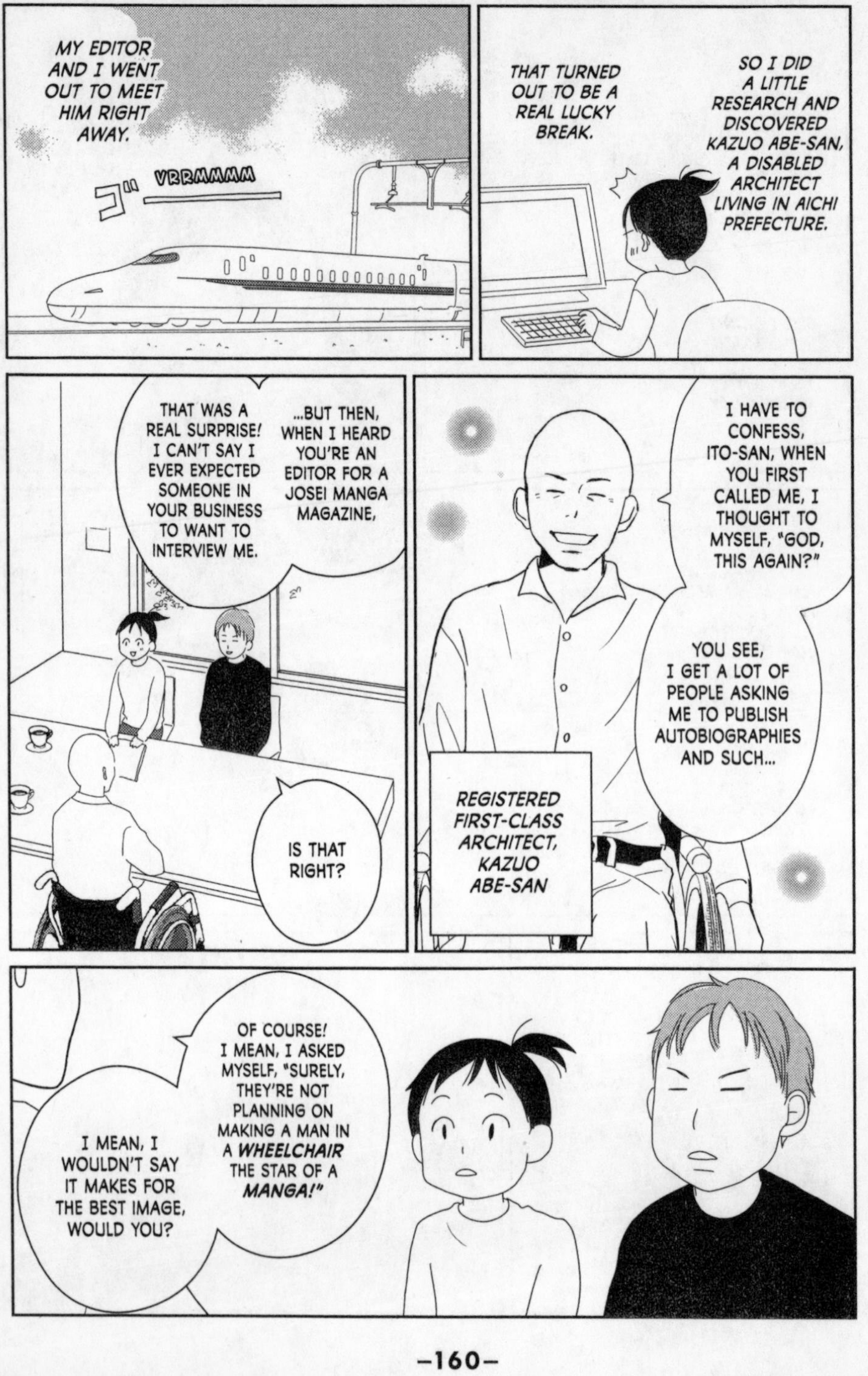
SO I DID A LITTLE RESEARCH AND DISCOVERED KAZUO ABE-SAN, A DISABLED ARCHITECT LIVING IN AICHI PREFECTURE.
THAT TURNED OUT TO BE A REAL LUCKY BREAK.
MY EDITOR AND I WENT OUT TO MEET HIM RIGHT AWAY.
ゴ
VRRMMMM
I HAVE TO CONFESS, ITO-SAN, WHEN YOU FIRST CALLED ME, I THOUGHT TO MYSELF, "GOD, THIS AGAIN?"
YOU SEE, I GET A LOT OF PEOPLE ASKING ME TO PUBLISH AUTOBIOGRAPHIES AND SUCH...
REGISTERED FIRST-CLASS ARCHITECT, KAZUO ABE-SAN
...BUT THEN, WHEN I HEARD YOU'RE AN EDITOR FOR A JOSEI MANGA MAGAZINE,
THAT WAS A REAL SURPRISE! I CAN'T SAY I EVER EXPECTED SOMEONE IN YOUR BUSINESS TO WANT TO INTERVIEW ME.
IS THAT RIGHT?
OF COURSE! I MEAN, I ASKED MYSELF, "SURELY, THEY'RE NOT PLANNING ON MAKING A MAN IN A *WHEELCHAIR* THE STAR OF A *MANGA!*"
I MEAN, I WOULDN'T SAY IT MAKES FOR THE BEST IMAGE, WOULD YOU?

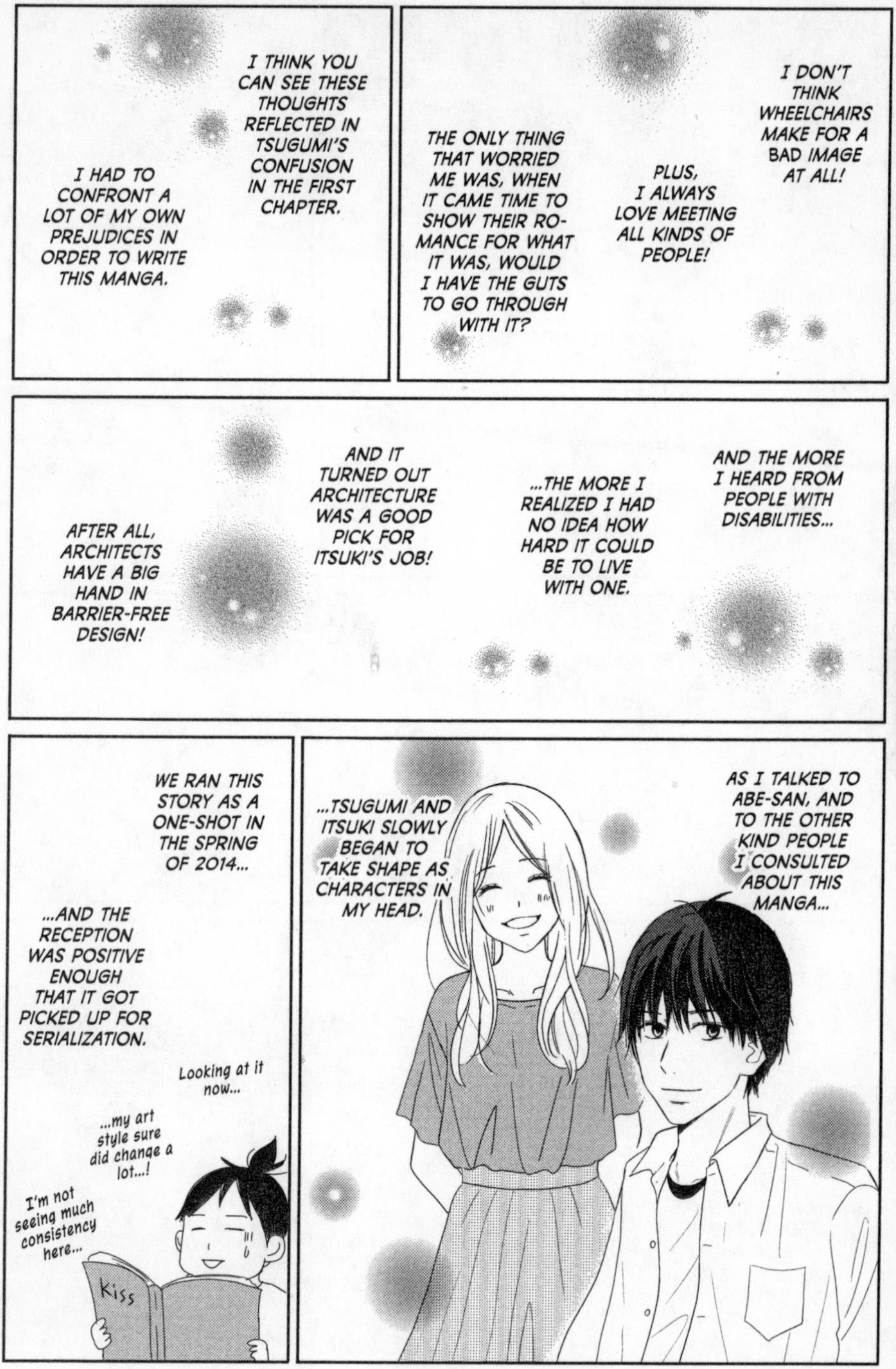
I DON'T THINK WHEELCHAIRS MAKE FOR A BAD IMAGE AT ALL!
PLUS, I ALWAYS LOVE MEETING ALL KINDS OF PEOPLE!
THE ONLY THING THAT WORRIED ME WAS, WHEN IT CAME TIME TO SHOW THEIR RO-MANCE FOR WHAT IT WAS, WOULD I HAVE THE GUTS TO GO THROUGH WITH IT?
I THINK YOU CAN SEE THESE THOUGHTS REFLECTED IN TSUGUMI'S CONFUSION IN THE FIRST CHAPTER.
I HAD TO CONFRONT A LOT OF MY OWN PREJUDICES IN ORDER TO WRITE THIS MANGA.
AND THE MORE I HEARD FROM PEOPLE WITH DISABILITIES...
...THE MORE I REALIZED I HAD NO IDEA HOW HARD IT COULD BE TO LIVE WITH ONE.
AND IT TURNED OUT ARCHITECTURE WAS A GOOD PICK FOR ITSUKI'S JOB!
AFTER ALL, ARCHITECTS HAVE A BIG HAND IN BARRIER-FREE DESIGN!
AS I TALKED TO ABE-SAN, AND TO THE OTHER KIND PEOPLE I CONSULTED ABOUT THIS MANGA...
...TSUGUMI AND ITSUKI SLOWLY BEGAN TO TAKE SHAPE AS CHARACTERS IN MY HEAD.
WE RAN THIS STORY AS A ONE-SHOT IN THE SPRING OF 2014...
...AND THE RECEPTION WAS POSITIVE ENOUGH THAT IT GOT PICKED UP FOR SERIALIZATION.
Looking at it now...
...my art style sure did change a lot...!
I'm not seeing much consistency here...
Kiss

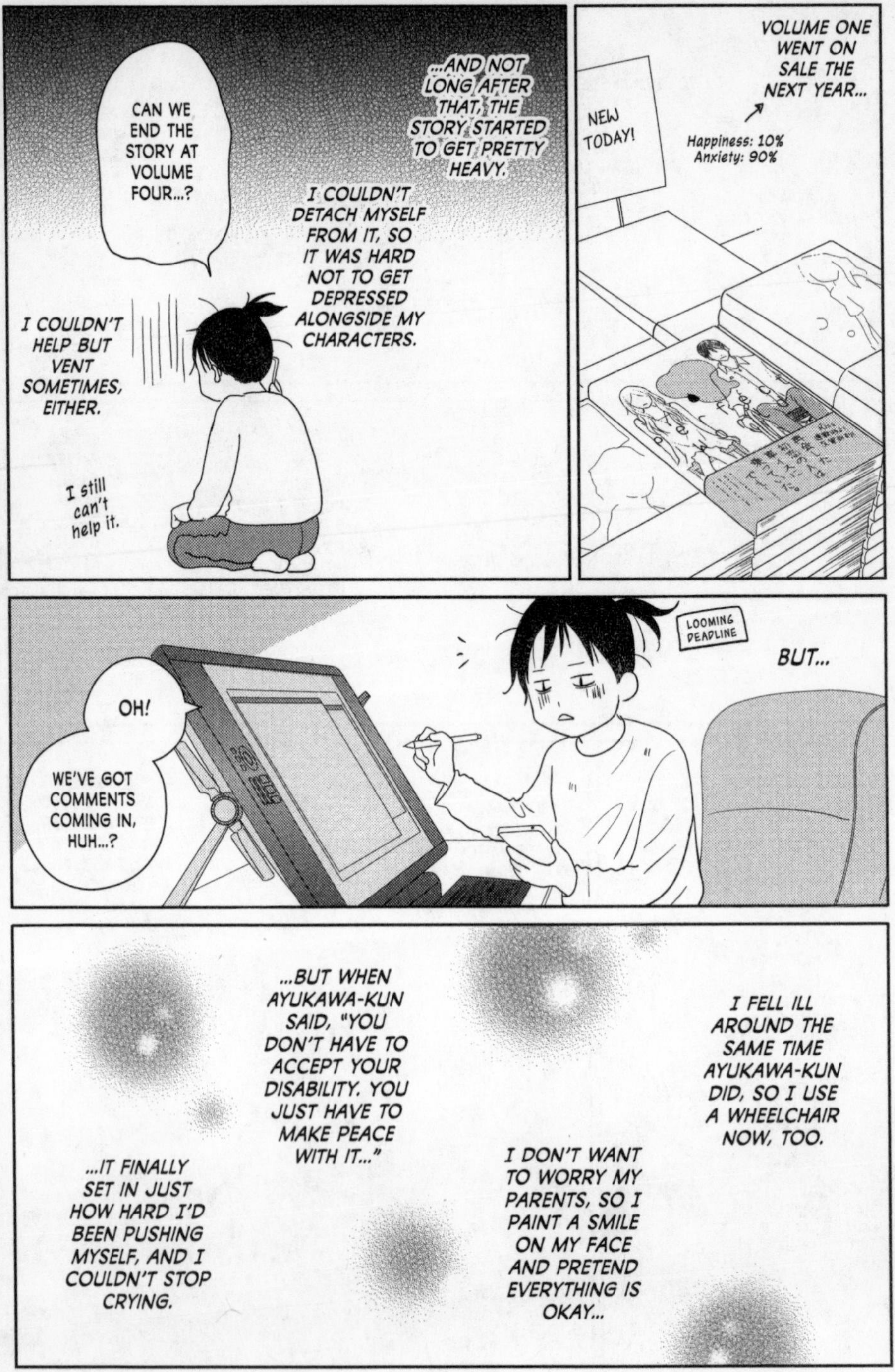
VOLUME ONE WENT ON SALE THE NEXT YEAR...
NEW TODAY!
Happiness: 10%
Anxiety: 90%
...AND NOT LONG AFTER THAT, THE STORY STARTED TO GET PRETTY HEAVY.
CAN WE END THE STORY AT VOLUME FOUR...?
I COULDN'T DETACH MYSELF FROM IT, SO IT WAS HARD NOT TO GET DEPRESSED ALONGSIDE MY CHARACTERS.
I COULDN'T HELP BUT VENT SOMETIMES, EITHER.
I still can't help it.
BUT...
LOOMING DEADLINE
OH!
WE'VE GOT COMMENTS COMING IN, HUH...?
I FELL ILL AROUND THE SAME TIME AYUKAWA-KUN DID, SO I USE A WHEELCHAIR NOW, TOO.
...BUT WHEN AYUKAWA-KUN SAID, "YOU DON'T HAVE TO ACCEPT YOUR DISABILITY. YOU JUST HAVE TO MAKE PEACE WITH IT..."
I DON'T WANT TO WORRY MY PARENTS, SO I PAINT A SMILE ON MY FACE AND PRETEND EVERYTHING IS OKAY...
...IT FINALLY SET IN JUST HOW HARD I'D BEEN PUSHING MYSELF, AND I COULDN'T STOP CRYING.

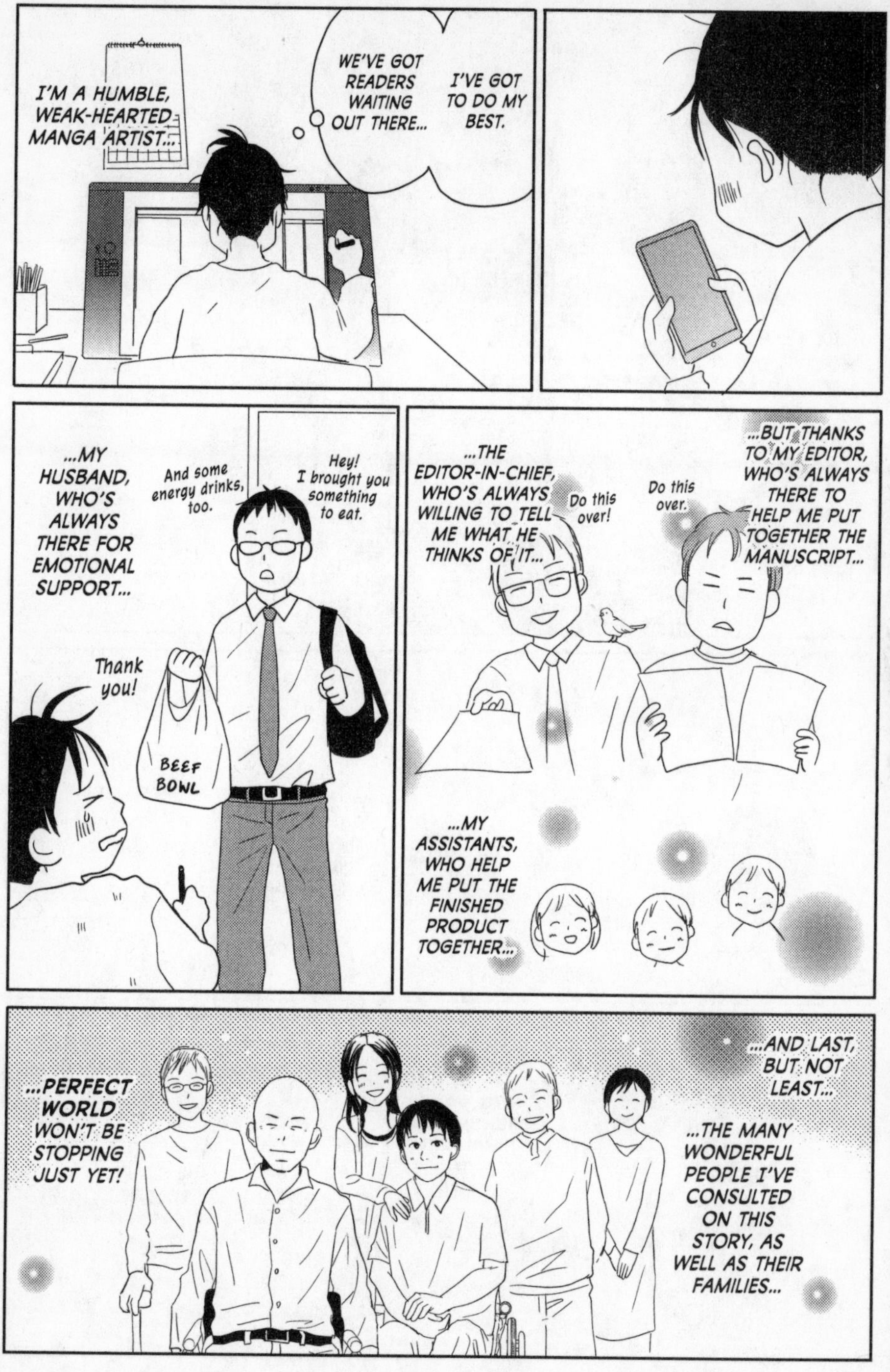
WE'VE GOT READERS WAITING OUT THERE... I'VE GOT TO DO MY BEST.
I'M A HUMBLE, WEAK-HEARTED MANGA ARTIST...
...BUT THANKS TO MY EDITOR, WHO'S ALWAYS THERE TO HELP ME PUT TOGETHER THE MANUSCRIPT...
Do this over.
...THE EDITOR-IN-CHIEF, WHO'S ALWAYS WILLING TO TELL ME WHAT HE THINKS OF IT...
Do this over!
...MY ASSISTANTS, WHO HELP ME PUT THE FINISHED PRODUCT TOGETHER...
Hey! I brought you something to eat.
And some energy drinks, too.
...MY HUSBAND, WHO'S ALWAYS THERE FOR EMOTIONAL SUPPORT...
BEEF BOWL
Thank you!
...AND LAST, BUT NOT LEAST...
...THE MANY WONDERFUL PEOPLE I'VE CONSULTED ON THIS STORY, AS WELL AS THEIR FAMILIES...
...PERFECT WORLD WON'T BE STOPPING JUST YET!

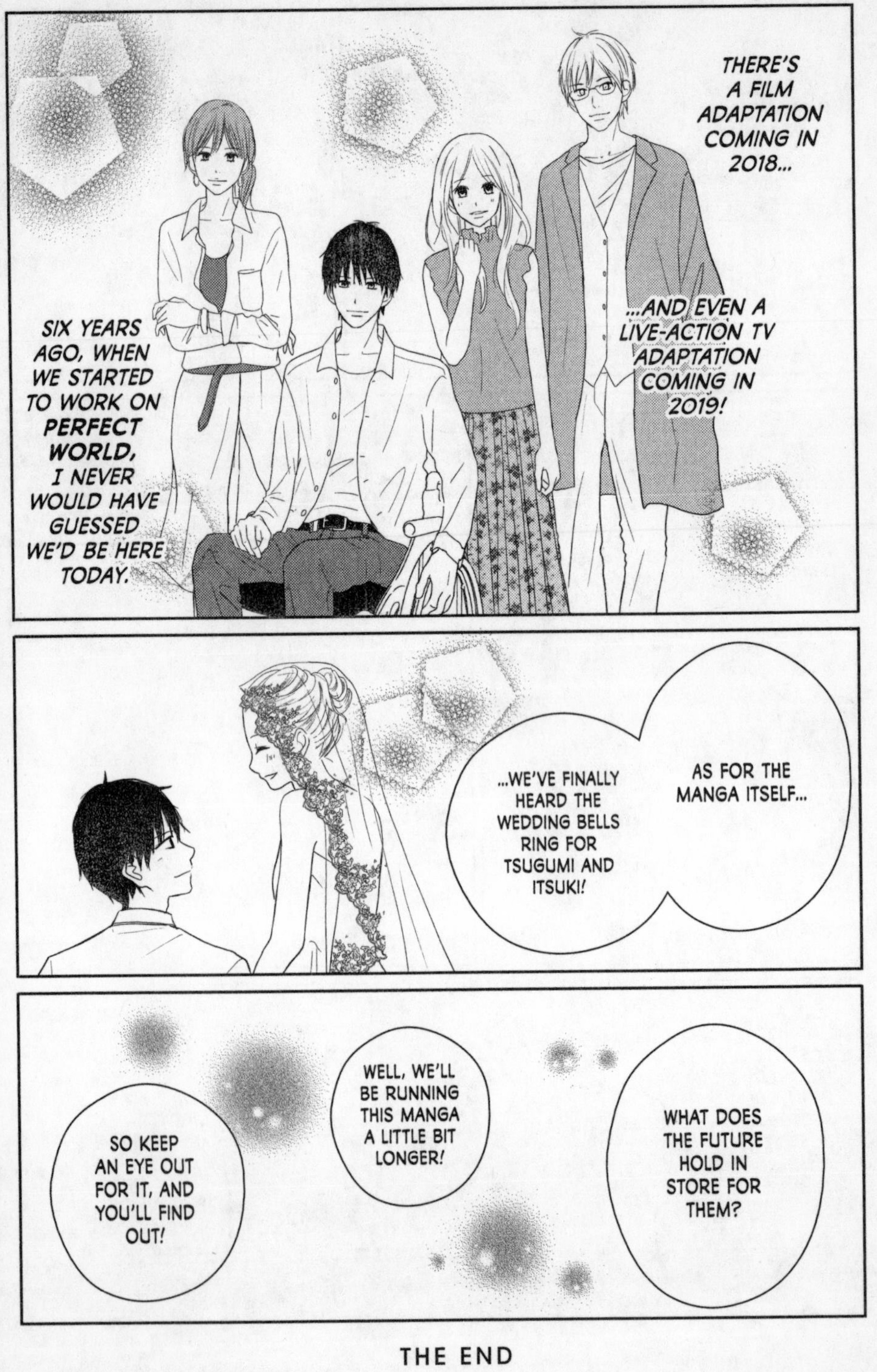
THERE'S A FILM ADAPTATION COMING IN 2018...
...AND EVEN A LIVE-ACTION TV ADAPTATION COMING IN 2019!
SIX YEARS AGO, WHEN WE STARTED TO WORK ON PERFECT WORLD, I NEVER WOULD HAVE GUESSED WE'D BE HERE TODAY.
AS FOR THE MANGA ITSELF...
...WE'VE FINALLY HEARD THE WEDDING BELLS RING FOR TSUGUMI AND ITSUKI!
WHAT DOES THE FUTURE HOLD IN STORE FOR THEM?
WELL, WE'LL BE RUNNING THIS MANGA A LITTLE BIT LONGER!
SO KEEP AN EYE OUT FOR IT, AND YOU'LL FIND OUT!

THE END

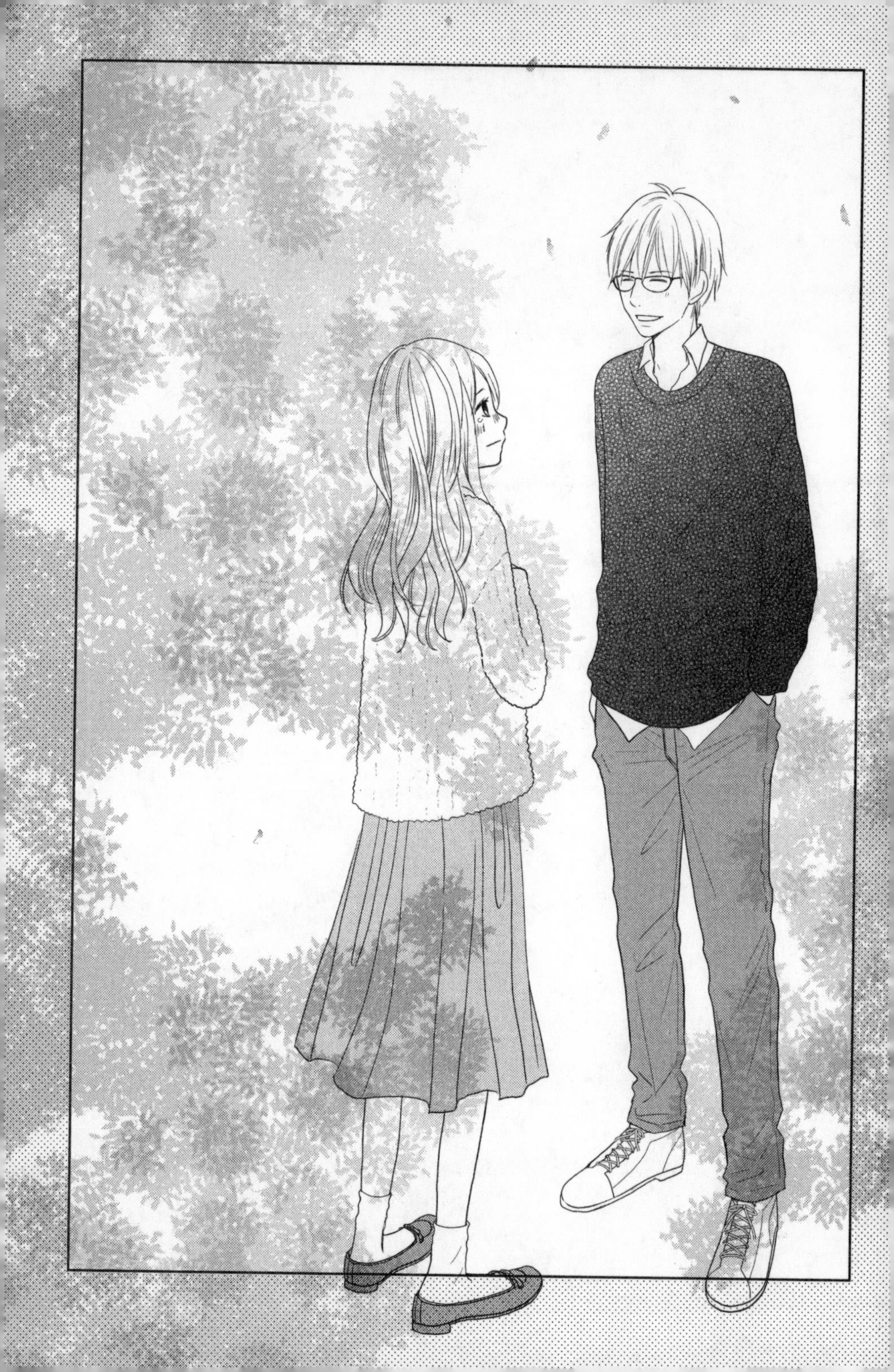

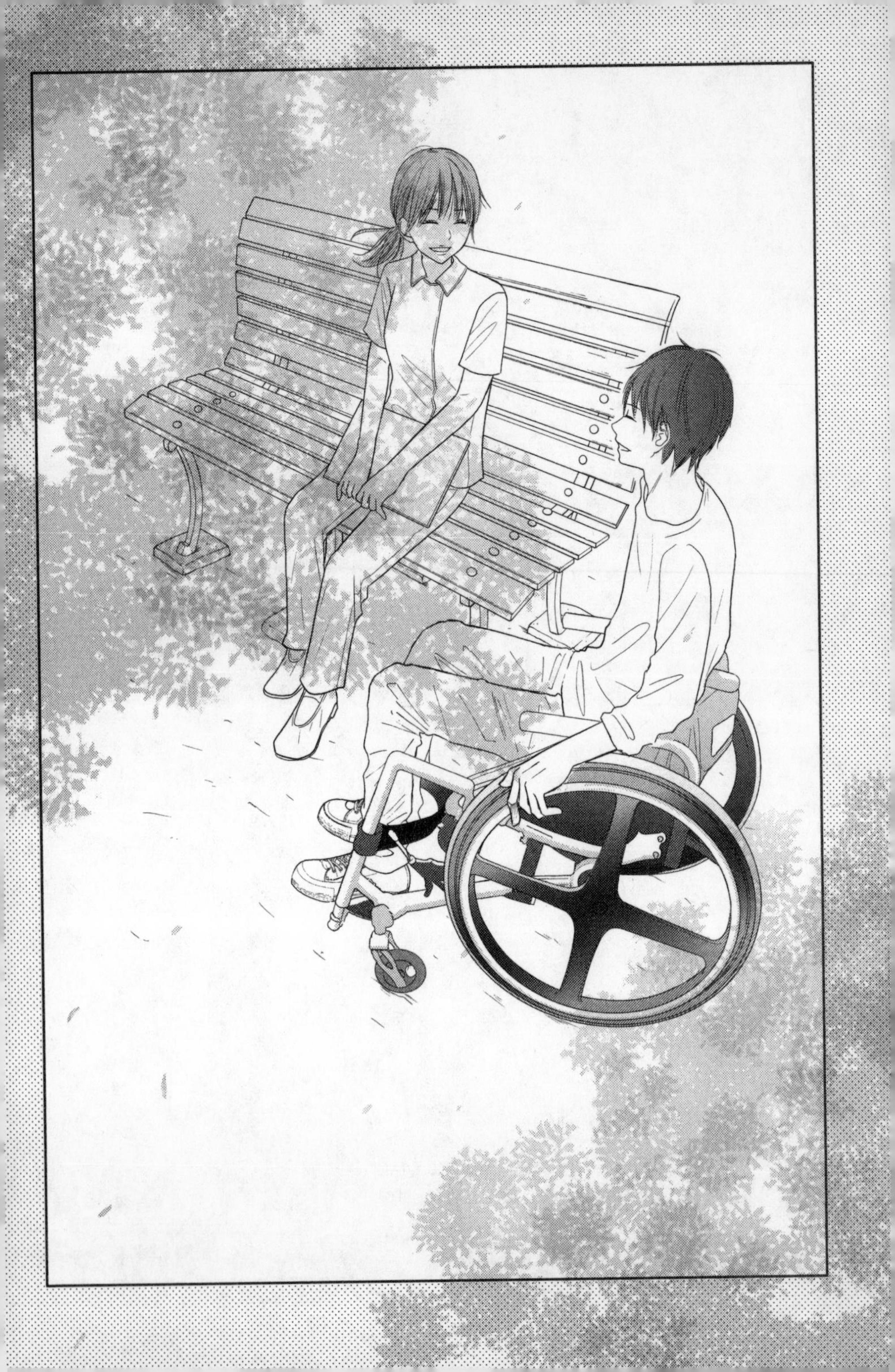

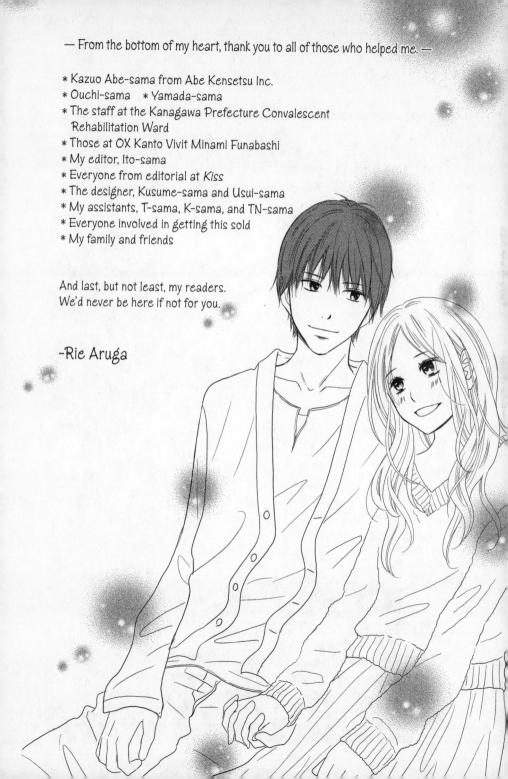

— From the bottom of my heart, thank you to all of those who helped me. —

* Kazuo Abe-sama from Abe Kensetsu Inc.
* Ouchi-sama * Yamada-sama
* The staff at the Kanagawa Prefecture Convalescent Rehabilitation Ward
* Those at OX Kanto Vivit Minami Funabashi
* My editor, Ito-sama
* Everyone from editorial at *Kiss*
* The designer, Kusume-sama and Usui-sama
* My assistants, T-sama, K-sama, and TN-sama
* Everyone involved in getting this sold
* My family and friends

And last, but not least, my readers.
We'd never be here if not for you.

-Rie Aruga

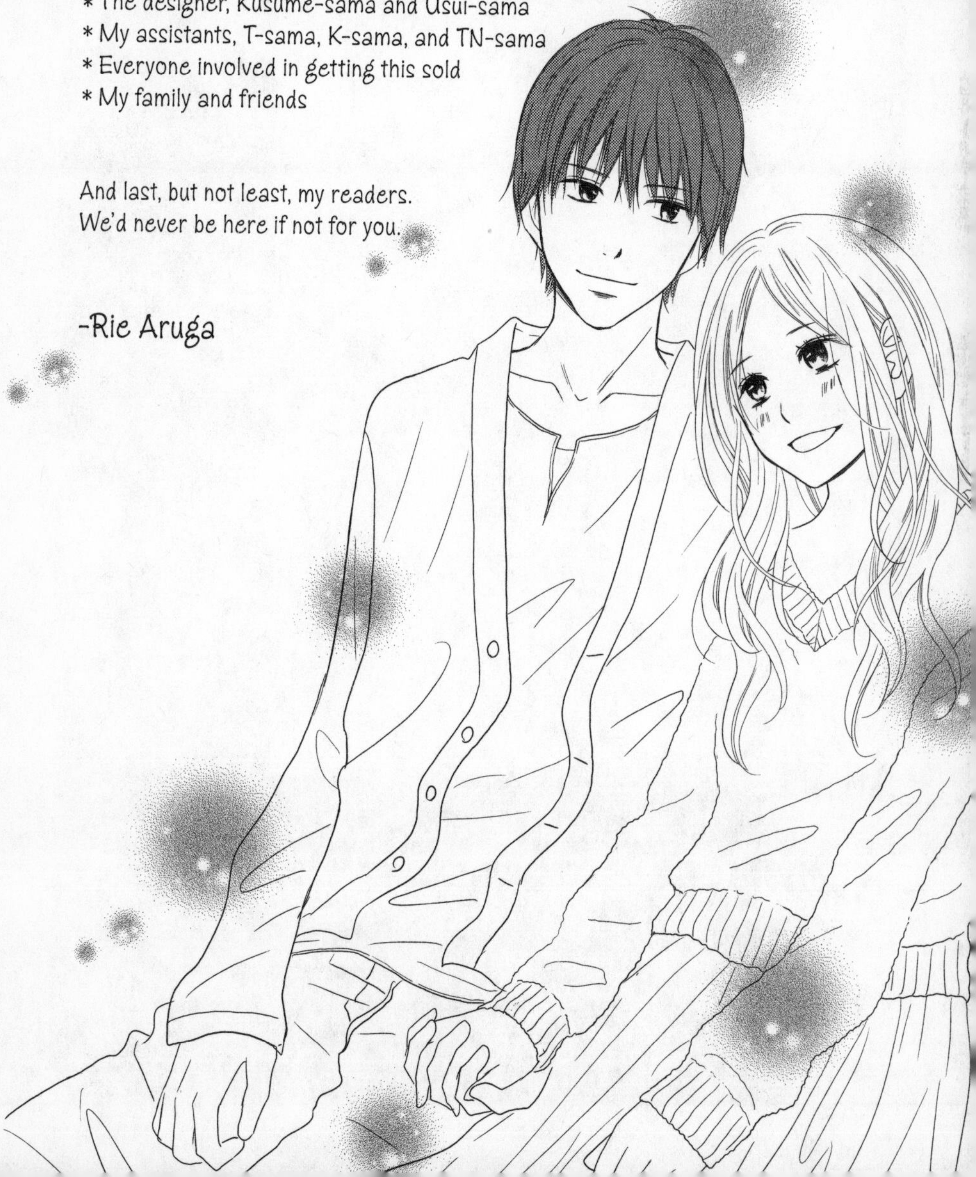

A SMART, NEW ROMANTIC COMEDY FOR FANS OF *SHORTCAKE CAKE* AND *TERRACE HOUSE*!

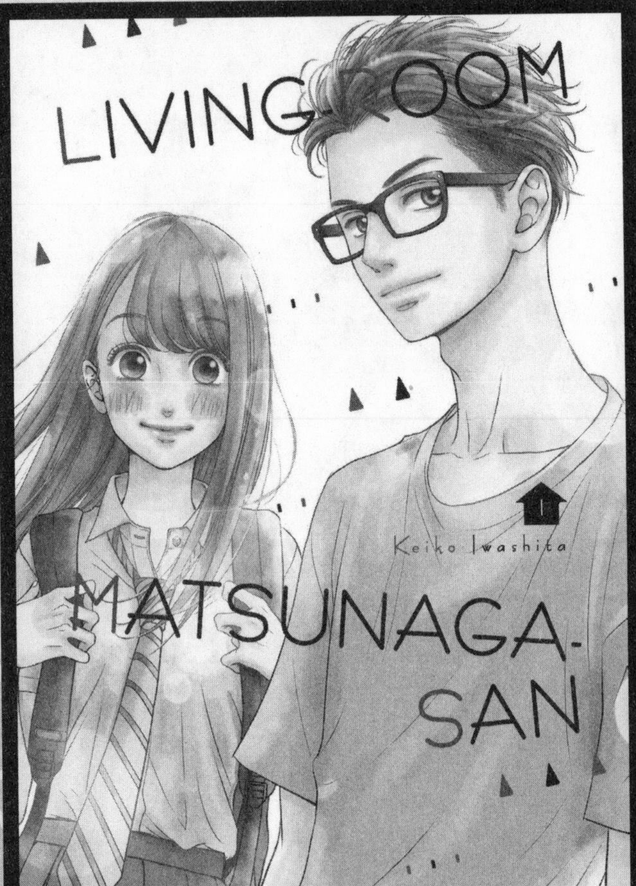
LIVING-ROOM
Keiko Iwashita
MATSUNAGA-SAN

A romance manga starring high school girl Meeko, who learns to live on her own in a boarding house whose living room is home to the odd (but handsome) Matsunaga-san. She begins to adjust to her new life away from her parents, but Meeko soon learns that no matter how far away from home she is, she's still a young girl at heart — especially when she finds herself falling for Matsunaga-san.

KC KODANSHA COMICS

The adorable new odd-couple cat comedy manga from the creator of the beloved *Chi's Sweet Home*, in full color!

Praise for *Chi's Sweet Home*

"Nearly impossible to turn away... a true all-ages title that anyone, young or old, cat lover or not, will enjoy. The stories will bring a smile to your face and warm your heart."

~School Library Journal

Sue & Tai-chan

Konami Kanata

Sue is an aging housecat who's looking forward to living out her life in peace... but her plans change when the mischievous black tomcat Tai-chan enters the picture! Hey! Sue never signed up to be a catsitter! *Sue & Tai-chan* is the latest from the reigning meow-narch of cute kitty comics, Konami Kanata.

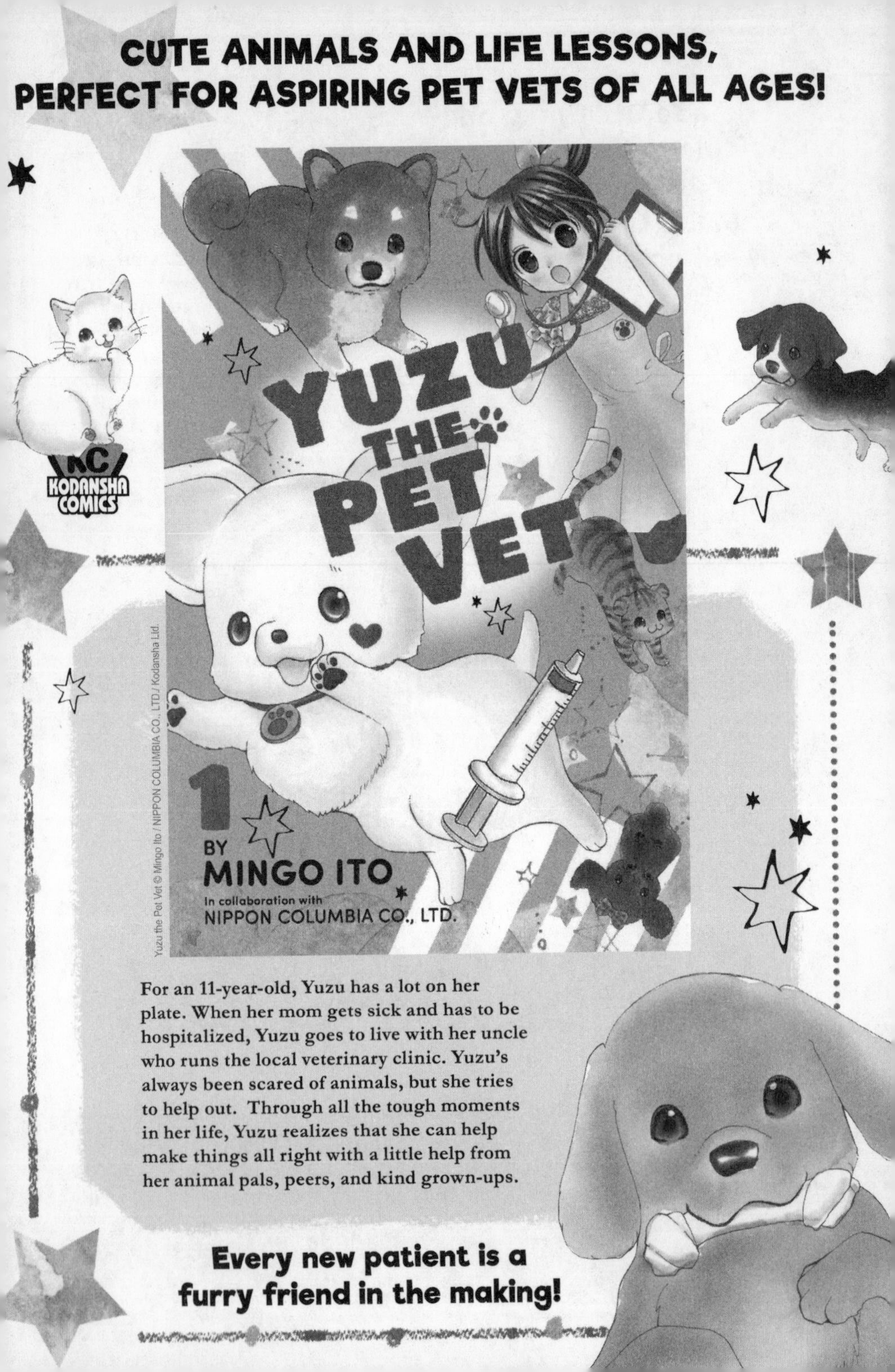

YUZU THE PET VET
1
BY
MINGO ITO
In collaboration with
NIPPON COLUMBIA CO., LTD.

Young characters and steampunk setting, like *Howl's Moving Castle* and *Battle Angel Alita*

Beyond the Clouds © 2018 Nicke / Ki-oon

A boy with a talent for machines and a mysterious girl whose wings he's fixed will take you beyond the clouds! In the tradition of the high-flying, resonant adventure stories of Studio Ghibli comes a gorgeous tale about the longing of young hearts for adventure and friendship!

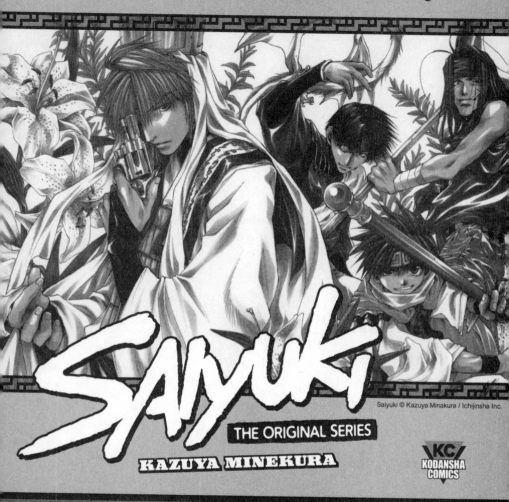

A Kodansha Comics Trade Paperback Original
Perfect World 9 copyright © 2018 Rie Aruga
English translation copyright © 2021 Rie Aruga

Published in the United States by Kodansha Comics, an imprint of Kodansha USA Publishing, LLC, New York.

Publication rights for this English edition arranged through Kodansha Ltd., Tokyo.

First published in Japan in 2018 by Kodansha Ltd., Tokyo as *Perfect World*, volume 9.

ISBN 978-1-64651-109-9

Original cover design by Tomohiro Kusume and Maiko Mori (arcoinc)

Printed in the United States of America.

www.kodansha.us

1st Printing
Translation: Erin Procter
Lettering: Thea Willis
Additional lettering: Sara Linsley
Editing: Megan Ling, Jesika Brooks
Kodansha Comics edition cover design by Phil Balsman

Publisher: Kiichiro Sugawara

Director of publishing services: Ben Applegate
Associate director of operations: Stephen Pakula
Publishing services managing editors: Madison Salters, Alanna Ruse
Production managers: Emi Lotto, Angela Zurlo